D0886803

THE REVIVAL OF
LABOR LIBERALISM

The Revival of
Labor Liberalism

ANDREW BATTISTA

UNIVERSITY OF ILLINOIS PRESS

URBANA AND CHICAGO

∞ This book is printed on acid-free paper.

Library of Congress Cataloging-in-Publication Data
Battista, Andrew
The revival of labor liberalism / Andrew Battista.
p.   cm.
Includes bibliographical references and index.
ISBN-13: 978-0-252-03232-5 (cloth : alk. paper)
ISBN-10: 0-252-03232-2 (cloth : alk. paper)
1. Labor unions—United States—Political activity—History.
2. Liberalism—United States—History. 3. United States—Politics
and government—20th century. 4. Working class—United States—
Political activity. 5. Progressivism (United States politics)
I. Title.
HD6510.B38   2008
322'.20973—dc22   2007023291

To the memory of
Rudolph E. Battista and Anne C. Battista
wonderful parents, delightful friends

CONTENTS

ACKNOWLEDGMENTS

It is a pleasure to acknowledge the assistance I received from many individuals and organizations in the research and writing of this book.

First and foremost, I wish to express my gratitude to the labor leaders and political activists who made my research possible by granting me interviews and access to the documentary records of the organizations that they led. In particular, I thank Douglas Fraser, Bill Dodds, Don Stillman, the late William Winpisinger, Heather Booth, the late Jack (Jacob) Sheinkman, David Dyson, Charles Kernaghan, and Barbara Briggs. I greatly appreciate the time, cooperation, and encouragement that each of these busy individuals provided. I also thank the many other union officials and political activists who consented to be interviewed and whose names will be found in the footnotes to this book. In addition, I gratefully acknowledge the assistance I received from Mr. Archie Motley and his staff at the Chicago Historical Society.

I am hard pressed to properly thank four exemplary colleagues at East Tennessee State University (ETSU) for the assistance and encouragement they gave me in the course of my research and writing. Professors Hugh LaFollette (now at the University of South Florida), Kenneth Mijeski, Scott Beck, and Weixing Chen were generous with their time and helpful in their comments or technical assistance on many of the chapters in this book. I cannot burden these valued colleagues with responsibility for the deficiencies of my book; I can thank them for their selfless contributions to whatever value it might possess. I also extend my gratitude to Ms. Betty Wagner, formerly the executive assistant in the Department of Political Science at ETSU, for expertly transcribing a long interview from a tape recording that was not always of the best sound quality. I am pleased to acknowledge, as well, that research for this book was made possible by a Presidential Grant-in-Aid and a Research Development Committee Grant from East Tennessee State University.

I thank two anonymous reviewers for the University of Illinois Press for their time and assistance. They helped me improve my writing style, saved me from some factual errors, and made important substantive comments, although constraints of space and stubbornness prevented me from responding to many of their criticisms and suggestions.

I am indebted to Laurie Matheson, Angela Burton, and Angela Buckley of the University of Illinois Press (UIP) for their professionalism and expertise in the process of publishing this book. I especially thank Laurie Matheson, acquisitions editor at UIP, for her invaluable support and constant cooperation.

I am grateful to three academic journals, *Labor History, Polity,* and *Diplomatic History,* for granting me permission to use materials that I had previously published in their pages.

Last, but certainly not least, I thank my wife, Kathie, and my son, Anthony, for the many ways, large and small, that they helped with this book. I deeply appreciate their tolerance, support, and cheerfulness, for longer than I had any right to expect.

INTRODUCTION

Unions and liberals profoundly shaped the development of American society and politics in the twentieth century. Their rise to power in the middle third of the century, between 1932 and 1968, dramatically changed social and political life in the United States; so, too, in very different ways, did their fall from power during the last three decades of the century. In both eras, of ascendance and decline, their fortunes were deeply entwined. Unions and liberals dominated the middle part of the century because they were strongly allied, and they declined in its final third because their alliance fractured. Unionism and liberalism rose together and fell together.

We know a good deal about the alliance between unions and liberals at the height of its power in the middle decades of the last century, because scholars have studied it extensively. The same cannot be said of that alliance in its period of decline. The decline of unionism and of liberalism have been analyzed often and well, but mainly as separate rather than linked developments. Moreover, it has apparently been widely—but incorrectly—assumed that, once the labor-liberal coalition fractured in the late 1960s, there simply was no coalition left to study. Most of the history of the alliance between unions and liberals since 1968 remains to be written. Until it is, we will not be in a good position to assess the coalition's prospects in the twenty-first century.

This book examines the history and politics of the labor-liberal coalition since 1968; it emphasizes two key and interrelated developments. First, as divisive issues fractured the labor-liberal coalition in the late 1960s, its decline led to numerous efforts to revive it. In time, these efforts did strengthen the coalition, but only to a limited extent, and more its internal coherence than its national influence. Second, the same contentious issues that fractured their alliance with liberals also divided some unions and labor leaders from others in the late 1960s. These political divisions catalyzed a broader factional conflict that culminated in a shift of power within the labor movement by 1995, one that further strengthened the labor-liberal coalition, if only modestly.

The link between these developments was the formation of a dissident, liberal wing of the labor leadership—often called the Reuther or Reutherite wing after its leader, United Auto Workers (UAW) President Walter Reuther—after the late 1960s. Over time, dissident labor leaders and their unions sought both to rebuild the labor-liberal coalition and to revive a union movement in decline. They tried to achieve these goals through new political organizations that they created between 1975 and 1986, including Democratic Agenda, Progressive Alliance, Citizen Labor Energy Coalition, National Labor Committee, Economic Policy Institute, and Jobs with Justice. A major purpose of this book is to record the history and analyze the politics of these organizations, neglect of which by scholars has so far deprived us of significant portions of the recent history of the labor-liberal coalition and of important grounds for assessing its prospects. Intensive case studies, based on archival and interview research, of the Progressive Alliance, Citizen Labor Energy Coalition, and National Labor Committee, and briefer profiles of the other three organizations, constitute the book's main contribution to original research and the key body of evidence for its central arguments.

The rise of an alliance between trade unions and liberals in the 1930s underlay the era of Democratic Party dominance and liberal governance that stretched from Franklin D. Roosevelt's New Deal through Lyndon B. Johnson's Great Society and enacted modern fiscal, welfare, labor, regulatory, and civil-rights reforms and policies. The decline of that coalition after the mid-1960s paved the way for an extended period of divided government in which an ascendant Republican Party and allied business and conservative interests typically held the initiative and sought, with varying degrees of success, to revise or repeal those earlier reforms and policies. The decline of the labor-liberal coalition was a product of both emerging rifts between unions and liberals and the waning political power of each of the partners. The splits between unions and liberals were precipitated by the rise of new social movements and political issues in the 1960s, which transformed the social base and political agenda of Democratic liberalism in ways that many unions found threatening. The waning political power of unions and liberals resulted from the end of the golden age of postwar economic growth in the 1970s and the political resurgence of business and conservatives that it favored, as well as from their own strategic failures and growing estrangement and changes in the structure of the American political economy.

That the labor-liberal coalition declined in the late 1960s is conventional wisdom in labor and political history.[1] Two dissents have been voiced to this view, however: one dates the decline of the labor-liberal coalition from the late 1940s, two decades earlier than the conventional view; the other denies that the coalition in fact declined and holds that it remains a vital influence in American politics.[2] Neither dissent is ultimately persuasive, though both rest on important arguments that cannot be lightly dismissed.

But some versions of the conventional wisdom have exaggerated the breadth and depth of the schism between labor and liberals and the decline of the coalition's power.[3] Important groups of unions and liberals maintained their coalition after the 1960s, its influence never utterly collapsed, and successive efforts to strengthen the alliance and its influence achieved at least limited success. Although the final third of the twentieth century was indeed a period of decline of the labor-liberal coalition, it was also one of efforts to reconstruct and strengthen it, efforts that have been all but ignored by both labor historians and political scientists. I emphasize this point not for sentimental or inspirational reasons, but in order to contribute to a fuller understanding of the history of the labor-liberal coalition and of its prospects for the future.

The rifts between labor and liberals that erupted in the late 1960s did not pit all unions and union leaders against liberals, at least not to the same extent. In fact, the rise of new social movements and political issues in the 1960s divided the labor movement itself, shattering the political harmony that had prevailed in organized labor since the merger of the American Federation of Labor (AFL) and the Congress of Industrial Organizations (CIO) in 1955. On the divisive issues of the 1960s, many important unions broke with other unions and the AFL-CIO and sided with liberals, in part precisely because they wished to preserve the labor-liberal coalition. By the latter half of the 1970s, these dissident or Reutherite unions, alarmed at the extent to which the political power of the labor-liberal coalition had declined, began to form new political organizations in an attempt to revive and strengthen that coalition. Through the Progressive Alliance, Citizen Labor Energy Coalition, National Labor Committee, and other organizations, the dissident or Reutherite wing of the union leadership sought to align labor with the new political forces that had transformed liberalism in the 1960s—including minorities, women, and middle-class issue activists—and to reassert labor-liberal influence in the Democratic Party and in national politics.

The immediate impact of these organizations on national politics and policy varied from minor to significant. Their importance lay chiefly in their combined and long-term influence on the revival of the labor-liberal coalition. Collectively and over time, these organizations made limited but real progress in reconstructing and strengthening the labor-liberal coalition. Even so, there is little cause for optimism about the coalition's future. It remains far weaker than the rival business-conservative alliance and on the defensive in national politics, and its prospects are limited by the continued decline of union density and the fragmentation of liberalism into distinct if overlapping New Deal, multicultural, and public-interest blocs.

The split between much of the labor movement and the "new liberals" of the 1960s had consequences for the internal politics of organized labor as well as for the labor-liberal coalition. Compared to the twenty-year (1935–55) schism between the AFL and the CIO, the period following the 1955 merger of the two federations was one of genuine political harmony in American labor. But this unity lasted only a decade, for it was disrupted by the political turmoil of the second half of the 1960s. Labor unity was initially sundered by the "Reuther-Meany split," which pitted UAW President Walter Reuther against AFL-CIO President George Meany on political, international, and institutional issues. Though it apparently ended with Reuther's isolation and then tragic death in 1970, the Reuther-Meany split in fact initiated a durable factional division in the U.S. labor leadership. A bloc of dissident unions formed in opposition to the positions of the AFL-CIO leadership on political, international, and institutional issues. The dissident or Reutherite wing of the labor leadership not only rejected the federation leadership's political stands that eroded the labor-liberal coalition; it also criticized the AFL-CIO's complacency about the decline in the unionized share of the workforce and refusal to promote labor organizing.

The political organizations that the dissident unions formed in the 1970s and 1980s were integral parts of this factional division and conflict in the labor leadership. These organizations were efforts to revive the labor-liberal coalition and its influence, but they were also attempts to forge a new model of labor politics distinct from that of the AFL-CIO. They sought to develop new political programs, strategies, and allies for organized labor; to revive the heritage of social unionism in the labor movement; and to adapt unions to the changing requirements of influence in American politics. In the view of dissident labor leaders, the rebuilding of the labor-liberal coalition and the development of new and more effective political strategies for the labor movement were necessary to rescue unionism from decline and marginalization. The new political organizations of the dissident unions were intended to take up these vital tasks, on which the leadership of the AFL-CIO had defaulted.

The Reuther wing of the labor leadership realized, however, that the future of organized labor depended on more than the rejuvenation of the labor-liberal alliance and the reformation of union politics. Dissident labor leaders from Walter Reuther through Jerry Wurf (president of the American Federation of State County and Municipal Employees) to William Winpisinger (president of the International Association of Machinists) believed that it also depended on change within the House of Labor. As they saw it, reversing the long trend of declining union density required—among other things, notably including reform of the nation's labor laws—a strong commitment to labor organizing, an expanded role for the AFL-CIO in the organizing process, and new and more effective organizing strategies, all of which in turn required institutional reform and leadership change in the labor movement. From the late 1960s on, the leaders of the dissident unions sought in various ways to effect these changes; their efforts were often politically maladroit and unsuccessful, but they fought the astonishing complacency of the federation leadership in the face of union decline.

The factional division in the labor leadership, then, was ultimately about the revival of a labor movement in decline. For the dissidents in the labor leadership, rebuilding the labor-liberal alliance, forging a new framework for labor politics, and developing effective institutional capacities and strategies for labor organizing were the keys to the revival of a strong and influential labor movement in the United States. For a quarter of a century after the late 1960s, the Reuther wing of unionism contended against the top leadership of the AFL-CIO and its allies among the more conservative unions to revive American unionism. The intensity of this factional split waxed and waned, and there were areas of accommodation and periods of rapprochement along the way. But this history of factional division over the future of the labor movement underlay the dramatic 1995 contest for the presidency of the AFL-CIO, which resulted in the election of the challenger and reform candidate John Sweeney. This outcome represented the first major shift of power within the U.S. labor movement since the 1955 merger and installed in the nation's labor federation an activist leadership committed to the revival of unionism and the labor-liberal alliance.

In ways shaped by the dissident unions and their political organizations, the Sweeney-led AFL-CIO altered labor's political and organizing strategies. By the late 1990s, these changes had strengthened labor's political influence and increased union membership. But these gains could not be sustained in the early years of the new century, when the old pattern of union political setbacks and membership decline resumed. It is likely that the nation's labor laws will have to be reformed if unions are ever to represent a larger and growing share of the workforce in the United States, and the AFL-CIO has made such reform a long-term objective. In the meantime, however, the resumption of union decline led to a new schism in the American labor movement, which in 2005 divided into rival labor federations for the first time since 1954.

In sum, I try in this book to illuminate the intertwined development of the labor-liberal coalition and the internal politics of the union movement since the late 1960s, especially through an examination of the history and politics of the Progressive Alliance, Citizen Labor Energy Coalition, and National Labor Committee, along with their predecessors and successors. In highlighting these organizations, I mean to emphasize the crucial role played in contemporary labor and political history by the Reutherite wing of the labor movement. These unions and labor leaders took the initiative to revive both unionism and the labor-liberal alliance. Their success is far from guaranteed; all that can be said with certainty is that the success or failure of their project will substantially determine the character of American society and politics in the future.

The plan of the book is as follows. The four chapters of Part I present the theoretical and historical background of this study. Chapter 1 defines the concept of the labor-liberal coalition and outlines the analytical framework by means of which I chart the rise, decline, and attempted revival of the labor-liberal coalition. Chapter 2 discusses the rise of that coalition in the 1930s and its accomplishments and limitations through the mid-1960s. Chapter 3 analyzes the decline of the labor-liberal coalition as a two-stage process, in which the internal unity of the coalition was first ruptured and then its external influence was further undermined.

Chapter 4 traces the reemergence of political divisions in organized labor in the latter half of the 1960s and the formation and development of rival leadership factions in the labor movement through the late 1970s. In all of these chapters, the central theme is the link between the fate of the labor-liberal coalition and the internal politics of the union movement.

Part II presents the detailed case studies of the political organizations of the dissident unions. Chapters 5–7 examine, respectively, the Progressive Alliance, Citizen Labor Energy Coalition, and National Labor Committee. Chapter 8 then uses these case studies to analyze the political strategy and the social bases of the dissident or Reutherite wing of the labor movement and contrasts them with the political strategy and social bases of the dominant or Meany wing of labor. This chapter also reviews and assesses alternative interpretations and various criticisms of the liberal or Reutherite labor leadership. The book's profiles of three other political organizations of the dissident unions are not included in Part II; they have been placed elsewhere to facilitate the narrative and to substantiate claims. Democratic Agenda is profiled in Chapter 4, and the Economic Policy Institute and Jobs with Justice are both profiled in Chapter 9.

Finally, Part III draws conclusions and makes arguments about the two central and interrelated issues of the book. Chapter 9 makes the case that the 1995 presidential election and leadership change at the AFL-CIO, the most important institutional developments in American labor in forty years, cannot be fully understood apart from their historical background in the quarter-century-long factional division in the labor leadership, and in particular from the influence of the political organizations of the dissident unions. This chapter also examines the record of the Sweeney-led AFL-CIO and the recent redivision of the labor movement into rival federations. Chapter 10 analyzes the ways in which and the extent to which the Progressive Alliance, Citizen Labor Energy Coalition, National Labor Committee, and other organizations of the dissident unions, as well as the 1995 leadership change at the AFL-CIO, contributed to the rebuilding and strengthening of the labor-liberal coalition in American politics. It also considers the sources of the continuing weakness and defensive position of that coalition in relation to its main competitor for political power, the business-conservative alliance organized through the Republican Party. Chapter 10, and the book, concludes with an analysis of the fragmentation of modern liberalism that, together with the ongoing decline of union density, limits the prospects for a strong and vital labor-liberal coalition in American public life.

PART 1

The Rise and Decline of the Labor-Liberal Coalition

CHAPTER 1

Understanding the
Labor-Liberal Coalition

The Concept of the Labor-Liberal Coalition

The ideas of a labor-liberal coalition and a labor–Democratic Party alliance have often been used to analyze and explain twentieth-century American politics and history. Although frequently used interchangeably, these two concepts should not be conflated, because the modern Democratic Party has never been a fully or uniformly liberal political party. During most of the twentieth century, the party was divided into liberal northern and conservative southern wings, and more recently it has been split into liberal and centrist factions with less definite regional bases. The concepts of a labor-liberal coalition and a labor–Democratic Party alliance partly overlap but are partly distinct. Is one analytically preferable to the other, then?

There are three reasons to prefer the concept of a labor-liberal coalition. The first is that it more accurately identifies the partners to the actual coalition, which was between unions and a *party faction.* Organized labor was allied only with the northern liberal wing of the Democratic Party, not its southern conservative wing, which for much of the twentieth century was as ardently anti-union as it was pro-segregation.[1] The second reason is that the concept of the labor-liberal coalition better expresses the political strategy of organized labor, which was not just to ally with the Democratic Party but to transform it into a coherent liberal political party. As Walter Reuther once expressed this aim, "We ought to bring about a realignment and get the liberal forces in one party and the conservatives in another."[2] In practice this meant, for most of the twentieth century, either expelling or transforming the southern conservative wing of the Democratic Party. Labor's two main efforts at this, in the late 1930s and in the years just after World War II, were largely unsuccessful, but by the mid-1960s it had at least helped to reduce the relative size and power of the southern Democratic delegation in Congress.[3] The third reason to prefer the concept of the labor-liberal coalition is that, unlike the idea of the labor–Democratic Party alliance, it does not deflect attention from labor's important ties with such liberal interest groups as Americans for Democratic Action (ADA), the National Farmers Union (NFU), and the National Association for the Advancement of Colored People (NAACP).[4] The idea of the labor-liberal coalition more readily subsumes these and other interest groups as well as the party faction.

While I prefer the concept of the labor-liberal coalition for these reasons, it would be wrong to make too much of the distinction between the two concepts or to dismiss the idea of the labor–Democratic Party alliance. After all, the liberals with whom organized labor has allied have typically been Democrats. Moreover, when, or to the degree that, the liberal wing of the Democratic Party has been dominant over other factions, the party could fairly be described as a liberal party. Indeed, the old southern conservative wing of the party shed its segregationist past and is now less powerful and less hostile toward labor.[5] Finally, insofar as labor has contributed money to the Democratic Party as an organization, not just to its candidates, and formally assumed seats on the party's executive body, the Democratic National Committee (although this did not occur until the 1980s), it has clearly established an organizational alliance with the Democratic Party. The concept of a union-party alliance is therefore legitimate and sometimes necessary. I shall also often use the phrase *labor–liberal Democratic alliance* as a terminological compromise.

Analytical Framework

In analyzing the rise, decline, and attempted revival of the labor-liberal coalition in subsequent chapters, I make assumptions and draw distinctions about its nature, development, and power. These should be identified and explained so that readers can more readily evaluate the analysis. Two premises about the labor-liberal coalition are especially important. The first is that each of the partners to the coalition, organized labor and the liberal wing of the Democratic Party, is an institution—or group or movement—that varies internally (in any given period) and changes over time in its social composition and political disposition. The second premise is that both the rise and the decline of the labor-liberal coalition were influenced by changes in the extent to which the social bases and political commitments of unions and liberal Democrats overlapped. The logic of these two premises is that the labor-liberal coalition and its evolution must be understood and analyzed as products of the *internal political dynamics* of both organized labor and Democratic liberalism.

Neither organized labor nor liberal Democrats can reasonably be conceived as an institution or group that is socially and politically homogeneous or static. Instead, at any given moment and over time, both unions and liberals vary among themselves in the social strata and political interests they represent. In a word, there are different types of unions and different kinds of liberals. Although this claim is not novel, it has not been made the starting point for analysis of the labor-liberal coalition, and its implications for understanding the development and dynamics of the coalition have not been explored. The formation, evolution, and power of the labor-liberal coalition have been deeply shaped by the inner diversity and change over time in the social bases and political commitments of both unionism and Democratic liberalism.

This does not mean that unionism and liberalism have no essential social and political content, or that there are no limits on the extent to which unions or liberals can vary among themselves or change over time and yet remain unions or liberals. Unions are organizations of workers that represent employee interests as bargaining agents in labor markets and workplaces and as party allies or interest groups in the political system. Modern liberals are advocates of active government, equality, and an inclusive and tolerant political community within the framework of individual rights and representative institutions. But these broad conceptions of the basic nature of unionism and liberalism, or reasonable alternative conceptions, allow for substantial differences among, and changes over time in, unions and liberals, both in their social composition and their political commitments.

Varieties of Labor

Studies of American labor commonly distinguish different kinds of unions, in a given period as well as over time.[6] Although no single classification of the main types of unions dominates the field of labor studies, one typology is widely used. It distinguishes four main types of unions: (a) craft, (b) industrial, (c) public employee, and (d) service-sector unions.[7] This typology distinguishes major blocs of unions by economic and social base, historical period, and political orientation. Craft, industrial, public employee, and service-sector unions represent employees in different occupations, industries, or sectors and with varied social profiles; emerged or grew to prominence in different eras; and developed distinctive political interests and strategies.[8]

Craft unions arose first and, through the American Federation of Labor, dominated American labor during the first third of the twentieth century. They organized workers by occupation, mainly the skilled trades in construction, transportation, printing, and other fields, and represented predominantly old-stock (of British or northern European descent) male workers. The market power of skilled workers led these unions to emphasize bargaining with employers as the method to advance worker interests. Craft unions engaged in political action to ensure the union legality and autonomy necessary to such bargaining, but most of them were anti-statist and opposed economic regulation and social provision by government. They also reflected the conventions of the dominant Anglo-American culture of the era.

Industrial unions emerged or grew in the 1930s and 1940s, and for two decades after 1935 maintained a separate labor federation, the Congress of Industrial Organizations. They organized workers by industry, regardless of occupation or skill level, chiefly in the new manufacturing industries like auto, steel, rubber, and electrical. Their memberships included large numbers of workers from southern and eastern Europe, and sometimes significant groups of black and female employees. The weak market power of less skilled workers inclined industrial unions to emphasize political action as well as collective bargaining to achieve employee interests and to favor an active role for government in managing the economy and providing social welfare. In many ways, industrial unions also promoted a more pluralistic culture.

Public-employee unions experienced their greatest growth in numbers and influence in the 1960s and 1970s, when they organized the swelling ranks of local, state, and federal government employees. Some of these unions organized on a craft basis, but the larger ones incorporated a mix of blue- and white-collar occupations, and many represented large female and black memberships. Public-employee unions are distinguished by a uniquely close relationship between political action and collective bargaining: because they bargain with government agencies and are usually denied the strike weapon, political influence is crucial to their bargaining success. They support expansion of the public sector, which boosts public employment and union membership, and have often been vigorous advocates of racial and gender equality. Since the 1970s, they have had their own department in the AFL-CIO.

Some service-sector unions also grew substantially in the last two decades or so of the twentieth century. The large ones organized a wide range of occupations in retail sales, health care, insurance, hospitality and leisure, and building maintenance. Their memberships are socially diverse, with large contingents of female, black, and Hispanic employees. The low-wage employment, diverse workforce, and limited unionization of the service sector incline these unions to support a broad political program of government regulation of the economy, expanded provision of social benefits, and multiculturalism. Some analysts have claimed that service-sector unions have particular difficulty mobilizing their dispersed and less educated members for political action, but this is not clear. These unions, too, have a separate department in the AFL-CIO.[9]

Over the course of the twentieth century, then, four successive blocs of unions grew to prominence in the U.S. labor movement. As they did, the social bases and political orientations of American unionism expanded and changed. By the last three decades of the century, the four types of unions coexisted, and to some degree competed for influence, within the labor movement and its federation. Because the typology of craft, industrial, public-employee, and service unions emphasizes historically successive and politically distinctive kinds of unions, it promises to help analyze and explain political divisions between unions and the evolution of the labor-liberal coalition.

As important as this typology is for understanding twentieth-century labor history and politics, it misses a key feature of the internal politics of American labor: its tendency toward bifactionalism. Twentieth-century unionism in the United States typically divided into two wings or factions, at least in regard to the broad social and political direction of the labor movement. Whether in a given period the labor movement comprised two, three, or four distinctive types of unions, the pattern of political division and alliance among them normally resulted in a bifactional structure, as is evident in three key eras of modern labor history.

The first and most obvious case of bifactionalism was the division of American labor into two separate union federations between 1935 and 1955. The AFL mainly represented the older craft unions among workers in skilled trades, whereas the CIO comprised the newer industrial unions among semi- and unskilled labor in modern mass-production industries. This division arose out of profound differences over how to organize the mass-production workforce, the importance of a political alliance with President Roosevelt and the Democratic Party, and support for activist government in economic management and social provision.

Second, for roughly a quarter-century beginning in the late 1960s, organized labor was divided into more conservative and more liberal wings, the former based most solidly in ex-AFL craft unions, with accretions of support from other types of unions, and the latter representing a coalition of industrial, public-employee, and a few growing service unions.[10] This later bifactional division of unionism did not assume the form of dual federations but rather of dominant (Meany) and dissident (Reuther) factions of the AFL-CIO. It reflected a schism within the labor movement over its relationship to the contemporary transformation of Democratic liberalism.

Finally, in 1995 organized labor split in two in the first contested election for the presidency of the AFL-CIO in its forty-year history. The election pitted an old-guard slate led by Thomas Donohue, the longtime secretary-treasurer of the AFL-CIO, against the "New Voice" ticket headed by John Sweeney, president of the Service Employees International Union (SEIU). The contest was fought over the strategies for, and the role of the AFL-CIO in, the revival of a union movement in decline, and it was won by Sweeney's more activist and reform-minded ticket. Although the pattern of union voting in this election was complicated, it exhibited a good deal of continuity with the Meany-Reuther factional split of the previous twenty-five years.[11] In this case, bifactionalism involved an outright struggle for control of the national labor federation.

The tendency toward bifactionalism in American labor reflects enduring differences between the relatively narrow economic bases, social composition, and political interests of craft unionism and the more varied economic bases, heterogeneous social profiles, and expansive political concerns of industrial, public-employee, and service-sector unions. Craft unions have always represented primarily skilled, white male workers in particular trades, and this narrow socioeconomic base has limited their political interests. They have sought to advance worker welfare mainly by controlling the supply of skilled labor, thus enhancing their bargaining power with employers. This strategy limited their political interests to securing the other conditions, legal and economic, of union bargaining power: government protection of the rights to organize, bargain, strike, and boycott, and government provision of subsidies (e.g., highway spending) and regulations (e.g., prevailing wage laws) that maintain employment levels and wage norms in the skilled trades. In addition, the social composition of craft unions rendered them culturally conservative, generally deferential to and protective of established racial, ethnic, and gender hierarchies (although the AFL supported female suffrage as early as the 1890s). Because they organized particular crafts, enrolled skilled workers, and represented relatively privileged social strata, craft unions tended to be exclusive and restricted in outlook and strategy; they rarely exhibited broad social and political sympathies, supported extensive programs of social reform or state-building, or formed durable alliances with other social forces.

By contrast, industrial, public-employee, and service-sector unions have all had wider and more varied socioeconomic bases that inclined them toward broader and more progressive social outlooks and political programs. Since all three types of unions organized multiple occupations, enrolled less skilled workers, and represented minority and female (as well as white male) employees, they developed broad economic concerns, relied on politics as well as collective bargaining to promote worker well-being, and encouraged cultural diversity. As organizations of (or including) low-skill workers who possessed less market power, these unions engaged in political action not just to prop up union power in collective bargaining, but to directly secure social benefits for workers and citizens, and they sought allies to bolster their political influence. As organizations of (or including) minority and female employees, they challenged traditional distributions of status and rights among racial, ethnic, and gender groups. Only broad political programs encompassing economic redistribution, social reform, and cultural pluralism could unite the heterogeneous members of industrial, public-employee, and service unions. These unions built on and generated wider social solidarities and a more inclusive and egalitarian outlook than did craft unions, and as a result they favored a more expansive social role for both the labor movement and the state.[12]

Despite real and important differences among industrial, public-employee, and service-sector unions, then, they have at times united in opposition to craft unions over the broad social and political direction of the labor movement. It also bears emphasis that this bifactionalism has assumed varied institutional forms, including separate labor federations, dominant and subordinate wings of a single federation, and outright contests for control of the labor federation.

Varieties of Liberalism

It is also clear that over the course of the past century, different kinds of modern liberals emerged in the United States and that many of them coexist today. Studies of twentieth-century American history and politics suggest a stunning variety of distinct and sometimes successive types of liberals, including New Deal and post–New Deal liberals, popular-front and anticommunist liberals, economic and cultural liberals, civil-libertarian and communitarian liberals, multicultural and public-interest liberals, and others.[13] These categories usefully evoke the range of different and sometimes opposed social strata and political interests that have worn the mantle of liberalism both over time and today, but they do not constitute a shared or systematic classification system. Different scholars distinguish different kinds of liberals and employ different terms or labels to designate them, depending on the historical periods or particular topics with which these scholars are concerned. Surprisingly little work has been done to develop a conceptually and historically grounded typology of liberals (and liberalisms) across the entire twentieth century, one that might provide a common framework and language for scholars.

For the purposes of this study, a particularly important distinction is between New Deal (or New Deal/Cold War) and New Politics liberals.[14] New Deal and New Politics liberals rose to power in successive periods, represented different generations and social strata, and advocated distinctive and at times conflicting policy agendas and political strategies. As a simple binary classification, this distinction does not permit a fine-grained analysis of the variations in or development of twentieth-century American liberalism. It does, however, usefully focus on crucial internal dynamics of Democratic liberalism in its period of decline, and for that reason it is indispensable for analyzing the evolution of the labor-liberal coalition from the late 1960s onward.

New Deal liberals, of course, rose to power in the 1930s under the leadership of President Franklin D. Roosevelt. As heirs of the Populist and Progressive movements, and in response to the Great Depression, they developed a commitment to active government to manage and regulate the economy, provide social welfare, and balance concentrated private power. Toward these ends, they recognized social (as well as civil and political) rights, expanded the authority of the national government, and promoted the growth of labor unions. New Deal liberals also embraced the currents of social pluralism and cultural modernism that flourished in the 1930s and 1940s. Yet, dependent on the votes of southern white Democrats in elections and in Congress, they largely accommodated the

South's Jim Crow system. During and after World War II, New Deal liberals forged principles of international activism and collective security in defense of democracy and open world trade. By the late 1940s, the uneasy wartime alliance with the Soviet Union shifted to superpower rivalry, and New Deal liberals thereafter supported Cold War foreign policy. New Deal/Cold War liberals achieved and maintained power through a broad electoral coalition that included workers, ethnic and religious minorities, white southerners, blacks, and the liberal middle class, as well as through alliances with industrial unions and other newly organized groups.[15]

New Politics liberals rose to prominence in the Democratic Party and national politics in the late 1960s and 1970s. Products of postwar affluence and higher education, they emerged from the civil rights, antiwar, feminist, environmental, and consumer movements and spoke for the nation's youth, minorities, women, and middle-class issue activists. New Politics liberals were not hostile to the economic and social welfare agenda of their New Deal/Cold War predecessors, but they were determined opponents of the war in Vietnam, racial and gender discrimination, and the degradation of the natural environment. Their fundamental commitments were to peace and international accommodation, racial and gender equality, and an enhanced quality of life. Like the social strata and movements they represented, New Politics liberals were a diverse lot; their unity in the 1960s and 1970s derived mainly from their shared opposition to the war in Vietnam and their common exclusion from power in the Democratic Party and national government. Their lack of influence made them critics of unrepresentative governmental and political institutions and advocates of bureaucratic, party, electoral, and other reforms. They gained power through reforms of the Democratic Party that gave them influence over its candidates and platforms, the organization of many new interest groups, and leveraging of their policy expertise, legal skills, and media savvy to reform public institutions and policies.[16]

As New Politics liberals organized and gained strength in the latter half of the 1960s, they challenged New Deal/Cold War liberals for control of the Democratic Party. By the late 1960s, then, Democratic liberalism was split between its established but declining New Deal/Cold War elements and its insurgent and rising New Politics forces. The ascendance of New Politics liberals not only split but also transformed Democratic liberalism, altering its social bases and political demands. And, because organized labor had been allied with New Deal/Cold War liberals for several decades, the insurgency of the New Politics liberals created deep tensions in the labor-liberal coalition and in organized labor itself. The division and transformation of Democratic liberalism in turn precipitated splits between labor and liberals and induced divisions between unions.

My emphasis on the distinction between New Deal/Cold War and New Politics liberals does not imply that liberalism, like unionism, has exhibited an enduring tendency toward bifactionalism. Instead, liberalism evolved from a unified to a bifactional and then to a multifactional movement over the course of the last century.

In the 1930s and 1940s, liberalism was a relatively unified movement. The overwhelming crisis of the Depression initially gave New Deal liberalism a unifying focus on economic relief, recovery, and reform and a central thrust toward class politics. Then the fascist threat and World War II reinforced liberal unity and extended it to the defense of democracy and a vision of a progressive and just international order. The early postwar years did bring to the surface tensions among liberals over civil rights, domestic communism, and relations with the Soviet Union. But when these tensions led Henry Wallace to run against President Harry Truman as the candidate of the Progressive Party in 1948, his weak showing revealed that the vast majority of liberals were aligned with Truman's New Deal/Cold War program.

Not until the late 1960s was liberal unity clearly and deeply sundered. The split between New Deal/Cold War and New Politics liberals inaugurated a period of bifactionalism in American liberalism. During the last two decades of the twentieth century, however, New Politics liberals themselves fractured, as the conditions that had once unified them—the war in Vietnam and their exclusion from positions of influence—ceased to exist. New Politics liberals divided into two broad camps: multicultural (or identity politics) liberals and public-interest liberals. Thus by the close of the twentieth century, American liberalism was divided at least three ways, adding New Deal/labor liberalism to the two varieties just mentioned. Some scholars believe that liberalism is even more fragmented than I have indicated, but there is wide agreement that liberalism is now multifactional.[17]

The Composition of the Labor-Liberal Coalition

The variety and evolution that characterize both unionism and liberalism have implications for the composition, organization, development, and power of their alliance. Who participates in the labor-liberal coalition, how it is organized, when and why it rises or declines, and how powerful or weak it is are all shaped by the divisions among, and change over time in, unions and liberals.

Political differences among unions and among liberals make it possible and even likely that, in any given period, a labor-liberal coalition will be composed of certain types of unions and/or certain kinds of liberals but not others, or at least will be supported more actively and strongly by some kinds of unions and liberals than others. To cite two examples, in the late 1940s the labor-liberal coalition included anticommunist but excluded popular front liberals, and in the late 1960s it was supported much more vigorously by industrial and public-employee unions than by craft unions. Analysis of the labor-liberal coalition at any moment of time should therefore specify which types of unions and liberals participate in the coalition and which do not, or what kinds of unions and liberals support it most actively and strongly.

The composition of the labor-liberal coalition in a particular period in turn helps to clarify and explain the terms of that coalition—that is, the goals and strategies around which the partners coalesce. Because unions and liberals differ politically among themselves, which particular unions and liberals join or strongly support a labor-liberal coalition and which do not will determine the goals and strategies the coalition pursues. For instance, because industrial unions were stronger supporters than craft unions of the labor-liberal coalition of the 1930s, that coalition quickly and firmly supported government-funded social insurance programs, about which craft unions were initially deeply ambivalent. Or, for another example, the exclusion of popular front liberals from the labor-liberal coalition of the late 1940s ensured that the coalition would support the Cold War.

Finally, over time, the emergence of new types of unions or of liberals might threaten, and compel change in, the composition and terms of an established labor-liberal coalition. To return to the last example, as of the late 1940s the terms of the labor-liberal coalition included support for the Cold War. Two decades later the war in Vietnam, a product of Cold War foreign policy, helped to generate a new type of liberal, New Politics liberals, who opposed the war in Vietnam and questioned the Cold War framework of U.S. foreign policy. The rise of New Politics liberals disrupted the established labor-liberal coalition, and as dissident unions moved to ally with New Politics liberals, the terms of their alliance included opposition to the Vietnam war, support for detente between the superpowers, and a new framework for United States policy in the Third World.

The Organization of the Labor-Liberal Coalition

The multiple and successive types of unions and of liberals also means that their alliance can be, and historically has been, organized in different ways. The labor-liberal coalition, like the union–Democratic Party alliance, is best understood as an organizational or institutional alliance, one between labor and liberal organizations that centers on the leaders, staff, and activists of these organizations and the institutional resources they control.[18] But there are different kinds and levels of labor and liberal organizations, and it is important to analyze both which ones ally in a given period and how the organizational bases of a labor-liberal coalition might change over time.

One type of labor organization that can participate in a labor-liberal coalition, and has at times served as labor's organizational base in that coalition, is the national labor federation. The AFL-CIO has strongly allied with liberals at various times, such as the period between 1955 and 1968, or the years since 1995. At other times the AFL-CIO has withdrawn from the labor-liberal coalition, at least on the crucial issues of the day, as was the case for a number of years after 1968 on such issues as the Vietnam war and reform of the Democratic Party. In any given period, whether the leadership of the labor federation decides to participate in or abstain from a coalition with liberals ultimately depends on which unions hold the balance of power in the federation.

It is wrong to assume, however, that the national federation is the only labor organization that can serve as the organizational base for unions in an alliance with liberals or the Democratic Party. The main alternative is an organized bloc of dissident unions that lacks control of the labor federation. Historically, when the labor federation has rejected or withdrawn from a labor-liberal coalition, dissident unions that favored such a coalition organized themselves to provide an institutional base for a labor alliance with liberals. This has been possible because in the United States the labor federation generally lacks the authority to compel its members unions to abide by its political decisions, and most unions maintain their own political operations and can act independently in national politics.[19]

Four organizational strategies are available to dissident unions that favor a labor-liberal coalition. First, because the labor federation is a complex organization, dissident unions might try to organize themselves to ally with liberals by uniting in and controlling some unit of the federation's organizational structure (a department, committee, political arm, etc.) that enjoys some degree of independence from central control. Second, they might seek outright control of the existing labor federation. Third, they could disaffiliate from the existing federation and establish a new one that they would control. Finally, a dissident bloc of unions might, while remaining affiliated to the existing federation, establish one or more political organizations independent of it in order to ally with liberals.

These are not only theoretical possibilities; all four options were in fact attempted by dissident unions during the twentieth century. The first strategy was tried in the mid-1930s when a small group of AFL unions, which were already organized on an industrial union basis, formed a Committee for Industrial Organization within the craft-union-dominated federation in order to ally with the Roosevelt administration and Democratic liberals and thereby promote the cause of industrial unionism in the modern mass-production industries. When, in short order, these unions were expelled from the AFL, they adopted the third strategy and organized themselves as a separate labor federation, the Congress of Industrial Organizations (CIO), through which they indeed pioneered the development of a labor alliance with Democratic liberals.

Beginning in the late 1960s, a bloc of industrial, public-employee, and (to a lesser extent) service-sector unions followed the fourth strategy and forged numerous political organizations, eventually including the Progressive Alliance, Citizen Labor Energy Coalition, and National Labor Committee, that sought to maintain a labor-liberal coalition at a time when the top leadership and dominant wing of the federation withdrew from such a coalition on crucial issues. Finally, in

1995, dissident unions took up the second strategy by supporting John Sweeney's "New Voice" slate and seeking direct control of the AFL-CIO through election of its top officers.

Various kinds of liberal organizations, too, can and have participated in the labor-liberal coalition. Liberal interest groups, from the National Farmers Union and the National Association for the Advancement of Colored People to the National Organization for Women and Friends of the Earth, have often allied with unions. Such interest groups have united with labor not only on national political and policy issues—civil rights laws, judicial nominations, trade agreements—but also in factional battles in the Democratic Party over its candidates, platform, and electoral strategies. Interest groups are likely to be especially important as an organizational base for the labor-liberal coalition when it is difficult for liberals to use party organizations to ally with unions, either because liberals are divided among themselves or because they face opposition from other factions in the Democratic Party.

Still, the party faction—the liberal wing of the Democratic Party—generally serves as the key institutional base for liberals allied with organized labor, because political parties continue to play the central roles in contesting elections, organizing government, and making public policy. But how is this party faction itself organized? What are the organizational bases of liberals in the Democratic Party, and how have they changed over time?

During the middle third of the twentieth century (roughly 1932–68), liberals had three important organizational bases in the Democratic Party, which they used to ally with the labor movement. First, liberals were strong in the state and local party organizations of the northern states. Second, they were based in the party's "presidential wing"—that is, the network of party organizations (Democratic National Committee, Democratic National Convention) and activists that contest presidential elections. And third, liberal Democratic Party activists and members of Congress sometimes formed intraparty or legislative caucuses like the Democratic Advisory Council and the Democratic Study Group.[20]

Beginning in the late 1960s, however, these bases of liberal organization and strength in the Democratic Party were disrupted by factional conflicts, first between New Politics and New Deal/Cold War liberals and later between liberals (of any stripe) and centrists in the Democratic Leadership Council.[21] Thus, in the late twentieth century, the era of liberal division and decline, liberals had to rely on other organizations to maintain their alliance with unions. In part, they relied on civil rights, women's, environmental, and other interest groups, which united with dissident unions in new coalitions like Democratic Agenda, Progressive Alliance, and Citizen Labor Energy Coalition. They also used legislative caucuses among liberal Democrats in Congress, including the Congressional Black Caucus, the Progressive Caucus, and the Populist Caucus, to ally with labor leaders and organizations. In fact, in this era the "congressional wing" of the Democratic Party, once the domain of the party's southern conservatives, became a more important and reliable base of labor-liberal influence than its presidential wing. Some urban and state Democratic organizations remained bases of liberal strength allied with unions in these decades, as well.[22]

In short, the organizational bases of the labor-liberal coalition are products of political division and conflict among unions and among liberals, and they change over time with the emergence of new types of unions or new types of liberals. Whether unionists rely on a central labor federation or an organized bloc of dissident unions to ally with liberals, and whether liberals rely on interest groups or party organizations to ally with unions, is determined by the shifting lines of division and balances of power among unions and among liberals, and between liberals and other party factions.

Finally, to view the labor-liberal coalition as an organizational alliance is to emphasize that it exists primarily among organizational elites—that is, the leaders, staff, and activists of labor and liberal institutions, rather than their rank-and-file memberships or mass constituencies. But the social composition and political disposition of union memberships and of liberal constituencies matter greatly to the labor-liberal coalition, because these shape the views, objectives, and strategies of union and liberal leaders and activists. To stress the organizational character of the labor-liberal coalition is not to deny the importance of the mass memberships or constituencies of unions and liberals to the ultimate fate of their alliance.

The Development of the Labor-Liberal Coalition

The emergence over time of new types of unions and new kinds of liberals alters the social composition and political orientations of unionism and liberalism, and thereby affects the development of their alliance. Both the rise and the decline of the labor-liberal coalition were shaped by changes in the degree to which organized labor and the liberal wing of the Democratic Party had common or overlapping social bases and political commitments.[23]

The formation of a viable labor-liberal coalition occurred only when unions and liberal Democrats began, in the 1930s, to represent the same social groups, or at least converging and overlapping constituencies, and thus to advocate similar ideological positions and policy demands. An early alliance between the AFL and the Democratic Party in the Progressive era floundered because the federation's skilled-craft labor base and anti-statist ideology were too narrow to help the party expand beyond its southern and agrarian base into northern working-class and urban constituencies.[24] By the mid- to late 1930s, however, the formation of the CIO and the electoral realignment that stretched from 1928 through 1936 gave the labor movement and the northern wing of the Democratic Party a common social base in the urban industrial working class, which, in conjunction with the Depression, committed both institutions to active government and a welfare-state program. The resulting organizational alliance endured, with considerable political success, for roughly a generation.

By the late 1960s, however, far-reaching social changes of the postwar era—the spread of affluence, expansion of higher education, growth of technical and professional occupations, and emergence of new social movements—transformed the social composition and political agenda of the liberal wing of the Democratic Party in ways that diverged from those of organized labor, especially its dominant wing, and this disrupted and weakened their coalition. The rise of a New Politics liberalism that was socially diverse but heavily concentrated among educated upper-middle-class professionals opened both a social gulf and political fissures between liberal Democrats and much of the union movement. This divergence in the sociopolitical foundations of unionism and liberalism was only the first of two major sources of decline of the labor-liberal coalition, but it was all the more important because it occurred just as both partners to the coalition came under political attack.

The disparity in the social bases and political views of labor and liberals that became apparent in the late 1960s deeply strained but did not end their coalition. The transformation of Democratic liberalism *threatened the terms of the existing labor-liberal coalition, and required their renegotiation if the coalition were to survive.* Specifically, the rise of New Politics liberals disrupted the existing labor-liberal coalition by challenging three of its terms: a policy agenda focused on economic and welfare-state issues, broad support for Cold War foreign policy, and a presidential nominating system in which party elites and high union officials played strategic roles. The labor-liberal coalition survived this challenge, though in shrunken and weakened form, because certain unions proved willing to renegotiate these terms and accommodate New Politics demands. The unions that proved most willing to do so constituted the dissident or Reuther wing of the labor movement and were, by and large, the unions whose memberships were socially heterogeneous and in that respect were closest in composition to the new social movements and New Politics liberals. Indeed, in the final decades of the twentieth century the social composition and political demands of unionism and liberalism began to converge once again, as racial minorities, public employees, women, and immigrants acquired greater prominence in the memberships of American unions, as well as in the constituencies of liberal Democratic politicians.

Change over time in the degree to which the sociopolitical foundations of unions and liberals either converge or diverge not only strengthens or weakens the prospects for their alliance but also alters its character and purposes. Organizational alliances can be distinguished into two types, instrumental and organic. Instrumental coalitions exist between institutions—say, economic and political institutions, or religious and political institutions—that represent different social groups and political demands and serve as a means to achieve the separate institutional goals of each partner. Instrumental coalitions are common and often effective but are also easily weakened or disrupted, because the partners lack any bond other than the mutual satisfaction of their separate goals. Organic coalitions exist between institutions that represent the same or overlapping social groups and promote the (resultant) shared principles and demands of the two partners. Such coalitions have deeper and stronger foundations than instrumental calculations of institutional self-interest; they emerge "naturally" from and rest on a shared social base and common political commitments. As a result, organic coalitions tend to be more ideological, cohesive, and stable than instrumental alliances.

The distinction between instrumental and organic coalitions can be applied to different stages of a single coalition over time, and indeed to different aspects of a coalition at a particular moment in time. So construed, the distinction illuminates the evolution of the labor-liberal coalition. That coalition has shifted over time between instrumental and organic stages, based on changes in the degree to which the social bases of unions and Democratic liberals overlapped. The AFL–Democratic Party alliance of the Progressive era was essentially instrumental in character, the labor-liberal Democratic alliance of the mid-1930s through the early to mid-1960s was a much more organic coalition, and in the 1960s and 1970s the labor-liberal coalition again assumed a more instrumental, and unstable, character as the sociopolitical foundations of Democratic liberalism diverged from those of the labor movement.

In each of these stages, though, the labor-liberal coalition in fact had both instrumental and organic characteristics and purposes. In every phase of their alliance during the twentieth century, organized labor and the liberal wing of the Democratic Party remained distinct organizations with discrete interests—bargaining power for unions, electoral success for liberal Democrats—that each hoped to maximize. But in every phase of their alliance there was also some overlap of constituencies and demands between unions and liberals that provided them with some common goals. To designate one stage of the labor-liberal coalition as instrumental and another as organic is to indicate the predominant character and purposes of the coalition in a particular period.

This way of thinking about the labor-liberal coalition suggests the limitations of a common interpretation of it as *essentially* an instrumental coalition, one that invariably serves as a means to achieve the separate goals of each of the partners.[25] In this view, the coalition is a product of a rational choice by union and party leaders to pursue their particular organizational goals by means of an alliance strategy, and it operates as a bargaining relationship between union and party leaders in which the power of each side to get what it wants from the other side depends on the resources it commands.[26] As powerful and illuminating as this approach is, it is too limited to adequately analyze the labor-liberal Democratic alliance. It misses the organic character of that alliance from the mid-1930s to the mid-1960s; obscures the evolution of the labor-liberal coalition by assuming that its character and purposes are fixed rather than variable; and ignores the mix of instrumental and organic characteristics and purposes that always characterizes the labor-liberal coalition in a given period.

The Power of the Labor-Liberal Coalition

The political power of the labor-liberal coalition is also shaped by the internal political dynamics of unionism and liberalism, though other factors are at least as important. The power of this coalition, and variations in it over time, are a function of five factors: (a) the strength of the coalition's internal bonds, (b) the density of the coalition, (c) the types and amounts of power resources mobilized by the coalition's partners, (d) the degree of institutionalization of the coalition, and (e) the power of the coalition's main political opponents.

The power of any coalition is partly determined by the strength of the bonds between its partners, or the breadth and depth of agreement between them on goals and strategies. This can be referred to as the internal strength or unity of the labor-liberal coalition. It is one element, but only one element, of the coalition's power or influence in the larger political system, which has other sources and is relative to the power of its political opponents. Thus the internal strength and the external power of the labor-liberal coalition (or any other alliance) are related but distinct phenomena. In the middle third of the twentieth century both the internal strength and the external power of the labor-liberal coalition were substantial; in the last third of the century both declined, though not to the extent that some have claimed.

Next, the political power of the labor-liberal coalition depends on its density—that is, the percentage of all unions and of all liberals that actually join or actively support the coalition, or the ratio of participating to nonparticipating unions and liberals. If political differences among unions or among liberals lead some unions or some liberals to refuse to join, withdraw from, or weakly support a labor-liberal coalition, then the coalition will be weakened. Beginning in the late 1960s, for example, the labor-liberal coalition was weakened by the refusal of the AFL-CIO and many of its unions to support the efforts of most liberals and the Reuther wing of the labor movement to end the war in Vietnam and reform the Democratic Party, and also by the lack of interest and support among some New Politics liberals (in environmental and government reform groups) for full employment policies. The power of the labor-liberal coalition will be maximized when unions are unified and liberals are unified in support of the coalition. The internal political dynamics of both unionism and liberalism shape the political power of the labor-liberal coalition through their effects on these first two determinants, the internal strength and density of the coalition.

The power of the labor-liberal coalition is also a function of the power resources that it, and each of its partners, is able to mobilize. A well-tested model of the power resources of union-party alliances in Western democracies emphasizes the size of union membership, the density of union organization (i.e., union membership as a percentage of the labor force), the degree of organizational unity and centralization in the labor movement, and the percentage of votes cast in elections for, and the duration of control of government by, parties of the left.[27] For the case of the labor-liberal coalition in the United States, this model should be modified or supplemented with additional power resources that are specific to liberals as a party faction and that expand labor resources beyond union membership and density. Resources specific to liberals as a party faction might include the percentage of Democratic voters who identify themselves as liberals, the percentage of votes cast for and of elections (both primary and general) won by liberal candidates, the percentage of members of Congress with strong liberal voting records, and the percentage of leadership positions in Congress held by liberals.

It is also important to recognize that the power resources of organized labor cannot be limited to measures of union membership and density. As Taylor Dark has shown, unions command a wide range of economic, electoral, and legislative resources that they can mobilize to influence national politics.[28] The decline of union density does not automatically produce decline in organized labor's political power or in the strength of the labor-liberal coalition, because unions can still mobilize impressive economic and political resources and even expand and improve the resources they devote to political action.[29] For instance, despite the continuing decline of union density, in the 1990s labor was at times able to increase the union shares of all campaign funds and of all votes cast in federal elections.

Another determinant of the power of the labor-liberal coalition is the forms and extent of organizational coordination and support between unions and liberals, or the ways and degree to which their coalition is institutionalized. Even if their internal bonds are strong and the power resources they mobilize are substantial, unions and liberals still might not develop effective means of coordination and support. Unions did not always have the effective campaign organizations that they eventually developed to support, through fund-raising and voter mobilization, liberal Democratic candidates for public office, and at other times they did not use these organizations to support certain liberal candidates. Liberal officeholders have not always routinely communicated with union leaders and staff about policy decisions or legislative strategy. In short, even a unified coalition possessed of considerable resources can weaken itself by inadequate organizational coordination and support between the partners.

Finally, the power of the labor-liberal coalition is relative to the power of its main competitors or opponents in national politics, which we can summarize as the business-conservative coalition. The latter's power is determined by the same factors as that of the labor-liberal coalition. After the late 1960s, and especially after the late 1970s, the power of the labor-liberal coalition in national politics declined relative to that of the business-conservative alliance.

Conclusion

The composition, organization, development, and power of the labor-liberal coalition are all products of the internal political dynamics of both organized labor and Democratic liberalism. Changes in the social composition and political disposition of organized labor and the liberal wing of the Democratic Party, the degree of unity or division among both unions and liberals, and the balance of power between different types or factions of unions and of liberals have been central to the evolution and fortunes of the labor-liberal coalition. Among other things, these variables determine whether or to what extent the social bases and political demands of unions and liberals overlap and therefore shape the character and prospects of the labor-liberal coalition.

CHAPTER 2

The Rise of the
Labor-Liberal Coalition

Precursor: The AFL–Democratic Party Alliance of the Progressive Era

The labor-liberal coalition was forged in the 1930s. This marked the first durable and potent political alliance for the modern American labor movement. An important precursor, however, was the organizational alliance between the AFL and the Democratic Party between 1906 and 1918. Although this labor-Democratic alliance of the Progressive era seemed successful and promising in 1916, it fell apart after World War I.[1] The AFL could not keep the Democratic Party in power in the congressional elections of 1918 or the presidential election of 1920, as the party lost working-class votes; at the same time, the party did little to protect AFL unions against mounting employer opposition after the war.[2] Subsequently, during the 1920s, conservative and business elements became dominant in the national Democratic Party, and the AFL, after endorsing Robert M. La Follette's Progressive Party candidacy in 1924, returned to its traditional nonpartisanship.[3]

It is striking how quickly and completely this early AFL-Democratic alliance collapsed. There were two reasons for this. One was that the alliance was unable to fulfill the instrumental purposes for which it was established. The alliance arose out of the separate institutional needs of the AFL for legal and political support for collective bargaining and of the Democratic Party for electoral support outside of its traditional southern and western strongholds. But in the Progressive era, neither the AFL nor the Democratic Party was well suited to deliver what the other needed. The AFL was still too narrowly based in skilled-craft labor and among native stock or northern European workers, and too attached to anti-statist ideology, to influence or speak for the larger and more diverse working class.[4] For its part, the Democratic Party provided only limited protection for unions during Woodrow Wilson's administrations and even less after Wilson and Progressive reform influence declined, due to the southern and western base of the party's electorate and congressional representation and to revived northern business influence in the party.[5]

Underlying this instrumental failure of the coalition was a second problem: the lack of strong social or ideological foundations for an AFL-Democratic alliance. The social composition and ideological orientations of the AFL and the Democratic Party were too dissimilar in the Progressive era and the 1920s for an organic coalition to arise between them.

The CIO Reformation and the Rise of the Labor-Liberal Coalition

The labor-liberal coalition that emerged in the New Deal era proved much more durable and successful. What happened between the Progressive and New Deal eras that made possible in the later period what had not been in the earlier one? Three developments stand out: (a) the party or electoral realignment that stretched from 1928 through 1936; (b) the Depression; and (c) the "CIO reformation" of American labor politics.[6] Only the last of these requires extended discussion.

National elections from 1928 through 1936 gradually realigned workers, minorities (blacks, southern and eastern Europeans, Catholics, and Jews), and urban residents with the Democratic Party, uniting them with the white South in a majority coalition.[7] Much of this realignment was spurred by the Depression and Franklin D. Roosevelt's campaigns and early New Deal programs, but some of it preceded these and was motivated by ethnoreligious developments. Apart from establishing it as the dominant party for a generation, the chief consequence of this realignment was to give the Democratic Party a strongly working-class and urban social base outside the South.

Along with its influence on the partisan realignment of key voting blocs, the Depression generated heightened worker militancy and class consciousness, which increased the demand for unionization (especially in mass-production industries) and promoted working-class political unity by submerging ethnoreligious differences.[8] More generally, it revived and strengthened demands for economic and social reform and shifted the center of ideological debate away from laissez faire and toward active government.

The rise of the CIO worked a reformation of the American labor movement in two ways: first by creating a type of unionism that differed from that of the AFL, and then by pressuring the AFL to grow and change. On the eve of the 1930s, the AFL was based mainly among skilled workers, typically old-stock American or northern European, organized into craft unions in the construction, railroad, local transport, entertainment, printing, and other trades.[9] The federation and many of its affiliated unions adhered to the ideology of "voluntarism," according to which unions were voluntary associations that were autonomous (i.e., subject to only limited AFL authority), nonpartisan, and reliant on their own economic power rather than on the state to secure rights and benefits for workers.[10] Voluntarism was or became an anti-statist ideology, never more so than in the 1920s when the AFL opposed wage and hour laws and unemployment insurance, fearful that such social legislation would undermine the support of workers for unions.[11] Consonant with its voluntarist ideology, the AFL practiced "business union-ism," which was concerned primarily with advancing the immediate economic interests of workers through collective bargaining and rested on a high dues–high benefits formula that only skilled workers could sustain.[12] The skilled labor base, craft structure, voluntarist ideology, and business unionism of the AFL made it reluctant and ill-equipped to organize the modern mass-production industries, by now the core of the U.S. economy, even when workers in them demonstrated in the 1930s that they wished to be unionized.[13]

As the CIO organized the auto, steel, electrical, rubber, and other mass-pro-duction industries in the latter half of the 1930s, it differed significantly from the AFL. It organized mostly semi- and unskilled mass-production workers in industrial unions. Its membership was more heterogeneous than that of the AFL, as it included many workers from southern and eastern Europe, as well as Afri-can-American and female workers.[14] It also rejected voluntarism as unsuited to the needs and interests of low-skill workers who lacked market power. As Ruth Horowitz has said, "New, more positive attitudes toward government, legisla-tion, political partisanship and activism arose with the formation of the CIO as an independent force in the American labor movement."[15] Horowitz observes that CIO leaders did not give a name to their ideology, and she simply calls it "antivoluntarism," but it could be characterized as New Deal liberal or perhaps social democratic.

Consistent with this outlook, the CIO practiced "social unionism," which the historian John Barnard has defined as "the use of unions to pursue the public good through political, social, and economic reforms."[16] CIO leaders themselves distinguished their version of unionism from that of the AFL in similar terms; as CIO President Philip Murray put it in 1944, "It is a new departure for American labor to lead . . . a national movement devoted to the general welfare just as much as to the particular interests of labor groups."[17] The more socially conscious and politically active unionism of the CIO derived from the (relatively) weak market position of unskilled workers, the inherently inclusive and egalitarian impulses of industrial unionism, the heterogeneous composition and diverse interests of its membership, and the urban concentration of the mass-production workforce (which among other things increased its electoral potential).[18]

The CIO not only differed from the AFL, it also compelled the AFL to grow and change by its competition and success as a rival labor federation. Competi-tion stimulated AFL organizing, and the federation's membership increased from under 3 million in 1933 to 4 million in 1939, by which time CIO membership was about 3.5 million.[19] The older federation actually proved more adept than the CIO at organizing new workers: by 1945, AFL unions enrolled 10 million workers whereas CIO organizations enrolled 4.5 million.[20] Further, once the CIO demonstrated the viability of industrial unionism, it found greater favor in the AFL, and some longtime craft unions in the federation began to organize on an industrial basis, although craft unionism remained the dominant force in the AFL.[21] The growth of organizing and of industrial unionism in the AFL gave it not only a larger but also a more economically and socially diverse membership. Finally, CIO competition and success also contributed to the modification of the AFL's nonpartisanship and anti-statism in and after the 1930s, although these did not go down quickly or easily.[22] It is surely true that these changes in the AFL reflected the impact of the Depression and the New Deal, but they also owed a great deal to the challenge thrown down to the older federation by the CIO, and in that sense the CIO worked a reformation of the entire American labor movement.[23]

The CIO reformation of American labor combined with the party realignment of 1928–36 and the Depression to make a strong and durable labor-liberal coalition possible in the 1930s. Together, these three developments strengthened the social and ideological foundations and enhanced the instrumental effectiveness of the labor-liberal Democratic coalition, particularly in comparison with the AFL-Democratic alliance of the Progressive era. First of all, these developments established considerable congruence or overlap in the social composition of organized labor and the northern Democratic Party. As J. David Greenstone put it: "In short, the 1930s were almost as critical a period for labor as for the Democratic Party *and in very much the same ways* . . . as a result of the realignment, the Democrats dramatically expanded their constituency to include the same groups of urban industrial workers and ethnic minorities that the CIO brought into organized labor."[24] Second, they also produced similar ideological dispositions in the two institutions. Given their diverse working-class and urban constituents and the economic crisis of the 1930s, both organized labor—particularly the CIO—and the Democratic Party advocated active government to achieve recovery and to enact economic and social reforms. The overlapping social bases and similar ideological inclinations of labor and the northern Democratic Party made their alliance more organic and gave it the solidity to endure inevitable political strains and setbacks.

Finally, the three developments made the labor-liberal coalition more instrumentally effective; each partner was better able to satisfy the institutional needs of the other. The strengthened working-class base and urban liberalism and the new majority status of the Democratic Party made it willing and able to enact favorable labor legislation, and the larger, more urbanized and diversified membership and expanded political commitments and resources of organized labor likewise made it willing and able to provide electoral and legislative support to

New Deal liberals. As unions and liberal Democrats both became more powerful in the 1930s, they became more valuable allies to each other.

Even more than indicated previoiusly, the rise of the CIO and the formation of the labor-liberal coalition were deeply intertwined and interdependent developments. The creation of the CIO was key to the development of a labor-liberal coalition, and that coalition was in turn crucial to the success and growth of the new labor federation. To begin with, it was precisely the opportunity to build a labor-liberal Democratic alliance that led a small group of leaders of AFL unions, led by John L. Lewis of the United Mine Workers and Sidney Hillman of the Amalgamated Clothing Workers, to establish the CIO. These leaders believed that the future of organized labor depended on organization of the strategic mass-production industries and that industrial unions, which would organize all the workers in a given industry regardless of their occupations or skill levels, were the appropriate means to accomplish that. They originally formed the CIO (Committee for Industrial Organization) in 1935 as a committee within the AFL to promote organization of the mass-production sector on an industrial union basis. Only after the AFL suspended the CIO unions in 1936—a clear indication of the AFL's resistance to organization of the new industries and to industrial unionism—did they eventually establish the CIO (renamed the Congress of Industrial Organizations) as an independent labor federation.

In forming the CIO, Lewis, Hillman, and their allies were chiefly influenced by political developments. They saw an opportunity—rooted in early New Deal policies, Roosevelt's need for reelection support, and the growing Democratic partisanship of workers—for labor to ally with Roosevelt and the Democrats and thus secure the political support necessary to unionize the mass-production workforce. They feared that AFL traditionalists, heedless of the economic significance and political requirements of organizing mass-production industry, would fritter away this opportunity. As Melvyn Dubofsky and Warren Van Tine put it: "Above all else, Lewis perceived the inseparable connection between New Deal politics and the successful organizing of mass-production workers. National politics, then, and not abstract disputes concerning the value of craft versus industrial unionism were decisive in the rift within the AFL and the emergence of the CIO."[25] Hillman's thinking was similar.[26]

Not surprisingly, then, on labor's side it was CIO unions that took the initiative in allying with Roosevelt and New Deal Democrats and in making the innovations in labor's ideology, policy preferences, and electoral activity necessary to that alliance. CIO leaders, even before they founded that body, immediately supported and actively promoted New Deal legislation ranging from the National Industrial Recovery Act of 1933 through the National Labor Relations Act and the Social Security Act of 1935 to the Fair Labor Standards Act of 1938; AFL leaders remained divided, dilatory, and passive even when they supported these measures.[27] CIO unions took the lead in forming campaign organizations (Labor's Nonpartisan League in 1936, Political Action Committee in 1943), making substantial contributions of funds, and conducting extensive voter mobilization on behalf of Roosevelt and New Deal liberals; again, AFL efforts in these areas lagged behind in time, scale, and intensity.[28]

It was also the new CIO unions that first capitalized on the assistance provided by labor's political allies. Following Roosevelt's reelection to a second term, the CIO used New Deal legal and political support to unionize the key auto and steel industries. Rank-and-file militancy; the dedication of activists; the leadership, strategies, and resources of the CIO; and other factors played roles in the organization of mass-production industry, but New Deal legal and political support was crucial.[29] Powerful political allies were necessary to the success and growth of the CIO.

The labor-liberal coalition that arose in the 1930s was thus an alliance of industrial unionism with New Deal liberalism. Based in the urban industrial workforce that both labor and New Deal Democrats came to represent in the 1930s, the terms (or goals) of this coalition were twofold. One was a commitment to active government and welfare state development, in the interest of economic recovery and stability in general and of the material well-being of workers and urbanites in particular. The other was the exchange of institutional benefits, legal and political protection for unions and electoral support for liberal Democrats. In this sense, the coalition was both ideological (or organic) and instrumental, founded on shared political commitments as well as group or institutional self-interests.

This labor-New Deal liberal alliance was fairly powerful and successful. It finally brought the industrial working class into full and effective participation in American public life. It was crucial to maintaining the Democratic Party in power during a decade and a half of economic crisis and world war. It enacted modern labor, fiscal, welfare, social-insurance, and regulatory policies that relieved economic distress and contributed to recovery. In the process, it extended unionism and collective bargaining to a historic peak of over one-third of the labor force and to the modern mass-production industries, and developed much of the modern welfare state in the United States, particularly at the national level. In these and other ways, the rise of the labor-liberal coalition shifted the balance of power among contending classes, parties, and ideologies; altered the agenda and policies of the state; and changed long-standing relations of power in the private economy. Finally, it made a major contribution to the defeat of the fascist powers in World War II and shaped a new international role for the United States. These should be understood as accomplishments of the *coalition* of industrial unionism and New Deal liberalism, for the power of each rested on their alliance.[30]

There were also limits to the power and achievements of this coalition during the 1930s and early 1940s, of course. One weakness was that it still had a relatively low level of institutionalization—that is, of regular and formal mechanisms of coordination and support between unions and liberal Democrats.[31] Another important limit on the power of the labor-liberal alliance was the continuing influence of the conservative coalition of southern Democrats and northern Republicans in Congress, which as early as the late 1930s moved aggressively against New Deal labor and social policies. Not the least of the weaknesses of the labor-liberal coalition was the ongoing division of the labor movement. Although labor had to split apart so that the CIO could respond to the opportunity to forge a strong labor-liberal alliance, in time the schism in organized labor would weaken that alliance as well as unionism itself. Finally, by the end of World War II, the alliance of industrial unionism and New Deal liberalism had not yet proved that it could create or sustain prosperity in peacetime, extend the benefits of collective bargaining or social insurance to groups of workers who remained excluded from both, complete the liberalization of the Democratic Party by transforming or expelling its southern conservative wing, or achieve racial equality.

The Evolution of the Labor-Liberal Coalition in the Post–World War II Era

The limitations of the labor-liberal coalition made it vulnerable to the revival of business and conservative influence during and after World War II, and in the immediate postwar years—a crucial and turbulent period in modern American politics—the advance of the coalition was largely halted in all three areas of its prior progress: union growth, electoral success, and welfare state development. Following the huge strike wave of 1945–46 and Republican victory in the 1946 congressional elections, the anti-union Taft-Hartley Act was passed in 1947 over President Truman's veto, and subsequent efforts to repeal the act failed.[32] Operation Dixie, the campaign launched by the CIO in 1946 to unionize the South—and to reconstruct the southern wing of the Democratic Party by creating an interracial working-class electorate that would sustain a liberal party leadership in that region—was decisively defeated.[33] Labor militancy also declined after the postwar strike wave, and in the decade after World War II, no new industries were organized and union density at best held steady at about 35 percent of the labor force.[34]

Further, the labor-liberal coalition's capacity to maintain firm Democratic control of national government was eroded. Republicans held majority control in Congress in 1947–49 and again in 1953–55, and of course occupied the White House from 1953 until 1961. The electoral difficulties of the coalition and the Democratic Party in those years were due to changes in the class composition of the electorate induced by rising prosperity; declining levels of class voting after 1948; the defection of southern white voters, beginning with the "Dixiecrat Revolt" of 1948, in response to civil-rights measures; the rise of communism and Cold War as cross-cutting issues; and President Eisenhower's popularity.[35] It seems likely that a reduced capacity to mobilize electoral support, due to the decline of party organization and to internal divisions in the labor movement, also played a role.[36]

With diminished influence over national government, the labor-liberal coalition's ability to set the public agenda and enact major new reforms was also constrained. During the Truman years, the Employment Act of 1946 and the Housing Act of 1949 were passed, and in 1950, Social Security coverage and benefits were extended. Evaluations of the 1946 and 1949 acts have varied, but neither would qualify as major new reforms on the New Deal scale, and the Social Security amendments of 1950 obviously represented an (important) extension of an existing program. The one Truman proposal of a major new reform, for national health insurance, was never adopted by Congress.[37]

If the power and progress of the labor-liberal coalition were checked in the second half of the 1940s, it is also true that in the political conflicts of those years the coalition was able to preserve its past gains and much of its earlier strength against strong business and conservative challenges, a point that has been obscured by some important scholars of the labor-liberal coalition.[38] First of all, as Dubofsky has pointed out, the gains that unions made during World War II in membership, density, industries organized, and institutional security were not reversed after the war, in sharp contrast to the aftermath of World War I, when union gains made during that war were rolled back and organized labor was gravely weakened.[39] Although clearly a defeat for labor, the Taft-Hartley Act as passed was less draconian than the original version of the bill, was not all that employers had hoped for, and weakened but did not repeal the Wagner Act.[40] Although union density only held even in the decade after 1945, union membership increased by close to three million in that period, from 14.32 million in 1945 to 17.02 million in 1954.[41]

Second, however much the electoral fortunes of the labor-liberal Democratic alliance shifted after World War II, the New Deal framework of party politics was maintained, if in attenuated form, through the 1950s, and the Democratic Party retained considerable strength in Congress throughout the period.[42] Finally, not only were the main economic and social reforms of the 1930s preserved, but the national government continued to grow after World War II as both civilian employment and social expenditures (on health, income security, education, and manpower programs) increased considerably through the 1940s and 1950s.[43]

Not only was the progress of the labor-liberal coalition checked (but not reversed) in the early postwar years, its political commitments were modified then as well, by economic growth and the onset of Cold War. The growth of the U.S. economy after World War II—contrary to widespread expectations of a return to depression conditions—muted earlier criticisms of capitalism and weakened the interest of unions and liberals in planning, industrial councils (for joint management of industry by business, labor, and state), and other economic reforms.[44] It also persuaded some Democratic politicians that existing New Deal programs were sufficient and, given that welfare state development was often blocked politically, encouraged industrial unions to turn to collective bargaining for new or expanded health, pension, and unemployment benefits.[45] At the same time, growth validated active government and the welfare state, proving that they could sustain prosperity, and enabled the government to finance rising social spending while also repaying the large public debt accumulated during the war. Thus, after World War II, the labor-liberal coalition exhibited less zeal for reform and a growing commitment to maintain private-sector growth.

But unions and liberals continued to favor and pursue welfare state development. They viewed private-sector growth and the welfare state not as alternatives but as mutually necessary and reinforcing: growth was needed to finance the welfare state, and social expenditures were needed to maintain aggregate demand and growth.[46] CIO unions believed that collective bargaining would serve as a spur to welfare state development, on the assumption that employers would not want to bear the costs of union-negotiated social benefits.[47] In the latter half of the 1950s the AFL-CIO worked with liberal Democrats in Congress to enact area redevelopment legislation (to promote employment in depressed regions), extend Social Security benefits to the disabled, and expand Social Security to include health insurance for the elderly.[48] Although these proposals were often blocked in the 1950s, the labor-liberal coalition revived them under the more favorable political conditions of the 1960s and launched a second phase of welfare state development.

More consequential for the labor-liberal coalition was the advent of the Cold War. Despite the anticommunism of liberal and labor leaders, including most CIO leaders, Depression-era politics allowed people in or close to the Communist Party to play important roles in the CIO and, to a much lesser degree, in some New Deal agencies, and later the fascist threat in Europe produced U.S.-Soviet cooperation during World War II. After the war, many labor and liberal leaders hoped to continue "popular front" alliances at home and "great power" cooperation abroad. CIO leaders initially resisted pressure to move against communists in the federation, and in 1945 the CIO joined the labor movements of the other victorious World War II allies, including the Soviet Union, in establishing the World Federation of Trade Unions (WFTU), the trade union version of "great power" cooperation.[49] (The AFL refused to join the WFTU, out of opposition to both the CIO and Soviet trade unions.) New Dealer Henry Wallace's 1948 Progressive Party presidential candidacy supported U.S.-Soviet cooperation.

But the vast majority of labor and liberal leaders soon aligned with the Cold War and domestic anticommunism. Developments in the CIO were particularly important. The proposal of the Marshall Plan in 1947 and especially Wallace's third-party campaign in 1948 shifted the CIO clearly into the Cold War/ anticommunist camp. Although unenthusiastic about Truman, with whom organized labor had a rocky relationship, CIO leaders strongly supported his election in 1948 because they needed Democratic support in order to repeal the hated Taft-Hartley Act. The support of the CIO's communists for Wallace thus appeared to CIO leaders as a sacrifice of fundamental trade union interests to those of a political party or even a foreign state.[50] Between 1948 and 1950, the CIO expelled eleven communist-led or -influenced unions with a combined membership of nearly one million workers, and in 1949 it joined the AFL, the British Trades Union Congress, and other labor bodies in forming the International Confederation of Free Trade Unions, which excluded communist unions.[51]

In effect, the terms of the labor-liberal coalition were expanded in the late 1940s, as unions and liberals became allied in support of anticommunism and Cold War as well as active government and the welfare state. The sources and consequences of this development remain matters of scholarly and political debate.[52] The anticommunism of New Deal liberals and organized labor in the late 1940s was principled and progressive in character. The anticommunist and Cold War orientation of the CIO, in particular, was fairly close to that of contemporary European social democratic labor movements and political parties.[53]

Over time, however, anticommunism and the Cold War did much to weaken and undermine the labor-liberal coalition. Unions and liberals at times practiced anticommunism in ways that contradicted trade union, liberal, or democratic values. Business leaders and conservatives used anticommunism to attack labor and liberals. The Cold War strengthened conservative social institutions and political forces, placed political and fiscal constraints on economic and social reform, and encouraged trade and other policies that weakened industry, workers, and unions. Cold War foreign policy made its supporters susceptible to alignment with reactionary and repressive regimes and movements.[54] Anticommunism at home and the Cold War abroad both had political dynamics that labor and liberals did not and could not control, because they were commitments of the political right as well, and labor and liberals did not establish clear differences between their version and the right-wing version of those commitments.

It took a very long time for liberal and labor leaders to grasp the ways that anticommunism and the Cold War corroded their moral authority and political power. By the time at least some of them did, the denouement of Cold War foreign policy, in Vietnam, had already deeply split the labor-liberal alliance. But that outcome was two decades in the future from the late 1940s, and rejection of anticommunism and the Cold War by the labor-liberal coalition at that time might well have exposed it to more severe repression as well as compromised its own principles.[55]

Apart from the Cold War, stalemate characterized American politics in the late 1940s; the power and progress of the labor-liberal coalition were checked, but business and conservative forces could not roll back New Deal reforms. In response to this stalemate, the labor-liberal coalition worked to strengthen its internal bonds, organizational capacities and resources, and political influence. In all these areas, the labor-liberal coalition did become stronger by the late 1950s or early 1960s.

In part, the bonds of mutual support between labor and liberals were tightened by adverse developments. The passage of anti-union legislation in the 1940s, including the Smith-Connally Act of 1943 as well as the Taft-Hartley Act four years later, and the atrophy of state and local Democratic Party organizations in the 1950s, which left unions as the only campaign organizations available to liberal politicians in many areas, made unions and liberal Democrats more dependent on each other for political support. But in addition, many CIO unions actively sought to solidify their alliance with liberal Democrats by abandoning lingering third-party hopes and expelling communist-led unions in and after 1948. Liberal Democrats in Congress responded in kind in the 1950s by promoting reforms of the lawmaking process that would facilitate the legislative goals of organized labor and other liberal groups.[56]

The labor-liberal coalition also developed greater organizational capacities and resources in the 1940s and 1950s. Passage of the Smith-Connally and Taft-Hartley acts persuaded the CIO to form its Political Action Committee in 1943 and the AFL to set up its Labor League for Political Education in 1948; these were the first solid and durable campaign organizations that unions built. The merger of the two federations in 1955 finally produced a unified political arm of organized labor in the form of the AFL-CIO's Committee on Political Education (COPE). Gradually, then, labor increased its capacity to mobilize campaign funds and voters in support of liberal Democrats.[57] Unions and labor federations enhanced their lobbying capabilities over the same period of time.[58] Moreover, liberal Democrats in Congress and in the party leadership formally organized themselves in the mid- to late 1950s, through such groups as the Democratic Advisory Council and the Democratic Study Group, in order to better formulate and promote a liberal policy agenda.[59] As they expanded and improved their organizational capacities and resources, labor and liberals also better coordinated their electoral and legislative activities.[60]

Besides strengthening its internal bonds and expanding its organizational capacities and resources, the labor-liberal coalition augmented its influence in national politics in two other ways beginning in the mid-1950s. First, the merger of the AFL and the CIO in 1955 strengthened the coalition's political influence. As rival labor federations with substantial social and political differences, the division between the AFL and the CIO since 1935 had been deep and bitter. Competition between the two spurred the growth of unionism, but it also had costs. Rivalry between AFL and CIO unions led to jurisdictional disputes, raiding of each other's members, collusive agreements with employers by some (mainly AFL) unions to preempt organizing drives by other (mainly CIO) unions, disputes over labor laws and their administration (because they might favor some unions over others), disruption of city and state central labor councils, endorsements of different candidates in some elections, and mutual public vilification.[61] These industrial and political conflicts weakened not only the AFL and CIO unions themselves but also the labor-liberal coalition, as liberal leaders understood. As early as 1938, President Roosevelt put Secretary of Labor Frances Perkins to work trying to unify the AFL and CIO.[62] "Unity talks" between the two federations were held periodically thereafter, but without good prospects of success until 1952.

By that time, a number of developments combined to promote unification of the two labor federations. One was the gradual narrowing of the industrial and political differences between the AFL and CIO, as both federations increasingly accommodated craft and industrial principles of organization and supported liberal Democrats, labor and welfare legislation, and Cold War foreign policy.[63] Another was mounting institutional strains in the CIO, including the dissension over and expulsion of communist-led unions, stagnant membership and precarious finances, and a debilitating rift between the presidents of its two largest unions, Walter Reuther of the UAW and David McDonald of the United Steel Workers of America (USWA). These and other institutional weaknesses made merger seem a reasonable alternative to organizational decline for many CIO leaders.[64]

A third and powerful impetus to merger was the accumulating threats to the institutional security of unions and the larger political context in which they materialized. Following on the heels of the Taft-Hartley Act of 1947, the Republican sweep of the White House and Congress in the 1952 elections, the proliferation of state "right to work" laws in the early 1950s, and President Eisenhower's appointment of an unsympathetic National Labor Relations Board made both AFL and CIO leaders much more conscious of the political costs of disunity.[65] These threats to union security were products of the shift in the balance of power in national politics in the early postwar years. Thus, as Alan Draper has said, "Both Meany and Reuther thought of merger in relation to the deteriorating political climate. They hoped that by consolidating the two organizations they would be able to check and reverse this trend."[66] A final factor was the strange coincidence that the longtime presidents of the two federations, William Green of the AFL and Philip Murray of the CIO, both died in 1952. Their deaths facilitated merger, in that their successors, George Meany and Walter Reuther, respectively, were younger and less embittered by the years of division.

The political importance of merger negotiations was indicated by the fact that, just as FDR had tried to promote them in 1938, so Eisenhower tried to obstruct them in 1952–53.[67] Nevertheless, by 1955 they resulted in an agreement to unify.[68] Because this decision reflected both a limited political convergence between the AFL and the CIO and rising concern over political threats to the institutional security of unions, the merger formed a labor movement unified and active in support of liberal Democrats, labor and welfare legislation, and the Cold War.

The increased unity and commitment to political action heralded by the 1955 merger strengthened organized labor and the labor-liberal coalition. Although the AFL-CIO could not prevent passage of the anti-union Landrum-Griffin Act in 1959, it contributed substantially to the election of Democratic presidents in 1960 and 1964, the progressive weakening of the conservative coalition in Congress in elections from 1958 through 1964, and the election of the most liberal Congress in nearly three decades in 1964.[69]

These electoral victories, and the weakening of the conservative coalition in Congress, were the second way that the labor-liberal coalition strengthened its national political influence. At least as much as restoring Democratic control of the White House, weakening the conservative coalition in Congress was crucial for reviving labor-liberal influence and resolving the stalemate in national politics since the late 1940s. The labor-liberal coalition weakened the congressional alliance of southern Democrats and northern Republicans by gradually electing to Congress—between 1958 and 1964—more Democrats from northern states, which reduced both the number of northern Republicans and the share of southern conservatives among Democrats in Congress.[70] It also diminished the power of the conservative coalition by reforming the Rules Committee in the House of Representatives.[71]

The growth of labor-liberal unity, resources, and influence set the stage for the civil rights and social welfare legislation enacted in the Kennedy-Johnson years. Dubbed the "Great Society" by President Johnson, this legislation included the Area Redevelopment Act, Manpower Training and Development Act, Civil Rights Act, Voting Rights Act, Economic Opportunity Act, Elementary and Secondary Education Act, Urban Mass Transportation Act, Medicare and Medicaid Acts (Title 18 and Title 19 Amendments to the Social Security Act), Clean Air Act, Clean Water Restoration Act, and others. These acts created such programs as Head Start, Legal Services, Job Corps, Neighborhood Youth Corps, Vista, Medicare and Medicaid, Comprehensive Community Health Centers, Model Cities, and more.[72] These laws and programs were an interrelated mix of civil rights, employment, antipoverty, education and training, urban and rural development, health care, and environmental policies, and comprised the largest expansion of the welfare state since the New Deal.

These Great Society policies were supported and enacted by an alliance of northern Democrats and liberal interest groups and social movements, notably including the recently unified union movement. Some scholars have downplayed the role of organized labor in the welfare state development of the Kennedy-Johnson years, emphasizing instead the militancy of the civil-rights movement, the expertise of policy intellectuals, or the strategies of corporate and state elites as decisive influences.[73] Although these influences were undoubtedly significant, the role of the unions was quite important also. Their contributions were threefold: (a) long years of public advocacy of employment, health insurance, and other social programs; (b) electoral activity that created the partisan and ideological composition of government necessary to Great Society lawmaking; and (c) extensive and effective lobbying, including participation in the development of legislative proposals and coordination of the lobbying efforts of other liberal groups.[74] It was just these contributions of unions in the Kennedy-Johnson years that led Greenstone to the conclusion that organized labor was by then "the most important nationwide electoral organization for the Democratic Party," "the single most important lobbying group within the party's welfare-oriented constituency," and "the core of the entire liberal lobby."[75]

Continuity and Change in the Labor-Liberal Coalition

The labor-liberal coalition of the mid-1960s, then, remained a potent welfare state alliance, and one that retained a substantial if eroding base of support in the working class, especially considering the increase in class voting in 1960 and 1964.[76] In that respect, at least, there are good grounds for emphasizing the continuity of the labor-liberal coalition between the mid-1930s and mid-1960s, rather than the sharp discontinuity—specifically, a marked decline in the coalition's class base, reform commitments, and political power after the mid- or late 1940s—that some scholars have stressed.[77] The political power of the labor-liberal coalition was checked in the late 1940s, and its reform potential was limited by the Cold War commitments it assumed at that time, but the coalition strengthened itself after the late 1940s, and the constraints of the Cold War were mostly felt after the mid-1960s. The most serious decline of the labor-liberal coalition occurred in and after the late 1960s, not the late 1940s.[78]

Still, neither the power of the labor-liberal coalition in the first half of the 1960s nor its continuity with the coalition of the 1930s should be exaggerated. The strong influence of the coalition over social legislation in the early and mid-1960s was not evident in economic policy or labor law. In two respects, the economic policy of the Kennedy-Johnson years revealed more business than labor-liberal influence, or at least an inclination to accommodate market-oriented growth strategies. First, the use of fiscal policy to provide macroeconomic stimulus relied on tax cuts, including investment tax credits, that were favored by business rather than the increased public spending that many liberals and labor leaders called for.[79] Andrew Martin later pointed out that the fiscal policy of the Kennedy and Johnson administrations was much like that of the Conservative Party in England at the time.[80] Second, Kennedy and Johnson often attached higher priority to low inflation than low unemployment and preferred less intrusive macroeconomic policies to more interventionist labor market policies to deal with employment problems, whereas unions and "urban liberals" in Congress had the opposite priorities and preferences.[81]

Further, even during the Johnson administration and 89th Congress, which passed the civil-rights and Great Society legislation, organized labor could not win repeal of section 14(b) of the Taft-Hartley Act, which permitted state "right to work" laws that ban the union shop. Although repeal passed the House of Representatives, in late 1965 and early 1966 it succumbed to a filibuster in the Senate that was supported by southern Democrats as well as most Republicans and fortified by small business and trade association opposition.[82] The conservative coalition in Congress had been weakened by the mid-1960s, but not enough to allow organized labor to overcome employer opposition, antimajoritarian Senate procedures, and a less than fully supportive Democratic president in pursuit of a more union-friendly labor law. The persistence of section 14(b) would help to keep the South a regional anti-union haven.

Finally, the labor-liberal coalition of the 1960s differed from that of the 1930s in the greater role that race played in the later coalition. The civil-rights movement of the 1950s and 1960s and the Voting Rights Act of 1965 altered the social composition and political demands of Democratic liberalism. From 1960 to 1972, the share of all Democratic votes cast by black voters in presidential elections increased from 7 to 21 percent.[83] The growing electoral clout of black voters combined with rising black unemployment, urban disorder, and a certain complacency about the structure of the U.S. economy to shape the agenda and legislation of the Great Society as much (or more) along lines of race as of class, distinguishing it to some degree from the New Deal.[84]

Still, as of the mid-1960s, the increased importance of the black vote to Democratic liberalism neither relieved liberal politicians of the need for union support nor differentiated the social base of liberalism from that of organized labor. In the presidential election of 1964, unionized workers provided 32 percent of all votes cast for the Democratic candidate, whereas black citizens supplied 12 percent.[85] And blacks constituted nearly as large a share of unionized workers as of Democratic voters, representing about 9 percent of union members at the time they constituted 12 percent of Democratic voters.[86] In the middle of the 1960s, there was still a strong social foundation for the labor-liberal coalition in the overlapping constituencies of organized labor and liberal Democrats; racial minorities simply loomed larger in both labor and liberal constituencies than in the 1930s.

In sum, the labor-liberal coalition recovered from the setbacks and constraints of the late 1940s to generate a second phase of social reform and welfare state development in the middle years of the 1960s. However impressive the influence and accomplishments of the labor-liberal Democratic coalition of that era were, it seems a mistake to view it as comparable to the union-party alliances of contemporary European social democracy. The smaller size and scope of the welfare state (as measured by the range of its programs and its share of national income), the priorities and mix of economic policies, and the character of labor laws in the United States all indicate significant differences at least in the power, and perhaps the ideology and program, of the labor-liberal Democratic coalition and European social democratic movements.[87] But just as the power and accomplishments of the labor-liberal coalition should not be inflated, neither should they be dismissed or downplayed, for both were still considerable in the middle years of the 1960s. In that period, the labor-liberal coalition was able, through public policies and collective bargaining, to manage and distribute the fruits of economic growth in ways that improved the economic and social status of both black and white workers. It would not be long before it would become clear what a fractured and weakened labor-liberal coalition meant for the disposition of both private power and public authority.

CHAPTER 3

The Decline of the Labor-Liberal Coalition

Introduction

The wave of labor-liberal reform concentrated in the mid-1960s was brought to a rather abrupt halt by the congressional elections of 1966. The Democratic Party retained majority control of Congress but lost four seats in the Senate and forty-seven in the House of Representatives, and many liberal and COPE-supported candidates were defeated. The most liberal and active Congress in three decades had been reined in by racial backlash.[1] Thereafter the labor-liberal coalition entered an extended period of decline, which had two distinct stages and sources.

In the first stage, between 1968 and 1972, the source of decline was internal, as conflicts erupted between organized labor and liberals. Particularly damaging were disputes over the war in Vietnam and reform of the Democratic Party. Underlying these conflicts was the rise of New Politics liberals, who differed in their social backgrounds and political concerns from the New Deal liberals with whom unions had long been aligned. The social and political gulf between organized labor and New Politics liberals weakened but did not destroy the labor-liberal coalition, for an important group of unions acted to preserve it by siding with the new liberals on the divisive issues.

In the second stage, which was concentrated in the years from 1978 through 1982, the sources of decline were primarily external: the end of the "golden age" of postwar economic growth and political attacks on unions and liberals by a rejuvenated business-conservative alliance. Following the recession of 1974–75, U.S. economic performance deteriorated, and an economy at once stagnant and inflationary undermined the labor-liberal coalition and aided the resurgence of a strong business-conservative alliance. This alliance further weakened the labor-liberal coalition by effectively attacking unions and liberals in labor markets and national politics.

The Rise of New Politics Liberals and the Disruption of the Labor-Liberal Coalition

Between 1968 and 1972, deep divisions emerged between labor and liberals over the Vietnam war and the Democratic Party's presidential nominations and nominating process. There were other tensions and disputes, to be sure, but they were less threatening to the survival of the labor-liberal coalition. The underlying source of the conflicts between labor and liberals over Vietnam and the Democratic Party was the rise of "New Politics liberals" in the late 1960s, which altered the social base and political demands of Democratic liberalism in ways that caused it to diverge from organized labor.

New Politics liberals were a diverse but related set of political forces that ascended to power in the Democratic Party in the late 1960s and early 1970s.[2] They comprised the more mainstream segments of the social movements of those decades, including the civil-rights, antiwar, women's, and environmental movements. New Politics liberals constituted a much larger and broader set of political forces than the New Left, the more self-consciously radical organizations—including Students for a Democratic Society (SDS) and the Student Nonviolent Coordinating Committee (SNCC)—that emerged mainly among university students in the early 1960s, criticized contemporary liberalism, and often served as the left wing of the new social movements.[3] As indicated by the movements in which they were active, New Politics liberals encompassed youth, minorities, women, and middle-class-issue activists. Between the mid-1960s and mid-1970s, they organized a variety of interest groups, including the National Organization for Women, National Women's Political Caucus, Common Cause, Public Citizen, Friends of the Earth, Environmental Defense Fund, and Consumer Federation of America, among others.[4]

The diverse social strata, protest movements, and interest groups that constituted the New Politics liberals had important links and shared interests. The civil-rights movement served as a model for the social movements that followed and shaped their organizational and political strategies. Opposition to the Vietnam war provided a focal point, a common issue, and opportunities for collaboration among the various New Politics groups and movements. Activists with backgrounds in the civil-rights and antiwar movements played important roles in founding and leading women's, public-interest, and other new citizen groups. Across the various New Politics movements and groups, the leadership and activists tended to be well educated, drawn from or destined for professional occupations, and thus of middle- or upper-middle-class status.[5] Last but not least, the various strata, movements, and groups that made up the New Politics liberals were all largely excluded from the corridors of power in the mid- to late 1960s, including the Democratic Party.[6]

Thus New Politics groups and causes, however varied, possessed a shared outlook and agenda that emphasized civil rights, cultural pluralism, international accommodation, quality-of-life issues, governmental and political reform, and participatory democracy.[7] They also had a common strategy, which was to gain power in national politics in and through the Democratic Party, especially by reforming and controlling its presidential nominating process.[8]

The rise of the New Politics groups and movements transformed Democratic liberalism, altering its social composition, organizational base, and political demands. In contrast to the working-class and trade-union base and the welfare state and Cold War commitments of New Deal liberalism, the New Politics made youth, minorities, females, and especially educated middle-class professionals central constituencies of Democratic liberalism. It also considerably enlarged the number and range of interest groups that provided organizational support (in election campaigns and legislative lobbying) for liberal Democrats. And it placed sociocultural, peace, and quality-of-life issues high on the agenda of Democratic liberalism. This social and political profile of New Politics liberalism reflected, in addition to the emergence of new social movements, key demographic and economic developments of the long postwar era: the baby boom, the extended prosperity, the vast expansion of higher education, and the growth of technical and professional occupations.[9]

As New Politics liberals rose to power in the Democratic Party in the late 1960s and early 1970s, then, the social bases and political demands of organized labor and Democratic liberalism began to diverge, weakening the prospects for a strong labor-liberal coalition. But although deep divisions and conflicts arose between labor and New Politics liberals, there were also areas and periods of agreement and collaboration between them. Peter Levy has shown that this was also true of the relationship between labor—especially what he calls the "social activist unions"—and the New Left.[10]

Organized labor confronted the demands of New Politics liberals—for racial and gender equality, consumer and environmental protection, peace in Southeast Asia and détente with the Soviet Union, and party reform—in three domains: (a) national policymaking, (b) the institutional rules and collective-bargaining practices of unions, and (c) the national Democratic Party. In the first arena, labor was able to accommodate many of the major New Politics demands. The AFL-CIO and many of its affiliated unions provided strong support for the Civil Rights Act of 1964 and the Voting Rights Act of 1965. The federation was even instrumental in securing inclusion in the 1964 legislation of a section on fair-employment practices that prohibited racially discriminatory employment decisions by unions as well as employers.[11] The AFL-CIO also supported the Equal Rights Amendment, and some unions—especially the American Federation of State, County and Municipal Employees (AFSCME), the Service Employees International Union

(SEIU), and the Communication Workers of America (CWA)—proved to be among the most active advocates of "comparable worth" (equal pay for comparable work) measures for women before both legislatures and courts.[12]

Further, as David Vogel has pointed out, the AFL-CIO was "the only organized political supporter of strong consumer protection" until the late 1960s, and thereafter unions usually remained allies of the newly organized consumer groups, as in the long but unsuccessful battle in the 1970s to establish a Consumer Protection Agency.[13] Trade unions were also "relatively strong supporters of environmental regulation" until U.S. economic performance deteriorated in the mid-1970s.[14] A notable area of cooperation between environmentalists and organized labor was occupational-safety and health legislation, including the Federal Coal Mine Health and Safety Act of 1969 and the Occupational Health and Safety Act of 1970.[15]

Thus the AFL-CIO and many unions made an effort to accommodate the public-policy priorities of New Politics liberals. At the same time, New Politics liberals often cooperated with labor in support of welfare state measures. Claims that New Politics liberals had "postmaterialist" values and demands, in opposition to the "materialist" outlook and interests of unions, are exaggerated and overgeneralized; civil-rights and women's groups always had a dual agenda encompassing social-welfare as well as civil-rights issues.[16] In the realm of national policy, then, the relationship between labor and New Politics liberals was often accommodative and cooperative. But, as will be seen below, this was not the case on the fundamental issue of the war in Vietnam (or on other aspects of Cold War foreign policy, including détente with the Soviet Union), the major policy conflict between labor and New Politics liberals through the mid-1970s. In the later 1970s, deteriorating economic conditions generated disputes over environmental, regulatory, and trade policies, but these were never as consuming or as damaging to the labor-liberal coalition as the war in Southeast Asia.[17]

The demands of New Politics liberals also impinged on the internal operations and collective-bargaining policies of trade unions. Civil-rights and women's organizations, as well as black and female unionists, forcefully questioned the extent to which unions provided equal opportunities and benefits for racial minorities and women, both within unions as institutions and in the labor contracts they negotiated with employers. They criticized the existence of racially exclusionary or segregated local unions (prior to the civil-rights legislation of the mid-1960s); the underrepresentation of minorities and women in skilled trades, apprenticeship programs, and positions of union leadership; and discriminatory seniority rules and grievance procedures.[18] Scholars linked to the civil-rights movement argued that the AFL-CIO in fact refused to implement the prohibition against racially discriminatory employment decisions by unions that the federation had supported politically in Title VII of the Civil Rights Act of 1964.[19] Union members filed charges of discriminatory treatment by unions with the Equal Employment Opportunity Commission and brought suits against them in federal courts. Black and female union leaders formed the Coalition of Black Trade Unionists (CBTU) in 1972 and the Coalition of Labor Union Women (CLUW) in 1974 to promote minority and female leadership in labor and to pressure unions and the AFL-CIO on minority and women's issues.[20]

Unions and labor leaders reacted in various ways to these criticisms and developments. Some angrily rejected them, whereas others, backed by sympathetic intellectuals, conceded problems but mounted a qualified defense of the overall record of unions and bargaining agreements on racial or gender issues. The latter argued, not without evidence, that the worst cases of exclusion and discrimination occurred in craft unions in skilled trades and that industrial, public-employee, and service-sector unions were more inclusive and egalitarian; that minorities and women derived substantial economic and social benefits from union membership; and that unions compared favorably with all other social institutions in the degree to which minorities had been integrated into both membership and leadership.[21] At least some unions also responded to inner turmoil and external criticism by voluntarily modifying their institutional and bargaining practices, though the extent and effectiveness of such changes evidently varied.[22]

These issues and disputes no doubt strained relations between organized labor and New Politics liberals, especially when, as with access to skilled trades and seniority rules, they became embroiled in extensive administrative regulation or court litigation. But they did not prevent cooperation in the realm of national policymaking (see above) or even in the arena of the national Democratic Party (see below). To a considerable degree, both unions and New Politics liberals limited the spillover effects of these issues and disputes on their relationships in other fields. In time, the heat of these controversies dissipated, in part because racial and gender inequities within the labor movement were reduced. In fact, even as those controversies played out, organized labor and the civil-rights and women's movements increasingly intersected. During the 1960s and 1970s, the proportions of blacks and females in the labor movement rose, largely because of the growth of unionization among teachers, hospital workers, and state and local public employees, and the organizing process in these sectors drew inspiration, energy, and support from the civil-rights and women's movements.[23]

The final site of engagement between unions and New Politics liberals was the national Democratic Party, particularly its presidential nominating process. In 1968, organized labor and New Politics liberals divided in their candidate preferences for the Democratic presidential nomination. New Politics liberals by and large supported antiwar candidates, either Eugene McCarthy or Robert Kennedy (before his assassination in early June). Labor leaders initially favored President Lyndon Johnson's renomination and then supported Vice President Hubert Humphrey upon Johnson's withdrawal from consideration.[24] Their support for Johnson and Humphrey—both New Deal/Cold War liberals—was based as much or more on domestic as on foreign policy considerations but did reflect continuing labor support for the war in Vietnam.

Vice President Humphrey won the nomination without having entered any of the Democratic presidential primaries, in which Senators McCarthy and Kennedy had both participated and won significant support. This was possible because in 1968 the Democratic Party still operated (for the last time) with its old nominating procedures, with most convention delegates chosen and controlled by state and local party leaders rather than selected and bound by pledges in primary elections or open caucuses.

New Politics liberals who had supported McCarthy or Kennedy viewed this nominating system as unfair and unrepresentative, and they determined to change it. They secured agreement at the 1968 convention to establish a party commission that eventually proposed sweeping changes in the party's nominating procedures.[25] Over the next four years, an intraparty battle occurred over the proposed changes in nominating methods and delegate selection rules, and much (but not all) of the labor movement opposed New Politics liberals in this party reform battle. In the 1972 Democratic nomination contest, which occurred under new rules as a result of the victory of reform forces, deep division was once again evident between New Politics liberals and much of the labor movement.

In sum, in the various public arenas in which they both had major interests at stake, the relationship between organized labor and New Politics liberals encompassed agreement and collaboration, deep and persistent division, and tensions that were reduced if not fully resolved over time. Labor and New Politics liberals were not invariably antagonistic, but the conflicts between them over Vietnam and Democratic Party reform severely strained the labor-liberal coalition, all the more so because many older New Deal/Cold War liberals had come to favor ending the war and reforming the party.[26] But while the conflicts over Vietnam and party reform seriously weakened the labor-liberal coalition, they did not destroy it, because on these divisive issues the labor movement itself split, and an important section of it sided with New Politics liberals against the top leadership and dominant wing of the AFL-CIO. This development, which has been ignored by some analysts of labor and liberalism, was essential to the preservation of a labor-liberal coalition, if a shrunken and weakened one, in American politics.[27]

New Politics Liberals and the Split in Organized Labor

After over a decade of relative unity in American labor since the 1955 merger of the AFL and CIO, by 1968 the war in Vietnam and the Democratic presidential nominating process had rekindled political discord between unions. As is well known, the AFL-CIO leadership was a strong and unwavering proponent of the U.S. war in Southeast Asia. Through each phase and every escalation of the war, the federation supported the objectives and policies of successive administrations; even the Nixon administration's widely censured invasion of Cambodia and resumption of bombing against North Vietnam in the spring of 1970 received the full support of President Meany and the majority of the Executive Council.[28] AFL-CIO leaders also missed few if any opportunities to condemn and red-bait even moderate opponents of the war, including those within the labor movement, but they reserved their harshest attacks for the youthful activists of the antiwar movement. (In 1965, 1967, and 1970, antiwar demonstrators in New York City were pummeled by prowar unionists.) The strongest and most enduring support for the Vietnam war within organized labor came from the building and construction trades and maritime unions, long a power base of Meany and the Executive Council majority, although various ex-CIO unions, like the Steel Workers under its then president, I. W. Abel, backed the war, as well.[29] A deep enmity developed between much of organized labor and the antiwar movement.[30]

It is less well known that opposition arose in American labor to the war in Vietnam, and to the AFL-CIO's steady support for it. Differences over Vietnam were among the disputes with George Meany that led Walter Reuther to withdraw the UAW from the AFL-CIO in 1968, although Reuther's own opposition to the war was slow to develop.[31] Indeed, until 1969, public opposition in organized labor to the Vietnam war was largely confined to the lower levels of trade union leadership. The major organized source of labor opposition to the war prior to this date was the Labor Leadership Assembly for Peace, which evolved from the Trade Union Division of the Committee for a Sane Nuclear Policy (SANE). Of the Assembly's five hundred member officials from various unions, only forty-five were high elected officers or staff of international unions, whereas the rest were local or regional union leaders.[32]

After 1969, however, opposition to the war extended to the top leadership of many international unions, a growing number of which publicly opposed the war by executive action or convention resolution. Moreover, between 1969 and 1972, a succession of labor committees arose to present an alternative labor voice on Vietnam and to end the war; these included the Alliance for Labor Action and the Labor Peace Committee in 1969, the National Labor Committee to End the War in Indochina in 1970, and Labor for Peace in 1972. Unlike the earlier Labor Leadership Assembly, these committees were typically organized and led by the presidents and vice presidents of international unions.[33] Among the more prominent of the unions that opposed the war were the UAW, American Federation of State, County and Municipal Employees, Amalgamated Clothing Workers, Amalgamated Meat Cutters, Oil Chemical and Atomic Workers, Retail Wholesale and Department Store Workers, United Electrical Workers, United Packinghouse Workers, American Newspaper Guild, International Longshoremen's and Warehousemen's Union (the West Coast longshore union), and United Farmworkers Organizing Committee.[34] These unions were drawn from the manufacturing, public, and private-service sectors, and most of them were former CIO unions.

The growth of opposition to the war in Vietnam among top leaders of numerous international unions after 1969 was due to the mounting economic costs and social dislocations of the war, the increasing political isolation of labor, and the fact that labor leaders were no longer constrained to endorse the war by their support for liberal Democratic administrations. It opened a breach between international unions that supported and those that opposed the war. This coincided with both a further growth of opposition among local and state labor bodies and a rising tendency for the labor opposition at all levels to demand an immediate and total withdrawal of all U.S. forces from Southeast Asia, with the result that organized labor became bitterly divided by the war.[35] The growing labor opposition never proved able to reverse the AFL-CIO's support for the war, but, as Levy has shown, it did allow for reconciliation and even coordinated political activity between a segment of organized labor and the antiwar movement.[36]

Unions also divided over reform of the Democratic Party's presidential nomination process and over the candidates for the party's nomination in 1972, issues that were closely linked to the war in Vietnam. Pressed by New Politics liberals angered by the outcome of the 1968 nomination contest, the Democratic Party established a Commission on Party Structure and Delegate Selection, popularly known as the McGovern-Fraser Commission. The commission proposed major changes in the party's nominating process, including the two key demands of the New Politics liberals, for primary elections (or open caucuses) as the means to select delegates to the party nominating conventions and for quotas to ensure fair representation of youth, minorities, and women at those conventions.[37] The AFL-CIO leadership opposed these reform proposals. As William Crotty observed in his study of party reform, "Reform threatened organized labor's preeminent status within national conventions and the AFL-CIO fought it tenaciously. . . . More often than not, labor (as represented by the AFL-CIO leadership) was to position itself in diametric opposition to the reform movement."[38] President Meany and other leaders feared that these reforms would undermine the federation's role as a power broker in Democratic nominating conventions, which rested on elite bargaining rather than electoral mobilization of union members.[39]

But several major unions—the UAW, AFSCME, Communications Workers, Machinists union, National Education Association, and Oil Chemical and Atomic Workers—dissented from the AFL-CIO's position and operated as an informal labor caucus in support of party reform.[40] Leaders of these unions were sympathetic to the claims of youth, minorities, and women for enhanced representation in the Democratic Party, and they believed that the use of primary elections to select convention delegates played to their strength as unions with effective political operations capable of mobilizing their members in elections.[41] Most of these industrial and public employee unions had CIO backgrounds and were or became opponents of the war in Vietnam. The reforms that they supported, and that the AFL-CIO opposed, were eventually approved by the Democratic National Committee and state legislatures and scheduled to take effect in 1972.

Thus the Democratic nomination contest of that year took place under the new rules established by the reform process. New Politics liberals united around the candidacy of Senator George McGovern, who had co-chaired the McGovern-Fraser Commission and whose nomination campaign benefitted from the reforms of the nominating process that the commission had proposed. By contrast, unions split among different candidates at different times (as some dropped out of the contest), including Hubert Humphrey, Senator Henry Jackson, Senator Edmund Muskie, and McGovern.

More critically, organized labor divided over the Democratic convention's choice of Senator McGovern as the party's presidential nominee. Following his nomination, the AFL-CIO Executive Council decided, in a lopsided vote that sustained President Meany's position, not to endorse McGovern. For federation leaders, McGovern's respectable record on labor's issues as a senator, which Meany himself had acknowledged just a few years earlier, was not enough to overcome his role as a leader of the antiwar and reform forces in the Democratic Party, especially because the McGovern campaign did little to attract union support.[42] AFL-CIO neutrality in the 1972 election was also, according to the veteran labor reporter A. H. Raskin, a convenient cover for the building trades and maritime unions that worked openly for the reelection of President Nixon.[43] By refusing to endorse the 1972 Democratic nominee, leaders of the AFL-CIO and many of its influential affiliates not only strained labor's organizational alliance with the party but also once again opposed the New Politics liberals who formed the core of McGovern's support.

But the AFL-CIO's decision did not sit well with some important unions. In response, several of the largest and most politically active unions, again including the United Auto Workers, the American Federation of State, County and Municipal Employees, and the International Association of Machinists, reduced their commitments of funds and personnel to the AFL-CIO's political arm, COPE, and expanded their own capacities for political action.[44] Moreover, despite the neutrality decision, at least thirty-three unions, representing a majority of unionized workers, formally endorsed McGovern for president.[45] Ultimately, the same unions that had supported party reform also established the Labor for McGovern Committee and campaigned strongly for the Democratic nominee.[46] Despite significant rank-and-file opposition and their own lack of enthusiasm, the leaders of these unions endorsed and campaigned for McGovern in order to support the Democratic Party and the liberal reform groups that were ascendant within it.

After the 1972 election, the AFL-CIO leadership remained unreconciled with party reform and the McGovern nomination. George Meany and other federation leaders played a leading role in the formation of the Coalition for a Democratic

Majority (CDM), which united labor leaders, Cold War Democrats like Senator Henry Jackson of Washington, and party regulars in opposition to the new nominating procedures and the New Politics liberals and in support of a bid by Senator Jackson for the Democratic nomination in 1976.[47] Realizing that it would not be possible to secure consensus within the AFL-CIO in support of Senator Jackson, however, the Executive Council officially renounced involvement in the 1976 Democratic presidential nomination process.[48]

This was yet another unacceptable decision to a number of key unions, nine of which—the UAW, AFSCME, Machinists, Communications Workers, NEA, Electrical Workers (IUE), Oil Chemical and Atomic Workers, United Mine Workers, and the Graphic Arts International union—therefore united in the Labor Coalition Clearinghouse. The purposes of the Clearinghouse were to coordinate the participation of its member unions in the 1976 Democratic primaries and caucuses, in order to maximize their influence at the party convention, and to serve as labor's electoral machinery for the Democratic candidate in the general election in case the AFL-CIO again remained neutral.[49] In the event, the federation proved willing to endorse and campaign for Jimmy Carter in the 1976 general election, and the Clearinghouse did not remain active beyond the presidential nomination contest of that year. But prior to the general election the Clearinghouse was widely viewed as a rival to COPE, and a leading journalist asserted that the "center of national labor influence in the Democratic Party" had shifted from the AFL-CIO to the Labor Coalition Clearinghouse and speculated that unless the federation altered its political strategy it risked an enduring schism in organized labor.[50]

In short, the labor movement itself divided over the war in Vietnam and over the Democratic Party's presidential nomination process. An important group of large and politically active unions broke with the established leadership of the AFL-CIO and supported New Politics liberals in opposing the war, reforming the party's nominating process and campaigning for the election of George McGovern. These unions dissented from the AFL-CIO not only on the substance of these issues but also on the strategic choice they posed to unions: whether or not to ally with the New Politics liberals rising to power in the Democratic Party. Again, although the AFL-CIO usually supported the main public-policy demands of the New Politics liberals, its conflicts with them over the war in Southeast Asia and the Democratic nomination process were sufficiently important and intense to threaten the labor-liberal coalition. By siding with New Politics liberals on those issues, the dissident unions—drawn from the sections of the labor movement that had always been most committed to that coalition—acted to preserve the labor-liberal alliance, even at the cost of deepening division within the house of labor. Just as labor disunity had proved necessary to the formation of the labor-liberal alliance in the mid-1930s, so it proved necessary to the preservation of that alliance in the late 1960s and early 1970s.

Stagflation and the Rejuvenation of the Business-Conservative Alliance

The election and administration of Jimmy Carter served as something of a transition between the first and second stages and sources of decline of the labor-liberal coalition. As in 1968 and 1972, so too in 1976, unions and New Politics liberals divided—among themselves as well as from each other—in their candidate preferences in a highly fragmented Democratic presidential nomination contest.[51] In contrast to the two previous general elections, however, labor (both wings) and New Politics liberals united in support of Carter's general-election campaign. Although Carter was a moderate southern Democrat and in many respects an unknown quantity, both labor and liberals had high hopes for his administration as he assumed office, because it was the first Democratic administration in eight years, the 1976 Democratic platform was quite progressive, and the party had solid congressional majorities.

But by the midpoint of Carter's term, many labor and liberal leaders were disappointed in his administration and the Democratic Congress, and rallied behind Senator Edward Kennedy's effort to push a more liberal program on the White House at a midterm party conference held shortly after the 1978 elections, in which many liberal Democrats had been defeated. Many of them also supported Kennedy's unsuccessful challenge to Carter in the 1980 Democratic primaries and caucuses.[52] This shift occurred because both organized labor and New Politics liberals suffered policy defeats and electoral setbacks in the Carter years, as his administration and congressional Democrats increasingly succumbed to two powerful and closely related forces: (a) stagflation and (b) the rejuvenation of the business-conservative alliance. Especially in the years from 1978 through 1982, these external forces further weakened the labor-liberal coalition in the second phase of its decline.

The end of the "golden age" of postwar economic growth can be dated from the recession of 1974–75. For the next two decades, rates of growth of output, productivity, and wages and family income tended to be lower than they were previously, and levels of unemployment, inflation, poverty, income inequality, and trade deficits tended to be higher.[53] The initial effect of this deteriorating performance of the U.S. economy in the mid-1970s was to intensify the political activity of organized labor and to revive the labor-liberal coalition. Unions won both an increase in the minimum wage and federal regulation of private pension plans, through the Employee Retirement Income Security Act (ERISA), in 1974. In addition, the labor-liberal coalition, including such New Politics liberals as civil-rights and environmental organizations, regrouped in support of the old goal of full employment, in the form of the Full Employment and Balanced Growth Act, also known as the Humphrey-Hawkins Act.[54] By the late 1970s, however, as stagflation—the conjunction of high unemployment and inflation—and import penetration came to dominate the U.S. political economy, the end of the postwar economic boom weakened the labor-liberal coalition in numerous ways.

For one thing, stagflation discredited the Keynesian policies of macroeconomic management on which labor and New Deal liberals had long relied.[55] More generally, it revived criticism of both union wage premiums and public spending as inefficient and inflationary, and it thereby fed the rise of anti-union and anti-statist sentiment.[56] The recession of the mid-1970s and the subsequent stagnation also exposed a crucial political weakness of New Politics liberals; as David Vogel put it, "having based their political program on policies designed to ameliorate the effects of economic growth, they had no practical solutions to offer when that growth appeared to have become problematic."[57] Further, the deterioration of U.S. economic performance after 1974–75 weakened the labor-liberal coalition by generating new policy disputes between unions and New Politics liberals over trade, environmental protection, and deregulation of transportation industries.[58] Finally, the changed economic environment increased the political leverage of the business community, for stagnation and heightened international competition increased the pressure on government to accede to the policy demands of business, all the more so because they also increased middle-class support for a probusiness agenda.[59]

As it cast serious doubt on the capacity of labor and liberals to manage the economy, the end of the postwar boom created political space for the ascendance of conservative and probusiness economic policies ranging from monetarism through deregulation to supply-side tax cuts. Straitened economic circumstances after the mid-1970s also provided an opportunity for a rejuvenated business-conservative alliance to attack and further disable unions and liberals. Even if business and conservatives accommodated themselves to organized labor and modern liberalism after World War II, such accommodation did not last much beyond the middle of the 1960s. By that time, conservatives were organizing to attack liberals and labor, and less than a decade later they were joined in the effort by a massive business mobilization. By the late 1970s, business-conservative efforts to weaken labor and liberals began to show results.

After the mid-1960s, American conservatism experienced both revival and transformation. Senator Barry Goldwater's landslide defeat in the 1964 presidential election seemed at the time to sound the death knell of conservative politics, but his campaign in fact initiated the development of new conservative organizations, activists, and strategies. Over the following decade or so, an enlarged, strengthened, and altered conservative movement emerged, one increasingly willing and able to sharply challenge liberal politics and policy.

Following Goldwater's defeat, conservatives formed new political organizations of many kinds: lobbying groups, political action committees, direct-mail operations, think tanks, legal foundations, single-issue organizations, grassroots groups, and media enterprises. Extensive networks of conservative activists, thinkers, publicists, policy experts, campaign consultants, fundraisers, and donors arose in and among these organizations. This revival of conservative political forces also changed the character and temper of conservatism, creating what has often been called a New Right in American politics. Compared to the mainstream conservatism of the Eisenhower era, this New Right was more aggressively ideological, more influenced by a strong religious wing of Christian conservatives, and more attuned to social and cultural (as well as economic) issues. The New Right was also innovative in its political strategies, which included mobilization of racial and gender backlash, a right-wing populism that appealed to "the people" against intellectual and bu-reaucratic "elites," and a progrowth economic strategy centered on tax cuts and deregulation.[60] These changes were crucial to the success of conservatism in the quarter-century after 1968, for they allowed it to develop a broader base of support, effectively challenge liberalism, and assemble winning coalitions in elections.

Many sources fed this revival and transformation of conservatism. It was in part a countermobilization against the new social movements of the 1960s and 1970s. It also drew from some of the same developments that had nourished those move-ments, especially the expansion of higher education and the growth of professional and technical occupations, which supplied the conservative reaction as well as the new social movements with an enlarged cadre of educated and skilled activists who had time and money to devote to politics. Of critical importance was the postwar growth of the sunbelt and of the wealth amassed by right-wing firms and families in that region. The initial opportunity for conservative revival and change emerged from southern resistance to the civil-rights revolution (as Goldwater's campaign showed); the formation of the Christian right was based heavily in the sunbelt; and sunbelt capital was crucial to the financing of many of the new conservative organizations and campaigns between the mid-1960s and mid-1970s. Economic and social changes ranging from postwar suburbanization to the stagnation of growth after the mid-1970s shaped the resurgence of conservatism also.[61]

Close on the heels of the conservative revival, American business launched both an anti-union offensive and a broader mobilization of business political power. In the first case, employers undertook to defeat unionization drives, undermine union bargaining power, rid themselves of established unions and contracts, and prevent changes in labor law favorable to unions. In pursuit of these goals, employers drew from a vast store of anti-union weapons and stratagems. They increasingly resorted to illegal as well as legal means to defeat unions in repre-sentation elections, especially the firing of union activists or sympathizers. They also frequently petitioned the National Labor Relations Board for decertification elections, by which existing unions may be decertified as bargaining agents for workers. Another method was to delay or refuse to negotiate a first contract with a certified union, which in time undermined employee support for the union. An even more common approach was concession bargaining, whereby employers demanded concessions on wages, benefits, and work rules from employees and their unions. Some firms used bankruptcy proceedings to abrogate contracts that they had negotiated. Others practiced "positive labor relations" to undercut employee desire for union representation. Many firms relocated facilities to non-union areas at home or abroad, or threatened to do so. Finally, employers made extensive use of the anti-union management-consulting industry and intensified lobbying against pro-union labor-law bills.

This anti-union employer offensive, too, had several sources and causes. The profit squeeze on manufacturing firms after the mid-1960s, and the heightened international economic competition that was one of its sources, played key roles. The widening differential between union and nonunion wages in the 1970s also helped to spur the employer offensive. Further, both the preexisting decline of unionization (and of public support for unions) and the weak penalties for commission of the "unfair labor practices" prohibited by the National Labor Relation Act (NLRA) reduced the costs to employers of opposing unions. Finally, the shift to Republican control of the White House and executive branch after 1968 undoubtedly encouraged the adversarial posture of business toward organized labor.[62]

The broader political mobilization by business in the 1970s aimed to expand its political organization, resources, activity, and influence in order to reduce tax and regulatory burdens and promote Republican and conservative control of government. The remarkable scope of this mobilization indicated how determined business was to achieve these goals. It encompassed the creation of public-affairs or government-relations departments in many firms; the increased representation of corporations in Washington, D.C., either directly by opening corporate lobbying offices in the capital or indirectly by hiring lobbying firms already located there; the formation of corporate and trade-association political action committees to finance election campaigns; the establishment of new and revitalization of existing business lobbying organizations, such as the Business Roundtable and the U.S. Chamber of Commerce; the increased involvement of corporate CEOs in Washington lobbying and of management personnel, shareholders, suppliers, and customers in grassroots lobbying; the financing of think tanks; political advertising in print and broadcast media, and efforts to cultivate more favorable media coverage of business; and growth of political alliances among different business interest groups.[63]

These efforts to augment the political power of business were motivated by the decline in profit rates in some sectors of the economy after the mid-1960s; the imposition, across many industries, of consumer, environmental, and occupational safety and health regulations between the mid-1960s and mid-1970s; the restoration of Democratic control of both the executive and legislative branches of the national government in 1976; and the desire of business for the autonomy and flexibility needed for "corporate restructuring" in the face of a stagnant but globalizing economy. Despite some scholarly controversy on the issue, it appears that this mobilization entailed a more class-wide and partisan orientation by business in national politics during the 1970s than had previously been the case.[64]

The conservative revival and the business mobilization (against both unions and liberals) were initially independent developments, for the most part. Mutual wariness between much of the nation's business leadership—with the important exception of sunbelt entrepreneurs—and the New Right, especially religious and social conservatives, kept them on separate tracks for a time. But as Thomas Edsall has argued, a "conservative convergence" occurred as the 1970s progressed, based on the "increasing intersection . . . of the interests of the right-wing ideological community, the business community, and the Republican Party."[65] Two developments encouraged this convergence: the growing representation of the New Right in Congress after 1976, which compelled both business leaders and the regular Republican party to accommodate it; and unified Democratic control of national government between 1977 and 1981, which provided a common enemy against which all three elements could unite.[66]

The alliance of the new conservative movement and a mobilized business community greatly strengthened the Republican Party, providing it with the money, organizational infrastructure, ideological coherence, and activists that allowed it to become increasingly effective in agenda-setting and electoral competition.[67] At the same time, the growing effectiveness of the Republican Party only enhanced the political influence of the new conservative movement and the mobilized business community. This conjunction of conservative revival, business mobilization, and the institutional and political strengthening of the Republican Party enabled damaging blows to be leveled against labor and liberals by the later 1970s.

And labor and liberals were weakened by those attacks. Union density—the percentage of the labor force that is unionized—declined from just over 30 percent in 1968 to just under 25 percent in 1980 (and then to under 21 percent in 1982, reflecting the impact of the recession of the early 1980s).[68] More than in the previous decade and a half, declining union density in the 1970s resulted from intensifying management opposition to unions. The growth of anti-union trade associations and especially of the anti-union management consulting industry, a dramatic increase in charges and findings of unfair labor practices by employers, the declining win rates of unions in representation elections, and the sharp growth in the incidence of decertification elections (called by employers) and in the number of members lost to unions through decertification elections all show that an escalating employer offensive was partly responsible for declining union density in the 1970s.[69] A hardened employer attitude against unions in that era also reduced the ability of unions to negotiate first contracts after achieving bargaining rights; forced union concessions on wages, benefits, and work rules; and dissolved once stable industrywide bargaining patterns into more decentralized bargaining.[70] In the sphere of industrial relations, then, unions were weakened over the course of the 1970s both in their coverage of the workforce and in their bargaining power, in good measure because of heightened management opposition.

Unions were also weakened in the realm of national politics by the conservative revival and the political resurgence of business. In congressional elections between 1976 and 1982, many prolabor incumbents, including a couple of north-eastern Republicans, were defeated—sixteen in the Senate alone, according to Edsall—and replaced by better-financed opponents who were much less sympathetic to unions.[71] An important study comparing the House of Representatives in the Eighty-ninth (1965–67) and Ninety-fifth (1977–79) congresses found that organized labor "lost far more key votes" on labor legislation in the Ninety-fifth than in the Eighty-ninth Congress despite having nearly as lopsided a Democratic majority as the earlier Congress.[72] The authors attributed this decline in labor's legislative success to moderating levels of support for labor, linked strongly to declining levels of liberalism, among House Democrats. This study included labor's defeat in the House on the common situs picketing bill in March 1977, but not the more serious defeat of the Labor Law Reform bill (which passed in the House) by Senate filibuster in June 1978. According to most accounts, an intensive business lobbying campaign was instrumental to the defeat of Labor Law Reform, although traditional political and institutional features of the U.S. Senate—the conservative coalition and the filibuster—also have a strong claim on responsibility.[73] Even the fall 1978 passage of the Humphrey-Hawkins Full Employment Act, one of labor's few policy victories of that era, was far from a major triumph, as the bill was substantially weakened before adoption, stronger versions having been firmly opposed by a unified business community.[74]

In addition, the astonishing growth of business political action committees during the 1970s meant that in 1976, business outspent labor in elections for the first time in a long while. Furthermore, business PAC growth was such that, although business generally became more partisan (i.e., Republican) in the late 1970s, more business money went to the Democratic Party (still the majority in Congress) than before. Between 1978 and 1980, the share of all campaign funds contributed to Democrats by labor fell from about 66 percent to 43 percent, "a development that helped make many Democrats more independent of trade unions and thus more responsive to pressures from business."[75] Even before the Republican victories in the 1980 presidential and Senate elections, then, unions were weakened in electoral politics (including campaign finance), in Congress, and in the Democratic Party.

Liberals, too, were weakened in the latter half of the 1970s, both in Congress and in the Democratic Party. The 1974 elections and subsequent institutional re-forms had already shifted power in Congress away from senior and more liberal Democrats to younger, more moderate ones.[76] The elections of 1978 then revealed the vulnerability of liberal Democrats to New Right attack, and when the Senate shifted to Republican control in 1980, twelve incumbent Democrats fell and sixteen new Republicans, most of them "ultraconservatives," were elected in the largest partisan turnover since 1958.[77] But the weakening of liberalism was not simply a matter of the declining number and institutional authority of liberal Democrats; it also involved a declining level of liberal commitment among the Democrats who remained in office or in positions of party leadership. The study referred to above comparing the House of Representatives in the Eighty-ninth and Ninety-fifth Congresses found a significant decline in the level of support among Democrats for liberal positions on issues between the late 1960s and the late 1970s.

By the latter date, the influence of liberals, of both New Deal and New Politics vintage, in the Democratic Party was also weakened. Already in the early 1970s, liberal influence in the Democratic Party, still constrained by the southern wing of the party, had been challenged by the organization of the anti-McGovern forces, including top leaders of the AFL-CIO, into the Coalition for a Democratic Majority (CDM), which advocated commitment to traditional values and Cold War foreign policy. A more serious threat to liberal influence arose when, "in the late 1970s and early 1980s, another Democratic faction emerged—the neoliberals."[78] As Nicol Rae, Kenneth Baer, and other analysts of the Democratic Party have noted, the neoliberals split off from the New Politics liberals and advocated market economics, fiscal conservatism, and a shift of support from labor to entrepreneurial (especially high-technology) elements, while maintaining mildly liberal positions on social and foreign-policy issues.[79] Senators Gary Hart and Paul Tsongas were perhaps the most prominent examples of Democrats with roots in New Politics liberalism who became neoliberals in and after the late 1970s. Also, in the early 1980s the national Democratic Party established a Democratic Business Council to raise money from business interests, in an effort to offset the major financial advantage of the Republican Party.[80] By the late 1970s, liberals largely lost the capacity to shape debate and set the agenda in Congress and the Democratic Party.

Conclusion

It is no easy matter to explain the decline of the labor-liberal coalition, and I do not claim to have provided a complete or definitive explanation. Most other explanations of union and liberal decline treat them as separate phenomena, when they are in fact linked and interdependent. Those that recognize the linkage often do not distinguish between the coalition's internal unity and its external power, as a satisfactory explanation must. Whether the focus is on unionism and liberalism as separate phenomena or on their alliance, there is of course the question of what kinds of explanation, what types and range of explanatory variables, are best able to account for decline.

Many explanations of the decline of unionism and liberalism emphasize either changes in economic and social structure or the strategies and policies of unions and liberals themselves. Some portray union or liberal decline as a direct consequence of such structural changes as the postwar spread of affluence and higher education, the relocation of industry from the snowbelt to the sunbelt, the shift of employment from manufacturing to service industries or from blue-collar to white-collar occupations, or the globalization of economic activity.[81] Others attribute it to such allegedly failed or misguided strategies and policies as (for writers on the left) bureaucratic business unionism, alliance with a capitalist political party, and

Cold War foreign policy, or (for those on the right) collectivist or redistributionist unionism, welfare statism, and rejection of Middle American cultural values.[82]

Economic and social changes and union and liberal strategies and policies undoubtedly contributed to labor-liberal decline. Of those listed above, the spread of affluence and higher education after World War II, the rise of the sunbelt, and Cold War foreign policy were among the economic and social changes and union and liberal strategies and policies incorporated into my account of labor-liberal decline. But structural and strategic explanations both have difficulties, and neither alone can provide an adequate account of labor-liberal decline.

The limitations of structural explanations have been revealed most clearly in major studies of union decline, which have shown that structural changes in the economy and labor force explain some but not most of the decline of union density. These studies have also indicated the analytical problem underlying the empirical weakness of structural explanations of union decline: they ignore the actual process of unionization and deunionization, which includes union organizing drives, employer opposition, representation and decertification elections, and the legal-political regulation of all of these.[83] In other words, they ignore the crucial ways that the impact of economic and social changes on union density is mediated by institutions and politics. The same logic, of the institutional and political mediation of structural change, applies to the decline of liberalism, as well.

Strategic and policy explanations of labor-liberal decline have other difficulties. As suggested above, ideological preconceptions have often influenced claims about which strategies and policies failed and caused union or liberal decline. Such explanations also too frequently fail to analyze the constraints under which unions and liberals made strategic or policy choices and to demonstrate that they had feasible alternatives. Further, unions and liberals always necessarily pursued multiple strategies and policies (industrial and political, domestic and foreign), but strategic or policy explanations rarely have tried to disentangle their consequences. Finally, and perhaps crucially, strategies and policies were not the only elements or determinants of the political conflicts in which unions or liberals were involved, yet such explanations tend to assume that failed strategies or policies explain why unions and liberals lost battles and declined.[84]

Union and liberal decline can be analyzed separately, but only to a point, because in both their rise and their fall, unions and liberals were deeply intertwined. The decline of the labor-liberal coalition, of both its internal unity and its external power, was a product of active political struggles—struggles that took place among unions and among liberals, between unions and liberals, and between the labor-liberal coalition and the business-conservative alliance—over issues from the Vietnam war through Democratic Party reform to stagflation. Economic and social changes and strategic and policy choices should be incorporated as elements of the national political developments and conflicts through which the decline of the labor-liberal coalition was most directly and decisively determined.

CHAPTER 4

Labor Redivided

From the 1955 Merger to
Factional Division in American Labor

The 1955 merger of the AFL and the CIO healed the most severe breach in the U.S. labor movement in the twentieth century. In the conventional view, the merger heralded a period of internal harmony in organized labor, extending to its political as well as industrial role and strategy. This was so for two reasons. First, the merger was in part a product of political convergence between the two labor federations since the late 1940s, in which the AFL moved leftward and the CIO moved rightward toward a common role in support of the Democratic Party, the welfare state, and Cold War foreign policy.[1] Second, as the AFL was much larger and more stable than the CIO at the time of merger, it largely controlled the new federation.[2] CIO President Walter Reuther's efforts to maintain the cohesion and influence of the industrial unions after the merger met with only limited success, so the CIO proved unable to press its remaining differences with the dominant AFL.

Although there is a good deal of truth in this conventional view, the postmerger harmony in organized labor was neither as deep-rooted nor as durable as some have assumed. Convergence between the AFL and CIO was limited and a less important cause of merger than political threats to the institutional security of unions, such as the resurgence of the Republican Party in the elections of 1946 and 1952, the Taft-Hartley Act of 1947, and the proliferation of state "right to work" laws in the early 1950s.[3] Further, by the late 1960s, differences within the labor movement over its political role and strategy emerged once again, as the labor leadership divided over the rise of New Politics liberalism and its signature issues. This political division in labor, moreover, was part of a more general schism over the fundamental issue of the decline and revival of unionism in the United States. Less than a decade and a half after merger, then, American labor was redivided over major political and institutional issues, and a deep and durable split opened between dominant and dissident wings of the labor leadership. Because the dissident wing rested in large part on ex-CIO unions and consciously sought to revive social activism in labor, this split suggests, contrary to an influential interpretation, that the 1955 merger did not represent the utter demise of the CIO and social unionism.[4]

The inherent significance of the political and institutional issues over which labor leaders divided meant that the post-1968 factional split in American labor was a crucial development. The future of the labor-liberal coalition would be shaped by the course and outcome of this split. So, too, would the future of the union movement itself. It is important, therefore, to understand the nature and development of the factional division in American labor. Toward that end, we must go beyond the discussion in the previous chapter to consider three aspects of the factional split in labor during the late 1960s and 1970s. (Chapter 9 will analyze the course of factional division in labor during the 1980s and early 1990s.)

First, it is necessary to explain more fully the division between unions and labor leaders over the transformation of Democratic liberalism wrought by the rise of New Politics liberals. Social, political, and institutional differences as yet undiscussed all help to explain why the dissident wing of labor was, but the dominant wing was not, willing to renegotiate the terms of the labor-liberal alliance to accommodate New Politics liberals. Second, the two wings of the labor leadership divided not only over national politics but also over the decline and revival of unionism in the United States, and it is crucial to grasp the terms and development of the factional debate over this fundamental issue. For the dissident unions, the restoration of a strong labor-liberal coalition in national politics was one part, but only one part, of a larger project to revive American unionism. Third and finally, the nature and course of the factional split in labor were bound up with a parallel fissure in American social democracy. The Meany and Reuther wings of labor allied, respectively, with Social Democrats USA and the Democratic Socialist Organizing Committee/Democratic Socialists of America, and these alliances shaped the political, international, and institutional conflicts between the two factions of labor.

Factional Division in Labor over New Politics Liberalism

The factional division that emerged in the labor leadership in the late 1960s was anticipated earlier in the decade by the eruption of heated disputes between Walter Reuther, then president of the AFL-CIO's Industrial Union Department as well as of the UAW, and federation president George Meany. Meany and Reuther had been the last presidents of the AFL and CIO, respectively, before the 1955 merger. Although both leaders desired and negotiated the merger, differences remained between them and the labor federations they led. By the early 1960s, the UAW leader had become frustrated with the failure of the AFL-CIO under President Meany to achieve his (Reuther's) high hopes for a unified labor movement. He publicly criticized Meany's leadership of organized labor, and in 1962 he came very close to withdrawing the UAW from the AFL-CIO.[5]

In 1966, Reuther resumed his public criticism of Meany, indicting his leadership of the AFL-CIO on numerous counts: failure to mount large-scale organizing campaigns, stifling of internal debate, the rigidity and hawkishness of the federation's anticommunist foreign policy, the indulgence of holding AFL-CIO conventions and council meetings at expensive Florida beach resorts, a tendency to alienate liberal allies among youth and intellectuals, and abandoning active public leadership in favor of private bargaining with powerful politicians.[6] The AFL-CIO, Reuther charged, lacked "the social vision, the dynamic thrust, the crusading spirit that should characterize the progressive, modern labor movement."[7]

To remedy some of these problems, Reuther proposed changes in the organizational structure, methods of operation, and policies of the AFL-CIO, but he won little support for these proposals. As his differences with Meany over Vietnam and other issues intensified, Reuther and the UAW finally disaffiliated from the AFL-CIO in 1968. Because no other unions followed Reuther's example, it appeared at the time that he and his views were isolated in the labor movement. This impression was reinforced when Reuther formed the Alliance for Labor Action (ALA) with an unlikely ally, the Teamsters union, for he had little success at recruiting other unions to join this potential rival to the AFL-CIO.[8] In addition, as Nelson Lichtenstein has pointed out, Reuther's critique of the AFL-CIO received little if any support from liberals outside the labor movement.[9]

In retrospect, however, Reuther's criticisms of the AFL-CIO and his decision to chart an independent course inaugurated the broader discord and division that would soon overtake American labor on both its relationship with New Politics liberalism and the decline of unionism. Reuther's apparent isolation reflected his political mishandling of his criticisms and disaffiliation rather than a lack of sympathy among other unions and labor leaders with the substance of his views. For, as the previous chapter showed, not long after Reuther's departure from the AFL-CIO, a number of other industrial unions, joined by rising public employee unions, also followed the path of dissent and independence—though not disaffiliation—from the federation. Thus, a dissident or Reuther wing of organized labor was reborn in the late 1960s in opposition to the dominant or Meany wing.

Following Reuther's tragic death in an airplane crash in 1970, leadership of this wing of labor was assumed by Jerry Wurf, president of the American Federation of State County and Municipal Employees. In the early 1970s, Wurf became the most outspoken critic of Meany's leadership of the federation, proposing organizational, operational, and policy changes in it similar to those that Reuther had advocated earlier, and he was a key figure in efforts to preserve the labor-liberal coalition.[10]

Wurf's leadership of the Reuther wing of labor symbolized the political alliance of rising public-employee unions with older industrial unions and reflected the growing role and influence of public-employee unionism in American labor.

The Meany and Reuther wings of organized labor had different institutional positions (within the AFL-CIO), social bases, and political interests. In the late 1960s and early 1970s, the Meany wing retained the dominant position it had achieved in the 1955 merger. It continued to hold the top executive offices (president and secretary-treasurer) and the Executive Council majority in the AFL-CIO and also controlled the federation's foreign-affairs apparatus—the Department of International Affairs—and its various overseas institutes. It maintained final authority over the federation's political arm (COPE) and legislative department, as well, although the Reuther wing had influence in both bodies. The base of this dominant wing of labor remained the ex-AFL craft unions, especially in the construction and transportation sectors of the economy. Both AFL-CIO President George Meany and his successor Lane Kirkland came from these unions, which also constituted the largest and most cohesive bloc on the Executive Council—on which they were overrepresented, compared to their share of the federation's membership—for several decades after the 1955 merger.[11] Meany's remarkable tenure as AFL-CIO president, from 1955 through 1979, rested on both his background in and loyalty to this bloc of unions and his willingness and ability to transcend it when necessary.[12]

Although they cooperated with New Politics liberals on numerous issues, Meany and the wing of labor he led had well-established views, interests, and alliances that precluded support for two key demands of the new liberals. They could not accept the demand to end the war in Vietnam because of their rigid anticommunist, Cold War ideology. In the view of the Meany wing of labor, communism was a monolithic, totalitarian, expansionist system that was incapable of change and with which there was no real prospect of peaceful coexistence, so that every challenge from it had to be met with decisive military force.[13] This ideology was not only deeply held by President Meany and other labor leaders, it was also institutionalized in the AFL-CIO's Department of International Affairs (DIA), which was directed by longtime Meany advisor Jay Lovestone, a former leader of the American Communist Party turned virulent anticommunist, staffed by people who shared Meany and Lovestone's views, and extensively financed by the U.S. government.[14] The Meany wing's support for the war also reflected its long-standing political ties to the foreign-policy bureaucracy of the federal government, dating from World War II and the early postwar years, and to the Cold War wing of the Democratic Party, symbolized by the close relationship of AFL-CIO leaders with Senator Henry "Scoop" Jackson.[15] In short, the demand to end the war and lessen Cold War tensions was incompatible with the ideological disposition, institutional interests, and political alliances of the Meany wing of unionism.

The demand to reform and open up the Democratic Party likewise threatened the established political position and alliances of the AFL-CIO leadership and the unions that supported it. The reform proposals of the New Politics liberals jeopardized the insider status and power-broker role, based on elite bargaining, that the Meany wing of labor had achieved in the presidential-nominating process of the Democratic Party.[16] Party reform also threatened the control over the nominating process exercised by party "regulars," the traditional leaders and professional politicians in the Democratic Party, especially those in the state parties and urban machines with which building-trades unions had long been aligned.[17] The Meany wing of labor opposed party reform in order to protect its existing influence in the Democratic nominating system and its settled alliance with party regulars.

More generally, as Taylor Dark has shown, precisely because it was the *dominant* wing of organized labor, the Meany faction held a privileged position in the Democratic Party, relative to the Reuther wing, that was placed at risk by the rise of the New Politics liberals. As the president of the AFL-CIO, Meany enjoyed access to and influence with Democratic administrations and congressional leaders that even Walter Reuther lacked, and Meany used his influence over appointments and the scheduling of bills to benefit unions that supported him and to marginalize the Reuther wing. By the access and influence they granted him, Democratic leaders bolstered Meany's power in the federation.[18] Meany and other AFL-CIO leaders worried that, in a reformed Democratic Party, an alliance of the Reuther wing with New Politics liberals might lead to a very different pattern of union access and influence and even shift the balance of power within the AFL-CIO.[19] Like the demand to end the war in Vietnam, the proposal to reform the Democratic Party jeopardized too many institutional and political interests for the Meany wing of labor to accept.

As it revived in the decade after the late 1960s, the Reuther wing of labor included the United Auto Workers (UAW), State County and Municipal Employees (AFSCME), Machinists (IAM), Clothing and Textile Workers (ACTWU), Oil Chemical and Atomic Workers (OCAW), United Electrical Workers (UE), Communications Workers (CWA), National Education Association (NEA), United Farm Workers (UFW), and, perhaps less centrally or continuously, the Mine Workers (UMW), International Union of Electrical Workers (IUE), Graphic Arts union (GAIU), Amalgamated Meat Cutters (MCBW), Longshoremen's union (ILWU), Newspaper Guild (TNG), and a few others. It was thus based mainly on ex-CIO industrial unions, some ex-AFL industrial unions such as the Machinists, and large and important public employee unions like AFSCME and NEA. The Reuther wing was distinguished from the Meany wing not only in the sectors of the economy from which it was drawn but also in the social composition of its union membership, as the dissident unions were more likely than the dominant ones to include less skilled workers and to have large black and female memberships.[20] Some unions in the Reuther wing, such as the Electrical Workers (UE) and the National Education Association (NEA), were not affiliated to the AFL-CIO; those that were affiliated remained, collectively, institutionally subordinate within the federation.

The Reuther wing of labor lacked the kinds of political views, interests, and alliances that precluded the Meany wing from accepting key demands of the New Politics liberals; indeed, it had incentives to accommodate those demands and forge an alliance with New Politics liberals. The labor leaders in the Reuther camp had inherited anticommunist and Cold War ideology, but of a different sort than that of the Meany wing, especially in regard to the ways that the United States and other Western countries should deal with communist states or movements. Reuther did not see communism as monolithic and unchanging but as polycentric and capable of liberalization under certain conditions. He believed that Western labor movements and governments should maintain relations—economic, diplomatic, cultural—with communist states and movements that would encourage peaceful change and liberalizing tendencies in them.[21] Although Reuther initially supported the war in Vietnam, after 1968, when he was no longer constrained by support for a Democratic president, these views led him to favor a negotiated settlement of the conflict and an end to the war.

Further, because dissident unions and labor leaders lacked the insider status and power-broker role that the Meany wing enjoyed in the Democratic nominating process, reform of that process did not threaten them and even offered them enhanced influence.[22] Moreover, because of its ideology and subordinate position in the AFL-CIO, the Reuther wing did not have such close ties with Cold War and "regular" Democrats or possess the same degree of access to and influence with Democratic administrations and congressional leaders as the Meany wing. The rise of New Politics liberals therefore not only did not threaten a privileged political position and established alliances but even offered some hope of improving the standing and influence of the Reuther camp in the Democratic Party and even, perhaps, in the AFL-CIO.[23]

In the years after 1968, the dissident labor leadership therefore proved willing, as the AFL-CIO leadership ultimately did not, to renegotiate the terms of the labor-liberal alliance. The rise of New Politics liberalism required such a renegotiation, because it differed from the New Deal/Cold War liberalism with which organized labor had allied in the 1930s and 1940s. It expanded the domestic-policy agenda of Democratic liberalism beyond New Deal economic and social-welfare issues, rejected or at least significantly revised the Cold War foreign policy of the older Democratic liberalism, and multiplied the social·strata and interest groups with claims to liberal Democratic leadership. The AFL-CIO leadership was open to expansion of the domestic agenda of liberalism, but not to rejection or serious revision of Cold War foreign policy (in Asia or elsewhere) or to power-sharing arrangements with other groups on the liberal wing of the Democratic Party. Dissident union leaders were open to all of these demands, for policy and power, of the New Politics liberals. There were three general and underlying reasons why the dissident unions, but not the AFL-CIO leadership and the dominant wing of organized labor, were willing to renegotiate the terms of the labor-liberal alliance.

First, the social base of the dissident unions was more congruent than that of the dominant unions in the AFL-CIO with the social base of New Politics liberalism. Despite class differences, the social composition of the dissident unions overlapped that of New Politics liberalism because of the comparative strength of minorities, females, and public employees among many dissident unions. To the degree that the social profile of the dissident unions was similar to and overlapped that of New Politics groups and activists, it generated in those unions a greater sympathy for the political demands of the new liberals.

Second, the dissident unions were a mix of industrial, public-employee, and service-sector unions, the kinds of unions that are most dependent on a broad liberal coalition to accomplish their political objectives and meet the needs and interests of their members. Such unions are far from identical in their interests and demands, but they all tend to have relatively broad and diverse memberships whose well-being depends on a wide range of public policies and services, from favorable macroeconomic policies through equal-employment-opportunity and sexual-harassment laws to high levels of public expenditure on education and health care. Today as yesterday, these kinds of unions have been the strongest supporters of active government and of a liberal coalition to sustain it.

Third, the dissident unions needed political allies not only to sustain active government but also to help shift the balance of power within the labor movement their way. The New Politics liberals were rising forces in the Democratic Party and national politics, and alliance with them offered some hope of enhancing the power of dissident unions in their own house as well as in party and national politics.

Factional Division in Labor over Union Decline and Revival

The rise of New Politics liberals and the need to renegotiate the terms of the labor-liberal alliance were not all that divided the dominant and dissident wings of the labor leadership. So, too, did the decline of organized labor and the need to revive it. The efforts of the Reuther wing of the labor leadership to raise these issues for debate and action, like its efforts to chart a new political strategy for labor, generated disputes with the Meany wing. In fact, the political divisions in labor were part of the more general split over union decline and revival.

Beginning in the 1960s, leaders of the dissident unions repeatedly denounced the decline of union density (i.e., the percentage of the labor force that is unionized), of labor's progressive social vision, and of the economic and political in-fluence of unionism, and they asserted the need for revitalization of the labor movement to solve these problems. Just as regularly, the Meany wing of labor downplayed evidence of decline and denied the need for change. In these intra-labor disputes over decline and revival, dissident union leaders identified three requirements for revitalization of the labor movement: (a) reorganization of the AFL-CIO, (b) expansion of organizing efforts, and (c) adoption of a new political strategy, especially one that would restore labor's alliance with liberals.

UAW President Walter Reuther was the first union leader to raise the issue of the stagnation of the labor movement and the imperative of reviving it. As early as 1961 he proposed that the AFL-CIO undertake large-scale organizing campaigns. Though the federation's Executive Council approved his proposal, it took no steps to finance or implement it. Reuther then proceeded on his own to provide financial and other support, through both the UAW and the federation's Industrial Union Department, for important organizing drives by the American Federation of Teachers (AFT) and César Chávez's National Farm Workers Association (which in 1966 became the United Farm Workers Organizing Committee).[24] But he was not done promoting broader change in the labor movement.

By 1967, Reuther had formulated a wide-ranging plan to revitalize the labor movement through reorganization of the AFL-CIO, massive organizing campaigns, and change of labor's political posture. He proposed that the federation be reorganized by expanding its Executive Council to make it more representative of the variety of unions in the AFL-CIO, reviving the smaller Executive Committee that had become inactive despite its important status in the federation's constitution, and regularly convening the General Board, on which all affiliates had a seat.[25] These proposals were clearly intended to shift institutional authority and control away from President Meany and the federation's dominant ex-AFL craft unions.[26]

Reuther also recommended that the AFL-CIO launch major new organizing campaigns among farm workers, the working poor, service-sector employees, and white-collar workers. He envisioned this organizing crusade as one that would be based on coordination among multiple unions and a strong role for the AFL-CIO, especially through control of financing (via a tax imposed on all unions) and of jurisdictional issues.[27] This model of organizing, probably inspired by the CIO of the 1930s, implied a greater degree of coordination and centralization than was characteristic of the AFL-CIO, which emphasized the individual union as the appropriate locus of organizing activity.

Finally, Reuther advocated that the AFL-CIO reorient its politics by more actively engaging economic policy, the war on poverty, civil rights, resource conservation, reconstruction of urban areas, easing of Cold War tensions, and other national and community issues, and by rebuilding alliances with liberals, intellectuals, and youth.[28]

Reuther submitted his program for revitalization of the labor movement as a resolution to the 1967 convention of the AFL-CIO, but in the midst of escalating disputes with George Meany he withdrew the resolution and demanded a special convention for the exclusive purpose of debating his program. Negotiations on this demand proved difficult, and before long the UAW disaffiliated from the AFL-CIO. The historian John Barnard later concluded that Reuther failed at the time to build support for his proposals among other dissident unions, was outmaneuvered by the crafty Meany, and so ended up withdrawing from the federation in isolation without having forced a full-scale debate on the issues.[29] The federation subsequently showed no interest in the issues of union decline and revival that Reuther's resolution addressed. Even though Reuther's efforts were politically inept, his criticisms of the AFL-CIO and proposals for change were serious, substantial, and detailed.[30] And although Reuther seemed isolated in 1968, it was not long before his successor as the leading dissident took up his cause.

In 1973, AFSCME President Jerry Wurf submitted to the biennial convention of the AFL-CIO another resolution that decried the decline of the labor movement and called for institutional reform, expanded organizing, and political change in order to revive it. Wurf's resolution identified the key problems of organized labor as declining union density, institutional disarray, and the weakening of labor's political influence and progressive social role. The rate of unionization, Wurf pointed out, had declined steadily since the early 1950s, to about one-quarter of the labor force.[31] The labor movement was further weakened by several institutional disorders: the three largest U.S. labor organizations (the UAW, NEA, and Teamsters) were not affiliated to the AFL-CIO; the federation's affiliated unions were divided and hostile because of jurisdictional conflicts; and the AFL-CIO lacked the mechanisms and authority to incorporate unaffiliated organizations and to prevent or resolve jurisdictional conflicts and union rivalries.[32] As a result, the AFL-CIO could not unify or coordinate the labor movement and in particular could not meet the urgent need to develop and carry out a "massive program to organize the unorganized."[33] Finally, declining union density and institutional disarray weakened organized labor's political influence and social role. The labor movement was less effective at shaping economic and social policies in the interests of low- and middle-income citizens, and it was not living up to its potential as an institution promoting social justice and progress.[34]

Wurf's resolution declared that "serious reforms" were needed in order to "reverse the decline of unionism," "strengthen and vitalize the AFL-CIO structure," and create a "more vital and more influential labor movement."[35] The main purpose of the resolution was to propose that the federation establish a Commission on the State of Unionism to study the decline of organized labor and recommend reforms that would revitalize it. But it also indicated the kinds of changes that Wurf considered most important. He recommended institutional reforms of the

AFL-CIO, including arrangements to bring unaffiliated labor organizations into the federation or at least to enhance cooperation with them; revision of union jurisdictional boundaries so that there would be fewer and broader jurisdictions with less overlap; and a process of mergers and consolidations among the federation's 113 affiliated unions.[36] John Herling subsequently reported that Wurf wanted to see the number of unions reduced to twenty-five or thirty at most.[37]

Another change that Wurf urged on the AFL-CIO was to "devot[e] more attention to organizing the unorganized."[38] As he repeatedly emphasized, the institutional reforms he proposed were necessary to enable the federation to co-ordinate affiliated unions and undertake large-scale organizing. In Wurf's view, only a substantial growth of union membership through organizing drives could ultimately restore labor's political influence, legitimize labor's claim to speak for all working people, and allow labor to fulfill its potential as a progressive social institution.[39] The final change that Wurf proposed to revitalize labor was political; in order to strengthen the labor movement, he counseled, "We should seek alliance with those outside the AFL-CIO who share our interests."[40]

Wurf's resolution received only perfunctory debate at the 1973 convention of the AFL-CIO. It was supported by some other dissident unions, but how many and how strongly is unclear.[41] Although the resolution was a product of extensive discussion within AFSCME, it does not appear that Wurf made any more effort than Reuther had to consult with or line up support from other dissident unions in advance. The report of the convention's Resolutions Committee found Wurf's diagnosis alarmist, his reform proposals drastic and unwise, and the present institutional arrangements of the AFL-CIO satisfactory, and it recommended "non-concurrence" with his resolution. The convention carried this recommendation by a voice vote.[42] The Resolutions Committee, it should be added, well understood the thrust of Wurf's resolution: "The resolution as submitted proposes by inference a drastic alternation [sic] in the powers of the federation to compel structural revisions which under the Constitution are voluntary, and to alter in a sweeping manner the constitutional relationship between the federation and its autonomous affiliates."[43] Like Reuther, Wurf believed that organizing success required a greater degree of central authority in and coordination by a reformed federation. The Resolutions Committee and the larger convention not only disagreed with this view, they also saw no reason to establish a Commission on the State of Unionism or to otherwise engage the issues of decline and revitalization that Wurf tried to raise.

Again, however, those issues could not be suppressed indefinitely. By 1977–78, a group of newly elected union presidents enlarged and reinvigorated the dissident wing of labor and raised the issue of union decline and revival yet again.[44] William Winpisinger, elected president of the Machinists union in 1977, was the most forceful critic of the AFL-CIO leadership and advocate of change in the labor movement among this group, but Douglas Fraser of the UAW, Glenn Watts of the

Communications Workers, and others shared many of his views. The concern of these new dissidents over union decline, their criticisms of the AFL-CIO, and their ideas about how the labor movement could be revitalized were similar to those of Reuther and of Wurf, who remained a leading dissident in these years. They decried the decline of union density, the erosion of labor's role and image as an agent of social justice and progress, and the weakening of labor's political alliances and influence. They criticized the AFL-CIO for contributing directly to these problems or for impeding their resolution. And they believed that institutional change, expanded organizing, and new political strategies were all necessary to revive labor.[45]

But owing to changed circumstances and the fate of Reuther and Wurf's earlier efforts, the dissident union leaders of the late 1970s modified their predecessors' ideas about union revival and abandoned their method of trying to promote it. Neither Winpisinger nor any other dissident submitted a grand reform resolution to an AFL-CIO convention in the hope of provoking debate and changing minds. Instead, the new dissidents followed a two-track strategy for promoting revitalization of the labor movement. First, they acted on their own to establish conditions for the revival of the labor movement, and second, they maneuvered to change the balance of power, and perhaps the leadership, of the AFL-CIO as a precondition of union revival.

Along the first track, individual unions—most notably the Communications Workers, but also the UAW, AFSCME, SEIU, and ACTWU—poured more resources into organizing drives, boosted efforts to educate and mobilize their existing members, and tried to create a more favorable public image of unions.[46] Further, in a move of Reutherite provenance, the dissident unions enhanced the organizing capacities of the Industrial Union Department (IUD) of the AFL-CIO by making its presidency a full-time position, increasing its resources (in part by persuading the UAW to rejoin the federation), and developing the strategy of "multiunion organizing campaigns."[47] A revamped IUD, the dissidents believed, could undertake the expanded and centrally coordinated organizing that was needed to revive union density but that the AFL-CIO under Meany would not attempt.[48] Finally, dissident unionists created organizations to rebuild political alliances and develop political strategies that would contribute to the revitalization of the labor movement.

The second track, altering the power balance and possibly the leadership of the AFL-CIO, was viewed as a precondition for implementing the kinds of reforms that Reuther and Wurf had earlier championed to revive organized labor. This was considered a possibility because of the considerable turnover of union leadership in the mid- to late 1970s. New leaders, generally recognized as more "progressive and aggressive" than their predecessors, rose to the presidencies of the Machinists, Communications Workers, Steel Workers, Electrical Workers, Government Employees, and other unions and then assumed seats on the federation's Executive Council.[49] As was widely expected, this development strengthened the liberal wing and its opposition to George Meany, and dissident union leaders acted to reinforce this trend.[50]

They strengthened the IUD to counterbalance the influence of the Building and Construction Trades Department within the federation, as well as to boost organizing.[51] They prevailed upon the UAW to reaffiliate to the AFL-CIO, in order to expand the resources of the IUD and augment the influence of the dissident bloc on the Executive Council and at conventions.[52] And dissident union leaders intensified their criticism of Meany's leadership and pressured him to step down. Winpisinger repeatedly and publicly urged the octogenarian president of the AFL-CIO to resign, explaining that Meany's departure was necessary for the revival of the labor movement: "Meany should pack it in. . . . In recent years, he's given labor the public image of aging, out-of-touch leadership, and of being a selfish special interest. . . . We need a fresh start. . . . I would like to see the federation reclaim the mantle of representing the underdog and all workers. That would rekindle the spirit, and organizing opportunities would open up and people would involve themselves in the struggle."[53] Although short of a frontal challenge to the dominance of the Meany wing of labor, these maneuvers strengthened the position of the liberal unions and their influence over the leadership of the AFL-CIO.

Dissident labor leaders of the late 1970s modified earlier views about the decline and revitalization of labor in one other way. By this time the dissidents were convinced that both heightened employer opposition to unions and current interpretation and administration of federal labor law were leading causes of union decline, and they emphasized them much more than Reuther and Wurf had. They strongly supported the Labor Law Reform bill, which proposed changes in labor law and its administration to facilitate union organizing, as essential to the revival of organized labor. In their support for this bill, the dissident unions were united with the Meany wing of the AFL-CIO. For by 1977–78, the continued decline of union density, and several years of criticism by dissident unions of its complacency about union organizing, led Meany's administration to agree that reform of labor law—which of course entailed no institutional, policy, or leadership changes in the AFL-CIO itself—was needed for successful union organizing.

But whereas the AFL-CIO leadership genuinely supported the Labor Law Reform bill, it did not attach the same priority to this legislative remedy for union decline as did dissident union leaders. The top officers and legislative department of the federation accorded higher priority to passage of the common-situs picketing bill, which was of concern only to construction trades unions, and they conducted their lobbying campaigns accordingly.[54] Leading dissident unions like the UAW, Machinists, and Communications Workers were the strongest supporters of the Labor Law Reform bill, as President Carter's top political advisor recognized.[55] The priorities of the AFL-CIO leadership, and the evident influence of the federation's Building and Construction Trades Department (BCTD) on them, distressed the dissident unions and confirmed their view that changes in the power balance and leadership of the federation were required if unionism were to be revived.[56]

Indeed, the defeat of labor law reform might well have spurred the dissident unions to mount a full-scale challenge to the dominant wing of the AFL-CIO in the late 1970s, but for several reasons did not. For one thing, the dissident unions rightly blamed defeat of the Labor Law Reform bill primarily on big business, conservative southern Democrats, and antimajoritarian Senate procedures, and their principal response to this legislative debacle was therefore to try to rebuild and strengthen the labor-liberal coalition in the Democratic Party and in national politics, particularly through the political organizations examined in this book. For another thing, George Meany finally decided to retire as president of the AFL-CIO in 1979 at the age of eighty-five, and this seems to have satisfied the desire of the dissident unions for leadership change. They did not contest Meany's succession by the federation's longtime secretary-treasurer, Lane Kirkland, despite the fact that he was Meany's ally and designated heir. Dissident labor leaders believed that Kirkland would lack the institutional influence and control that Meany possessed, be a more open and tolerant president, and have to take account of their strengthened position in the federation.[57] At the same time, despite their strengthened position, the liberal unions still lacked the votes on the Executive Council or in the convention to topple the dominant wing.[58]

Although they modified Reuther and Wurf's views, Winpisinger and other dissident labor leaders of the late 1970s kept alive their predecessors' concern about the decline and revival of unionism. Throughout the 1960s and 1970s, then, a fault line ran through the labor leadership over this fundamental issue. For the Reuther wing of labor, concern over the decline of unionism was the deepest source of dissent from the strategies and policies of the AFL-CIO under George Meany, and revival of the labor movement through institutional reform, expanded organizing, and a new political posture was the defining and abiding commitment of the dissident labor leadership. Across those two decades, on the other hand, the dominant or Meany wing of labor exhibited an astonishing complacency about this crucial issue, repeatedly refusing even to inquire into the dimensions and sources of union decline or to engage in serious debate about potential solutions to the problem.

The efforts of dissident labor leaders to address the pressing problem of union decline and to promote a revival of organized labor were sometimes half-hearted, often politically un-astute, and usually of limited effectiveness. But not only did the Reuther wing of the late 1960s to late 1970s acquit itself well in comparison with the somnambulant Meany wing, it also laid the groundwork for more consequential efforts to revive the labor movement in the late 1980s and mid-1990s, as will be shown in a later chapter.

Factional Divisions in Labor and in
American Social Democracy

The rift that opened in the labor movement in the late 1960s was soon followed by a similar split in the Socialist Party, by then a small party without a visible leader—Norman Thomas, the party's longtime leader and frequent presidential candidate, died in 1968—but still an organized expression of social democracy in the United States. In 1972–73, the Socialist Party fractured into three groups over the war in Vietnam. Two of these groups were Social Democrats USA (SDUSA) and Democratic Socialist Organizing Committee (DSOC). SDUSA, the right wing of the old Socialist Party, strongly supported the war in Vietnam and so opposed the antiwar movement. DSOC represented part of the left wing of the old Socialist Party, opposed the war in Vietnam, and was open to activists from the new social movements and New Left. Both SDUSA and DSOC were admitted as U.S. representatives to the Socialist International, the organization of labor, social democratic, and socialist political parties around the world, but the two groups were sharply opposed ideologically and politically.[59] The conflict between the Meany and Reuther wings of the labor leadership quickly became entwined with the split between SDUSA and DSOC, and this involvement shaped the course of relations between the two wings of labor and gave their disputes a sharper ideological edge.

SDUSA was a tiny organization, numbering fewer than one thousand members, and retained only a genealogical connection to social democracy.[60] In the 1970s, it forged two alliances that allowed it to exercise influence beyond its limited numbers. One was with the emergent "neoconservative" movement among some Democratic intellectuals and politicians and the closely related Cold War wing of the Democratic Party, led by Senator Henry Jackson. Neoconservatives—including among others Norman Podhoretz, Irving Kristol, Ben Wattenberg, Nathan Glazer, and Daniel Patrick Moynihan—rejected the ascendant New Politics liberalism in the Democratic Party, especially its antiwar component, and criticized the errors and excesses of Great Society programs.[61] Following George McGovern's defeat in 1972, SDUSA leaders and activists joined with neoconservatives to form a factional organization in the Democratic Party, the Coalition for a Democratic Majority (CDM), which advocated a more conservative or hard-line approach to social issues and foreign policy and supported Senator Jackson's bid for the Democratic presidential nomination in 1976. Although this latter effort failed, the SDUSA–neoconservative–Senator Jackson nexus exerted ideological and policy influence in the Democratic Party, even as it prepared the ground for effective Republican attacks on the party.[62]

The other alliance that SDUSA formed was with the Meany/Kirkland wing of the AFL-CIO. One of President Meany's top advisors, Tom Kahn, was a prominent SDUSA member, Meany and other federation leaders worked closely with

SDUSA to form the Coalition for a Democratic Majority, and SDUSA members obtained staff positions in the federation's Department of International Affairs (DIA) during Meany's reign. The alliance grew closer after Lane Kirkland succeeded Meany to the presidency of the AFL-CIO in 1979. Both Kirkland and federation Secretary-Treasurer Thomas Donohue were close to SDUSA (Donohue married a SDUSA activist). Because SDUSA was preoccupied with foreign affairs and characterized by a militant Cold War ideology, it is not surprising that its greatest role and influence in the AFL-CIO was in the DIA. Tom Kahn was appointed director of DIA, and another SDUSA member, Eugenia Kemble, served as executive director of the department's Free Trade Union Institute (FTUI) during Kirkland's tenure. Members of SDUSA held many other staff positions in the DIA, and also in the federation's A. Philip Randolph Institute (which dealt with civil-rights issues), Department of Organization and Field Services, and other units. Some AFL-CIO affiliates were also closely linked to SDUSA, none more so than the American Federation of Teachers, whose president, Albert Shanker, was a member, and the staff of which included many SDUSA members.[63]

SDUSA secured employment for prominent members and influence in a major (if declining) social institution from its alliance with the AFL-CIO. The federation leadership also benefitted from the alliance, in the form of knowledgeable, politically sophisticated, and ideologically compatible staff in its important Department of International Affairs, strengthened ties to the Cold War wing of the Democratic Party, a rare conservative voice supportive of organized labor, and, in the 1980s, expanded access to government agencies and funds in the realm of foreign affairs. For the Reagan administration SDUSA recruited activists like Carl Gershman and Arch Puddington for positions in Ambassador Jeane Kirkpatrick's mission to the United Nations, the National Endowment for Democracy (NED), the Kissinger Commission on Central America, and Radio Free Europe. At least in part through ties to SDUSA, Kirkland gained a seat on the Kissinger Commission and, along with AFT President Shanker, on the board of NED, and the AFL-CIO's Free Trade Union Institute became a leading recipient of NED grants.[64]

If the Meany/Kirkland wing of labor linked its fortunes with SDUSA, the dissident or Reuther wing allied with the Democratic Socialist Organizing Committee (DSOC), which was led by Michael Harrington, Norman Thomas's successor as the most prominent American socialist of his generation. In 1982, DSOC, with a membership of five thousand, merged with the New American Movement, an organization of New Left veterans, renamed itself Democratic Socialists of America (DSA), and claimed between seven and eight thousand members.[65] DSOC/DSA was an explicitly socialist organization that nonetheless sought to play a role in mainstream national politics. As Harrington later explained it, DSOC/DSA aspired to influence the "mass left," that is, the new social movements of the 1960s and the liberal wing of the Democratic Party. Concerned about the fragmentation and weakening of this mass left, and about the tendency of many in it to dismiss the working-class and trade unions, the mission of DSOC/DSA was to organize "a broad liberal labor coalition within the Democratic Party."[66] DSOC/DSA therefore adopted a strategy of coalition building between organized labor, or more precisely "the antiwar wing of the AFL-CIO," and the new social movements.[67] In Harrington's view, this was the way that DSOC/DSA could strengthen the mass left and have an impact on national politics while continuing to uphold and propagate socialist values.

By the mid-1970s, leaders of several dissident unions began to play an active role in DSOC. Dissident unionists were attracted to DSOC/DSA partly because of their affinity for its social democratic ideology and their respect for Michael Harrington, but probably even more because of its strategy for influencing mainstream national politics through the formation of a labor-liberal coalition in the Democratic Party. Leaders and staff of the UAW, IAM, AFSCME, ACTWU, and other unions were early members and supporters of DSOC. Somewhat later they were joined by national, regional, and/or local leaders and staff of the USWA, CWA, SEIU, and other unions.[68] These union leaders and staffers joined DSOC/DSA as individuals and did not formally affiliate their unions as organizations, but the unions they led made up much of the core of the dissident wing of organized labor.

DSOC's effort to organize a labor-liberal coalition in the Democratic Party began in 1975 with the formation of a group called Democratic Agenda (DA). An alliance of notables from various movements and organizations (labor, feminist, environmental, religious), this group sought to promote a liberal agenda for the Democratic Party. It was financed by AFSCME, IAM, and UAW, based on support for the project by the presidents or vice presidents of these unions, respectively, Jerry Wurf, William Winpisinger (who eventually became vice chair of DSOC/DSA), and Douglas Fraser.[69]

According to Michael Harrington, the influence of Democratic Agenda on the 1976 platform of the Democratic Party made it one of the most liberal platforms in the party's history.[70] President Carter's budget and economic policies, however, led DA to submit resolutions to the Democratic Party's 1978 midterm convention that criticized those policies as antithetical to the party platform. Although its resolutions failed to win the support of a majority of delegates, DA's role at this convention helped, in Harrington's view, to inspire Senator Edward Kennedy's liberal challenge to Carter's renomination in 1980.[71] But Kennedy's bid for the Democratic nomination also failed and, owing to an organizational crisis that DSOC suffered in the early 1980s, Democratic Agenda ceased to exist after 1982. It had taken initial steps toward coordinating disparate liberal groups and movements and reasserting their voice in the Democratic Party, but it cannot be credited with the kind of impact on national politics that Harrington had hoped to achieve.

As it recovered from its crisis, DSA in 1986 launched Democratic Alternatives as a successor to Democratic Agenda, and once again, dissident unions financed the effort.[72] Though little has been written about it, Democratic Alternatives was apparently formed to battle the new factional organizations—the Democratic Leadership Council (DLC) and the Democratic Policy Commission (DPC)—of centrist Democrats seeking to moderate the party's image and agenda.[73] It was unsuccessful at this task, since the centrist or "New Democrat" faction of party elites that DLC and DPC represented was ascendant in the Democratic Party, at least its presidential wing, after the mid-1980s.[74] The death of Michael Harrington just three years after the launching of Democratic Alternatives surely weakened the group.

Although it cannot be said that either Democratic Agenda or Democratic Alternatives had a major or lasting impact on the Democratic Party or the "mass left," the efforts of DSOC/DSA to rebuild a labor-liberal coalition in the party were nevertheless of some significance. Following the strained relations between organized labor and the liberal left during the late 1960s, DSOC provided an early forum for discussion and joint action between the two camps that promoted their reconciliation. DSOC/DSA allowed leaders and staff of the dissident unions to ally with two groups that were in the process of becoming Democratic Party activists: social democratic intellectuals, and veterans of the social movements and New Left of the 1960s. It seems clear that the involvement of Douglas Fraser, William Winpisinger, Jerry Wurf, Jack Sheinkman, and other dissident labor leaders in DSOC/DSA, Democratic Agenda, and Democratic Alternatives helped to inspire them to build organizations like the Progressive Alliance, Citizen Labor Energy Coalition, and National Labor Committee to revive the labor-liberal coalition.

Just as SDUSA and the AFL-CIO leadership both benefitted from their alliance, so DSOC/DSA and the dissident union leadership both gained from theirs. For a relatively small and ideological organization like DSOC/DSA, cooperation with dissident unions provided financial support for its political projects, opportunities to influence major institutions like organized labor and the Democratic Party, and perhaps staff employment for some of its members and activists. The alliance supplied the dissident unions with talented and committed activists to assist in the rebuilding of a labor-liberal coalition in the Democratic Party, support for the labor movement from intellectuals skilled in policy and public debates, and—through DSOC/DSA's membership in the Socialist International and Michael Harrington's wide contacts among social democratic influentials in Europe and elsewhere—enhanced access to social democratic union and party leaders abroad. The relationship of dissident unions with DSOC/DSA after the mid-1970s helped to revive among them the extensive knowledge of and contacts with European social democracy that Walter Reuther and the UAW had in the 1960s.[75]

The alignment of the Meany and Reuther factions with SDUSA and DSOC/ DSA reinforced and sharpened the political differences and rivalry between the two wings of the labor leadership. Nowhere was this more evident than on international and foreign-policy issues. When William Winpisinger of IAM and Jerry Wurf of AFSCME supported DSOC's 1980 conference titled "EuroSocialism and America," which brought leaders of Europe's labor and social democratic parties to New York City to discuss their trade-union and party strategies, AFL-CIO President Lane Kirkland tried unsuccessfully to pressure the German Marshall Fund to withdraw its financing of the conference. Although Kirkland and DIA director Kahn portrayed the conference as an international trade-union meeting that only the AFL-CIO had the right to convene, they more likely felt that the conference bestowed a mantle of legitimacy on DSOC rather than SDUSA as the standard-bearer of social democracy in the United States.[76]

More important, the links between the two wings of labor and the split in American social democracy added fuel to the intralabor division over U.S. policy and AFL-CIO activity in Central America in the 1980s. SDUSA members in the Reagan administration helped to plan and execute U.S. policy in Central America, and SDUSA members in the federation's Department of International Affairs guided the AFL-CIO's own operations in the region, whereas DSA, like its social democratic counterparts in Europe and Latin America, opposed U.S. and AFL-CIO policies in Central America, as did the dissident unions.[77]

The interweaving of the factional splits in organized labor and organized social democracy also sharpened ideological and strategic differences between the Meany and Reuther wings of unionism. It certainly intensified their division over Cold War foreign policy. More generally, SDUSA pulled the Meany wing of labor closer to domestic neoconservatism, while DSOC/DSA pulled the Reuther wing closer to the outlook of European social democracy. The Reuther wing had always had a basically social democratic outlook, but their alliance with DSOC/DSA after the mid-1970s seems to have given dissident union leaders and activists a deeper and more self-conscious commitment to social democratic views.[78]

In addition, its ties to SDUSA strongly reinforced the political strategy of the dominant wing of the labor movement, especially its alliance with the Cold War wing of the Democratic Party and the foreign-policy bureaucracies of the federal government, its rejection of the cultural and international orientation of New Politics liberals, and its penchant for insider bargaining in party and national politics. The links between the Reuther wing and DSOC/DSA likewise facilitated the efforts of the dissident unions to chart a new political strategy for labor based on accommodation of New Politics liberals, opposition to rigid Cold War foreign policy, and a stronger commitment to social democratic reformism.

Finally, the pairing of the Meany wing with SDUSA and of the Reuther wing with DSOC/DSA potentially raised the stakes of the institutional rivalry between the two factions of the labor leadership. Any significant shift of control over the AFL-CIO from the Meany wing to the Reuther wing might terminate a secure employment base for SDUSA activists and create one for DSOC/DSA activists.

The rival organizations of social democrats, especially SDUSA, had more than politics at stake in the factional split in labor, though what role they played in the maneuvering between the Meany and Reuther wings for control of the federation is unclear.

The alignments between factions of organized labor and of organized social democracy proved long-lasting, and their international, ideological, strategic, and institutional implications shaped the course of labor's internal politics right through the 1995 upheaval at the AFL-CIO.

The Politics of the Reuther Wing, 1978–82

The second stage of decline of the labor-liberal coalition, between 1978 and 1982, initially exacerbated the split in the labor leadership. Following the defeat of the Labor Law Reform bill in the summer of 1978, dissident labor leaders stepped up their public criticism of George Meany. Echoing Walter Reuther's complaints of a decade earlier, they criticized the inability or unwillingness of the AFL-CIO president to tolerate dissent, promote union organizing, strengthen ties with liberals, and respond forcefully to the growing influence of anti-union business and conservative forces.[79] More important, they redoubled their own efforts to restore a strong labor-liberal coalition and to find a more effective union political strategy, by building new and independent political organizations. William Winpisinger of IAM and Douglas Fraser of the UAW were the first dissidents to respond to the marked decline of the labor-liberal alliance in and after 1978. In the spring of that year, Winpisinger formed the Citizen Labor Energy Coalition, and the following autumn, Fraser organized the Progressive Alliance.

In time, however, the post-1978 decline of the labor-liberal coalition also had a contrary impact on the internal politics of the union movement (see Chapter 9). Particularly after the elections of 1980 brought to power the most conservative and anti-union Republican administration since before the New Deal, as well as a Republican majority in the Senate, there were strong pressures and incentives toward "labor unity," and a limited and conditional rapprochement between the dominant and dissident wings of the labor leadership emerged.

But this concordance was barely arranged before the Reagan administration's policy in Central America drove another wedge between the rival blocs of labor leaders. As AFL-CIO support—which was strong but not uncritical—for the administration's policies in Nicaragua and El Salvador threatened to further undermine relations between labor and liberals, in 1981 another dissident labor leader, Jack Sheinkman of the Amalgamated Clothing and Textile Workers Union (ACTWU), organized the National Labor Committee in Support of Democracy and Human Rights in El Salvador, in order to oppose U.S. policy in the region and to develop a new foreign-policy and international role for American labor.

Between 1978 and 1982, then, the dissident labor leadership established three new political organizations. Products of the further decline of the labor-liberal coalition and intensified conflict with the dominant wing of unionism, these organizations were established to restore a strong labor-liberal coalition and an influential union movement, and were more or less vigorously opposed by the AFL-CIO. We turn now to the history and politics of the Progressive Alliance, Citizen Labor Energy Coalition, and National Labor Committee.

PART 2

The Revival of the Labor-Liberal Coalition: Case Studies

CHAPTER 5

The Progressive Alliance

Introduction

As Douglas Fraser, president of the United Auto Workers union, convened the founding meeting of the Progressive Alliance in Detroit on October 17, 1978, the mood among the delegates was one of enthusiasm and hope. Such sentiments had become increasingly rare among unionists and liberals during the previous two years. After all, despite a Democratic White House and Congress, unions and liberals had suffered legislative defeats on labor, consumer, regulatory, tax, and energy policies, as the political climate shifted in a probusiness and conservative direction.[1] Now, however, one of the largest and most liberal unions in the country had assembled a new national coalition of over one hundred organizations from the labor, civil-rights, feminist, environmental, community-organizing, and other movements. *The Economist* declared it "a conclave of American liberalism such as it has been impossible to assemble since before the Vietnam war."[2] Not only was a new spirit of cooperation evident among unions and liberals, but the Progressive Alliance promised a bold and wide-ranging effort to effect change. According to its "Statement of Principles," the Alliance intended to "create an alternative to the direction in which our country appears headed" and to "develop and implement new programs for achieving social, political and economic justice in America."[3] *Newsweek* quoted a determined and optimistic delegate at the Detroit meeting as saying, "We're going to get some leverage and make people in Washington pay attention."[4]

Yet, less than three years later the Progressive Alliance was disbanded, having made only a minor impact on American politics. Its inability to realize its potential and achieve its aspirations, or for that matter even to survive, deeply disappointed many of its participants and sympathetic observers, who struggled to figure out what had gone wrong.[5] There is no denying that, however auspicious its birth, the Progressive Alliance proved to be a short-lived coalition that did not carry any of its initiatives through to completion. In that sense, it failed.

But that is not the whole story. For during its short life, the Progressive Alliance launched significant reform campaigns, had success in the early stages of those campaigns, and retained the support of most of its member organizations. What is most striking, and curious, about the Progressive Alliance is that it was disbanded despite having made progress in its two major campaigns, for party reform and corporate accountability, and despite the will of its member groups to maintain the coalition. Until it suddenly lapsed into inactivity and was dissolved, the Alliance suggested the promise of a revived labor-liberal coalition.

Progress and promise, then, were just as much a part of the Progressive Alliance as failure and disappointment. Both sides of its story are instructive about the politics of the dissident unions and the problems and prospects of labor-liberal revival. Indeed, part of the significance of the Alliance lay in its role as a model, both positive and negative. The Progressive Alliance was one of the earliest of the many organizations formed by the dissident wing of American labor to forge a new model of union politics and rebuild the labor-liberal coalition. Those that came later followed some of the promising directions that it charted and also learned from some of its mistakes. As a result, the later organizations lasted longer and enjoyed greater, if still limited, success.

Origins of the Progressive Alliance

The Progressive Alliance was largely the creation of Douglas Fraser and his union, the United Auto Workers. Three developments prompted Fraser to organize the Alliance. Two of these, the defeat of the Labor Law Reform bill and the failure of the Carter administration and Democratic Congress to enact the party's 1976 platform, made painfully clear just how much union and liberal influence had declined, and provided Fraser's immediate motivations for organizing the Alliance. The third, the division in the labor leadership since the late 1960s, served as a background condition that shaped the way he responded to those developments.

Douglas Fraser's decision to organize the Progressive Alliance sprang most directly from the defeat of the Labor Law Reform bill by Senate filibuster in late June of 1978. Organized labor's top legislative priority for the Ninety-fifth Congress, the modest bill sought to prevent employer defiance of labor law in order to protect the legal right of workers to organize and bargain collectively.[6] It nonetheless suffered defeat in a Democratic Senate "at the hands of an unprecedentedly broad coalition of business groups," which waged against the bill "one of the most intense legislative campaigns in the history of Congress."[7] A critical role in this campaign was played by the nation's largest corporations, including many in the Labor-Management Group and Business Roundtable, purported centers of corporate pragmatism.[8]

Fraser was the first labor leader to act in response to this defeat, initially by resigning from the Labor-Management Group, a private consensus-building and advisory body composed of corporate executives and union officials.[9] In his July 1978 letter of resignation, he denounced the campaign against Labor Law Reform as "the most vicious, unfair attack upon the labor movement in more than 30 years" and called it evidence that "leaders of the business community, with few exceptions, have chosen to wage a one-sided class war today in this country."[10] Concluding that cooperation with business was now untenable, Fraser's letter announced the intention of the UAW to "reforge links with those who believe in struggle" and to "form new coalitions."[11] This was the first public declaration of Fraser's plan to organize the Progressive Alliance; three months later, it was formally launched.

As historian David Brody has argued, the role of the Labor Law Reform battle indicates that the genesis of the Progressive Alliance lay in the destabilization of the postwar system of industrial relations, which had been established and governed by an accord between business and labor.[12] Under the terms of this de facto accord, unions gained organizational security and workers won the prospect of negotiated increases in wages and benefits, along with a system of industrial jurisprudence at the workplace; in return, business secured industrial stability and guarantees of its "managerial prerogatives"—that is, its unilateral right to decide strategic business issues such as pricing, investment, location of production, and technical change.[13] The defeat of Labor Law Reform registered the breakdown of the economic and political balance of forces that had sustained this accommodation. Fraser himself viewed this defeat as proof that business had "broken and discarded the fragile, unwritten compact previously existing during a period of growth and progress."[14] The Progressive Alliance was a product of and response to the disruption of the postwar truce between business and labor.

Of equal or greater importance to the formation of the Progressive Alliance was the failure of the Carter administration and the Democratic majorities in Congress to enact key planks of the party's 1976 platform. Douglas Fraser and other labor and liberal leaders considered that platform highly progressive, so they expected major legislative gains when the Democratic Party captured the White House and retained its substantial congressional majorities in the 1976 elections.[15] By 1978, however, many of these leaders were bitterly disappointed, not only by defeat of Labor Law Reform but also by defeat of common-situs picketing, by lack of progress toward national health insurance, and by the results of presidential and/or congressional action on the minimum wage, the Humphrey-Hawkins full employment bill, tax reform, and energy policy.[16] What Fraser termed the "irresponsibility" of the Democratic Party's elected officials toward the 1976 platform was one of the central problems that the Progressive Alliance was formed to address.[17]

In Fraser's view, the failure of the Democratic Party to enact its progressive 1976 platform reflected three underlying problems in the institutional and political structure of the party. The first was the growing influence of business in the party, because of its "money power" and an increasingly bipartisan corporate political strategy.[18] The second problem was the absence of institutional mechanisms by which the party's elected officials could be held accountable for enactment of the party platform, a problem symptomatic, in Fraser's view, of the deplorable lack of principle and responsibility in the U.S. party system.[19] These two ultimately rested on a third and fundamental problem: the fragmentation of liberal political forces, which dissipated their potential power in the Democratic Party. Hence a "principal motivation" in Fraser's decision to form the Alliance was the need to coordinate liberal political forces in order to assert their full collective power in the Democratic Party.[20]

Finally, the origins of the Progressive Alliance lay in the decadelong division of the labor movement into rival Meany and Reuther wings. Having disaffiliated ten years earlier over Walter Reuther's disputes with George Meany, Fraser and the UAW could not now turn to the AFL-CIO to mount a response to fresh defeats on labor law and party platform (although this would soon change). Indeed, because the UAW had long held the AFL-CIO leadership culpable in the breach between labor and liberals, it was in any case unlikely to turn to the federation for help in rebuilding the labor-liberal alliance. Instead, Fraser naturally turned to the other dissident unions, whether inside or outside the AFL-CIO, to assist in organizing and leading the Progressive Alliance.

Those unions obliged and joined with the UAW to form the core and directive group in the Progressive Alliance. In addition to the UAW, they included the American Federation of State, County and Municipal Employees (AFSCME); International Association of Machinists (IAM); National Education Association (NEA); Communications Workers of America (CWA); Graphic Arts International Union (GAIU); United Food and Commercial Workers (UFCW); and Oil, Chemical and Atomic Workers (OCAW). These unions helped to organize the Progressive Alliance, provided the bulk of its funding, occupied its strategic leadership and staff positions, and retained a controlling influence over its agenda and activities.[21] Without denying the specific and central role of Douglas Fraser and the UAW in the formation and leadership of the Progressive Alliance, that coalition must also be understood as an effort by a larger bloc of dissident unions to craft a new model of labor politics and restore a strong alliance with liberals.

These origins suggested, and its actual founding confirmed, that the Progressive Alliance would have three purposes. First, it was conceived as an anticorporate coalition that would enable unions and liberals to enter the fray against the "one-sided class war" that business had initiated. Second, the Alliance would serve as a labor-liberal caucus or faction in the Democratic Party, in order to promote "party reform aimed at creating a stronger, more accountable, more ideological Democratic Party."[22] Third, the Alliance was organized to develop a new political role for labor and to rebuild and strengthen the labor-liberal coalition in national politics. As Douglas Fraser conceived it, the Progressive Alliance would be "the old coalition" plus "the new groups" that had formed in the 1960s and 1970s.[23] In other words, the long-standing alliance of unions with New Deal liberals would be updated by including the new social movements among youth, minorities, women, and others. Reconstructing the labor-liberal coalition was central to the plans of the Reuther wing of the labor leadership to reform the Democratic Party and to challenge corporate power.

The Progressive Alliance and the Democratic Party

At its first meeting, some delegates proposed that the Progressive Alliance organize a new, third political party.[24] Although the Alliance never officially ruled out this possibility, the third-party option was not a live strategic issue in the Alliance and was never seriously discussed.[25] Douglas Fraser had already declared that a third party was "not a good idea at the present time; it just wouldn't work."[26] Even apart from Fraser's opposition, there was no substantial support in the Alliance for a third-party venture, for its constituent groups and movements had all been incorporated into the Democratic Party.

But if the Alliance was a Democratic coalition, it was also one born of rising dissatisfaction with the current drift of the party. In launching the Alliance, Fraser proposed that its "strategy" should be to reform or transform the Democratic Party.[27] The formation of the Alliance was an attempt to establish a labor-liberal caucus or faction in the Democratic Party in order to contest for power in it and to reform its structure and program. The alliance pursued this party caucus or factional strategy in four principal ways.

First, the alliance sought to coordinate the groups and movements on the Democratic Party's liberal wing. In the view of Fraser and others, organizational fragmentation and political competition among liberal forces had weakened them and made the party vulnerable to business and conservative influence. By providing the organizational means to aggregate the interests and coordinate the activities of liberal groups and movements, the alliance intended to reassert their power in the Democratic Party.[28]

Second, the alliance promoted a more progressive agenda and program for the Democratic Party. The staff of the Alliance's Progressive Issues Project prepared position papers on such issues as the proposed balanced budget amendment, national health insurance, plant closures, state and local tax reform, and the Equal Rights Amendment and distributed them among party leaders and activists by means of a computerized mailing list of some twenty thousand people.[29] At the 1980 Democratic National Convention, the Alliance submitted an "Economic Bill of Rights," modeled on President Franklin D. Roosevelt's proposal of the same title in his 1944 State of the Union address, for incorporation in the party platform.

It proposed "extending to all citizens the basic elements of a decent existence" by means of publicly guaranteed economic rights to employment, a living wage, decent housing, medical care, a quality education, and adequate social insurance; it also called for "an extension of democracy into and over the big corporations."[30] Though the Alliance failed to win its incorporation in the 1980 platform, the "Economic Bill of Rights" was an elaborate proposal that symbolized support within the party for a more advanced social democratic program.

For more long-term programmatic influence in the Democratic Party, the Alliance established an Issues Commission to generate innovative solutions to economic and social issues and to integrate them into a comprehensive agenda and program.[31] Prominent intellectuals were recruited to serve on the Issues Commission, and it did produce a certain amount of research and policy formulation in the areas of macroeconomic and social-welfare policy.[32] However, such work as the Commission accomplished was not widely circulated in the Democratic Party, and most of the Commission's ambitious plans remained unfulfilled as a result of the Alliance's brief life span.

Third, the Alliance took initial steps to develop linkages and support relations with the Democratic Party's liberal and progressive candidates and elected officials. The Progressive Issues Project was intended to provide a source of intellectual and political support for Democratic candidates and officeholders, especially at state and local levels. Also, at the time of its demise, the Alliance had under consideration a proposal to organize a progressive caucus in the Congress; the Alliance would supply the caucus with policy advice and political support, and the caucus would press the Alliance's legislative and budgetary goals.[33] These examples indicate an inclination to establish the Alliance as an organizational base for the coordination of the Democratic Party's liberal candidates and officeholders with its liberal interest groups and constituencies.[34]

Fourth and finally, the Progressive Alliance sought institutional reform of the Democratic Party to ensure the accountability of party officeholders for enactment of the party platform. The objective of "platform accountability" was a fundamental one for Douglas Fraser; it was the pivot of his conception of the Democratic Party as a "responsible party," one that would be ideologically coherent, programmatically oriented, organizationally strong, and accountable to its members.[35]

At the 1980 Democratic National Convention, the Alliance submitted a "Resolution for a Commission on Party Accountability" calling for establishment of a special party committee to consider reforms that would "yield an effective and disciplined effort to implement the Platform of the National Democratic Party."[36] The Alliance's "Resolution" was adopted by the convention, and subsequently the Democratic National Committee (DNC) created a Platform Accountability Commission and charged it to conduct hearings and issue a final report in 1984. Terry Herndon, executive director of the National Education Association and a key supporter of platform accountability in the Progressive Alliance, was named as one of the chairpersons of the commission.[37]

Entirely successful to this point on a matter of high priority to Douglas Fraser and others, the Progressive Alliance was nevertheless officially disbanded before the Platform Accountability Commission even began its work, leaving it without an organized base of support in the Democratic Party.[38] The outcome was predictable. The Platform Accountability Commission's final report was a mere two pages in length and confined to generalities; it simply advocated the accountability of elected officials for enactment of the party platform without recommending specific institutional reforms to guarantee such accountability. Of all the reform commissions created by the Democratic Party since 1968, the Platform Accountability Commission was almost certainly the least consequential.[39]

The willingness of Fraser and other leaders to dissolve the Alliance after they had secured establishment of the Platform Accountability Commission reflected the failure of this particular reform objective to unify and mobilize the various organizations and constituencies that composed the Alliance. Platform accountability and party reform were high priorities for a group of union leaders, party activists, and intellectuals in the Alliance but seem not to have been for other key groups in the coalition, including the civil-rights, feminist, and community-organizing groups.

The Progressive Alliance was ultimately of minor consequence as a labor-liberal caucus or faction in the Democratic Party. It failed to achieve the institutional reform necessary to party accountability, and there is no evidence that it substantially influenced the agenda or program of the party, except perhaps on the issue of plant-closing legislation (discussed in following paragraphs). Still, the Alliance took up the important challenge of creating an *organized* labor-liberal caucus in the Democratic Party, developed many of the components of an effective party caucus or factional strategy, and showed early promise in executing the strategy (e.g., in gaining establishment of the Platform Accountability Commission). Had the Alliance endured, it might well have made a greater impact as a labor-liberal factional organization in the Democratic Party.

It is also true, however, that the Progressive Alliance's party caucus strategy always contained a serious flaw, one that would have limited its effectiveness even if the coalition had survived. When it incorporated, the Alliance decided to obtain a tax-exempt status, 501(c)(3), that prohibited direct electoral activity by the coalition. In fact, more than tax-exempt status led the Alliance to accept limitations on its electoral activity. The prohibition on direct electoral activity allowed the Alliance to defuse an impending division between supporters of President Carter and those of Senator Edward Kennedy for the 1980 Democratic presidential nomination.[40] Though disenchantment with Carter was rife in the Alliance, some of its member organizations either favored Carter's renomination—a prominent example was the National Education Association, which was bound to Carter for establishment of the Department of Education—or at least were disinclined to challenge an incumbent eligible for reelection.

This prohibition of electoral activity prevented the Alliance from enhancing its influence over the party's candidates and officeholders by either presenting its own candidates or extending or withholding support for self-declared candidates in the party's primary elections. It also limited the Alliance's ability to use primary elections as opportunities to promote its agenda and program and to mobilize the party electorate behind it. A full-fledged party caucus strategy required concerted participation in the party's candidate nomination processes; but as a large and diverse coalition, the Alliance was exposed to rival candidacies and divided candidate preferences among member organizations, so that intraparty electoral activity had the potential to disrupt the coalition. Alliance leaders were quite conscious of this tension and resolved it at the expense of the party faction strategy.

Anticorporate Politics

Shortly after the Progressive Alliance formed, Douglas Fraser declared corporate wealth and power the chief obstacles to equality, justice, and democracy, and "misuse of corporate power" the common enemy of all the classes and groups in the coalition. He advocated that the coalition conduct a "broad yet targeted anti-corporate offensive" in order to recast public debate around the proposition that "corporate irresponsibility is the problem" and to mobilize public support for "corporate accountability."[41] As a result, the Alliance initiated three projects intended to challenge the power and prerogatives of corporate business.

The first anticorporate initiative focused on the role of corporate money in politics and was stimulated by the explosive growth of corporate and trade-association political action committees (PACs) after 1974. The Alliance's Political Process Commission planned to conduct research into the scale and impact of corporate investment in electoral politics, publicize the issue of corporate campaign money, and propose changes in the Federal Elections Campaign Act (FECA) to control more strictly the political uses of business money.[42] In early 1980, the Alliance published its research on corporate PACs in a report titled "The Private Use of the Public Interest: Business Spending in American Politics."[43] But thereafter, the Alliance was inactive on the issue, and no legislative campaign to amend FECA was ever mounted. In effect, the issue was displaced by the Political Process Commission's preoccupation with platform accountability in the Democratic Party.

A second initiative involved the development and promotion of liberal alternatives to the economic strategies and policies advanced by corporate and conservative interests in response to the stagflationary economy of the 1970s.[44] This task fell to the Alliance's Issues Commission, which established an Economic

Policy Subcommission headed by prominent liberal and left-wing economists.[45] Although it intended to pursue an ambitious program of research, public discussion, and policy formulation, the subcommission managed only to produce a few discussion papers and pamphlets, in part because of problems arising from the divergent theoretical and political orientations of the economists who directed it.[46]

It is noteworthy, however, that research originally commissioned by the Alliance led to an important analysis of stagflation and critique of corporate/conservative economic strategies: *Beyond the Waste Land: A Democratic Alternative to Economic Decline,* by Samuel Bowles, David Gordon, and Thomas Weisskopf.[47] *Beyond the Waste Land* developed a strategy of wage-led growth that the Alliance might have promoted as an alternative to probusiness policies, but the coalition folded before the project it had commissioned came to fruition. It should also be mentioned that in March of 1980, the Alliance sponsored a well-attended conference in Washington, D.C., to examine the corporate/conservative attack on social regulation and to devise strategies for the maintenance and extension of occupational, environmental, and consumer health and safety protections.[48]

The third anticorporate initiative was carried further and conducted more vigorously than the other two. Prompted by Don Stillman—the UAW's director of Governmental and International Affairs, who played an important role in the Progressive Alliance—Fraser and the Alliance's Executive Board early on committed the coalition to a campaign against the economic dislocations generated by plant closings and the mobility of private capital.[49] Although this campaign was never governed by an articulated strategy, it came to have several elements.

The first step was to promote public awareness of the causes and consequences of plant closure. For this purpose, the Alliance commissioned a comprehensive study of plant closures and relocations, by Barry Bluestone and Bennett Harrison, and published their report in 1980 under the title *Capital and Communities: The Causes and Consequences of Private Disinvestment.*[50] Demand for this study was such that the Alliance reprinted it three times within six months and then published a condensed edition to widen its accessibility.[51] The Alliance also produced a radio documentary and other media projects to publicize the issue of plant closings.

A second part of the campaign was the organization of a new labor-community coalition to combat plant shutdowns and relocations in Pennsylvania. In late 1979, the Alliance placed a representative (a UAW official) in Philadelphia to organize a Delaware Valley Coalition for Jobs. The coalition was successfully organized and was active in the Philadelphia area and at the state level.[52] For reasons that are not clear, the Alliance did not attempt to replicate this coalition in other communities or states.

The third component was to assist and coordinate existing state and local coalitions that were seeking to control or remedy plant closings through community action, legislation, or collective bargaining. The Alliance convened regional conferences on the problem of plant shutdowns and migrations, in Columbus, Ohio, in April 1979; in Boston in January 1980; and in Portland, Oregon, in April 1980. All three conferences were heavily attended and appear to have galvanized and unified local and statewide campaigns against plant closings in their regions. Demands for more of these conferences outstripped the capacity of the Alliance to provide them.[53] Also, in January 1980, the Alliance and the Conference on Alternative State and Local Policies jointly published a "Plant Closings Strategy Packet" designed to aid and coordinate citizen-labor coalitions across the country by providing detailed information on the status and content of federal and state plant-closing laws and bills, on state and local groups active on plant-closure issues, and on resources available to such groups.[54]

The fourth and final element of the Alliance's campaign comprised initial steps to promote national legislation to regulate plant closings. The Alliance released the report *Capital and Communities* in its entirety to the Joint Economic Committee of Congress and to the House and Senate Labor Committees, and Professors Bluestone and Harrison delivered extensive testimony to the House Committee on Small Business in early 1980.[55] The Alliance called for further congressional hearings and advocated national plant-closing legislation. Had the Alliance proceeded further with a national legislative campaign, it could have proposed the controls and remedies recommended by Bluestone and Harrison, including federal monitoring and regulation of capital flows, requirements for prior notification of plant closings, and mandated severance payments to workers and redevelopment funds to localities affected by closures or relocations.[56]

Although the Alliance's campaign against unregulated plant closures and capital mobility was not carried through to its planned conclusion, it was the most significant and successful activity of any kind undertaken by the Alliance, and it held the greatest potential for the coalition to mobilize a larger movement for economic reform. No other Alliance activity generated an equivalent level of outside interest and response or served as well to relate the Alliance to emergent concerns and mobilizations at the grass roots. Moreover, as a broad coalition of national organizations, most of which had state and local affiliates, the Alliance was well suited both to encourage the further formation of grass-roots coalitions and then to coordinate and lead a national campaign for plant-closing legislation. Promising, if halting, steps in this direction were taken by the Alliance before its demise.

Whether these steps contributed to the passage of the Worker Adjustment and Retraining Notification (WARN) Act of 1988, which required firms with more than one hundred employees to give them sixty days' advance notice of plant closures or mass layoffs, is impossible to know for certain. Organized labor had pressed for passage of such legislation since 1974, and the Alliance was dissolved some seven years before WARN was enacted, so the Alliance itself was clearly not the crucial influence. But strong public support was critical to the passage of WARN, and it seems likely that Alliance activity raised both media coverage and public awareness of the plant-closing issue and demonstrated to labor leaders and liberal Democrats what a potent issue it could be.[57] In any case, WARN as enacted was not the same legislation that unions had proposed, since it was weakened with a host of exemptions before passage. As a result, it often proved ineffective at ensuring advance notification of plant closures to workers and communities.[58]

The Progressive Alliance aimed its anticorporate initiatives at important components of business power—campaign funds, macroeconomic policy influence, control of private investment—and demonstrated skill and promise in the prosecution of those initiatives, even though they were not carried through to completion. Questions have been raised, however, about the depth of the Alliance's commitment to anticorporate politics, or at least about its will and capacity to sustain such a politics had it survived longer than it did. For even as the Alliance was conducting its "anti-corporate offensive," stagflation, foreign competition and import penetration, and massive job loss in key firms and industries led Alliance labor leaders toward cooperation and alliances with employers in order to preserve jobs and maintain union influence.

An early instance of this process, with special relevance for the Alliance, was the case of Chrysler, which was hurtling toward bankruptcy in 1979, endangering the jobs of 140,000 employees and union members. This prospect led Douglas Fraser and the UAW to lobby jointly with Chrysler to secure federal loan guarantees, negotiate major wage concessions to the firm, and assume a seat on the Chrysler board of directors.[59] According to the executive director of the Alliance, this pattern of UAW-Chrysler cooperation, however necessary, served to moderate or even reverse the anticorporate rhetoric that had pervaded Fraser's inauguration of the Progressive Alliance.[60]

Although the Chrysler case was unique in many respects, two other examples illustrate the general tendency of foreign competition and import penetration to turn many Alliance unions toward political coalitions with business on trade issues. First, after 1978, the UAW entered into a lobbying coalition with the Big Three domestic automakers to obtain quotas on Japanese auto imports; by 1981, this joint effort had led to "voluntary restraint" by Japan on its level of auto exports to the United States.[61] Second, in 1980, eight of the leading unions in the Alliance also joined the Labor–Industry Coalition for International Trade (LICIT), an alliance of large firms and unions in basic industry that sought more aggressive trade policies, trade-law enforcement, and federal assistance to industry in order to advance the competitive position of U.S. business in world markets.[62] In a 1983 report, the members of LICIT declared that "cooperative efforts by industry and labor, such as the Labor–Industry Coalition for International Trade, have convinced those of us involved that an often surprisingly broad range of consensus exists (or can be developed) among labor, management, and government on issues affecting the future of American industry."[63]

Furthermore, stagflation and deindustrialization also led many Alliance and other labor leaders to favor the development of corporatist arrangements for management of the economy—that is, institutional mechanisms for the joint negotiation of sectoral and national economic objectives and policies by the top leaderships of business, labor, and government. In order to control the burst of inflation in the later 1970s, Alliance labor leaders like Fraser and William Winpisinger, president of the Machinists union, called for a national incomes policy in which wages, prices, and all types of income would be subject to controls negotiated among business, labor, and government. Admitting that business might not be prepared to accept the new "social contract" entailed in such an incomes policy, Fraser indicated that "if [industry] were willing to take that step, I'd be willing to work with them."[64] In the 1980s, most labor leaders also advocated a national industrial policy in which representatives of business, labor, and government would in concert plan microeconomic and capital allocation policies to shape the pace and direction of industrial development. For organized labor, such an industrial policy seemed to hold the promise of preserving jobs in unionized manufacturing sectors and of enhancing labor's control over the industrial process despite declining union coverage of the workforce.[65]

To some, both inside and outside the Progressive Alliance, these developments indicated a weakening commitment, a reversal of course, or even a lack of seriousness to begin with, by the Alliance's labor leadership toward anticorporate politics.[66] Although it contains a kernel of truth, this judgment is for the most part unreasonable and at odds with the available evidence. The cooperation and alliances with employers into which many Alliance unions entered were tactical moves intended to preserve the jobs of union members and the institutional viability of unions in the face of powerful adverse economic pressures. Both these pressures themselves (from economic stagnation, intensified trade competition, and massive loss of unionized employment) and the resultant political alliances with employers to some extent diverted union attention, resources, and activity from anticorporate politics and economic reform. But it is unreasonable to suppose that Alliance unions could have avoided such tactics and erroneous to think that they abandoned anticorporate politics in favor of them. The union turn toward tactical cooperation and alliances with employers did not cause the dissolution of the Progressive Alliance (although the devastation of UAW membership by a stagnant domestic economy and rising import penetration did play a major role). And the demise of the Alliance did not represent the end of anticorporate politics by its member unions, because they continued to practice it through the Citizen Labor Energy Coalition, Jobs with Justice, and other organizations of the Reuther wing of the labor leadership.

The Demise of the Progressive Alliance

On April 15, 1981, two years and six months after its founding meeting, the Executive Board of the Progressive Alliance officially disbanded the coalition. In a letter announcing the decision to its member organizations, Douglas Fraser explained that "it did not seem possible . . . to sustain an appropriate level of interest and funding for the continuation of the Alliance."[67] The Executive Board's action was foreshadowed several weeks earlier when Fraser decided that he could not continue as chair of the Alliance.[68] Indeed, given that the Alliance had already been inactive for several months, the board's decision seems merely to have confirmed that the Alliance was a defunct organization.

Yet it might have been possible to salvage the Alliance at the time the Executive Board acted. Prior to the board's decision, a plan had emerged whereby Terry Herndon, executive director of the National Education Association, would succeed Fraser as chair of the Alliance. The plan initially had Fraser's approval, and many members of the Alliance felt strongly that the coalition should be preserved. But the succession plan did not carry the day, perhaps because a few Alliance unions opposed it, but more likely because Fraser's attitude toward the Alliance changed.

In order to explain the demise of the Progressive Alliance, it might help to begin by disposing of two explanations that do not contribute much to understanding its dissolution. First, the decline of the Alliance was not a product of serious disputes between unions and liberals, or between any of the coalition's member groups, over either policy issues or political strategies. There were problems of coalition building in the Alliance (see following paragraphs), and some issues did prove, or might in time have proved, divisive in the coalition. But with the partial exception of the Carter-Kennedy split, which was managed, there is no evidence that the Alliance was ever plagued by explosive conflicts of interest or principle among its member organizations.[69] The brief life span of the Progressive Alliance did not mean that unions and liberals were politically incompatible.

Second, the Progressive Alliance was not disbanded because the UAW and other unions abandoned the strategy of independent labor politics, coalition building with liberals, and social reform in favor of regroupment in the AFL-CIO, political alliances with employers, and a narrow and defensive trade union agenda. The UAW and other Alliance unions did indeed move in these directions, even as they led that coalition. Douglas Fraser negotiated the reaffiliation of his union to the AFL-CIO during the last year of the Progressive Alliance, and the UAW approved it in April of 1981, the very month the Alliance was disbanded.[70] In addition, as was shown in preceding paragraphs, midway through the Alliance's abbreviated life cycle the UAW and other coalition unions entered into political alliances with employers in search of federal subsidies or trade protection. Alliance unions also advocated trade, incomes, and industrial policies that, to many observers, seemed intended to bolster the declining fortunes of these organizations and their members rather than address broader issues and serve wider interests.[71] For instance, for several years after 1980, the primary legislative objective of the UAW was "domestic content" legislation to require that a percentage of all cars sold in the U.S. market be composed of American-produced parts.[72]

But these moves did not represent a strategic retreat or reversal by the co-alition's unions that explains the dissolution of the Progressive Alliance, as has been claimed.[73] Through the Citizen Labor Energy Coalition, Jobs with Justice, and other organizations, the UAW and other unions continued to practice the broad political strategy of the Progressive Alliance long after it was disbanded. The movement of Alliance unions toward regroupment in the AFL-CIO, politi-cal alliances with employers, and a narrow and defensive trade-union agenda constituted not a retreat from independent labor politics, revival of the labor-liberal alliance, and social unionism, but a second political track alongside it, one that was dictated by the severe economic and political pressures that dissident unions—particularly those in the manufacturing sector—faced in the late 1970s and early 1980s. Some will insist that these two political tracks were contradic-tory, and there certainly were tensions between them. But the fact remains that the Reuther wing of the labor leadership pursued both tracks, and pursued them seriously, at the same time. (These issues are discussed further in Chapter 8.)

An explanation of the demise of the Progressive Alliance lies elsewhere than in labor-liberal conflict or shifting union strategy. The decline of the Alliance had four distinct but intersecting sources: the crisis of the U.S. auto industry, problems of coalition building, the multiple political functions the Alliance assumed, and the outcomes of the 1980 election cycle. This combination of internal and external problems explains the key stages of the decay and dissolution of the Progressive Alliance—the lapse of the coalition into inactivity, Douglas Fraser's decision to step down as chair, and the failure of the succession plan—that preceded the formal termination of the coalition by its Executive Board.

In light of his central role in the Progressive Alliance, Douglas Fraser's decision, made no later than March 1981, that he could not continue as chair was a serious blow and was followed within a month or so by the official termination of the Alliance. The principal reason for Fraser's decision was the escalating crisis of the U.S. auto industry, a compound of domestic stagnation and import penetra-tion, which had already decimated his union's membership and was threatening further devastation. The looming collapse of Chrysler obviously commanded much of the UAW leadership's time and attention from at least mid-1979.[74] More broadly, the state of the domestic auto industry at the time confronted the UAW with massive membership losses: from 1979 to 1981, essentially the life span of the Alliance, UAW membership declined from over 1.5 million to over 1.2 million.[75] These problems meant that Fraser's "own union constituents were relying on him to devote his full attention to the parlous condition of the automobile industry";

a UAW official explained Fraser's decision to step down as chair of the Alliance by saying, "Our membership was not going to understand any extracurricular forays."[76]

Fraser's decision to step down inevitably posed problems for the Alliance, and not only because he had supplied the coalition with much of its vision and direction. At least as important, his union had been the coalition's principal benefactor, contributing far more cash and in-kind services to it than any other member organization, and under the circumstances, Fraser's decision to step down as chair surely entailed a marked reduction in the level of the UAW's contribution. These problems were not insuperable, though, and as was indicated earlier, a will to maintain the coalition was apparent and a succession plan was developed before the Executive Board formally dismantled the Alliance.

Some Alliance insiders explained the failure of the succession plan by claiming that a few Alliance unions—more responsive to the concerns of the AFL-CIO leadership than most unions in the coalition, and with votes or influence on the Alliance Executive Board—vetoed it in deference to the federation's opposition to the National Education Association as an unaffiliated organization.[77] But Douglas Fraser's position was almost certainly more decisive. He had initially supported the succession plan, and had he remained committed to it, his influence on the Executive Board would likely have prevailed. He ultimately decided, however, that the Alliance was not worth saving. As he explained, "I, on the other hand, felt strongly that we shouldn't have an organization just for the sake of having an organization. . . . If you're going to have an organization, at least it should fulfill in some measure any objectives for which it was organized, and we weren't doing that. . . . If you're not fulfilling the function for which you were intended, you should face up to it and dissolve, and that's what we did."[78]

On its face, this view is puzzling. The Alliance, after all, had in fact made progress on both of its key objectives: reform of the Democratic Party to make its officeholders accountable for enactment of the party platform, and placing issues of corporate power and responsibility on the public agenda. The progress that had been made on these goals surely helps to explain why many of its member organizations wished to preserve the Progressive Alliance. Fraser's view that the Alliance had proved ineffective and was not worth saving presumably referred to problems that, in his judgment, rendered further progress unlikely.

First and foremost were problems of coalition building. Fraser felt that the Progressive Alliance had never really gelled, had not truly united its member organizations and groups, and he attributed this lack of unity to what he called the "big umbrella" model of coalition building that the Alliance had adopted.[79] By this he meant that the Alliance was a large national coalition that embraced a wide range of groups and interests, and that it therefore confronted a dilemma. The dilemma was that a broad national coalition could work—that is, make significant gains on issues—only with an agenda limited to a few key issues, but a limited agenda made it difficult to build or sustain a broad national coalition. Fraser had tried to unite the Alliance's member groups and organizations around a limited agenda of party reform, corporate power, and economic policy, but it had not worked. Too many other groups in the coalition demanded attention to their priorities, which could lead only to an agenda so broad that the coalition would be unable to make progress on any particular issue. In his words, "You had so many groups with so many different interests, and that complicated the matter. . . . You're dealing with fifty-five issues and that's really never a good way to advance a program. That was very troublesome to me."[80] In short, in Fraser's view, the Alliance had not achieved the important purpose of overcoming liberal fragmentation, and its preservation could be purchased only at the cost of its programmatic effectiveness.

Fraser was not the only insider to perceive problems of coalition building in the Alliance, but others had a different understanding of their nature and cause. Some former staff members claimed that union dominance impaired coalition building in the Alliance. In their view, the dominant position and role of the coalition's unions reduced the interest and participation of important nonlabor groups, notably civil-rights and feminist organizations, by relegating them to a token role and limiting the coalition's agenda to labor's priorities.[81] They saw this as a key cause of the decay of the Alliance.

In many ways, unions did dominate the Progressive Alliance, because they organized and financed it. It is certainly possible that union dominance had corrosive effects that weakened the coalition. But if so, it was not because the Alliance unions used their controlling position to shape the coalition's agenda around the specific institutional or group interests of labor, for such issues as U.S. trade policy or federal labor law were never even raised in the Alliance. Alliance labor leaders sought to emphasize the common interests of the coalition's partners, but they defined these common interests in terms of traditional party and class/economic issues (reform of the Democratic Party, anticorporate initiatives), into which gender, racial, environmental, and other priorities were not fully or equally assimilated. If union dominance was a problem, then, the problem was not that it permitted labor to pursue particularistic interests but that it permitted labor to define the coalition's general interests. But there is little evidence either from the documentary record or from interviews that union dominance was a direct cause of the collapse of the Alliance. As other former leaders and participants in the Alliance credibly argued, union dominance was acceptable to most nonlabor groups, who recognized the need for a broad labor-liberal coalition, believed that they would benefit from it, and understood that only the unions possessed the resources necessary to sustain it.[82] Indeed, the evidence suggests that most of the nonlabor groups (as well as the unions) wished to maintain the Alliance at the time it was dissolved.

Another problem that might well have reduced the effectiveness of the Progressive Alliance, although it is not clear how large it loomed in Fraser's thinking, was the coalition's attempt to perform three distinct political roles or functions: (a) party caucus or faction, (b) think tank, and (c) mass mobilization. As was shown earlier, the Alliance was established in part as a labor-liberal caucus or factional organization in the Democratic Party, in order to make it a more progressive and responsible party. In addition, one of Douglas Fraser's motivations in organizing the Alliance was to restore a strong liberal voice to a public debate increasingly dominated by the right. He was particularly concerned about the rise and influence of conservative think tanks like the American Enterprise Institute (AEI) and the Heritage Foundation, and he hoped that the Alliance could serve as an effective competitor on the left.[83] Toward this end, the Alliance recruited many prominent liberal and left intellectuals to engage in research, publication, and policy formulation. Given the alienation of so many intellectuals from organized labor since the late 1960s, the Progressive Alliance was quite significant as an effort—and not the last—by the Reuther wing of the union leadership to revive the once strong bonds between intellectuals and the labor movement. The final political role of the Progressive Alliance, mass mobilization, was initially less central than the party faction and think-tank functions but gathered strong support within the coalition over time. It was most evident in the Alliance's effort to mobilize and coordinate a national campaign, including grass-roots organizing, for legislation regulating plant closures.

At the time the Alliance was created, labor-liberal forces urgently needed organizations to perform all three of these vital functions. But it is doubtful whether any single organization could have effectively performed all of them at once, and the Alliance's attempt to do so seems to have strained and weakened it. Above all, the Alliance did not have the financial and staff resources to effectively perform all three functions. Even had the Alliance concentrated all of its funding and staff on think-tank activity, it still would not have competed on equal terms with Heritage or AEI. The Alliance created separate organizational units to carry out the three roles, but there was little coordination among them, and they competed for resources. All in all, the attempt to perform all three political roles seems to have stretched the Alliance too thin and either did reduce or in time would have reduced its effectiveness at each function.

Finally, and crucially, the outcomes of the most recent election cycle affected the fate of the Progressive Alliance. Fraser's decision to step down as chair of the Alliance, and then the official termination of the coalition by its Executive Board, followed by just four and five months the November 1980 election of Ronald Reagan to the White House and of a Republican majority to the Senate. Because the overarching purpose of the Alliance was, as its founding "Statement of Principles" declared, to point the country in a new and progressive direction and to achieve economic, social, and political reforms, the 1980 election results apparently led to the conclusion that the Alliance had not worked and now faced such bleak prospects that there was no reason to maintain it.

But the general elections of 1980 were not necessarily the critical ones in this respect. Both the documentary record and the recollection of participants indicate that the Progressive Alliance became inactive after President Jimmy Carter's renomination as the Democratic Party's presidential candidate in August of 1980. In fact, if not officially, Carter's renomination took the life out of the Alliance. Much of the impetus to the formation of the Alliance came from labor-liberal frustration with Carter's policy record during the first half of his term. Moreover, although the evidence does not suggest that the Alliance was deliberately formed to serve as a vehicle—whether for Senator Edward Kennedy or someone else—to challenge Carter's renomination, many of the coalition's member organizations did in fact support Senator Kennedy's challenge. When Carter won renomination, it must have seemed to Fraser that the policies the coalition advocated would have little chance of adoption and that platform accountability, an issue that always carried anti-Carter implications, was unlikely to be achieved. As of August 1980, it was clear that, under the best of circumstances, the labor and liberal groups in the Alliance would have to live and work with Carter for another four years and that the continuation of the Alliance would only complicate that already difficult task. Michael Harrington, who regretted the termination of the Alliance, argued that "political reality" in the wake of the 1980 election cycle convinced some Alliance leaders that their coalition was now futile, but he speculated that had Senator Kennedy won the 1980 nomination contest, the fate of the Progressive Alliance might have been different.[84]

The dissolution of the Progressive Alliance was something of an overdetermined outcome, one caused by multiple and independent but converging influences. The crisis of the U.S. auto industry and of UAW membership, problems of the coalitional strategy the Alliance adopted, the overburdening of the Alliance with several difficult political roles or functions, and the results of the 1980 Democratic nomination contest and presidential and Senate elections all contributed to its untimely demise.

The Progressive Alliance, the Dissident Unions, and the Labor-Liberal Coalition

The Progressive Alliance was very much the creature of UAW President Douglas Fraser and the union he led. Fraser created the Alliance and defined much of its program and strategy, and his union was its primary patron. The large number (over one hundred) of unions and liberal organizations that enrolled in the Alliance testified to the wide respect that Fraser commanded in the world of labor-liberal politics. So closely was the Alliance identified with its founder that it was often referred to as "Doug Fraser's group." In creating and leading the Alliance, Fraser acted in the tradition of UAW politics established by Walter Reuther, who was at the center of labor-liberal politics in the United States from the end of World War II until his death in 1970, as exemplified by his leadership of Americans for Democratic Action from 1947 onward and his establishment of the Citizens' Crusade Against Poverty in the mid-1960s.[85] The extent to which the Progressive Alliance relied on the leadership and patronage of Douglas Fraser and the UAW, however, rendered it vulnerable to the crisis that afflicted the union as the U.S. auto industry slumped after 1979.

But the Progressive Alliance was never just "Doug Fraser's group." It was also a collective effort by the larger dissident or Reuther wing of the U.S. labor leadership to establish an alternative labor politics to that of the AFL-CIO. The presidents, officers, and staff of at least eight other important unions played vital roles in the financing and leadership of the Alliance, and yet other unions participated in it to varying degrees. Along with Douglas Fraser and the UAW, they sought to fashion an independent labor politics committed to revival of the labor-liberal alliance, economic and social reform, public controls on corporate power, and reconstruction of the Democratic Party. In its attempt to forge such a politics, the dissident wing of the labor leadership both demonstrated its fidelity to the tradition of social unionism initiated by the CIO and distinguished itself from the politics of the AFL-CIO during the 1960s and 1970s. That dissident labor leaders proved unwilling to sustain the Progressive Alliance for more than a few years at most did not mean that they had abandoned this project, which they continued to pursue through other organizations even as the Alliance dissolved.

And, of course, the Progressive Alliance would not have existed without the membership and participation of its many nonlabor liberal organizations. Although the level of support for and activity in the Alliance varied considerably among these liberal groups, there is no doubt that many of them were deeply committed to the coalition and favored its maintenance at the time it was dissolved. The Alliance showed that the will to revive the labor-liberal coalition existed among many liberal leaders and groups as well as in a wing of organized labor. And many liberals continued to ally with unions in other organizations after the Alliance had passed from the scene.

Although the disbanding of the Progressive Alliance dashed the hopes of many at the time, it is important not to make too much of the collapse of that coalition. The Alliance should be viewed as a particular and early effort in a broader and long-term process of rebuilding a vital labor-liberal alliance. Many other efforts proved more enduring and successful, partly because union and liberal leaders and activists learned from the experience of the Alliance. Compared to the latter, subsequent attempts to forge a new union politics and revive the labor-liberal coalition either managed to avoid a profound crisis of a leading union or developed a more genuinely collective leadership, limited and more clearly defined their issue agendas, and developed more specialized political roles or functions. But these successor organizations remained true to the basic program and strategy of the Progressive Alliance: independent labor politics, coalition building between unions and liberals, economic and social reform, control of corporate power, and reasserting labor-liberal influence in the Democratic Party. In fact, both the similarities and differences were already evident in an organization that was a contemporary of the Progressive Alliance, the Citizen Labor Energy Coalition.

CHAPTER 6

The Citizen Labor Energy Coalition

Introduction

In popular memory, the 1970s has always suffered in comparison with the 1960s. In reality, as momentous as the earlier decade was, the later one was at least as significant for its economic, political, and cultural developments. In the 1970s, two key and closely related features of postwar America came to an end: (a) robust economic growth and (b) plentiful and cheap energy. Though important for many other things, from *Roe v. Wade* through Watergate to the Iranian hostage crisis (not to mention disco), the 1970s was most crucially the decade of stagflation and energy crises. Energy crises were an integral part, though not the only source, of both stagnation and inflation. As such, they helped to reshape American politics, in particular to undermine the power of the labor-liberal coalition. The energy crises of the 1970s demanded a response from that coalition; that response came when representatives from nearly seventy labor and liberal groups gathered at the DuPont Plaza Hotel in Washington, D.C., in April of 1978 to organize the Citizen Labor Energy Coalition (CLEC).

The founding of CLEC was a bold stroke, for this new coalition aspired to represent workers and consumers, fight the powerful energy industry, and change government policy during the second energy crisis, which commenced with a new round of energy price increases in 1978–79. And CLEC had another, equally ambitious purpose: to revive and strengthen liberal politics by coalition building between unions, citizen organizations, and public interest groups. CLEC made limited yet significant progress toward these goals by the mid-1980s, when it was absorbed into a larger organization. An important but neglected episode in contemporary labor and political history, as well as in the energy crisis, CLEC's experience should not be lost to memory and reflection.

Origins and Development of CLEC

The Citizen Labor Energy Coalition was assembled by Heather Booth and William Winpisinger, leaders in the citizen-organizing and trade-union movements, respectively, and two of the most important figures of contemporary progressive politics. Booth was a veteran of the civil-rights movement and New Left. Her husband, Paul Booth, had been a leader of Students for a Democratic Society (SDS) who, as Peter Levy has pointed out, represented the most pro-union segment of the New Left; he eventually became director of organizing for one of the nation's largest unions.[1] Meanwhile, in 1973, Heather Booth founded the Midwest Academy, a Chicago training school for labor, community, and political organizers. Booth and the academy developed close ties to several statewide citizen groups that had also been formed in the 1970s by activists from the social movements of the 1960s and thus became part of a nascent citizen-organizing movement. Discussions about political strategy led Booth and other organizers from this movement to decide that the citizen groups should be linked with unions and other organizations in a national coalition mobilized around energy issues. When she and her colleagues proposed the plan to William Winpisinger, the new president of the International Association of Machinists (IAM), he readily agreed to the project.[2]

Winpisinger, a veteran of World War II and an auto mechanic by trade, rose to the presidency of the 920,000–member IAM in 1977. As a social unionist who admired Walter Reuther, he believed strongly in the labor-liberal alliance, so it is not surprising that he joined Booth in organizing CLEC. He helped plan and chaired its founding conference, recruited unions and solicited union funding for CLEC, and committed considerable IAM financial and in-kind resources to it. In doing so, Winpisinger rejected the lingering hostility of top AFL-CIO leaders toward the New Left. Federation President George Meany tried to dissuade Winpisinger from working with Booth because of her New Left background, but as Booth recalled, "Wimpy called me . . . and I told him what I believed and told him the things that I was, and he said, 'Good!'"[3]

Organizing CLEC was a delicate task. Eight months of consultation and planning among the Midwest Academy, the citizen groups, and the Machinists and other unions were required before the founding convention was held. The critical issues in these discussions were the authority structure of the coalition and its stance on nuclear power. The first issue was settled by an agreement that CLEC would be governed by an executive committee with seats equally apportioned among unions, citizen groups, and public interest organizations, and that for an initial period each of these three constituencies would have a veto over committee decisions. The second issue was resolved by a decision that CLEC would take no position on nuclear power, even though nearly all of the groups that joined CLEC, including the unions, opposed it. This decision allowed the Oil, Chemical and Atomic Workers Union (OCAW) to join CLEC and eliminated a major source of potential friction between CLEC and the AFL-CIO and its building and construction trades unions. It also cost CLEC the support of Ralph Nader and some environmental groups.[4]

At CLEC's founding convention, Heather Booth was chosen executive director and William Winpisinger president of the new coalition. This nicely symbolized the alliance of social unionism and New Left–derived citizen organizing that was at the core of CLEC. Though initiated by citizen groups, CLEC's formation and development depended critically on labor participation and support. In addition to IAM, fifteen international unions enrolled in CLEC at the start and another six joined slightly later. These unions supplied much of CLEC's leadership and resources, including, along with its president, one-third of its Executive Committee members, the vast majority of its funds raised from member dues, and most of the in-kind assistance on which it relied. And important if informal leadership roles in CLEC were played by Douglas Fraser, president of the United Auto Workers; Jerry Wurf, president of the American Federation of State, County and Municipal Employees; and William Hutton, director of the National Council of Senior Citizens, a group with close ties to labor.[5]

Booth, Winpisinger, and their allies formed CLEC in response to both the energy crisis and the decline of liberal politics. They recognized that the energy crisis had made energy issues central to economic performance and government policy and believed that it pitted the well-being of workers and consumers against corporate power and profits. They therefore organized CLEC to provide a popular voice on energy issues and to fight for an outcome of the energy crisis favorable to workers and consumers. But CLEC's founders focused on the energy crisis for strategic as well as substantive reasons. They thought it would serve better than other issues to unify working and middle-class citizens and organizations in opposition to corporate priorities and laissez-faire policies and thus to mobilize a liberal coalition that would eventually engage other issues. Indeed, although the energy crisis supplied the issue and opportunity for CLEC's founders, the decline of liberal political forces—labor, the New Deal coalition, the social movements of the 1960s—provided their deeper motivation. They hoped to revive and strengthen liberal politics by uniting the citizen-organizing, trade-union, and public-interest movements.[6]

The citizen groups and unions also had particular institutional motives for forming CLEC. For the citizen-organizing contingent, CLEC was a means to build their emerging movement, which at the time comprised only five statewide, multi-issue citizen groups. They hoped that an energy alliance with major unions would furnish them with the issue and resources to create new citizen groups in many states and link them in a national organization. They were not disappointed. CLEC largely built the national organization called Citizen Action—created in 1979 by the same citizen-organizing groups that initiated CLEC—by forming energy coalitions in twenty-five states and later encouraging their evolution into multi-issue groups affiliated with Citizen Action. Between 1983 and 1985, CLEC itself was gradually absorbed into Citizen Action, where it shifted to nonenergy issues and eventually declined.[7]

For its unions, CLEC was a means of restoring some of the labor movement's waning vigor and influence. To begin with, Winpisinger and his fellow union leaders believed that CLEC could help labor recoup its public support, by showing that energy firms rather than unions were responsible for stagflation and by linking labor with the anticorporate activism of citizen, consumer, and environmental groups. Winpisinger also thought that an alliance with the new citizen groups would rekindle organized labor's appreciation of grass-roots political activism. As he put it, referring to the young organizers and activists in these groups, "These people were great neighborhood participants. They knew how to go out and organize things and raise money, punch doorbells, arrange demonstrations. And all of that I thought was awfully important to labor trying to do something with its political agenda."[8] Finally, Winpisinger expressed the deep concern of many union leaders about labor's political alliances when he emphasized that CLEC would rebuild "some of the bridges that George Meany had burned over the years."[9]

By the late 1970s, then, both citizen organizers and social unionists saw coalition building as a way to strengthen their own movements while also reinvigorating liberal politics. They believed that coalition building among unions, citizen groups, and public-interest organizations was possible, despite past tensions and differences, because all three now shared an anticorporate ideology, agreed on a wide range of policy issues, needed political allies and support, and were aligned with the Democratic Party. CLEC's founders were also convinced that coalition building among these movements would in fact strengthen liberal politics, in two ways. It would do so first by combining the specific resources and competencies of each of the three movements. CLEC would revitalize liberal politics by integrating the mass base and organizational and financial resources of unions with the grass-roots organizing and direct-action techniques of citizen groups and the policy expertise and lobbying skills of public-interest organizations. Second, CLEC's leaders and staff believed that their coalitional strategy was innovative in a way that would strengthen liberal politics. CLEC would be a national alliance but, unlike liberal alliances of the past, it would have a "solid local power base" in state and local coalitions, which would fortify CLEC's national campaigns with "grass-roots organization and political action."[10]

This strategy required CLEC to engage in extensive organization building. The national coalition established its headquarters in Chicago but also set up a Washington, D.C., office to handle legislative strategy and lobbying. It mobilized its resources—leadership, staff, policy expertise, communications, funding—effectively if somewhat unevenly. CLEC drew its leadership (president, secretary-treasurer, Executive Committee) from the heads of its member labor, citizen-action, and public-interest groups. As a result, its leadership was proven and skilled but limited in the time and effort it could devote to CLEC. It was thus all the more important that CLEC assembled an experienced and talented staff of more than twenty organizers, lobbyists, publicists, campaign strategists, administrators, and policy experts. This staff was drawn from the citizen-organizing and public-interest groups in CLEC, often had backgrounds in the social movements of the 1960s, and exercised considerable initiative in the coalition.[11]

The national coalition's other key resources were communication networks and funds, the former in substantial but the latter in short supply. Its unions provided CLEC with extensive and ready-made networks of communication and mobilization that greatly assisted its organizing and legislative campaigns. CLEC's financial resources, on the other hand, were a constant problem and certainly no match for those of the energy industry. Its major income sources were dues and contributions from unions and grants from foundations and the federal government. Half a dozen unions—IAM, UAW, AFSCME, SEIU, NEA, UFCW, and the AFL-CIO, after Lane Kirkland replaced Meany as president—paid annual dues of $5,000 to $10,000, and other unions paid lesser dues. Unions also made financial and in-kind contributions of widely varying amounts, the Machinists' union being by far the largest benefactor. Counting contributions as well as dues, a reasonable estimate is that unions accounted for about 40 percent of CLEC's annual income, which ranged from half a million to a million dollars. Insofar as its funds were internally generated, CLEC was a labor-subsidized coalition, but except for IAM, the unions did not invest significant shares of their resources in CLEC, which thus had to commit great time and effort to securing foundation and federal monies. In 1982, CLEC created a new staff position devoted entirely to fund-raising, but by 1983 the coalition suffered a financial crisis from which it never fully recovered.[12]

Much of CLEC's early history was spent building the state and local energy coalitions. To do this, CLEC held planning conferences and hired organizers in each of six regions (New England, Mid-Atlantic, South, Midwest, California, Pacific Northwest) between late 1978 and early 1979. It then targeted ten states for intensive and another fifteen states for lesser levels of organizing activity. Regional organizers worked with state and local affiliates of CLEC's member organizations to build the state coalitions, and state organizing was most successful where CLEC's major unions—IAM, UAW, AFSCME, SEIU, USWA, UFCW, NEA—were strong.[13]

By mid-1980, CLEC claimed twenty-five state energy coalitions, which varied in structure, composition, and level of activity. Twelve were created anew by CLEC on the model of the national coalition, with organizational membership, dues, functioning committees, and paid staff, whereas the rest were preexisting mass-membership and multi-issue organizations that assumed the role of state energy coalitions. Some of the state coalitions were in fact confined to one or a few large cities or had a low level of organization and participation. Also, CLEC was unable to establish a significant base in the South. Nevertheless, the building of many new state coalitions and the creation of a broader network of state energy groups was a substantial organizing accomplishment, carried out in less than two years and with limited resources.

CLEC's state coalitions were granted considerable autonomy to pursue particular state and local energy issues but were expected to assist CLEC's national educational and legislative campaigns by means of local media and publicity work, mobilization of members for public events, and congressional district operations to supplement national lobbying with local pressure. They were integral to CLEC's efforts to address and resolve the energy crisis.[14]

CLEC and the Energy Crisis

Based on its analysis of the nature and sources of the energy crisis, the Citizen Labor Energy Coalition proposed principles for a new national energy strategy and waged several campaigns for energy policies that would resolve the crisis. In CLEC's view, the energy crisis was one of drastic price increases but not genuine supply shortages. CLEC acknowledged the roots of this crisis in U.S. dependence on foreign oil and the power of the international cartel of oil-producing nations. It always emphasized, however, the domestic source of the crisis: a small group of giant, integrated oil and gas firms owned and controlled most energy resources and deeply influenced public energy policy, enabling them to supply and price energy to their advantage. According to CLEC, these firms contrived shortages and raised prices in order to increase profits, extend their ownership of energy resources, and leverage major policy changes. Hence in CLEC's view the crisis was fundamentally about "power over the development and allocation of energy resources."[15]

CLEC argued that there were two possible outcomes of the energy crisis. A pro-industry resolution of the crisis—featuring deregulation, tax concessions, and further concentration of the industry—would only increase corporate control of energy resources and economic welfare, to the detriment of the majority of Americans. The other possibility was a more rational and democratic disposition of energy resources based on the interests of workers and consumers and an enlarged role for the public sector. CLEC's mission was to fight for the latter outcome.[16]

Accordingly, CLEC proposed four principles of an energy strategy that would serve worker and consumer interests: just and affordable energy prices; job creation and preservation; deconcentration of the energy industry; and safe energy sources. Affordable energy prices were a basic human right for residential consumers and a condition of competitiveness for industrial users. Energy policy should also maximize employment, and conservation and solar technologies had good prospects for job creation and preservation. Fair prices and full employment further required that concentration of ownership and control in the energy industry be broken up and a public energy corporation established as part of a more competitive industry structure. Finally, choice or promotion of energy sources should be based on their safety for workers, consumers, and the environment. CLEC believed that energy policies based on these principles would win majority support and stabilize the economy.[17]

By 1979, CLEC had elaborated these principles into a comprehensive energy policy proposal called the Citizens' Energy Program (CEP), which had several provisions. First, it called for the reimposition of price controls on natural gas, crude oil, and refined products. Second, it advocated federal grants and tax credits to subsidize energy costs for low- and moderate-income citizens. Third, the CEP proposed that oil firms be required to operate at maximum capacity during supply shortages and that a special prosecutor be authorized to investigate contrived shortages and price gouging. A fourth provision promoted a more competitive energy industry by such measures as elimination of oil-industry tax subsidies, prohibition of oil-company mergers and acquisitions, divestiture of the major oil firms, and establishment of a public energy corporation. Fifth and finally, the CEP called for mandatory conservation standards, a solar-development bank, and incentives for energy-efficient building and retrofitting in order to create jobs through conservation and alternative energy sources. This ambitious program was introduced into Congress as the Citizens' Energy Act by Rep. Toby Moffett (D-CT) and Sen. Howard Metzenbaum (D-OH). Though never approved in its entirety, elements of this act—a Solar and Conservation Bank, low-interest loans and grants for homeowner and renter energy investments, fuel assistance and weatherization funds for low-income families—were incorporated into legislation that Congress passed in 1980.[18]

CLEC's bid to shape energy policy, however, centered not on wholesale passage of the Citizens' Energy Act but on four legislative campaigns based on provisions of that act. CLEC mounted two of these campaigns at the state level, where it sought to reform utility service and rates and to impose taxes on oil-company profits. The other two campaigns were conducted at the national level, where CLEC promoted conservation and solar technology and fought to maintain or restore price controls on oil and natural gas. CLEC's battle for price controls, called the "Campaign for Fair Energy Prices," was always its primary policy objective.[19]

CLEC's first state-level campaign, for reform of electric and natural gas service and rates, was launched in the fall of 1978. Because of sharp rate increases, member organizations of CLEC were already engaged in utility reform campaigns in a dozen states when it was formed, and CLEC quickly recognized the issue's popularity and potential to build state energy coalitions. CLEC ultimately waged utility-reform campaigns in twenty-five states over a five-year period. These campaigns targeted state legislatures, public-utility commissions, and utility firms and sought direct rate relief, more equitable rate structures, bans or limitations on utility shutoffs during winter months, and, in some states, establishment of elected regulatory commissions. With support from the Carter administration, the Department of Energy, and Senator Edward Kennedy (D-MA), this campaign enjoyed considerable success. CLEC won bans or limitations on winter utility shutoffs in at least twenty-three states; direct rate relief for residential customers in several states; and more equitable rate structures in up to twenty states.[20]

CLEC's second state-level campaign, for new or strengthened state taxes on oil companies, was initiated by the energy coalitions of Connecticut, New York, and Massachusetts. Their state legislative victories on oil taxation prompted national CLEC to develop similar campaigns in a dozen or more states by late 1981. The coalition waged these campaigns on grounds of tax fairness, fiscal stability, and regional equity, arguing that new or strengthened taxes on oil companies were needed to remedy their nonpayment or underpayment of taxes, to relieve the distress of state finances, and to stem the financial drain from energy-consuming to energy-producing states. The oil-tax campaigns proposed that states adopt "excess profits" taxes and a "unitary" accounting system, whereby states tax a share of a multinational firm's worldwide income or profits.[21]

CLEC's campaign for state taxation of oil firms was not very successful. Though it did win legislative victories in Connecticut, New York, Wisconsin, Minnesota, and Massachusetts, in most of these cases the victories were limited (tax loopholes were closed), vetoed, or judicially weakened. The campaign was undermined by the oil companies' threat, carried out in some states, to pass tax increases on to consumers in higher product prices, and by a federal court ruling that it was unconstitutional for Connecticut's tax on oil firms to prohibit them from passing the tax through to consumers in higher prices.[22]

One of CLEC's two national campaigns promoted conservation and solar technology as rational energy policies that would also preserve and create jobs. CLEC's general objective in this campaign was to increase employment-generating investments in conservation and solar technologies. Thus it sought to increase federal grants and loans to firms, public agencies, and households for conservation and solar improvements. It also pressed for bank and utility financing of residential conservation and solar investments at below-market interest rates. Lastly, CLEC wanted state and local governments to adopt conservation and solar requirements for the building or retrofitting of public facilities. To achieve these goals, CLEC participated in the Carter administration's 1978–80 "Solar Policy Review"; launched model state campaigns for employment growth through conservation and solar technology in Ohio and Massachusetts; and conducted a publicity campaign to increase public use of existing tax credits and low-interest loans for weatherization improvements.[23]

The conservation and solar campaign was, however, a secondary one for CLEC. Its sole accomplishment, congressional authorization in 1980 of a Conservation and Solar Bank to finance homeowner and tenant improvements, proved an insubstantial victory. Not only was the bank's initial appropriation inadequate, but the Reagan administration refused even to organize the bank until ordered to do so by a federal court a year and a half later, and by this time CLEC was preoccupied by other battles.[24]

CLEC's primary national initiative was the "Campaign for Fair Energy Prices," which sought to maintain and extend federal price controls on oil and natural gas, the major U.S. energy sources, in order to ensure economic stability and distributive justice. This campaign was a response to the main trend of national energy policy at the time, the deregulation of energy prices, and was always CLEC's highest priority because of its great economic and distributional stakes.

In the case of oil, CLEC waged a yearlong fight against President Carter's 1979 order of a phased decontrol of crude-oil prices and his proposal of a windfall-profits tax on oil companies, which was intended to make decontrol politically acceptable. CLEC argued that decontrol of oil prices was not justified by either production costs or the promise of new production. It also contended that decontrol would increase both inflation and unemployment. This in turn would impose a great burden on consumers and workers while bestowing on major oil firms a windfall profit (little of which would be captured by the proposed tax) that would facilitate their goal of monopolizing ownership of energy resources. To build support for bills—HR3621 and S396, sponsored, respectively, by Rep. Thomas Luken (D-OH) and Sen. Henry Jackson (D-WA)—that would block Carter's order and maintain oil price controls, CLEC combined Washington lobbying with local pressure on members of Congress and carried out a campaign to expose oil-industry profiteering. The central event of CLEC's battle against decontrol was the October 17, 1979, Big Oil Day, which attracted up to 100,000 people to protests in 120 cities. Big Oil Day received extensive media coverage and secured CLEC's reputation as the leading grass-roots voice on energy issues.[25]

Despite these efforts, CLEC failed to reverse the decontrol of oil prices. In March of 1980, Congress accepted Carter's decontrol order and passed a windfall-profits tax. As this occurred, CLEC dropped its original opposition to the tax and helped to pass a stronger version over weaker ones. Estimated to raise $227 million in revenues, the tax still left the industry a nice chunk of the windfall profits expected from decontrol over the coming decade and, in any case, was a necessary concession to win decontrol. Though it failed to achieve its policy goal, CLEC's oil campaign earned it national recognition and a place in the energy-policy arena. It also allowed CLEC to hone its political skills for the even bigger fight over natural gas.[26]

CLEC's natural-gas campaign had three stages, the first being its unsuccessful effort to defeat the Natural Gas Policy Act (NGPA) of 1978, which provided for phased decontrol of natural-gas prices and concluded one of the most complex and ferocious legislative battles of the postwar era. Having been formed a mere six months prior to passage of the act, CLEC was forced to join the battle over NGPA at a late stage and just as it was building itself into a functioning coalition. Under these adverse circumstances, CLEC managed to wage a surprisingly strong campaign of public education, Washington lobbying, and local pressure on members of Congress in over twenty states. But CLEC and other opponents lost a crucial procedural vote on NGPA by the razor-thin margin of 206–207, and the act was then passed by Congress and signed by President Carter on November 9, 1978.[27] The NGPA raised the ceiling price of new (post–April 1977) gas on the interstate market and gradually decontrolled it by 1985. This was a considerable victory for the oil and gas industry, but an incomplete one because it did not meet all of the industry's demands. CLEC consoled itself that it had at least led the opposition to gas deregulation and come close (on the procedural vote) to derailing a major bill backed by powerful corporate interests.[28]

The second stage of the campaign was CLEC's successful 1981–82 battle to block President Reagan's plan to accelerate the schedule and extend the scope of gas deregulation contained in the NGPA. In conjunction with the AFL-CIO, CLEC won from a majority of House members written pledges of opposition to further deregulation of gas prices either by Congress or by the Federal Energy Regulatory Commission (FERC). This preemptive mobilization of congressional resistance—effected by pressure CLEC exerted in the home districts of over two hundred House members, reinforced in thirty-six districts by a door-to-door canvass to generate constituency support—deterred President Reagan from submitting a decontrol bill to the Ninety-seventh Congress and dissuaded FERC from raising gas prices by administrative means. CLEC viewed this as its major energy-policy victory and claimed that it saved several million jobs for workers and tens of billions of dollars for consumers. It is also true that this victory staved off NGPA deregulation for only three years.[29]

Therefore, in the campaign's third and final phase, CLEC went on the offensive in the Ninety-eighth Congress (1983–84) to enact the Natural Gas Consumer Relief Act (NGCRA), which retained price controls on old gas, extended controls on new gas until 1987, and lowered the well-head price of natural gas. Largely crafted by CLEC and introduced into Congress in March of 1983, the NGCRA was dubbed by *Congressional Quarterly* the leading alternative to President Reagan's new bill, introduced in February, to decontrol old as well as new gas prices.[30] CLEC's fight for passage of the NGCRA included a media campaign, direct lobbying of Congress, a door-to-door canvass in fifty targeted congressional districts, and the September 24, 1983, Gas Protest Day, held in forty cities in thirty-five states. This aggressive effort failed to win passage of the NGCRA, however, for CLEC was unable to gain the support of the crucial House Energy and Commerce Committee. CLEC was not strong enough to re-regulate and roll back natural-gas prices, but it was able, along with the AFL-CIO and others, to prevent the Reagan administration and gas industry from accelerating and widening price decontrol. In the face of this stalemate, Congress abandoned the gas-price issue in the summer of 1984. This ended CLEC's "Fair Energy Price Campaign" and roughly coincided with the end of CLEC as an independent organization.[31]

CLEC's policies and campaigns suggest five conclusions about its role and significance in the energy crisis. First, CLEC was an anticorporate coalition that challenged the power and priorities of the dominant energy firms and opposed a pro-industry resolution of the energy crisis. Of course, CLEC lost the war over how to resolve the energy crisis, especially because it was unable to halt the tide of energy price deregulation. This inability stemmed from the superior power of the energy industry—which, in the words of the energy policy expert Walter Rosenbaum, "exhibits one of the highest concentrations of corporate wealth, market power, and government influence among any U.S. economic sector"—and the growth of conservative control of government after 1978.[32] It is also true that CLEC failed to mount a serious campaign for the two key reforms it proposed of the industrial structure of the energy sector: more vigorous antitrust enforcement and formation of both a public energy corporation (to compete with private firms) and a federal oil-purchasing authority (to assume the import function and break the link between OPEC and the oil majors). But otherwise, CLEC vigorously fought the energy industry both in the court of public opinion and in policy-making arenas. Its anticorporate challenge was sufficiently strong to arouse the vigilance and resistance of the energy industry and to win modest victories over it in its public-utilities and natural-gas campaigns.[33]

Second, CLEC was a proworker and proconsumer coalition that fought for energy policies ensuring affordable prices and high and stable employment. It strengthened consumer interests in the energy crisis through its mass base and grass-roots capabilities, which existing consumer groups generally lacked. It also enabled an important group of unions to assert workers' stakes in the energy crisis more publicly and forcefully than organized labor had done previously, especially by linking energy policy to the traditional labor goal of full employment. Moreover, CLEC made strides toward overcoming past conflicts between unions and consumer groups and uniting them based on their shared opposition to corporate power. And CLEC's policy victories yielded clear if limited gains for consumers and workers.

Third, CLEC functioned, by circumstance more than design, as a regional coalition representing broad northeastern and midwestern interests in the energy crisis. Because of the geographical distribution of its member unions and citizen groups, CLEC and its state and local coalitions were concentrated in the Northeast and Midwest and had little presence or strength in the South. Thus it is not surprising that the energy policies CLEC advocated, notably price regulation, expressed economic interests and public preferences typical of energy-consuming rather than energy-producing areas. CLEC sought to resolve the energy crisis on terms favorable to the energy-consuming northeastern and midwestern states that it represented, regions that in fact bore the economic and fiscal brunt of the crisis.[34]

Fourth, CLEC was a liberal coalition that fought for distributive justice and active government in its attempt to resolve the energy crisis. It portrayed the energy crisis as a conflict over the distribution of the costs and benefits of energy production and consumption among classes and regions, and its most valuable role in that crisis was to force these crucial distributional issues to the center of policy debates and to promote egalitarian solutions to them. Moreover, in an era of resurgent laissez-faire, CLEC argued cogently that only a strong and active public sector could manage the problems of energy production and consumption in ways consistent with economic stability and social justice.

Fifth and finally, CLEC's impact in the energy crisis was certainly modest but not insignificant. Given the waning power of liberal politics at the time, even CLEC's limited impact on energy policy can be considered an accomplishment.

CLEC and Liberal Politics

CLEC was created, in part, precisely to remedy this decline of liberal influence in American politics. It sought to do this through a four-part strategy of coalition building among labor, citizen, and public-interest groups; organization and mobilization at state and local levels; participation in party and electoral politics; and renewal of the populist tradition. This strategy, and the institutions it produced, made a worthy contribution to liberal politics, even if CLEC did not fundamentally reverse the fragmentation and weakness of liberalism.

As CLEC's founders expected, their coalition-building strategy did strengthen liberal politics, both during and after the energy crisis. During the energy crisis, CLEC led the opposition to the energy industry and shaped energy policy to a degree that was quite modest but probably unmatched by any other left-of-center group. It was able to do this because it allowed labor, citizen, and public-interest groups to forge a unified energy agenda and program and to coordinate their various skills and resources—electoral activity, lobbying, grass-roots mobilization, direct action, canvassing, policy research, media campaigns—so as to maximize their influence.[35]

CLEC also fortified liberal politics beyond the energy crisis, by building Citizen Action and forging durable links between unions and citizen-organizing groups. By the late 1980s, Citizen Action, with twenty-five affiliated state groups and a membership over two million, had become a potent electoral force in a number of northeastern and midwestern states. As a result, it also achieved influence in the Democratic Party and bolstered the party's liberal wing, and even shaped the national policy agenda with its campaigns to reauthorize the Superfund program and to reform health care. All this lead the journalist David Moberg to describe Citizen Action in 1986 as "the largest, most effective grass-roots force on the left in American politics."[36] Moreover, many of the CLEC unions continued to finance Citizen Action, participate in its state affiliates, and collaborate with it in electoral and policy campaigns well into the 1990s.

Yet, CLEC's coalition building also had limitations as a strategy for strengthening liberal politics. These limitations derived from CLEC's focus on energy issues, which was simultaneously the coalition's chief strength and main weakness. Energy issues were tailor-made to unite unions, citizen groups, and public-interest organizations, and CLEC's focus on them undoubtedly helped to make it a coherent and cohesive coalition that could concentrate its activity and resources for maximum policy effect. But CLEC's focus on energy issues also had three unfortunate consequences.

The first was that CLEC never explored the full range of common interests that existed among its constituent movements or the full scope of influence that their alliance might exert. CLEC's founders did not assume that the shared interests of labor, citizen, and public-interest groups were confined to energy issues, but CLEC did not test how far, or across what range of issues, those shared interests extended. And the coalition's exclusive focus on energy issues obviously limited the range of issues and policies that it could influence.

The second consequence was the absence of major organizations representing minorities and women. CLEC did not exclude these groups, but its focus on energy issues did not attract them or elicit strong support and participation from them. As a result, CLEC did not coordinate the full range of liberal groups and movements, which limited its potential to lead and strengthen liberal politics.

The third consequence was that CLEC did not survive the fading of the energy crisis as an independent organization. As a single-issue coalition, CLEC began to wane as the energy crisis abated, owing to the resolution of domestic energy policy battles and the stabilization of world energy supplies and prices. As this occurred, CLEC might have survived by converting itself into a multi-issue coalition, which was the intention when the coalition was founded. Some of the citizen groups, however, preferred to concentrate their efforts on developing Citizen Action rather than on converting CLEC into a multi-issue coalition. This decision was influenced by the limited resources of citizen groups, but, as several CLEC leaders and staff emphasized, it also reflected emerging divisions in the citizen-organizing movement over its political strategy and alliances. With support for the conversion of CLEC into a multi-issue coalition ebbing, and with the coalition already in dire financial straits, the unions supported its integration into Citizen Action. For all practical purposes, this spelled the end of CLEC as an organized and active labor–citizen–public interest alliance at the national level. These movements, however, continued to cooperate in Citizen Action and in later organizations.[37]

The second element of CLEC's political strategy was its commitment to organization building and popular mobilization at state and local levels. As shown above, CLEC's organization building at state and local levels was substantial and durable. Its ability to mobilize popular participation was also impressive. It used direct action (protests and demonstrations), congressional district operations, and the door-to-door canvass to activate people on energy issues. It had a demonstrated capacity to mobilize hundreds or thousands for state and local actions and up to a hundred thousand for national actions, ranging from letter-writing and petition drives through voting and lobbying to public rallies and marches. It mobilized not only members of CLEC's affiliated organizations but also people with no connection to CLEC or to energy issues, thereby engaging new participants in energy-policy battles and liberal politics.[38]

A good example of CLEC's skill at mobilizing grass-roots participation was its success at building congressional resistance to President Reagan's plan to accelerate the decontrol of natural-gas prices. CLEC used congressional district committees, set up by its state and local coalitions, to organize "accountability sessions" with representatives in two hundred targeted districts. These sessions mobilized unionists, senior citizens, and members of community groups to articulate CLEC's anti-decontrol position and solicit pledges of support for it from members of Congress, and then to monitor the votes of legislators and hold them accountable in subsequent elections. In thirty-six of these districts, CLEC also conducted canvasses that mobilized thousands of citizens for letter, telephone, and petition drives in support of the accountability sessions. These local efforts were crucial to CLEC's ability to block accelerated deregulation of natural-gas prices.[39]

In the recent history of liberal interest groups and alliances, CLEC is notable for its commitment to and effectiveness at grass-roots organization and mobilization. Its development of the canvass as a method of mobilization and recruitment was especially influential, as Citizen Action and other progressive groups later used the CLEC canvass on issues like toxic-waste cleanup and health-care reform.

The third part of CLEC's strategy, participation in party and electoral politics, evolved slowly and hesitantly, because its citizen and public-interest groups were traditionally antipathetic toward it. But circumstances compelled CLEC to enter party and electoral politics. For one thing, CLEC was a coalition of Democratic voting blocs, but one opposed to the energy policies of an incumbent Democratic administration. For another, CLEC's citizen and public-interest groups were stunned by the electoral resurgence of the Republican right in 1980, which forced them, under prodding by Heather Booth, to rethink their antipathy toward party and electoral politics. Finally, the course of CLEC's campaign to maintain price controls on natural gas forced it to recognize once and for all that the success of its legislative agenda depended on electoral activity.[40]

CLEC's first and only substantial foray into electoral politics, in the congressional and state elections of 1982, was targeted on thirty-five House and Senate races crucial to the natural-gas battle and was coordinated with the AFL-CIO. CLEC conducted a door-to-door canvass to mobilize voters and provide information on candidates; disseminated research on energy-industry campaign contributions; solicited pledges from candidates to oppose further decontrol of gas prices; and endorsed candidates. It is doubtful that CLEC made financial contributions to candidates in 1982, as its political action committee (PAC) was evidently established only in time for the 1984 elections. Still, thirty of the thirty-five congressional candidates CLEC supported in 1982 were elected, ten for the first time, and the leaders of CLEC's state coalitions in West Virginia and Connecticut were elected to the House of Representatives and the state legislature, respectively. CLEC's initial electoral activity, especially its use of the canvass, was impressive and augured well for the future, but by the 1984 elections, CLEC was in transition and decline and its electoral activity was very modest.[41]

Although CLEC's electoral activity supported Democrats, the coalition also functioned as a reform faction in the Democratic Party, seeking to change the energy policies of a Democratic administration by participating in the party's internal decision making. Toward this end, CLEC was active in the 1978 and 1982 Democratic Party midterm conferences, in the 1979–80 Democratic Party platform hearings, at the 1980 Democratic national convention, and with the Democratic National Committee.[42]

CLEC's electoral and partisan role left an imprint on liberal politics. It was in and through CLEC that citizen-organizing groups entered electoral and party politics, eventually playing a significant role through Citizen Action and the State and Local Leadership Project, organized by Heather Booth to train candidates and campaign workers after she stepped down as executive director of CLEC. CLEC also contributed to liberal electoral activity by resuscitating the use of the door-to-door canvass for voter mobilization, candidate and issue information, and fund-raising. Finally, the factional role that CLEC played in the Democratic Party helped to revive populist and class politics among a segment of congressional Democrats.[43]

The final aspect of CLEC's strategy was renewal of populist politics. CLEC's populism had four interrelated elements: (a) a focus on economic issues that could unite the working and middle classes; (b) opposition to corporate economic and political power; (c) mobilization of ordinary citizens to give them voice and influence; and (d) insistence on egalitarian distribution of resources and sacrifices (in the energy crisis). CLEC's populism was implicit in its practice more than it was consciously theorized, but CLEC and its offshoot, Citizen Action, served as models for the development of an explicit populist strategy that many on the left came to advocate during the 1980s and 1990s for building a progressive majority in American politics.[44]

CLEC's populism and later elaborations of populist strategy were responses to two developments. The first was the decline of the class-based New Deal coalition and the associated transformation of liberalism. From the mid-1960s on, the working- and lower-middle-class base and majority status of the New Deal coalition were eroded by the rise of divisive social and foreign-policy issues, and liberalism became identified more with such issues and their respective constituencies (racial minorities, women, antiwar activists) than with working-class economic issues. The second development was the rise of right-wing populism, which appealed to the sociocultural conservatism and patriotism of many non-affluent voters and was integral to Republican electoral advances from the late 1960s onward. For CLEC and later strategists, left-populism was a form of class politics and the only strategy capable of circumventing sociocultural divisions, undermining the appeal of right-wing populism, and building a progressive majority.[45]

CLEC successfully united working- and middle-class political forces (unions, citizen organizations, public-interest groups) in opposition to corporate and conservative priorities, and it demonstrated that skillful use of populist appeals could mobilize considerable public support. Its role and accomplishments in the energy crisis arose in part from its populist politics, and to that extent, CLEC would seem to confirm the left-populist strategy. Because of its narrow focus on energy issues, however, CLEC neither permitted a general test of the strategy nor confronted the crucial problem of populist coalitions historically: their vulnerability to disruption by racial politics. CLEC's record spoke well for the left-populist strategy but did not seal the case for it.[46]

In sum, CLEC made both institutional and strategic contributions to progressive politics. Institutionally, CLEC served as the key political organization of the popular left in the second energy crisis, and it also largely built Citizen Action and its network of state and local groups, which functioned as a "progressive grass-roots infrastructure," to use Heather Booth's description, on a broad range of issues and campaigns for more than fifteen years.[47] Strategically, CLEC developed an innovative plan to regenerate liberal politics and tested it with some success. The core of CLEC's strategy was its novel alliance of labor unions with the citizen-organizing movement and public-interest groups. But it was the conjunction of national coalition building with grass-roots organization and mobilization, party and electoral politics, and populist renewal that made CLEC's strategy original and important. CLEC's experience left open the question of whether this strategy could accommodate a broader range of groups and issues, but the coalition's accomplishments at least suggest that it had potential as a way forward for liberal politics.

CLEC, the Dissident Unions, and the Labor-Liberal Alliance

The Citizen Labor Energy Coalition bore many similarities to its contemporary, the Progressive Alliance, and its experience confirms much of what the Alliance suggested about the politics of the dissident unions and the prospects for labor-liberal revival. But CLEC also differed from the Alliance in key ways and was a longer-lasting and more successful political organization. It therefore offered more positive lessons to the dissident unions and suggested brighter prospects for labor-liberal revival. Still, even CLEC's success was limited and had costs that should not be overlooked.

The broad similarities of the Citizen Labor Energy Coalition to the Progressive Alliance were evident in its formation, purposes, structure, program, and strategy. Like the Alliance, it was formed and led by a leading dissident labor leader, whose union served as its primary patron. Again like the Alliance, CLEC was also the project of a larger wing of the labor movement, for other dissident unions and labor leaders played key roles in its organization and leadership, too. Indeed, five of CLEC's seven core unions—those most active and important in organizing, funding, and leading it—were also among the eight core unions of the Progressive Alliance (the five were UAW, IAM, AFSCME, NEA, and UFCW). Further, CLEC was established for the same political purposes as the Alliance, to develop an alternative labor politics and to revive the labor-liberal alliance. It was therefore structured much like the Alliance, as a coalition between dissident unions and other liberal groups and organizations. Finally, like the Alliance, CLEC focused its program on economic issues and anticorporate reforms and based its strategy on coalition building and factional politics in the Democratic Party.

Given these similarities, it is not surprising that CLEC's record over a period of six or seven years corroborates much of what the Alliance revealed about the dissident unions and the revival of the labor-liberal coalition. That record confirms that the dissident unions were trying to develop an independent labor politics based on coalition building with liberals, progressive positions on broad economic and social issues, anticorporate reforms, and organizing the liberal wing to contest for power in the Democratic Party. It also confirms that the will to rebuild the labor-liberal alliance existed among other liberal groups and movements as well as among dissident unions, that dissident unions and many liberals shared important interests and ideals, and that uniting unions and liberals would strengthen both. As a more durable and successful organization than the Progressive Alliance, the Citizen Labor Energy Coalition boosted the confidence of dissident labor leaders in their political project and of both unions and liberals in the prospects for strengthening their alliance.

But the explanation for why CLEC proved more durable and successful lies in its differences from the Alliance, evident in the same areas as its similarities. To begin with, CLEC's formation and leadership were not dominated by William Winpisinger, IAM, and its other core unions to the extent that the Alliance's were by Douglas Fraser, UAW, and its other core unions. This was so because CLEC was conceived, initiated, and partly organized by Heather Booth and others in the citizen-organizing movement and because CLEC's staff, which initiated and directed much of the coalition's activity, was drawn from its citizen groups. CLEC was more nearly a partnership between its founding leaders and organizations than the Alliance was, and as a result, it experienced fewer problems of coalition building and was less vulnerable to the economic problems and membership losses that its patron suffered (although IAM did not experience the kind of severe crisis that the UAW did).

Further, although it had the same political purposes as the Alliance, CLEC had a clearer and more central *substantive* purpose: to resolve the energy crisis on terms favorable to workers and consumers. The Alliance developed an important and popular policy objective, public regulation of plant closings, but that objective coexisted with other issues and was overshadowed by the goal of platform accountability in the Democratic Party, which probably seemed to many in the Alliance to be a mere party rule. Because its mission was always centered on the energy crisis, a momentous public issue of great stakes and high drama, CLEC was able to fashion a focused and appealing program and to unify and mobilize its member groups around it, precisely what Douglas Fraser felt the Alliance had been unable to do.

CLEC's more focused mission and program also limited the range of liberal groups and movements that it recruited or attracted. CLEC was a coalition of unions, citizen groups, and public-interest organizations; the Alliance contained those three and several more, including minority and women's groups. It was bound to be easier for CLEC to unite and coordinate its more limited range of constituent groups. That CLEC in fact did this more effectively than the Alliance is indicated not only by its longer life and greater success but also by the judgments rendered by the leaders of the two coalitions. Whereas Fraser concluded that the Alliance model of a "big umbrella" coalition had not worked, Winpisinger and Booth evaluated CLEC's coalition building more positively. Winpisinger argued that "[CLEC] rebuilt bridges between the labor movement and community activists that had long been either burned or dormant, and created a grass-roots level dialogue between citizen organizations and the labor movement, and it has paid off in a million different ways."[48] Booth emphasized that CLEC played a significant role in overcoming the legacy of estrangement between organized labor and the New Left: "It formed alliances where previously there had been enormous barriers. . . . There had been an enormous divide that had been created over a long period of time, in part as a legacy of the Cold War, in part as a legacy of divisions that occurred in the 1960s between the student generation and an older generation. . . . [CLEC] was a way to find some common ground."[49]

Finally, CLEC's political strategy differed in two important ways from that of the Alliance. The first was CLEC's embrace of electoral politics. CLEC obtained the tax-exempt status 501(c)(3) only for the CLEC Foundation, its education and research arm, which left CLEC itself free of restrictions on electoral and lobbying activity. Prior to the 1984 elections, CLEC also established a political action committee, which allowed it to engage in campaign finance as well as other forms of electoral activity. The second way CLEC's strategy differed was its greater emphasis on building organizations and mobilizing citizens at state and local levels. CLEC's leaders did not consider electoral politics a threat to coalition unity, perhaps because of its more limited range of constituent groups, and they were convinced that national political influence rested on grass-roots organization and activism, a view that reflected the influence of the citizen-organizing movement.

In many ways, the Progressive Alliance and the Citizen Labor Energy Coalition represented the two horns of the dilemma of coalition building identified by Douglas Fraser. The Alliance included a wide range of liberal groups and movements but could not (in Fraser's view) unite them around a manageable program; the coalition had a focused program that unified its constituent groups but coordinated a narrower range of liberal groups around a single issue. Of the two coalitions, CLEC was the more successful: it lasted longer, exerted greater (though quite modest) influence over public policy, and left a substantial institutional legacy. For this reason, it can be argued that CLEC's model of coalition building was superior to that of the Alliance and that later political organizations of the dissident unions were closer to the CLEC than the Alliance model. It is important, though, not to lose sight of the costs of the CLEC model—namely, the limited range of groups it included and issues it influenced. CLEC proved a useful way to rebuild the labor-liberal coalition, but it could not be the only way.

CHAPTER 7

The National Labor Committee

Introduction

Nothing did more to undermine the unity of the labor-liberal coalition in the 1960s than the war in Vietnam. Just when the efforts of Democratic Agenda, Progressive Alliance, Citizen Labor Energy Coalition, and other organizations to restore that unity seemed to be paying off, President Ronald Reagan decided to overcome the "Vietnam syndrome" and revive Cold War interventionism in Central America. Opponents of President Reagan's policy in that region often drew an analogy between it and the war in Vietnam. In many ways the analogy was dubious, but in one respect it was on the mark: Reagan's policy toward the nations of the Central American isthmus threatened another labor-liberal rupture over foreign affairs.

That policy did indeed once again split the labor movement and pit liberals against the leadership of the AFL-CIO. But in contrast to the war in Vietnam, President Reagan's policy in Central America served to unite labor and liberals as much as to divide them. The key to this difference lay in the formation of yet another political organization of the dissident unions, the National Labor Committee in Support of Democracy and Human Rights in El Salvador (hereafter the National Labor Committee, or NLC). The rise of this important organization can be understood only against the backdrop of the crisis in Central America and the responses of the Reagan administration and AFL-CIO to it.

The 1980s was a decade of political and military crisis, and foreign involvement, in most of Central America, especially El Salvador and Nicaragua. Amid growing landlessness and poverty, armed insurgencies as well as reformist political oppositions arose in the 1970s against the military governments of both countries, but the course of the conflicts differed in the two nations. In Nicaragua, an insurrection led by the Sandinista National Liberation Front (FSLN) toppled the government of Anastasio Somoza in 1979, and the Sandinistas soon consolidated control over the Junta of National Reconstruction that assumed power upon Somoza's fall.

Throughout the 1980s, the leftist Sandinista regime was opposed and attacked by counterrevolutionary forces known as the Contras, which were organized and financed—sometimes officially, sometimes covertly—largely by the government of the United States.

In El Salvador, guerrilla groups united in the Farabundo Marti Front for National Liberation (FMLN) in 1980, and in the same year political opposition groups coalesced in the Democratic Revolutionary Front (FDR) and allied with the FMLN. Over the next decade, the FDR/FMLN waged both armed and political struggle against a succession of Salvadoran governments that were, even when headed by the centrist Christian Democratic President Jose Napoleon Duarte, dominated by rightists in the legislature, courts, military, and paramilitary death squads. The FDR/FMLN could not dislodge the government, but neither could the government and military defeat the armed opposition. El Salvador was locked in a bloody civil war in which some seventy-five thousand people lost their lives during the 1980s, mostly at the hands of the Salvadoran military.[1]

The Reagan administration viewed the Sandinista revolution in Nicaragua and the rebel insurgency in El Salvador through the prisms of the Cold War and the decline of U.S. global power in the wake of Vietnam, the Soviet invasion of Afghanistan, the hostage crisis in Iran, and other developments. It considered the Nicaraguan revolution and Salvadoran guerrilla war to be products of Soviet and Cuban intervention and regarded both the Sandinista regime and the FMLN rebels as Marxist-Leninist and totalitarian. The Reagan administration further viewed the Central America crisis as yet another indication of, and challenge to, waning American authority in the world, but also as an opportunity to restore U.S. influence.

Constrained by public and congressional opposition from direct military intervention, the Reagan administration organized and sustained the Contras in order to destabilize the Sandinista government and provided both military and economic aid to the Salvadoran government in the hope of defeating the FMLN guerrillas and their political allies. The U.S. government under President Reagan supported the opposition in Nicaragua but the government in El Salvador, yet the objective of U.S. policy in both countries was the same: to prevent the left from exercising power in America's own "back yard." The Reagan administration's provision of military aid to the Nicaraguan Contras and the Salvadoran government was, however, at times conditioned, reduced, or even halted by the Congress, which led the administration into the Iran-Contra scandals that undermined its policies in the region.[2]

Although the AFL-CIO strongly opposed the election and domestic policies of Ronald Reagan, its views and positions on the Central America crisis were broadly similar, though not identical, to those of his administration. Like the latter, the federation's top leaders and Department of International Affairs (DIA) emphasized Soviet and Cuban sponsorship of the Nicaraguan revolution and the Salvadoran guerrilla insurgency and insisted on the Marxist-Leninist and totalitarian character of the Sandinistas and the FMLN. Not surprisingly, then, they supported U.S. military aid to both the Salvadoran government and the Nicaraguan Contras. Sometimes the federation supported this military aid unofficially or with formal conditions attached, and it advocated that military aid be accompanied by programs of land reform and economic development. In these ways, the positions of the AFL-CIO were more nuanced than the policies of the Reagan administration. Fundamentally, though, it supported the administration's Cold War view of the crisis in the region and insistence on military resolution of the conflicts there.

The Cold War orientation of AFL-CIO policy was also evident in its own operations in Central America. The AFL-CIO and its foreign-policy arm for Latin America, the American Institute for Free Labor Development (AIFLD), recognized and supported only those trade unions and labor federations that were aligned with the Salvadoran government or against the Sandinista regime. They shunned all labor organizations that espoused leftist or nationalist ideologies or that supported the Nicaraguan government or the Salvadoran rebels.[3]

Dissident unions and labor leaders reacted differently to the crisis in Central America. They quickly, publicly, and forcefully opposed Reagan administration policy in the region and AFL-CIO support for it. They dissented from both the Cold War premises and military solutions of Reagan administration and federation responses to the crisis and fought against them in national politics and inside the AFL-CIO. They argued that the crisis in Central America had indigenous social and political sources, could be resolved only by political negotiations between governments and oppositions, and required American unions to practice international labor solidarity untainted by Cold War considerations, and they sought to build support for these positions in both the labor movement and national politics. These views and actions of the dissident unions contrasted not only with those of the AFL-CIO in the Central America crisis but also with their own during the Vietnam war. For in the 1980s, the dissident unions *immediately* joined liberals in opposing U.S. policy in Central America and *clearly* established an alternative labor voice on that policy. For this reason, the domestic political dynamics of U.S. policy in Central America differed from those of the Vietnam war, particularly in uniting as much as dividing unions and liberals.

The National Labor Committee was the vehicle of this union dissent and opposition to U.S. and AFL-CIO policy in Central America. NLC played a significant role in the U.S. Central America peace movement that opposed the Reagan administration and influenced congressional action on Central America. It also provoked the most open and serious foreign-policy debate in organized labor in several decades and developed a new foreign-policy and international role for labor distinct from the Cold War orientation of the AFL-CIO. In these ways, the

National Labor Committee made a considerable contribution to rebuilding the labor-liberal coalition in the United States.

The Formation of NLC

The National Labor Committee was created in September of 1981 by Jack Sheinkman, then secretary-treasurer of the Amalgamated Clothing and Textile Workers Union (ACTWU). Douglas Fraser, president of the United Auto Workers (UAW), and William Winpisinger, president of the International Association of Machinists (IAM), agreed to serve with Sheinkman as cochairs of NLC, and David Dyson, director of ACTWU's Union Label Department, assumed the position of executive director. Sheinkman, Fraser, and Winpisinger recruited NLC's membership gradually over a period of three or four years. By the October 1985 convention of the AFL-CIO, at which a sharp debate took place over U.S. policy in Central America, NLC was at full strength, with twenty-five members from twenty-three unions, including many of the federation's largest and most important affiliates. That NLC was able to recruit and retain this membership was no small accomplishment. As Dyson explained, "Putting a national committee together. . . . it was a real act of independence, defiance, a real vote of no confidence in the way the AFL-CIO was handling the Central America policy question and the question of unions in Central America."[4] Referring to AFL-CIO officials, Sheinkman concluded this line of thought: "They did everything they could to undermine us and to get some of the international [i.e., union] leaders to withdraw, but I'm proud that over the years we not only held fast but added [members]."[5]

Membership in NLC was restricted to presidents of national unions—with the temporary exception of Sheinkman himself, who rose from secretary-treasurer to president of ACTWU in 1987—for three reasons. First, at the time NLC was founded, lower levels of trade-union leadership and activists were already being mobilized by emerging local labor committees opposed to U.S. policy in Central America. Second, as NLC was going to dissent from the rigidly anticommunist approach of the AFL-CIO, its founders excluded nonlabor groups and individuals in order to protect it from red-baiting by the federation, which had a long history of discrediting dissenters in labor by claiming outside leftist influence on them. Finally, national union presidents had the positions and legitimacy that would enable NLC to most effectively challenge the views of the AFL-CIO and provide an alternative labor voice on Central America in national politics.[6]

Most of the union presidents in NLC joined as individuals, but they represented their respective unions in the Committee. In most cases, the membership of union presidents in NLC signified a larger commitment by their unions, or at least the broader leaderships of their unions, to the National Labor Committee, as two facts indicated. First, eleven unions were represented in NLC by successive presidents. Second, two unions, SEIU and CWA, formally instructed or informally pressured their presidents to join NLC. To a considerable degree, NLC was a committee of unions as organizations as well as of union presidents as individuals. Three kinds of unions supplied the bulk of NLC's member presidents. As of 1985, thirteen (57 percent) were based in manufacturing industries, four (17 percent) in government employment, and two (9 percent) in the service sector; no more than one NLC union came from any other industrial sector. Opposition to Cold War foreign policy in Central America was thus concentrated among unions in the manufacturing and public sectors, for reasons explained in the following pages.[7]

Member unions varied in their level of participation in and contribution to NLC. Until it merged with another union in 1995, ACTWU was the principal sponsor of NLC and devoted far more time, effort, and resources to the Committee than any other union. Indeed, NLC was in many ways Jack Sheinkman's project, the product of his initiative and political views. Four other unions—UAW, IAM, AFSCME, and NEA—played a vital role in the National Labor Committee and, along with ACTWU, constituted its core unions. They supplied the cochairs of the Committee, were among its earliest and permanent members, made significant financial or organizational assistance available to it, and participated extensively in NLC's political activities. An intermediate group of about twelve unions made a more modest contribution to NLC, and the remaining half-dozen unions played a limited role in the Committee.

In 1985 the combined membership of NLC unions was just under 7.2 million, a majority of the unionized workforce. NLC could thus claim to speak for a large number of unionists and citizens, which is an important resource for political action. Its other resources were limited, though not as meager as might initially appear. NLC unions made annual contributions of up to five thousand dollars to the Committee, with smaller unions contributing less. These were small sums for unions. NLC also secured grants from a few progressive foundations, but none of the grants exceeded fifteen thousand dollars. It is probable that NLC's annual budget was under $150,000 during the 1980s. On the other hand, NLC's core unions periodically gave additional money to the Committee and also provided it with substantial in-kind assistance, including staff services. NLC's own staff was small—limited to just two people in the 1980s—but talented and dedicated. David Dyson, the executive director, was the sole staff during NLC's first three years and performed this role while still working as director of ACTWU's Union Label Department. He nonetheless managed to devote a great deal of time and effort to the Committee, and his personal contribution to NLC was enormous. Beginning in 1984, NLC added a full-time national organizer, first Daniel Cantor and later Charles Kernaghan.[8]

Just as member unions and their presidents were not required to make substantial cash or in-kind contributions to NLC, neither were they required to devote significant time or effort to it or to compromise their personal or organizational autonomy. The Committee did not even hold regular meetings, which would have required considerable time and travel by union presidents. Further, NLC avoided issues and alliances that were divisive within the Committee, and member unions were free to participate or not in activities like fact-finding missions to Central America or the 1987 Mobilization for Justice and Peace in Central America and Southern Africa. NLC essentially operated on principles of voluntary participation and consensus decision making. By reducing the political obligations and organizational burdens on presidents and their unions, this minimized the costs of membership in NLC and facilitated recruitment and retention of members. It also left the Committee short of resources and rather insubstantial as an organization.[9]

Yet, despite organizational weaknesses, NLC proved capable of meaningful political action. Its limited organizational resources and capacities were not a severe problem, because NLC's own resources were not all that it could draw upon. Being composed of unions that conducted and financed their own political operations, all NLC needed to do was to coordinate these unions and their political activities. Much of NLC's legislative lobbying, for example, was conducted and financed by its member unions separately, but after consultation and coordination through NLC. Moreover, NLC utilized the local labor committees, with their committed and skilled activists at the grass-roots level, in its political work. Combining these other resources and capacities with its own enabled NLC to undertake the kinds and amounts of political activity required by its objectives.

Those objectives were first broached publicly in a March 26, 1982, advertisement that NLC placed in the *New York Times,* which suggested that NLC had political, international, and institutional objectives, though the last was only implied in the ad. As a later NLC document put it, the Committee was organized to play the three roles of "interest group," "solidarity catalyst," and "labor caucus."[10]

The National Labor Committee's domestic political objective was to oppose and change U.S. policy toward El Salvador. Above all, Sheinkman and his colleagues wanted to prevent direct U.S. military intervention in El Salvador, end U.S. military aid to the Salvadoran government, and redirect U.S. influence toward promoting a negotiated settlement of the conflict in that country. Once the National Labor Committee expanded its agenda to include Nicaragua, it worked throughout the decade to end U.S. aid to the Contras. The Committee's opposition to U.S. policy in Central America extended to the Cold War premises of that policy. As Sheinkman said of the Salvadoran civil war, "In my view, it was a battle that had nothing to do with the Cold War. . . . It was an indigenous revolution arising from political circumstances that had their roots long before, back in the whole economic and political structure of El Salvador."[11] Thus an underlying political goal of the Committee was to challenge the Cold War framework of U.S. foreign policy, and it argued repeatedly that the conflicts in Central America were caused not by communist subversion or Soviet intervention but by long-standing poverty and injustice.[12]

The Committee's international objective was to support the efforts of the Salvadoran people to secure democratic and human rights, including the rights to free and fair elections, to freedom of thought and expression, to live and work free of fear, and to organize trade unions. As NLC leaders believed that in El Salvador workers (including peasants), unions, and labor leaders were the principal victims of political repression, they were chiefly concerned with defending the right of Salvadoran workers to form unions and, through them, to bargain with employers, strike, and participate in political life. They established NLC to supplement the work of traditional human-rights groups, by focusing more clearly and forcefully on worker rights, and to develop and expand the practice of international labor solidarity.[13]

The Committee's institutional objective was to promote within the labor movement a new international outlook and role, different from that of the AFL-CIO. Sheinkman has emphasized that NLC "was not organized as a direct confrontation" with the AFL-CIO, and it is true that NLC rarely publicly criticized the federation or its controversial arm in Central America, the American Institute for Free Labor Development (AIFLD). Nonetheless, because for three decades the AFL-CIO had monopolized control of foreign affairs and remained uncompromisingly anticommunist, the very formation of NLC was a challenge to the federation, and that challenge only grew as NLC fought within the federation to alter labor's official policies on El Salvador and Nicaragua.[14]

NLC and U.S. Policy in Central America

Of NLC's three objectives, the most urgent was to oppose and change U.S. policy toward Central America. In a series of reports on labor and politics in El Salvador and Nicaragua, the National Labor Committee criticized the Reagan administration's policy of providing military aid to the Salvadoran government and Nicaraguan Contras. It disputed the administration's Cold War justifications of that policy and presented alternative views of the sources of conflict, the character of governments and oppositions, and the status of labor and human rights in El Salvador and Nicaragua.[15]

NLC argued that the civil war in El Salvador was rooted in long-standing underdevelopment, poverty, and injustice and was precipitated by state repression of the popular protests against those conditions that exploded in the late 1970s. It argued that Salvadoran president Duarte, who served from 1984 through 1989, and his centrist Christian Democratic Party did not hold real power in El Salvador and served mainly to continue the flow of U.S. military aid. The Salvadoran right retained effective control of the state through the influence of Roberto D'Aubuisson's National Republican Alliance (ARENA) party in the National Assembly, the predominance of rightists in the judiciary, and the continued role of the army as the arbiter of power in El Salvador. As a result, during Duarte's tenure democratic rights (of association, expression, and personal security) continued to be denied, state repression and death-squad activity were reduced but not ended, and no real progress was made toward land reform, prosecution of military officers responsible for massive human-rights violations, or negotiated settlement of the civil war. Moreover, trade unions could not function freely in El Salvador and indeed had been a special target of state repression and right-wing violence in that country since 1979–80. NLC staff testified to Congress in 1988 that nearly six thousand unionists had been killed in El Salvador during the decade. NLC considered the main opposition force, the Democratic Revolutionary Front/ Farabundo Marti Front for National Liberation (FDR/FMLN), an ideologically diverse movement that represented major social forces in El Salvador.[16]

NLC further argued that the Reagan administration's policy of military aid in fact undermined its stated objectives of restoring peace and democracy and strengthening the political center in El Salvador. Military aid, NLC claimed, failed to address the underlying sources of the conflict, strengthened the military–right wing alliance and stiffened its resistance to political negotiations, and thus prolonged the war in El Salvador. For all these reasons, NLC opposed military aid to the Salvadoran government. It insisted that only a settlement negotiated between the government and the FDR/FMLN could achieve peace and democracy in El Salvador and supported various plans for political negotiations, including the Contadora process and the Arias Plan.[17]

The National Labor Committee did not share the Reagan administration's view of the Nicaraguan government as a totalitarian regime. It did express reservations about Sandinista ideology, criticize limitations of democratic process in Nicaragua, and call on the Sandinista government to halt harassment of opposition trade unions. But the Committee argued that opposition unions were allowed to exist and press their demands on the government, seemed sympathetic to the view that restrictions on the right to strike were induced by the pressures of war, and insisted that in Nicaragua there was no repression of unions or murder and torture of union leaders as in El Salvador. The National Labor Committee was highly critical of the Nicaraguan Contras. It argued that the Contras had no substantial social base or public support in Nicaragua and functioned as a proxy army for the United States in an effort to destabilize the Sandinista regime. The Committee urged the U.S. government to end military aid to the Contras, stop blocking Nicaraguan access to international aid and credit, and resume bilateral talks with the Nicaraguan government. It also called for talks between the Sandinista government and opposition forces in the framework of the Contadora process, which sought a negotiated peace throughout Central America.[18]

In order to change U.S. policy in El Salvador and Nicaragua, NLC engaged in four types of political activity: (a) publication of reports on conditions in

Central America based on fact-finding missions to the region, (b) sponsorship of speaking tours of the United States by Salvadoran unionists, (c) congressional lobbying, and (d) mobilization of popular protest. First, between 1983 and 1990, NLC conducted five fact-finding missions in El Salvador and Nicaragua and then published four reports on labor and political conditions in those countries. Three of the delegations that NLC sent on these missions included members or staff of the U.S. Congress, and all of the delegations met with workers and union officers (some imprisoned), business leaders, government and military officials (including President Duarte in 1985), and religious leaders and human-rights activists in the two Central American countries. Publication of the reports was often timed to influence congressional votes on military aid to the Salvadoran government or Nicaraguan Contras, and they were widely distributed among unions, the public, the media, and members of Congress. Patterned after the work of human-rights groups like Americas Watch and Amnesty International, these missions and reports were the chief means by which NLC carried out two of its most basic functions: monitoring labor rights in Central America and influencing policy debates in the United States.[19]

Second, between 1986 and 1990, NLC sponsored three speaking tours of the United States by Salvadoran labor leaders. The Salvadorans delivered speeches, held press conferences, gave interviews to the media, and had meetings with American union leaders and members of Congress. The tours were intended to increase awareness in the U.S. of continuing abuses of labor and human rights in El Salvador and to encourage a shift of U.S. policy away from military aid and toward support for a political settlement of the Salvadoran civil war.[20]

Third, NLC lobbied Congress. Committee staff presented testimony at congressional hearings, and NLC union presidents wrote letters and made telephone calls to Democratic leaders and swing votes in the House of Representatives. Just as important, NLC assisted and coordinated both Washington and grass-roots (congressional district) lobbying by its constituent unions and by allied local labor committees on Central America. NLC staff monitored relevant legislation and votes in Congress, sent out "Legislative Alerts" to notify member unions and other groups of upcoming congressional debates and votes, supplied these unions and groups with information and arguments, and worked with House Democratic leaders to target swing votes in the House for lobbying. When NLC's ultimate objectives (terminating military aid to the Salvadoran government and Nicaraguan Contras in favor of political negotiations) were not on the congressional agenda, it lobbied for lesser but important goals like retaining human-rights conditions on military aid and reducing or withholding such aid. In the effort to halt or reduce Contra aid, NLC joined lobbying coalitions such as Countdown '87 and Central America Working Group.[21]

Fourth, together with religious leaders from various churches, NLC unions cosponsored the April 25, 1987, Mobilization for Justice and Peace in Central

America and Southern Africa, a protest demonstration held in both Washington, D.C., and San Francisco. NLC executive director David Dyson, a principal strategist and organizer of the mobilization, believed that dramatic protest politics was necessary to revive a stalled U.S. Central America peace movement because, as he said, "The one thing this movement hasn't had is a popular presence, or a street presence." At the same time, he wanted the mobilization to establish the mainstream character of the movement and thus favored sponsorship of it by labor and religious leaders rather than the smaller activist and ideological groups in the movement. The mobilization drew about one hundred thousand people in Washington, D.C., and about thirty thousand in San Francisco, making it the largest and most publicized event conducted by the U.S. Central America peace movement. It had been timed to influence an anticipated spring vote in Congress on Contra aid; when the postponed vote was finally taken in the fall, Congress denied the large aid package President Reagan had requested, but it is unclear what role the mobilization played in that outcome.[22]

In these efforts to change U.S. policy in Central America, NLC followed a threefold strategy—of cooperation with local labor committees, coalition with nonlabor groups, and coordination with liberal Democrats in the House of Representatives—to maximize its political influence. First of all, it cooperated with many of the local labor committees that had formed to protest U.S. policy in Central America. Some twenty-seven of these cross-union committees existed nationwide, mainly in larger cities on the two coasts and in the Great Lakes states, though only fifteen or so were well organized and effective. Although NLC had helped to organize many of these local committees, it did not charter them as chapters or branches, as it did not want to be identified with those local committees that openly embraced the FMLN and Sandinistas or that were influenced by a sectarian leftist group on the West Coast. But NLC worked closely with the local labor committees in the East and Midwest. It was in regular communication with them and involved them integrally in lobbying Congress, sponsoring U.S. tours by Central American labor leaders, and mobilizing unionists for the 1987 demonstration. Working with the local committees increased the resources (e.g., activists and communication networks) and strategic options (e.g., grass-roots lobbying) available to NLC.[23]

A second NLC strategy was coalition politics. The committee's founders had pledged publicly "to join with other segments of American society, such as religious, community, and human rights groups" in the effort to promote democracy and human rights in El Salvador. The most important alliance that NLC formed was with churches. As indicated earlier, David Dyson devised a "labor and religion formula" for sponsorship of the 1987 Mobilization for Justice and Peace in Central America and Southern Africa. This union-church alliance continued in a lobbying coalition called Countdown '87, organized to oppose President Reagan's bid for major new Contra aid; in a 1988 fact-finding mission to El Salvador that issued a report titled *Labor Rights Denied: El Salvador;* and in a 1989 "Labor-Religious Dialogue for Peace in El Salvador," held in New York City and chaired by Jack Sheinkman, which urged the Bush administration and Congress to end military aid to El Salvador and to support a regional peace process in Central America.

NLC's relationship with churches was facilitated by the fact that David Dyson was an ordained Presbyterian minister who had for two decades linked the worlds of religious faith and labor activism. NLC leaders believed that its alliance with churches enhanced both the legitimacy and the effectiveness of the committee's opposition to U.S. policy in Central America. Jack Sheinkman explained that this alliance was "a very important, very helpful linkage, because you might find a 'red' priest or a 'red' nun but it's not very likely, so they couldn't label us that. There were some American church groups doing yeoman's, and God's, work there as far as I was concerned, working very effectively. . . . so we worked very closely. . . . We helped them and they helped us."[24] In addition to cooperating with churches, NLC also worked with human-rights groups, particularly Americas Watch.[25]

Finally, NLC sought to augment its influence by coordinating much of its political activity with sympathetic liberal Democrats in the House of Representatives. It worked closely with Reps. Gerry Studds, David Bonior, Joseph Moakley, Michael Barnes, Edward Boland, and others to organize and conduct its speaking tours by Salvadoran unionists, its lobbying campaigns, and even its fact-finding missions to Central America. Liberal House Democrats helped to ensure that Salvadoran labor leaders were granted visas to the United States and agreed to meet with them; worked with NLC to identify the representatives who were swing votes on Contra aid and the key unions in their districts; and sent members of their staffs on NLC fact-finding missions, or even joined an NLC delegation to Central America, as Rep. Gerry Studds did in 1989. Like other groups opposed to U.S. policy in Central America, NLC recognized the Democratic-controlled House as the main locus of dissent to that policy within the national government and cooperated with like-minded representatives in order to more effectively challenge Reagan administration policy.[26]

What influence did NLC have on U.S. policy in Central America, and how successful was it in accomplishing its objectives? To begin with, congressional and interest-group opponents of the Reagan administration's Central America policy were unable to wrest control of the policy-making agenda from the White House until the Iran-Contra scandal broke. Moreover, the administration prevailed over its opponents in crucial mid-decade legislative battles—over provision of military aid to the Salvadoran government following the inauguration of President Duarte in 1984, and over restoration of funding for the Nicaraguan Contras in 1985 and 1986 after Congress had let it expire—that fixed U.S. policy in Central America for several years. These were critical defeats for all opponents of Reagan's policy, including NLC.[27]

But Congress shaped U.S. policy in Central America in ways that constrained the administration and were consistent with, if short of, the objectives of the U.S. Central America peace movement. It prevented the administration from acting on any plans it might have had for direct U.S. military intervention in Central America; supported Central American efforts, like the Arias peace plan, to resolve the conflicts in the region through political negotiation and cessation of external interference; and frequently reduced, often conditioned, and sometimes halted U.S. military aid to the Salvadoran government and the Nicaraguan contras. To what extent did these congressional actions result from the influence of the U.S. Central America peace movement and its various components?[28]

Many scholars have argued that the U.S. Central America peace movement, and broader public opinion, were key to forming and sustaining congressional resistance, such as it was, to Reagan administration policy in the region. There is a consensus among these scholars that the most important segment of that movement was the groups based in churches or religious faith, such as Sanctuary, Pledge of Resistance, and Witness for Peace. It is likely that unions were second to churches in undergirding the influence of the U.S. Central America peace movement. This was the conclusion of a central figure in the movement, Cindy Buhl, of the Central America Working Group, a lobbying coalition, who told Christian Smith that "the two strongest constituencies I worked with were the churches and unions."[29] The National Labor Committee was certainly the main union-based organization in the Central America peace movement at the national level.[30]

The Committee itself claimed credit for two specific legislative victories: (a) persuading the Senate Appropriations Committee in 1985 to withhold ten million dollars in military aid to El Salvador pending progress in the prosecution of the murderers of two American labor advisors in that country, and (b) persuading the Western Hemisphere Subcommittee of the House Foreign Affairs Committee in 1989 to include labor-rights provisions among the conditions placed on aid to El Salvador. The one big legislative battle that NLC claimed to have played a "major role" in was the final defeat of Contra aid in February of 1988, although the Committee had previously acknowledged that such aid was vulnerable because of the Iran-Contra scandals. Beyond specific policy battles, Jack Sheinkman believes that NLC's contribution was to make labor repression a focal point of U.S. public awareness and debate on Central America: "We tried to raise the element of trade unionists being killed, of peasants being killed. . . . Our hope was to bring the issue into a different focus to the public."[31]

The Conflict between NLC and the AFL-CIO

In addition to changing the policies of the Reagan administration in Central America, the National Labor Committee sought to alter the foreign policies of the American labor movement and to assist the efforts of Salvadoran workers to achieve labor and democratic rights. The AFL-CIO, especially its president and Department of International Affairs (DIA), traditionally controlled the labor movement's foreign policies. Throughout the postwar era, it maintained a strongly anticommunist international outlook and supported the Cold War foreign policies of U.S. administrations. Although the federation claimed to oppose equally regimes of the right and left that denied the right of free association, and to support all legitimate trade unions, it was in fact more inclined to oppose regimes of the left than of the right and to support moderate than leftist unions.

It is thus not surprising that the federation's views on Central America were close to those of the Reagan administration. Like the administration, the AFL-CIO emphasized Soviet and Cuban sponsorship of the Nicaraguan revolution and the guerrilla insurgency in El Salvador, portrayed the Salvadoran government under Duarte as democratic and centrist and generally praised its record on labor and human rights, dismissed the FDR/FMLN as Marxist-Leninist, denounced the Sandinista regime as a totalitarian dictatorship, and evinced considerable sympathy for the Nicaraguan Contras. These views predisposed the AFL-CIO to support the Reagan administration's policies in Central America.[32]

As the National Labor Committee opposed the views and policies of the Reagan administration in Central America, then, it also came into conflict with the AFL-CIO. This conflict was waged both in the governing bodies of the federation, especially the Conventions of 1983, 1985, and 1987, and in national policy-making arenas, mainly Congress. The issues in dispute were U.S. military aid to the Salvadoran government and Nicaraguan Contras and political negotiations between governments and oppositions in those countries.

The National Labor Committee not only lobbied Congress for termination of military aid to the Salvadoran government, it also tried to pass resolutions favoring termination of such aid at the biennial conventions of the AFL-CIO from 1983 on. The federation always defeated these resolutions and lobbied Congress against termination. Given the bipartisan congressional support for military aid to El Salvador from 1984 through 1989, however, the critical policy issue was whether to retain and strengthen the human-rights conditions on military aid that Congress had legislated. Both NLC and the AFL-CIO officially supported human-rights conditions on military aid. For NLC this was a second-best position, whereas the AFL-CIO was constrained to support conditionality because two of its AIFLD employees had been murdered by Salvadoran soldiers in 1981 while working on the land-reform program in that country.

Because the Reagan administration routinely certified human-rights improvements in El Salvador, conditionality had not halted the flow of aid. The National Labor Committee therefore lobbied Congress to impose more and stronger conditions on aid, to reject the administration's certification of human-rights progress, and to halt or substantially reduce military aid. By contrast, the AFL-CIO argued throughout the decade that the human-rights conditions on military aid had been met and that the aid should be supplied; fended off NLC convention proposals to oppose the administration's certification of human-rights progress in El Salvador; and in 1990 advised affiliated unions not to lobby for a House bill, strongly supported by NLC, that proposed a 50 percent reduction in military aid to El Salvador. Thus, despite formal agreement on human-rights conditions, the AFL-CIO favored provision of military aid to the Salvadoran government whereas NLC opposed it.[33]

A related issue was that of political negotiations between the Salvadoran government and the FDR/FMLN. At the 1983 and 1985 conventions of the AFL-CIO, NLC was able to win inclusion in the foreign-affairs resolutions of provisions calling for negotiations between government and opposition in El Salvador and stating that a negotiated settlement was preferable to a military solution in that country. The 1987 convention then voted unanimously to support the Arias peace plan for Central America. The AFL-CIO as well as NLC thus officially supported political negotiations, but this apparent agreement again masked at least strategic differences and probably different goals.

The AFL-CIO saw U.S. military aid and Salvadoran political negotiations as complementary, whereas NLC viewed them as contradictory. The federation accepted the Reagan administration's claim that military aid was necessary to prevent outright victory by the guerrillas and to force them to the negotiating table. NLC believed that military aid undermined negotiations by inducing the Salvadoran military to continue the war and pursue military victory. At the least, the AFL-CIO and NLC disagreed about what policies of the U.S. government would contribute to a negotiated settlement of the Salvadoran civil war. But it is difficult to avoid the impression that the AFL-CIO's official support for political negotiations in El Salvador was forced on it by the need to compromise with NLC, for the federation consistently promoted a view of the Salvadoran government and the FDR/FMLN that legitimated the administration's goal of military defeat of the insurgents through substantial military aid to the government.[34]

In the case of U.S. military aid to the Nicaraguan contras, NLC clearly and consistently opposed it, whereas the position of the AFL-CIO was ambiguous. The federation's hostility to the Sandinista regime nearly equaled that of the Reagan administration, and in the first half of the 1980s the AFL-CIO was already deeply involved with opponents of the regime through its support of an anti-Sandinista labor federation, the Confederation of Trade Union Unity (CUS), the role of the federation's Free Trade Union Institute (FTUI) in channeling National Endowment for Democracy funds to the anti-Sandinista newspaper *La Prensa,* and the involvement of several AFL-CIO unions in the pro-Contra lobbying group Prodemca (Friends of the Democratic Center in Central America). Yet, as of the mid-1980s, the AFL-CIO had not officially endorsed military aid to the Contras, and Lane Kirkland even rebuffed administration entreaties for his explicit support. There were three reasons for this: the Nicaraguan labor federation the

AFL-CIO supported did not favor U.S. military aid to the Contras even though it opposed the Sandinistas; Kirkland was miffed that the Reagan administration had ignored the Kissinger Commission's recommendation to provide funds for economic and social development in Central America; and the AFL-CIO hoped to avoid a deep and public split over Contra aid within the labor movement.[35]

Such a split came anyway, in a bitter debate at the October 1985 convention of the AFL-CIO, which eventually passed a compromise resolution that neither endorsed nor opposed military aid to the Contras but did call for political negotiations in Nicaragua as well as in El Salvador. The AFL-CIO's neutrality permitted unions to go their own way when, in the spring of 1986, President Reagan requested $100 million in military aid for the Contras. NLC unions lobbied against the request, several unions lobbied for it through Prodemca, and the AFL-CIO leadership took no official stand. At the 1987 convention, NLC achieved another compromise resolution that placed the AFL-CIO in opposition to U.S. military aid to the Contras "as well as" to Soviet and Cuban aid to the Sandinista regime. Moving the federation from neutrality to opposition on Contra aid was a clear NLC victory, though one limited by the continuing support of some AFL-CIO unions for Contra aid.[36]

The final votes on Contra aid during the Reagan administration occurred in the spring of 1988, when the House of Representatives voted down Reagan's last efforts to secure military aid. NLC lobbied intensively against Contra aid during these votes. Though it was on record as opposing Contra aid, the AFL-CIO simply sat out the issue rather than lobby against the aid. Although some unions still supported Contra aid, in these final votes the voice of labor was represented most clearly by NLC. Although for the last half of the 1980s the AFL-CIO officially supported political negotiations in Nicaragua and was neutral or opposed to military aid for the Contras, it continued to espouse a view of the Sandinista regime that confirmed the Cold War arguments of the Reagan administration and legitimated its policies toward Nicaragua.[37]

The Question of International Labor Solidarity

Conflict between NLC and the AFL-CIO over Central America concerned not only U.S. government policy but also the labor movement's own role in the region. The central issue here was what kinds of unions and labor federations in Central America the U.S. labor movement would support and, therefore, how the principle of international labor solidarity would be defined. The AFL-CIO and AIFLD recognized and supported only unions and federations that opposed the Sandinista regime or supported the Salvadoran government. Indeed, in El Salvador the AFL-CIO and AIFLD helped organize and finance three separate labor federations during the 1980s but abandoned each in turn when it began to criticize the Duarte government, bringing charges that the federation subordinated its proclaimed purpose of building trade unionism to the exigencies of U.S. foreign policy.

The National Labor Committee, on the other hand, recognized and maintained contact with pro-Sandinista as well as anti-Sandinista labor organizations in Nicaragua and with leftist and opposition unions and federations, such as the National Union of Salvadoran Workers (UNTS), in El Salvador. Jack Sheinkman explained why: "So when we took actions, we didn't care what federation—whether Christian Democrats, the so-called left wing, or a centrist organization—any trade unionist that came under attack, a kidnapping, whose life was threatened, we were out there defending. We made no distinction, because our feeling was very simple: a move against one group was a move against all."[38] Sheinkman strongly protested the AFL-CIO's habit of describing UNTS as a "guerrilla front," the term used by the Salvadoran right to legitimate its repression of UNTS, and NLC defended and aided UNTS unions when they waged strikes or suffered repression.[39]

Disputes over which unions and federations should be supported underlay further conflicts over two key activities of NLC: sending delegations on fact-finding missions to Central America, and sponsoring speaking tours of the United States by Central American labor leaders. It was NLC's fact-finding missions and speaking tours that first provoked a hostile response from AFL-CIO leaders (who initially underestimated the Committee), because they challenged the federation's traditional monopoly over the conduct of labor's international operations and over information and arguments about labor and politics in Central America. AFL-CIO President Lane Kirkland and the directors of the federation's Department of International Affairs (DIA), Irving Brown and, after 1985, Tom Kahn, were particularly upset that these missions and tours established contact with and support for Central American labor organizations that the federation did not recognize or approve and that they threatened to influence the state and local labor federations that are directly chartered by the AFL-CIO.[40]

The AFL-CIO reacted to this challenge in two ways. On the one hand, it sought to discredit and undermine the fact-finding missions and speaking tours by red-baiting their Central American participants and (to a lesser degree) U.S. sponsors and by discouraging or prohibiting involvement with them by the federation's affiliated unions and state and local labor federations.[41] Federation President Kirkland and DIA Director Kahn pressured state and local central labor bodies in particular to avoid any missions or tours not operated or cleared by DIA, and they issued shunning orders against unions not recognized by the AFL-CIO.[42] On the other hand, the federation also sent its own fact-finding missions to El Salvador and Nicaragua, issued new reports on labor and politics in those countries and disseminated them more widely in the labor movement, held seminars and conferences for state and local labor leaders to explain AFL-CIO foreign policy, sponsored its own speaking tours of the United States by approved Central American labor leaders, and published a new DIA newsletter on foreign affairs. Both responses tried to reassert the federation's institutional and ideological control in the domain of foreign policy, but the second one did so in ways that contributed to a healthy debate that expanded knowledge, dialogue, and participation within the labor movement in matters of foreign affairs.[43]

The most dramatic aspect of NLC's distinct conception of international labor solidarity was the network and campaigns it organized to defend Salvadoran unionists subjected to or threatened with imprisonment, torture, or murder by the government or death squads. This defense network developed from its first fact-finding mission to El Salvador in 1983, when the NLC delegation met with imprisoned leaders of the union of hydroelectric workers, STECEL, who had been held without trial since their arrest for strike activity in 1980. NLC organized an international campaign that won the release of the STECEL leaders from prison in 1984. But in the face of renewed death threats against the STECEL leaders from right-wing death squads, David Dyson and Don Stillman went to El Salvador and, together with representatives of human-rights groups and of the Dutch government, met the STECEL leaders as they were released from prison and provided them with a protective escort to the airport to ensure their safe passage to the Netherlands. The AFL-CIO called for the release on bond and speedy trial of the STECEL leaders, yet it condemned the strike for which they were arrested and apparently refused their plea for further support.[44]

The National Labor Committee thereafter maintained this defense network, which included its own member unions, local labor committees on Central America, the Canadian and a half-dozen European labor federations, and religious and human-rights groups. Because of its contacts in El Salvador, NLC would learn quickly (sometimes within two hours) of the arrest or abduction of union leaders in that country and would mobilize the network to secure their release or safety. The campaigns involved sending letters and telegrams to the Salvadoran government to demand the release or protection of the union leaders, enlisting members of Congress and of European parliaments to lend their support and intervene with the Salvadoran government, and sometimes sending people to El Salvador to assist endangered unionists. Among other campaigns, NLC mounted particularly important ones in defense of leaders of unions representing teachers (ANDES) and telecommunications workers (ASTTEL), unions that the AFL-CIO did not support.

Given the brutality of the repression in El Salvador, at times NLC could not defend but only try to locate the bodies of "disappeared" trade-union and peasant leaders. Some of the ten trips that David Dyson made to El Salvador in the 1980s had that purpose, as he painfully recalled: "In the early days when I was down there I used to go out to the dump, I did that twice, and tried to look for people that we knew. It is just [pause], I was never the same after I did that. I visited the morgue once too, looking for people."[45] Perhaps as many as forty Salvadoran union leaders were saved from prison, torture, or death by this defense network.

Both Jack Sheinkman and David Dyson believe that NLC's campaigns in defense of Salvadoran unionists were its most important contribution. Others recognized the importance of NLC's defense network and campaigns, as well as its broader effort to make labor rights a foundation of U.S. foreign policy. In 1989, NLC was given the Letelier-Moffitt Human Rights Domestic Award by the Transnational Institute (affiliated with the Institute for Policy Studies) in recognition of its contributions to labor rights in El Salvador and to the human-rights movement.[46]

American Labor and Cold War Foreign Policy

The conflict between NLC and the AFL-CIO was ultimately a conflict over Cold War foreign policy. Explaining it requires explaining both why the AFL-CIO adhered to Cold War foreign policy and why a particular group of unions dissented from it in the 1980s. What, then, were the sources of the AFL-CIO's support for Cold War foreign policy? As the Cold War took shape between 1947 and 1950, American labor's support for U.S. foreign policy was, as Robert Zieger, Denis MacShane, and others have argued, rooted in a principled and (especially in the case of the CIO) progressive anticommunist outlook. Leaders of both the AFL and the CIO rejected Soviet and communist ideology and practice as authoritarian and incompatible with independent trade unionism and a free society, and on this ground they opposed the expansion of Soviet and communist influence. Other influences reinforced and intensified American labor's anticommunist outlook and support for U.S. foreign policy in the early Cold War, including the historic influence of the Catholic church on American unions, the large number of CIO members of Eastern European origin, and the strong identification of unions and labor leaders with the state as a result of the New Deal and World War II. Still, a principled opposition to communist and Soviet ideology and conduct was the wellspring of union support for the early Cold War, just as it was for most New Deal liberals, American socialists and independent radicals, and European social-democratic labor movements and political parties.[47]

Beyond the mid-1960s, however, AFL-CIO support for U.S. Cold War foreign policy cannot be explained in this way, at least not entirely. For by that time, major consequences of the Cold War, unanticipated in the late 1940s, had led many liberals in the United States, social-democratic labor and party leaders in Europe, and indeed some American unions—like Walter Reuther's United Auto Workers—to rethink their commitment to the Cold War. These consequences included the nuclear arms race, political and fiscal constraints on domestic social reform, the alignment of the United States with repressive anticommunist regimes throughout the Third World, and above all the war in Vietnam. Combined with the increasingly polycentric character of the communist world, these developments led many liberals and social democrats in the United States and Europe to favor détente and arms control between the superpowers, to oppose American support for authoritarian regimes and U.S. military intervention abroad, and to propose new principles—whether peaceful coexistence, universal human rights, third-world economic and social development, or others—to guide U.S. foreign policy. This shift of attitude was based not so much on abandonment of underlying anticommunist principles as on judgments about the costs, moral and political as well as economic, of a militarized Cold War.[48]

But the AFL-CIO leadership was deeply resistant to this tendency among American liberals, European labor movements, and some U.S. unions. It remained committed to a particularly hawkish version of anticommunism and Cold War, exemplified by its unstinting support for the war in Vietnam, its fierce opposition to détente, its own international operations in Latin America and Asia, its inability to understand and accept the desire of the German and other European labor movements for accommodation with the Soviet Union, and its broad sympathy for U.S. policy in Central America in the 1980s. What accounts for this persistence of militant Cold War foreign policy in the AFL-CIO right through the 1980s, even as many of its longtime allies had revised or abandoned Cold War commitments?[49]

The strongly anticommunist views of the AFL-CIO's only two presidents during the Cold War era, George Meany and his successor Lane Kirkland, and the considerable authority they wielded within the federation over foreign-policy issues, were certainly important to the persistence of a Cold War outlook in the AFL-CIO. But economic, bureaucratic, and political factors powerfully reinforced and strengthened the ideological dispositions of these leaders and helped to ensure broader (but not universal) support for Cold War foreign policy within organized labor, especially among ex-AFL craft unions in the construction and maritime trades. To begin with, Cold War military spending sustained high levels of employment in highly unionized defense industries, and it became all the more important to preserve this base of union jobs in and after the mid-1970s—when it was potentially threatened by the end of the Vietnam war, détente, and arms control—because rates of unemployment began to rise then even as rates of union density continued to fall.

Further, the elaborate bureaucratic apparatus in charge of the federation's international affairs, including the Department of International Affairs and its four overseas institutes in Europe, Latin America, Asia, and Africa, helped to sustain a hard Cold War outlook in the AFL-CIO. This apparatus received extensive funds from the U.S. government, amounting to nearly forty million dollars in 1985, and was led and staffed by hawkish anticommunists drawn from Social Democrats USA. The financial benefits, ideological orientation, and institutional influence of this foreign-affairs bureaucracy all contributed to maintaining a Cold War posture in the AFL-CIO.

Finally, the AFL-CIO's durable commitment to hawkish Cold War policy also reflected important political alliances that the federation had developed, and wished to maintain, with key foreign-policy agencies of the United States govern-ment—including the Department of State, United States Agency for International Development, and U.S. Information Agency—and with leaders of the Cold War wing of the Democratic Party, such as Senator Henry Jackson of Washington.[50]

But what, then, explains the rise of NLC? What developments and conditions promoted the growth of dissenting foreign-policy views within segments of or-ganized labor? Economic, institutional, and especially political influences all con-tributed to the formation of NLC and the allied local labor committees on Central America. To begin with, economic developments and conditions spurred growing labor opposition to U.S. and AFL-CIO policy in Central America among certain types of unions. Many manufacturing unions became disenchanted with Cold War, interventionist foreign policies because they so often sustained authoritarian regimes of the right that repressed unions and maintained low-wage labor forces with which American workers had to compete. Public-employee unions also increasingly opposed such foreign policies because they shifted resources from domestic to defense spending. The deep recession of the U.S. economy in the early 1980s intensified such concerns. These economic factors explain the predominance of manufacturing and public-employee unions in NLC's membership.[51]

The rise of NLC and the local labor committees also had institutional roots, in developments within organized labor. Most of the unions that joined NLC had opposed the war in Vietnam and subsequently shared a history of political dissent from the top leadership of the AFL-CIO. NLC was thus part of the larger and ongoing conflict between rival leadership factions in American labor. Two other institutional developments may well have influenced the rise of new foreign-policy views in labor. Impressionistic evidence suggests that the growing influ-ence in organized labor of activists from the social movements (antiwar and civil rights) of the 1960s, many of whom had assumed low- and midlevel union staff positions, was a key factor in the rise of the local labor committees and an indirect influence on the formation of NLC. Also, though relevant empirical evidence is mixed, it is possible that the rising numbers and percentages of black, Hispanic, and female unionists contributed to the development of dissident foreign-policy views in labor.[52]

Ultimately, various political influences, broadly construed, were decisive in the formation of NLC. First of all, most of those who founded or joined NLC acted on moral or ideological convictions opposed to U.S. military intervention in support of repressive regimes and to AFL-CIO "shunning" of leftist workers and unions abroad. Second, the formation of NLC was deeply influenced by the political impact of the Vietnam war on organized labor. David Dyson was em-phatic on this point: "He [Sheinkman] had been very troubled by the silence of the American labor movement on Vietnam. You can't underestimate the effect that had on progressive trade unionists in this country. They were humiliated that they had not been able to be part of that debate from the institutions they worked for. . . . When we saw the Central America thing brewing there was this thought that we're going to have to organize fast or else we're going to get frozen out of the debate as we did in the 1960s."[53] Finally, labor opposition to U.S. policy in Central America was undoubtedly fueled by the fact that that policy was conceived and carried out by a conservative Republican administration that was strongly anti-union. As government in the Reagan era became much more adversarial toward organized labor and ceased to provide it with either legal protection or social reform, labor's incentives to support the government's foreign policies were greatly reduced, allowing dissent to those policies to mount.[54]

The Transformation of NLC in the 1990s

The 1990s proved to be a decade of change for the National Labor Committee. At the beginning of the decade, the Committee shifted its focus from foreign policy to the global economy. Then, in the mid-1990s, NLC was reorganized from a coalition of unions into a small, independent staff organization with substantially reduced ties to organized labor. NLC became a very different kind of organization than it had been in the 1980s, though it maintained the earlier commitment to defense of labor rights.

NLC shifted its focus from foreign policy to the global economy in response to two developments. One was the peace process that concluded the military conflicts in Central America. Following the Esquipulas Peace Accord of August 1987, which established a framework for political negotiations throughout Central America, peace agreements were reached between the Sandinista government and the Contras in April of 1988 and between the Salvadoran government and the FMLN in December of 1991. The second development was, in Jack Sheinkman's words, the "increased economic integration" of the Americas, the growth of trade and investment among the nations of the Western hemisphere.[55] Although NLC did not oppose this in principle, it feared that integration with low-wage economies and their multiplying export-processing zones—industrial enclaves of cheap labor that enjoyed preferential access to the U.S. market—in the southern hemisphere would exert downward pressure on employment, wages, and labor standards in the United States. As Sheinkman wrote in a 1991 NLC report, "The struggle for worker rights in El Salvador and the other countries in Central and South America has never been more important than it is now to the labor movement in the U.S. and Canada. . . . In the absence of effective worker rights in the region, increased economic integration will only exacerbate the already fierce wage competition which threatens the jobs, wages, and living standards of workers throughout the Americas."[56] NLC would now defend labor rights against threats from an unregulated global market rather than from authoritarian regimes sustained by the Cold War foreign policy of the United States.[57]

NLC's reorientation toward the global economy was guided by Charles Kernaghan, who became executive director in 1990 when David Dyson returned to the ministry. In 1992, Kernaghan launched NLC on a campaign to expose and end the role of the U.S. Agency for International Development (AID) in financing the development of export-processing zones in Central America and enticing U.S. firms to relocate to them. An effective media campaign, in which NLC collaborated with the CBS news program *60 Minutes* and portrayed AID as using taxpayer money to "export jobs" from the United States to low-wage zones offshore, led Congress to prohibit AID from using its funds to establish export-processing zones in foreign countries, induce U.S. firms to relocate offshore, or support projects that violated internationally recognized labor rights. The success of this campaign brought several additional unions, and more union money, into the National Labor Committee.[58]

By 1995, however, the Committee ceased being a coalition of unions, and by 1997 the small, independent staff organization that remained formed a new board of directors drawn from academia, churches, the media, think tanks, and a few unions. It is not certain from the available evidence why NLC was reorganized, but two events likely caused or contributed to the change. Most important, in 1995, ACTWU merged with the International Ladies Garment Workers Union (ILGWU) to form the Union of Needletrades, Industrial, and Textile Employees (UNITE), and as Jack Sheinkman was ready to retire, the presidency of the new union was assumed by ILGWU president Jay Mazur. Although UNITE continued to support NLC and Mazur joined the committee's new board of directors in 1997 (as did Jack Sheinkman and David Dyson), they did not, and under the pressures of merger perhaps could not, assume the role of sponsorship and leadership that ACTWU and Sheinkman had played. In addition, 1995 was the year in which a major change of leadership occurred at the AFL-CIO; following the retirement of Lane Kirkland, NLC member John Sweeney was elected to the presidency of the federation over longtime AFL-CIO secretary-treasurer Thomas Donohue. This change enabled NLC unions to pursue their international goals and strategies through the AFL-CIO and thus reduced their need for a vehicle like the National Labor Committee.

After 1995, the new NLC devoted itself to a campaign against the resurgence of sweatshops in the global apparel industry. Through exposure of the abusive labor practices of offshore clothing manufacturers under contract to major U.S. retail firms, the dominant force in the apparel industry, NLC sought to mobilize public pressure on these firms to accept responsibility for and improve their contractors' labor practices. More precisely, NLC demanded that large retail firms develop labor standards and agree to independent monitoring, preferably by human-rights groups, of their contractors' labor practices to ensure compliance with those standards. The main targets of this campaign were the Gap, Wal-Mart, and Disney, all icons of American popular culture as well as leading apparel retailers.[59]

NLC's anti-sweatshop campaign enjoyed some success. It focused media and

public attention on the revival of sweatshops and labor abuses in the global economy; influenced then Labor Secretary Robert Reich and President Bill Clinton to
convene a fashion-industry "summit" and form a "White House Apparel Industry
Partnership" to recommend voluntary labor standards that would end sweatshops;
and pressured the Gap and Wal-Mart to agree to independent monitoring of
contractors. It appears, however, that these achievements effected only limited or
formal changes in the labor practices of the global apparel industry, and some have
questioned whether NLC's emphasis on corporate labor codes and independent
monitoring ignores or even obstructs more effective solutions to the proliferation of sweatshops, such as unionization and collective bargaining, government
regulation, and labor standards in trade agreements. Undaunted, in the late 1990s,
NLC expanded its anti-sweatshop campaign to include Asia (as well as Central
America and the Caribbean) and the demand that large U.S. retailers disclose
the names and locations of all their offshore contractors.[60]

Conclusion

Considered as a discrete organization, the National Labor Committee made three
important contributions that have not been fully or properly recognized. First,
it was a key component of one of the major social movements of the 1980s, the
U.S. Central America peace movement, which played an important role in the
most divisive foreign-policy issue of that decade. The few extant studies of this
movement have rightly emphasized its origins and base in the religious community, evident in organizations like Sanctuary, Witness for Peace, and Pledge
of Resistance. The National Labor Committee and the local labor committees on
Central America suggest, however, that trade unionism was another important
social base of this movement. Indeed, a political alliance of churches and unions
was at the core of the U.S. Central America peace movement and provided it with
the combination of moral authority and political influence that allowed it to shape
public opinion and congressional action on Central America.[61]

Second, NLC contributed to debates over the foreign policy of the United
States government and the AFL-CIO. Its distinctive contribution to criticism
of Cold War foreign policy was its emphasis on the deleterious impact of that
policy on labor rights in developing countries. For NLC, denial of labor rights
by U.S.-supported regimes helped to generate the central problem of the world
economy: gross disparities among nations in wage levels and in labor and social
standards, which threatened the gains that workers and unions had struggled to
achieve in the United States and other advanced countries. Without denying that
many NLC unions sought trade protection for their members, it is important to
emphasize that NLC's solution to the problem of global labor competition was
not simply to wall off the U.S. market, but to raise wages and labor and social
standards in the developing world through establishment of effective labor-rights

and labor movements. Toward that end, NLC advocated that promoting respect for labor rights abroad should be a basic objective of U.S. foreign policy and that support for trade unions overseas should be the cornerstone of organized labor's international role.

Third, NLC helped to overcome a substantial obstacle in the way of rebuilding a strong labor-liberal coalition in American national politics. The AFL-CIO's firm support for the war in Vietnam badly damaged that coalition, and thereafter its reliable adherence to Cold War foreign policy continued to divide organized labor from liberals. The National Labor Committee, and the local labor committees informally allied to it, finally made a forthright break with the Cold War foreign policy of both the U.S. government and the AFL-CIO, a step that was all the more important because it occurred at a time of intensification of the Cold War and involved unions representing a majority of the unionized workforce. A major reason for NLC's break with Cold War foreign policy was its corrosive impact on labor's domestic political alliances. The National Labor Committee expressed the dissident labor leadership's view that a new labor foreign policy was necessary to rebuild the labor-liberal alliance.

Of course, as an attempt to rebuild the labor-liberal alliance the National Labor Committee was not a discrete organization but part of a larger effort that also included the Progressive Alliance, Citizen Labor Energy Coalition, and other organizations. Both its similarities to and differences from these other organizations shed further light on the politics of the dissident unions and the prospects for labor-liberal revival.

The National Labor Committee confirms much of what the Progressive Alliance and Citizen Labor Energy Coalition had indicated about the identity and politics of the dissident unions. Because its member unions in general, and its core unions in particular, corresponded so closely to those of the Alliance and the Coalition, NLC corroborates what those organizations suggested about which unions and labor leaders belonged to the dissident wing of labor and exercised leadership in it. The National Labor Committee also reinforces what earlier organizations revealed about the politics of the dissident unions, including their commitment to independent (of the AFL-CIO) labor politics, cooperation with liberals, coordination and strengthening of the liberal wing of the Democratic Party, and even emphasis on economic issues and anticorporate reforms. Although NLC was not itself a labor-liberal coalition, it practiced coalition politics with liberal religious and human-rights groups. And when the conflicts in Central America were resolved by the early 1990s, NLC shifted its focus from foreign-policy to global-economic issues and sought reforms of corporate labor practices in world markets.

NLC also bears out conclusions about the prospects for labor-liberal revival drawn from the experience of the Alliance and the Coalition. The willingness of religious and human-rights groups to work closely with the National Labor

Committee once again showed that liberals as well as dissident unions were interested in rebuilding the labor-liberal alliance. And the limited but significant policy influence exerted by the dissident unions, churches, and human-rights groups allied in the U.S. Central America peace movement again suggests that coalition building strengthened both labor and liberals.

But the National Labor Committee also differed from earlier organizations of the dissident unions, and the differences give a fuller picture of the politics of the dissident unions. Most obvious and important, NLC reveals another key element of the politics of these unions: opposition to Cold War foreign policy. Though it originated during the Vietnam war, opposition to Cold War foreign policy became a central and open political commitment of the dissident unions only in and through NLC. This opposition extended to the international operations of the AFL-CIO as well as those of the U.S. government, and through NLC the dissident unions effectively linked their critique of Cold War foreign policy to the crucial issues of labor rights and solidarity in a global economy.

Another distinctive feature of NLC was the particular liberal groups with which the dissident unions in it allied (outside if not inside the Committee itself), namely, religious and human-rights groups. It was not that these groups were altogether absent from the Alliance or the Coalition, but that they were the closest and most important allies of the dissident unions in NLC, because they were the liberal groups most active on Central America. In short, the National Labor Committee expanded the range of liberal groups with which the dissident unions made or restored a strong alliance.

Finally, although its predecessors had emphasized economic issues and anticorporate reforms, NLC was the first organization of the dissident unions to take up seriously the new problems of the global economy, including not only trade but also production, investment, labor competition, and worker rights. NLC helped the dissident unions, and perhaps the entire labor movement, make the transition from the end of the Cold War to the emergence of the global economy.

CHAPTER 8

The Political Strategy
and Social Bases of the
Dissident Unions

Introduction

The years from 1978 through 1982 were harsh ones for unions and liberals. Legislative setbacks, electoral defeats, collective-bargaining reverses, membership losses, and declining public approval were among the misfortunes they suffered. Unions and liberals responded in various ways to these calamities. One important response was the formation of the Progressive Alliance, Citizen Labor Energy Coalition, and National Labor Committee. These organizations were not disconnected. They were all formed and led by unions in the dissident wing of organized labor, they all allied these unions with liberal groups and movements, and they all sought to rekindle social activism in the labor movement and to rebuild a strong labor-liberal coalition in national politics. They constituted a coherent response to the further decline of unionism and liberalism between 1978 and 1982.

It does not diminish the indispensable role of liberals in (or alongside) them to acknowledge that the Alliance, Coalition, and Committee were a political project of the dissident labor leadership. Though the Citizen Labor Energy Coalition was a partial exception, these organizations were initiated, organized, subsidized, and led by the dissident unions. Through these organizations, dissident labor leaders tried to develop a new political strategy for the labor movement, different from that of the AFL-CIO and its dominant unions. We can now consider the Progressive Alliance, Citizen Labor Energy Coalition, and National Labor Committee collectively rather than individually, in order to learn more about the dissident unions and their political project. What do these organizations reveal about the political strategy of the dissident unions? What does their membership tell us about what kinds of unions were dissident unions that favored a new political strategy for labor? How did these unions and their political strategy differ from those in the dominant wing of American labor?

The Alliance, Coalition, and Committee also provide us with new information and evidence to assess competing analyses of labor politics in the late 1970s and early 1980s. Finally, these organizations, and the dissident labor leaders who formed and led them, were criticized at the time, amid debates about the way forward for unions and liberals. It is worth considering these criticisms, as well.

The Political Strategy of the Dissident Unions

Taken together, the Progressive Alliance, Citizen Labor Energy Coalition, and National Labor Committee developed a labor political strategy that had five components. The first and most obvious was coalition building with liberal groups and movements. Even the National Labor Committee, which, unlike the Alliance and Coalition, did not include nonlabor groups in its membership, formed alliances with churches and human-rights groups. That all three organizations practiced coalition politics indicates that it was considered an indispensable strategy for labor politics by the union leaders who formed and led them. The three organizations allied unions with different liberal groups and movements because they addressed different issues (e.g., consumer groups were more suitable allies than human-rights groups on energy issues, but vice versa on foreign-policy issues), and possibly because unions were searching for the most compatible and reliable partners. But together these organizations allied unions with a wide range of liberal groups, including civil-rights and women's organizations, the citizen-organizing and public-interest movements, and religious and human-rights groups. Many of these derived from the New Politics movement that had transformed liberalism over the previous decade, because the dissident unions understood that they had to ally with New Politics liberals in order to rebuild the labor-liberal coalition.

The second component of the new strategy was factional politics in the Democratic Party—that is, organizing liberal Democrats to assert their influence in the party. Dissident labor leaders like Douglas Fraser and William Winpisinger were disturbed by the conservative drift of the Democratic Party in the late 1970s and early 1980s, a development they attributed largely to growing business influence in the party and to divisions among liberal groups and movements.[1] Therefore theAlliance, Coalition, and Committee attempted not only to unite various liberal groups and movements (including unions) but also to coordinate them with the Democratic Party's liberal officeholders and candidates. Moreover, these organizations contended against moderate to conservative Democrats in the Carter administration and Congress over both internal party affairs (the party's rules and platform) and national policy (economic, energy, and foreign policy). Through the Progressive Alliance, Citizen Labor Energy Coalition, and National Labor Committee, dissident labor leaders assumed a more active and self-conscious factional role in the Democratic Party in order to reverse the decline of its liberal wing.

The third element of the strategy was anticorporate or populist reform. The union leaders who formed PA, CLEC, and NLC had been incensed by what UAW President Douglas Fraser called the "one-sided class war" that the business community had waged against the working and middle classes and their communities.[2] They responded by championing reforms that would impose a greater measure of social control and responsibility on corporate business. This was a major thrust of both the Progressive Alliance and the Citizen Labor Energy Coalition, with their campaigns to limit the role of corporate money in elections, hold firms accountable for the social costs of plant closings, and impose price and other regulations and increased taxes on energy corporations. Even the National Labor Committee, initially devoted to foreign-policy issues, turned to anticorporate reform campaigns—to curb the relocation of U.S. business overseas and to halt the growth of sweatshops—when the conflicts in Central America were resolved. As CLEC's leaders in particular conceived them, anticorporate reforms would be part of a broader strategy of economic or left-populism that could undercut the right-wing populism that had enabled conservatives to gain ground among the nonaffluent by articulating, and inflaming, their social and cultural grievances.

Opposition to Cold War foreign policy was the fourth component of the political strategy of the dissident unions. Again, a major reason for this opposition was that, since Vietnam, AFL-CIO support for Cold War foreign policy had divided labor from most liberals, weakening both. Dissident union leaders believed that they had to develop a new foreign policy for the union movement if they were to rebuild the labor-liberal alliance. Another source of union opposition to Cold War foreign policy was its role in draining resources from domestic social spending and in generating a global economic order that threatened workers and unions everywhere. Opposition to Cold War foreign policy was difficult for those dissident unions—including the UAW, IAM, USWA, OCAW, UE, and IUE—that represented defense-industry workers, and they often lobbied in favor of the specific weapons systems on which their own members' jobs depended even as they opposed Cold War policies and big defense budgets.[3] Still, the dissident unions strongly advocated a new foreign policy based on promotion of labor and democratic rights and regulation of the world market rather than on prosecution of a militarized Cold War.

The final element in the political strategy of PA, CLEC, and NLC was the modernization of labor's interest-group tactics. As Taylor Dark has shown, in the late 1970s the AFL-CIO remained wedded to a strategy of insider bargaining among a limited number of groups and elites, a strategy that had been discredited by a decade of change in American politics.[4] The dissident unions recognized this problem and tried to expand and update the techniques of influence available to labor. In particular, they developed two techniques increasingly used by a wide range of organized interests, including business: grass-roots lobbying and activism, and issue (or policy) research and advocacy.[5] The Alliance, Coalition, and Committee all organized local bodies that, in addition to pressuring local authorities, influenced Congress through grass-roots lobbying (constituent lobbying of representatives and senators in their home districts and states) and direct action (rallies and demonstrations). Further, all three organizations attached great importance, and devoted significant shares of their limited resources, to conducting research, issuing reports and publications, and communicating with the public through the media. The Progressive Alliance even had (unfulfilled) aspirations of competing with business-financed conservative think tanks like the Heritage Foundation and American Enterprise Institute. Much more than the AFL-CIO of that era, these organizations took seriously the need for unions to mobilize grass-roots support and to compete in the arena of public opinion.

This, then, was the strategy that dissident unions developed through the Progressive Alliance, Citizen Labor Energy Coalition, and National Labor Committee. It was an alternative to the politics of the AFL-CIO, especially the federation's rejection of New Politics liberals in favor of Cold War and regular Democrats as allies, its occasional (1972, 1976) withdrawals from presidential and party politics, its recent pursuit of a narrow labor agenda over broad social concerns, its hawkish anticommunism, and its reliance on insider bargaining in Washington, D.C., over more public and activist methods of political influence. The new strategy of the dissident unions aimed to ensure a future for both the labor movement and liberal politics. But what kinds of unions dissented from the politics of the AFL-CIO, how did they differ from the dominant unions in the federation, and what explains their commitment to social unionism and liberal politics?

The Social Bases of the Dissident Unions

The unions that formed PA, CLEC, and NLC differed from the dominant unions of the AFL-CIO in the tradition of unionism (AFL craft unionism or CIO industrial unionism) from which they descended, the industrial sectors they organized, and, probably, the social composition of their memberships. In the AFL-CIO of 1978, when both PA and CLEC were organized, ex-AFL unions outnumbered ex-CIO unions seventy-three to twenty-six, a margin of nearly three to one. From the 1955 merger through (in fact, well beyond) the end of the 1970s, ex-AFL unions continuously controlled the presidency of the federation and 70 to 75 percent of the seats on its executive council. More specifically, the dominant bloc of unions in the AFL-CIO throughout this era was the ex-AFL craft unions that represented predominantly white male workers in the construction and transportation sectors of the economy. These unions supplied both AFL-CIO presidents—George Meany and Lane Kirkland—and held 40 percent of the council seats in this period, even though they contained, in 1978, only 24 percent of the federation's combined individual membership.[6] They tended to have narrow public-policy goals focused on maintenance of employment levels, union power, and wage norms in their own industries through public subsidy and regulation.[7]

By contrast, ex-CIO unions were disproportionately represented in PA, CLEC, and NLC. Of the thirty-seven unions that joined one or more of these organizations, nineteen were ex-AFL unions, fifteen were former CIO unions, and three (NEA, UFW, NFLPA) had no premerger affiliation with either body. However, these numbers represented only 26 percent of the ex-AFL unions but 58 percent of the ex-CIO unions in 1978. Ex-CIO unions were overrepresented among PA, CLEC, and NLC unions compared to their share of all AFL-CIO unions (40 percent compared to 25 percent), whereas ex-AFL unions were underrepresented (51 percent compared to 72 percent). Moreover, the unions that played the most significant roles in the Alliance, Coalition, and Committee were even more disproportionately drawn from the CIO. Fifty-five percent of the core unions (those that founded, provided leadership and resources, and were most active) in these organizations, and 78 percent of those unions that joined all three organizations, were ex-CIO unions.[8]

Finally, several of the ex-AFL unions in the three organizations, notably the Machinists (IAM), Service Employees (SEIU), Food and Commercial Workers (UFCW), and Ladies Garment Workers (ILGWU), had long ago evolved into CIO-style industrial unions.[9] Because IAM, SEIU, and UFCW were among the core unions of the three organizations, virtually every union among the dozen or so that led PA, CLEC, and NLC reflected the industrial unionism of the CIO rather than the craft unionism of the AFL.

The unions that comprised the Alliance, Coalition, and Committee also differed from the dominant unions in the AFL-CIO in the sectors of the economy they organized. The sectoral distribution of the thirty-seven unions that joined PA, CLEC, or NLC was as follows: twenty-one (58 percent) from the manufacturing sector, five (14 percent) from the public sector, five (14 percent) from the private service sector, three (8 percent) from the construction sector, one (3 percent) from the communications sector, and one (3 percent) from the agricultural sector. Both manufacturing and public-employee unions were overrepresented in PA, CLEC, and NLC compared to their shares of all AFL-CIO unions, by 58 percent to 48 percent for manufacturing unions and 14 percent to 10 percent for public-employee unions. By contrast, construction- and transportation-sector unions were underrepresented in the three organizations compared to their shares of all AFL-CIO unions, by 8 percent to 12 percent for construction unions and by 0 percent to 14 percent for transportation unions.[10] Not a single transportation sector union joined PA, CLEC, or NLC, and although three construction-sector unions joined, in fact none of them was active in these organizations. Thus an alliance of manufacturing, public- employee, and service-sector unions anchored the dissident wing of the labor movement, in contrast to the bloc of construction and transportation unions that dominated the leadership of the AFL-CIO.

Finally, it is likely, but not certain, that the unions that joined the Alliance, Coalition, and Committee differed from the dominant unions in the AFL-CIO in the racial and gender composition of their memberships. Unfortunately, systematic data on the social composition of individual unions do not exist, but some limited or indirect evidence is available. In 1978 there were ten unions with at least 250,000 female members, and eight of those unions joined PA, CLEC, or NLC.[11] In addition, unions that had unusually high percentages of African-American members (UAW, USWA, AFSCME) or Hispanic members (UFW, ACTWU, ILGWU) at the time also joined and often led these organizations.[12] Lastly, Bureau of Labor Statistics data indicate that in 1980 the percentages of females and of blacks among union members were generally higher in the manufacturing, public, and private service sectors, from which PA, CLEC, and NLC unions were drawn, than in the construction and transportation sectors, from which the dominant unions in the AFL-CIO were drawn. Blacks constituted 13.9 percent, 16.9 percent, and 17.2 percent of union members in the manufacturing, public, and private service sectors, respectively, but 14.1 percent and 9.5 percent of union members in the transportation and construction sectors. Females made up 21.8 percent, 24.9 percent, and 52.9 percent of union members in manufacturing, public employment, and services, respectively, but only 10.3 percent and 1.5 percent of union members in transportation and construction.[13]

In sum, ex-CIO unions (or more generally industrial unions), those in the manufacturing, public, and service sectors, and probably unions with relatively large female and/or minority memberships were the most likely to join and lead the Progressive Alliance, Citizen Labor Energy Coalition, and National Labor Committee. Compared to the craft unions in construction and transportation that retained disproportionate control of the AFL-CIO, these unions were more committed to social activism and liberal politics. Why?

As J. David Greenstone and Ruth Horowitz showed, the CIO unions that formed in the 1930s and 1940s favored active government and the welfare state, developed broad social sympathies and political programs, and needed and acquired allies because they organized socially heterogeneous low-skill and low-wage employees in national labor markets.[14] These unions developed a liberal or even social-democratic approach to politics that in many cases—classically the Clothing and Textile Workers and Auto Workers unions—became an enduring union political culture.[15] Contemporary service-sector unions also tend to represent low-wage and socially heterogeneous workforces, with similar political results.[16] Although the obvious dependence of public-employee unions on government certainly explains much of their inclination toward liberal politics, both public- and service-sector unions were shaped politically by their comparatively large proportions of female and minority members. Not only were the disadvantaged economic and social status and more liberal outlooks of these groups an influence, but the growth of these unions coincided with and drew energy and support from the civil-rights and women's movements.[17]

Alternative Views of Labor Politics

This analysis of the split between the dominant and dissident wings of American labor, and of the political strategy and social bases of the dissident unions, is broadly compatible with some important recent studies of contemporary labor history and politics, such as those by Peter Levy and Taylor Dark.[18] But other writers on labor politics have provided different accounts of the dissident unions and of the internal politics of the labor movement, and it is important to consider these alternative views, especially in light of information and evidence derived from the Progressive Alliance, Citizen Labor Energy Coalition, and National Labor Committee.

One alternative account comes from the conservative labor economist Leo Troy. In his view, the main political development in organized labor during the last few decades was the rise of public-employee unionism. According to Troy, the growth of unionism in the public sector and its decline in the private sector, the higher rate and greater stability of union density in the public than the private sector, the concentration of organized public employees in relatively large unions, and the greater geographical dispersion of public- than private-sector unions all contributed to a shift in the balance of power in the labor movement away from private-sector and toward public-employee unions.[19]

Further, Troy argued that public-employee and private-sector unions increasingly had conflicting political goals: the former naturally favored expansion of the welfare state and of the broader economic role of government, and thus the "socialization of income and wealth"; the latter opposed such goals because their members bore the costs of redistribution as taxpayers, suffered from the inflation that government growth generated, and faced declining employment as capital was siphoned out of the private sector to finance public-sector growth.[20] Finally, given their political interests and growing power, public-sector unions were the source of the growing tilt in the labor movement toward policies of "government intervention" and "collectivism."[21]

It would be difficult to find an analyst of American labor who would not agree that the growth of public-employee unionism in the 1960s and 1970s was a major development with important institutional and political implications for organized labor. Public-employee unions have indeed become more influential in the AFL-CIO, and there are political differences between public- and private-sector unions, as liberal analysts have also noticed.[22] But many of Troy's specific claims were weakly supported and are contradicted by evidence in this and other studies.

In fact, Troy presented little empirical evidence of any kind for the claims that the key political division in organized labor was between public- and private-sector unions and that the former supported while the latter opposed expansion of the welfare state and the broader economic role of government. It appears that he arrived at these claims deductively, from assumptions he made about the economic interests of public- and private-sector employees, rather than inductively, from observation of labor politics. Moreover, the composition and history of the Progressive Alliance, Citizen Labor Energy Coalition, and National Labor Committee—not to mention a host of predecessor and successor organizations—suggest that the principal fault line in the labor movement did not run between public- and private-sector unions, that many private-sector and public-employee unions had shared interests and cooperated extensively in politics, and that the largest single bloc of unions supporting welfare-state liberalism remained ex-CIO industrial unions. As this book and other studies show, in every major political conflict in organized labor since the late 1960s—the Vietnam war, reform of the Democratic Party, the McGovern nomination, U.S. policy in Central America, the 1995 contest for the presidency of the AFL-CIO—the alignments *cross-cut* rather than paralleled the distinction between public- and private-sector unions, and the liberal position was represented by a coalition of private- and public-employee unions, not by the latter alone.

The liberal journalist Thomas Edsall advanced another account of labor politics. He argued that traditionally liberal unions in the manufacturing sector retreated into a narrow and defensive trade-union politics under the pressure of the profound economic problems they faced in the 1970s and 1980s.[23] Along with scholars like David Vogel and Walter Galenson, Edsall stressed that in those years recession, import penetration, deregulation, deindustrialization, and declining membership led once reform-minded industrial unions to demand trade protection, domestic content legislation (which requires the domestic manufacture of a fixed percentage of the parts of automobiles or other products sold in the United States), market regulations, and industrial policies to preserve union employment and wages.[24] These writers typically focused on the Auto Workers and Steel Workers unions to make their case, but other studies suggested that the same trend was evident in other industrial unions like the Clothing and Textile Workers, Machinists, and Communications Workers.[25] Furthermore, in the view of most of these writers, the increasingly narrow and defensive politics of these unions would inevitably repel rather than attract liberal support for organized labor. As Edsall put it, the "defensive posture" of these unions was "just the kind of posture that drives off potential allies."[26]

Though it identifies an important aspect of their public demands at the time, this is an incomplete and unbalanced view of the politics of dissident industrial unions in the 1970s and 1980s. These unions did make demands for trade, regulatory, and other policies that can reasonably be described as narrow and defensive in that they were intended to stanch the erosion of employment, union bargaining power, and wage norms in specific industries. But it is far from clear that they could have avoided doing so under the circumstances, and Edsall and like-minded authors did not propose alternative strategies, less narrow and defensive, by which beleaguered industrial unions might have represented and protected their members and dealt with the economic problems plaguing their industries.

Further, it is not true that dissident industrial unions responded to those economic problems only by making narrow and defensive policy demands. They also sought to enhance the productivity and competitiveness of their firms and industries, by means of concessions to employers on wages and work rules and experiments with new work arrangements and labor-management relationships (all of which were controversial within the union movement).[27] And the trade, regulatory, and industrial policies that these unions advocated were not all narrow and defensive. Many of them were general strategies for the entire manufacturing sector that dissident industrial unions explicitly, and plausibly, justified as serving broad working-class and national interests by preserving a high-wage employment base, maintaining the viability of industries critical to national security, boosting productivity and competitiveness, and reducing skyrocketing trade deficits.[28]

Last, Edsall and other writers who emphasized the narrow and defensive politics of industrial unions in the 1970s and 1980s simply ignored the organizations that those unions established to revive social activism in the labor movement and the labor-liberal alliance in national politics. None of those writers made any mention of the Progressive Alliance, Citizen Labor Energy Coalition, or National Labor Committee, each of which was founded by a union in a distressed manufacturing industry. As these organizations practiced coalition politics, engaged broad public issues, and promoted economic and social reforms, they show that the dissident unions, including those from the manufacturing sector, were not frozen into a narrow and defensive political posture and were able to attract liberal allies.

Finally, Kim Moody, an author and labor activist on the left, provided yet another perspective on the dissident unions and internal labor politics. He considered the political differences between the Reuther and Meany wings of labor much less important than the model of "bureaucratic business unionism" that they shared. Because of the postwar evolution of the CIO, unions in the Reuther wing mirrored those in the Meany wing in three crucial respects: (a) they mainly sought to negotiate the highest price—the best wages and benefits—for labor through bargaining with employers, (b) their bureaucratic structure stifled rank-and-file participation and controlled or canalized worker militancy, and (c) they accepted a subordinate position in the Democratic Party that provided few benefits to them or their members. By the late 1970s and early 1980s, according to Moody, this model of unionism had trapped liberal and conservative unions alike in declining union density, massive job losses, concession bargaining, and a depoliticized and demobilized working class. Thus the Reuther wing of labor was not a genuine alternative to the Meany wing and had no better prospects of leading a revival of organized labor or progressive politics.[29]

The more significant split in the labor movement, Moody argued, was that between top leaderships and insurgent rank-and-file movements in many unions, including liberal ones. These insurgent movements arose either to dislodge corrupt union leaders (Miners for Democracy, Teamsters for a Democratic Union) or to resist the concession bargaining and labor-management cooperation schemes to which union leaders had agreed (Steel Workers Fight Back, New Directions caucus in the UAW). In Moody's view, these rank-and-file insurgencies championed worker solidarity and militancy, confrontation with employers, and union democracy and, in conjunction with efforts to establish a Labor Party, embodied or prefigured a model of unionism distinct from "bureaucratic business unionism" and capable of reviving the labor movement.[30]

Moody's view of both the dissident unions and the rank-and-file insurgencies is unpersuasive. His analysis of the postwar evolution of the CIO into a "bureaucratic business unionism" subordinated to the Democratic Party, shared with other writers on the left like Mike Davis and Michael Goldfield, is overdrawn.[31] To be sure, over the course of the postwar era the CIO unions practiced an increasingly formalized contract unionism, relied more heavily on enlarged administrative apparatuses for both collective bargaining and political action, and received diminishing benefits from their alliance with the Democratic Party.[32] But these writers exaggerate the extent to which dissident unions, ex-CIO or otherwise, abandoned social unionism, stifled meaningful rank-and-file participation, and lost support from the Democratic Party. They neglect or blithely dismiss substantial arguments and evidence that the liberal unions played a key role in the development and passage of Great Society civil-rights and social-welfare legislation, allowed significant rank-and-file participation in the selection of union leaders and ratification of contracts, and secured at least defensive benefits from the Democratic Party even in recent decades.[33]

The view of the evolution of the CIO by these writers colored their assessment of the political organizations established by the dissident unions in the late 1970s and early 1980s. To Moody and Davis's credit, they were among the few who paid attention to the Progressive Alliance, Citizen Labor Energy Coalition, and National Labor Committee. But they rushed to judgment without careful investigation or detailed knowledge of them. They dismissed these efforts to revive social unionism and the labor-liberal alliance as ineffective and possibly insincere. Moody's judgment of PA, CLEC, and NLC as "the stillbirth of a new social unionism" summarized their view.[34] Although the achievements of these organizations were modest, they did make contributions both on substantive issues and to the strengthening and updating of the labor-liberal coalition. Further, the dissident unions were the key historical source of the 1995 leadership change at the AFL-CIO, and PA, CLEC, and NLC shaped the political strategy of the new federation leadership. Thus the political organizations of the dissident unions were more consequential than these critics allowed; they more likely marked the rebirth than the stillbirth of a new social unionism.

Moody's analysis and evaluation of the rank-and-file movements is also dubious. He exaggerates the scope and significance of these movements and their disputes with established union leaders. Such conflicts were not characteristic of unionism in general but were largely confined to unions in the manufacturing sector and reflected the deep changes and problems peculiar to that sector after the early 1970s. Although manufacturing-sector unions remained vitally important to the U.S. labor movement, it does not seem likely that developments confined to these unions, but largely absent from the increasingly important public and service-sector unions, would have the importance for the future of organized labor that Moody attributed to them. Indeed, the rank-and-file insurgencies appear to have been a transitory phenomenon of the 1970s and 1980s that had little success or influence outside the Mine Workers and Teamsters unions, the only cases outside the manufacturing sector, where the problem was corruption.

Further, Moody's claim that militant rank-and-file movements constituted the most important alternative to "bureaucratic business unionism" is implausible. The examples of rank-and-file militancy that he discusses revolved mainly around economistic demands and contractual issues, and neither these nor the rank-and-file movements against corrupt leadership generated broad social and political demands or commitments to organizing nonunion workers. His work seems in fact to indicate that rank-and-file militancy reproduces rather than overcomes the limitations of business unionism. Moreover, it is far from clear that rank-and-file movements against concessions represented the interests of all workers in an industry (i.e., a broad class interest), as Moody believed, rather than the particular interests of workers in a given enterprise or locality.

The American labor movement of the last third of the twentieth century remained sufficiently large and varied that no single account of its politics, including the one developed here, is likely to identify and explain everything of importance. But the rival accounts considered in preceding paragraphs do not provide credible alternatives, in part because they ignored or misjudged the Progressive Alliance, Citizen Labor Energy Coalition, and National Labor Committee.

Criticisms of the Dissident Unions

The efforts of the dissident unions to develop a new political strategy through the Progressive Alliance, Citizen Labor Energy Coalition, and National Labor Committee met with various criticisms at the time. Some of them came from the AFL-CIO leadership. Leaders in the dominant wing of organized labor were normally circumspect about publicly criticizing their dissident counterparts, yet they openly reproached the dissidents and their political organizations on two points: their opposition to U.S. foreign policy in Central America, and their willingness to ally with political activists from the New Left. Federation leaders criticized these positions of the dissidents as unwise policy and unsound strategy but did not effectively refute the dissidents' view that these positions were necessary in order to revive the labor-liberal alliance.

Most of the criticisms of dissident labor leaders and their political organizations came from the left, especially the segment of it that espouses the "rank-and-file" perspective. Activists and writers of this tendency criticized the political strategy of the dissident unions on four grounds: (a) it built only elite alliances with leaders of other liberal groups and movements rather than the more important coalitions at the base between union members and community groups; (b) it sought social change through the Democratic Party when the space for reform in that party had been closed by growing corporate and neoliberal influence in it, leaving an independent labor or left party as the only way to mobilize workers and create pressure for change; (c) it neglected the labor organizing that was necessary to boost union membership; and (d) it rejected the rank-and-file militancy and confrontation with employers that were needed to revive union power.[35]

These criticisms are less than compelling. As national organizations, PA, CLEC, and NLC were indeed "elite" or leadership alliances, but as the case studies showed, they had strong grass-roots components. This was particularly true of CLEC, which painstakingly built a network of state and local energy coalitions, and NLC, which helped to form and cooperated with the many local committees on U.S. policy in Central America. Even the Progressive Alliance organized the Delaware Valley Coalition for Jobs as a labor-community alliance to oppose plant closings or relocations. All three organizations indicate that dissident labor leaders were committed to promoting labor-community alliances that would unite and activate local unionists and members of other groups.

In their criticism of engagement with the Democratic Party and insistence on an independent labor party, advocates of the "rank-and-file" perspective pass too lightly over difficult issues. They ignore the fact that major sections of the working class and important social movements remain strongly committed to the Democratic Party. They elide the significant political costs that a third-party strategy could entail for unions, especially the loss of such protection as the Democratic Party still provides against the anti-union legislative agenda of the Republican Party and its employer allies. Above all, they neglect the major obstacles that the U.S. electoral system places in the way of all third parties.[36]

It is true that PA, CLEC, and NLC did not directly address the pressing problem of declining union density, but it is not true that dissident labor leaders showed no concern for this problem or made no efforts to promote labor organizing.

From Walter Reuther through Jerry Wurf to William Winpisinger, dissident labor leaders tried in various ways to revive large-scale union organizing, although their efforts were generally ineffective. By the mid- to late 1980s, as the next chapter will show, dissident union leaders achieved institutional reforms and innovations that are now widely regarded as having improved the organizing capacities of the labor movement, if not union density itself, and formed a new political organization, Jobs with Justice, that did directly address the problems of union decline and labor organizing. The efforts of the dissident unions, from the late 1960s on, to focus the labor movement on the problem of union decline, and the institutional reforms and organizing strategies that they proposed to reverse it, also influenced the organizing commitments and strategies of the Sweeney regime that came to power in the AFL-CIO in 1995.

Finally, the criticism that the political strategy of liberal union leaders was not up to the task of rebuilding union power because it rejected rank-and-file militancy and confrontation with employers rests upon dubious assumptions. Critics like Kim Moody simply take it for granted either that workers will automatically respond with militant opposition to employer demands for concessions, at least if "labor bureaucrats" do not discourage or repress it, or that militancy can be readily induced or mobilized by the right leaders or activists. But this essentialist or voluntarist approach to militancy neglects the social conditions that promote or impede it, and historical and empirical evidence does not support assumptions about the automatic emergence or mobilizability of worker militancy in response to employer offensives or economic distress.[37] Moreover, having argued cogently that the balance of class power had shifted decisively in favor of capital, Moody and other critics leave unexplained how militant worker confrontation with employers could possibly succeed.

Activists and writers of the "rank-and-file" perspective are strongly antipathetic toward the labor leadership, and indeed toward large and centrally administered labor organizations, fearing that these inhibit the model of "class struggle unionism" that they favor. It is more than a little ironic that such critics advocate a decentralized labor movement when a substantial body of comparative research indicates that, across the capitalist democracies, the most centralized labor movements are the most class-oriented and the most powerful.[38] None of this is meant to disparage militancy, union democracy, or even confrontation with employers, which are desirable or necessary for any labor movement. They do not, however, exhaust the sources of union power or constitute a viable strategy for labor under any and all circumstances.

Other writers on the left also questioned the political strategy of the dissident unions. Thomas Ferguson and Joel Rogers criticized their labor-liberal coalition strategy as outdated. They claimed that even at its height in the 1960s, the labor-liberal coalition had been unable to control the Democratic Party or effect a major redistribution of power in American society, and that the prospects for such a coalition were even less promising in the late 1970s and 1980s, given the decline of unions and liberals and the growing influence and shifting priorities of corporate and elite interests in the Democratic Party. They argued that it was more important for organized labor to develop a substantive program that would at once unify it and restore its public image as a progressive force, and recommended that the demand for a shorter work week serve as the core of that program.[39]

Ferguson and Rogers' critique of the labor-liberal coalition strategy was ill-considered. It devalued the achievements of the labor-liberal coalition of the 1960s. Remarkably, it ignored the fact that the decline of labor and liberal influence was due, in part, precisely to the fracturing of their coalition after the late 1960s and could therefore be restored only by rebuilding that coalition. Indeed, it overlooked the fact that, by virtue of its minority status, organized labor has no choice but to adopt a coalition strategy. Finally, coalition building with liberal groups and movements is hardly inconsistent with the development of the labor movement's substantive political program; dissident labor leaders rightly saw coalition politics precisely as the means to develop a union program that would regain progressive and public support.

The most sympathetic of the critics of the dissident unions was Stanley Aronowitz. He accepted the coalition strategy of these unions but argued that more was required. First, he urged the dissident labor leadership to more vigorously and forthrightly reconstruct the ideological basis of unionism. He argued that dissident union leaders should plainly declare their opposition to capital and its priorities, avoid integration into corporatist and neoliberal plans for management of the economy, and undertake the educational and other activity necessary to move their unions and members beyond the confines of "contract unionism." Second, like Ferguson and Rogers he also emphasized the importance of labor developing a coherent economic and social program based on its ideological commitments, though he recommended a much more expansive program than a shortened work week. Finally, Aronowitz recommended that unions and their social movement allies adopt a "party within the Democratic Party" strategy. The labor-liberal coalition, in other words, would have to constitute itself as an organized faction in the Democratic Party, with its own program and candidates, and contest for power within the party.[40]

The first two of these recommendations are perplexing. The Progressive Alliance, Citizen Labor Energy Coalition, and National Labor Committee would seem to indicate that dissident labor leaders were moving in precisely the ideological and programmatic direction that Aronowitz urged upon them. His few comments on these organizations suggest, however, that he found them ideologically vague and insufficient.[41] In any case, Aronowitz's final recommendation was correct in its implication that the dissident unions had not developed or pursued a "party within the Democratic Party" strategy to its fullest extent. Although PA, CLEC, and NLC all entailed a more self-conscious factional role for labor and its liberal allies in the Democratic Party, those organizations did not fully achieve or institutionalize a "party within the party" strategy, because they did not yield a durable factional organization with a formal party program, procedures for candidate recruitment, or campaign apparatus. The Progressive Alliance had the greatest potential for evolution into such a factional organization, making its early demise all the more significant.

Interestingly, scholars of American labor have begun to question why unions have not run their own candidates in Democratic Party primary elections, noting that failure to do so is a self-imposed limitation on labor's political influence.[42] As long as the current electoral system remains in place, this is a more promising approach for unions than formation of an independent labor party. But this point is also valid for the labor-liberal alliance, which must recruit and run its own candidates in Democratic primaries if it is to pursue a full-blown factional strategy.

Conclusion

Dissident unionism reemerged in the American labor movement in the late 1960s. A decade later, in a rapidly deteriorating political environment, the formation of the Progressive Alliance, Citizen Labor Energy Coalition, and National Labor Committee marked a new stage in the development of the dissident unions and their political project. Through these organizations, labor's dissident wing stepped up its efforts to revive the labor movement as a progressive social institution and the labor-liberal alliance as a vital political force. The Alliance, Coalition, and Committee also signaled the growing independence of the dissident unions from the AFL-CIO and its dominant unions. They developed a new political strategy for labor based on coalition building with new liberal groups and movements, factional politics in the Democratic Party, anticorporate reform and populism, opposition to Cold War foreign policy, and modernization of labor's political tactics.

The Alliance, Coalition, and Committee did not achieve a stunning reversal of labor and liberal fortunes. It is doubtful that anyone, including the dissident labor leaders who formed them, expected them to. But the organizations of the dissident unions were not without accomplishments, including modest influence on major public issues, the growing cohesion and assertiveness of the dissident unions, and a significant strengthening of the internal bonds and political capacities of the labor-liberal coalition.

Amid the ongoing decline of both union density and liberal electoral success, these accomplishments encouraged dissident labor leaders to continue their efforts to revive unionism and liberalism. In the second half of the 1980s, they formed new political organizations to develop and extend the political strategy of the earlier ones. The Alliance, Coalition, and Committee, then, were not a onetime effort of the dissident unions but instead laid the groundwork for later efforts in a continuing project of labor and liberal revival. By the 1990s, this project also led the dissident unions to intensify efforts to change and redirect the nation's labor federation. The internal politics of the labor movement then heated up considerably.

PART 3

The Past and Future of Labor-Liberal Politics

CHAPTER 9

Toward, and Beyond, 1995

Introduction

In October of 1995, John Sweeney defeated Thomas Donohue for the presidency of the AFL-CIO. Not only was this the first contested election in the forty-year history of the merged federation, but the outcome represented the victory of an insurgent campaign—self-labeled the "New Voice" campaign and later dubbed the "Sweeney Rebellion"—over the longtime secretary-treasurer and current interim president (since the resignation of Lane Kirkland, which was forced by the insurgents) of the AFL-CIO.[1] This outcome sharply altered the balance of power between the dominant and dissident wings of the labor leadership and led to significant changes at the federation. During the very public and highly charged campaign, the slate of insurgent candidates promised to reconstruct and revitalize the labor movement, and in the decade following its election the Sweeney team changed the organizational structure of the AFL-CIO and adopted new strategies to rebuild the economic and political power of organized labor.

The 1995 election and its outcome were the most important institutional developments in the American labor movement since the 1955 merger. They did not occur out of the blue; they were products of the evolution of the internal politics of organized labor since the late 1960s. A full explanation of the 1995 upheaval at the AFL-CIO must include the quarter-century-long schism in the U.S. labor leadership and the political organizations of the dissident unions, for they were an important historical source of and political influence on the "Sweeney Rebellion" and the new regime at the AFL-CIO. The genesis of the leadership change at the federation, the motives and goals of the insurgents, the course and outcome of the election, and the composition and strategies of the new AFL-CIO leadership cannot be fully understood apart from the prior efforts of the dissident unions and their political organizations to revive social activism, liberal politics, and union organizing in the labor movement.

By 1995, the split in the labor leadership between the dominant and dissident wings had a long and complicated history, the first decade (1968–78) of which was analyzed in Chapter 4. As this chapter will show, the split continued through the 1980s and early 1990s, though it followed a shifting course. In the 1980s, the differences between the two blocs of labor leaders narrowed and their relationship improved. In part this improvement was due to the stark new threat posed to the labor movement by the Reagan administration, which naturally encouraged unions to place greater emphasis on labor unity. But it was also attributable to the fact that the AFL-CIO, awakened by the threat of "Reaganism" and under its new and more flexible president, Lane Kirkland, finally began to accommodate the demands of the dissident unions for changes that would enhance the political and organizing capacities of the labor movement. To be credible, any effort to ground the 1995 earthquake at the AFL-CIO in the long-standing split between the Meany and Reuther wings of the labor leadership must acknowledge the reduction of factional hostilities in the 1980s, especially the efforts of the federation leadership to accommodate the dissident unions.

But, contrary to the judgment of some observers of organized labor, the breach between the Meany and Reuther wings of the labor leadership never fully healed in the 1980s, and the dissidents never abandoned their path of independent action to revive unionism and rebuild the labor-liberal alliance.[2] The pressures and incentives toward a rapprochement between the two wings of the labor leadership were counteracted throughout the 1980s by their deep and bitter disputes over U.S. and AFL-CIO policies in Central America and other foreign-policy issues. Moreover, however much Lane Kirkland's AFL-CIO moved to accommodate dissident concerns about union decline and revival, leaders of the dissident unions remained skeptical of the rival leadership faction and continued to act independently to rejuvenate unionism and the labor-liberal alliance. Thus, in the second half of the 1980s they established two new organizations, the Economic Policy Institute and Jobs with Justice, to extend and refine the political and organizing strategies that they had developed earlier.

Then, in the 1990s, yet another round of political setbacks pushed the factional split to the breaking point. When the hope inspired in the labor movement in 1992 by the return of unified Democratic control of the national government dissolved in just two years in a string of harsh political defeats, this split erupted into a major upheaval as dissident labor leaders finally concluded that the revival of unionism required leadership and organizational change at the AFL-CIO. The victory of John Sweeney's "New Voice" reform slate in the 1995 election represented the long-delayed triumph of the Reuther wing of labor in the battle for control of the nation's labor federation.[3]

The Sweeney regime, then, came to power at the AFL-CIO through a factional conflict over the revival of unionism, and over time it would inevitably be judged by its record on union revival. In the second half of the 1990s, the Sweeney leadership made important progress in reviving both the membership and the political influence of organized labor. But with the turn of the new century and millennium, the old pattern of union decline and political setbacks resumed. This led, just a decade after the Sweeney Rebellion, to another and even more serious round of disputes and division in the American labor movement.

AFL-CIO Accommodation of the Dissident Unions

The second stage in the decline of the labor-liberal coalition, in the years between 1978 and 1982, initially exacerbated the split in the labor leadership and led the dissident unions to establish new and independent political organizations. But when the outcomes of the 1980 elections escalated the political threat to organized labor, a different internal dynamic was set in motion within the labor leadership. The election of a deeply conservative and anti-union president and Senate majority in 1980 created pressures and incentives toward "labor unity" that affected both factions of the labor leadership, especially because this new political situation promised to intensify the employer attack on unionism. In the face of these threats, dissident unionists began to mute their criticisms of the AFL-CIO leadership, and the UAW reaffiliated to the federation in 1981.[4] At the same time, the new AFL-CIO leadership (Lane Kirkland having succeeded George Meany to the federation presidency in 1979), finally forced by the 1980 elections to face up to the declining fortunes of unionism, began to recognize the need for change to strengthen organized labor. The gulf between the two wings of the labor leadership narrowed.

This apparent rapprochement occurred on terms more favorable to the dissidents than to the Meany wing. For, given the prior strengthening of the dissident bloc in the latter half of the 1970s and the threatening new political environment, AFL-CIO President Lane Kirkland was strongly pressured to confront the decline of organized labor and to accommodate the views of the dissidents about how to revitalize it. During the 1980s, the AFL-CIO in fact took a number of steps to revive organized labor, and these encompassed several of the organizing efforts, institutional innovations, and political changes that the dissident unions had long advocated.

To begin with, between 1981 and 1983, the AFL-CIO increased the dues of affiliates in order to expand both organizing and political efforts.[5] The federation used some of this increased revenue to launch the Houston Project, a major organizing campaign—with a $1 million budget and over twenty organizers—that was jointly planned and carried out by the AFL-CIO and over twenty of its affiliated unions.[6] Intended to "crack the Sun Belt," the project was not particularly successful, among other reasons because of the deep recession and high unemployment that plagued the Houston economy just as the organizing campaign got under way.[7] But the Houston Project symbolized a new federation attitude toward labor organizing and was innovative in the significant planning, financial, and coordinating role that the AFL-CIO played in a large-scale organizing campaign.

In the early 1980s, the AFL-CIO also took steps to recuperate its political influence. In 1981 it staged a "Solidarity Day" demonstration in the nation's capitol against the Reagan administration's domestic policies that exhibited a greater openness to mass protest as a political tactic and that helped to improve relationships between the federation and the various liberal groups and movements that participated.[8] In the same year, the AFL-CIO initiated Legislative Action Committees (LACs), which mobilized rank-and-file union members to lobby legislators in their home districts, in nine congressional districts. An attempt to develop a capacity for grass-roots lobbying that the federation had previously lacked, the number and resources of the LACs were expanded later in the decade.[9] Also in 1981, the federation convened a Political Works Committee to develop a strategy to augment labor's political influence. Over the next few years, the AFL-CIO carried out the main components of the resulting strategy, including a substantial increase in the level of labor's financial contributions to (mainly Democratic) candidates and to the Democratic National Committee (DNC), securing expanded representation of union officials on the DNC, and procedures for a unified AFL-CIO prenomination endorsement of a Democratic presidential candidate (which went to Walter Mondale in 1984).[10]

In 1982 the AFL-CIO established a Labor Institute of Public Affairs to promote a more favorable public image of organized labor, largely through television advertising financed by the institute's $2 million annual budget.[11] The federation also instituted a program, designated the "face-to-face" or "one-on-one" program, to mobilize more union members as voters through direct contact with them by shop stewards and other union activists.[12] These and other measures strengthened the influence of organized labor in the national Democratic Party, but it is much less clear whether or to what extent they improved its position in national politics and policy making.[13]

Perhaps the best known of the AFL-CIO's efforts at revival in the first half of the 1980s was the formation in 1982 of a Committee on the Evolution of Work, chaired by the federation's secretary-treasurer, Thomas Donohue, to review the problems confronting workers and unions and to recommend solutions. Following an initial report released in 1983, the committee issued its second and more important report, titled *The Changing Situation of Workers and Their Unions*, in 1985.[14] The report analyzed the decline of union density and other changes in the labor market and workforce and recommended measures to promote the "renewal and regeneration" of organized labor.[15] It emphasized increased employer opposition to unions, the failure of labor law to protect worker rights, and the changing sectoral composition of employment in its explanation of declining union density, but it also called attention to problems in the policies and practices as well as the image of unions.[16] Thus the report recommended an extensive set of changes in the labor movement, including new methods to represent worker interests, ways to increase the participation of members in their unions, improved methods of public communication, new and improved methods of labor organizing, and institutional reforms ("structural changes") to make the labor movement more effective, including new guidelines and procedures to facilitate union mergers.[17]

These recommendations provided the framework for the federation's efforts at revitalization during the second half the 1980s. In that period, the AFL-CIO established procedures and offices to mediate or arbitrate disputes over organizing jurisdictions, so that organizing drives could proceed more effectively.[18] It organized an Office on Comprehensive Organizing Strategies and Tactics to help affiliates devise new methods by which to achieve union recognition or contracts from hostile employers.[19] The federation also set up a special office to assist nine of its affiliates in a campaign to unionize Blue Cross/Blue Shield employees. Along with its significance as an organizing drive in a major service industry, the Blue Cross/Blue Shield campaign was intended to serve, as Lane Kirkland said, "as a demonstration project for other multi-union organizing efforts."[20] In 1985 the biennial convention of the AFL-CIO agreed to a program to strengthen state and local central labor bodies and to increase the participation of local unions in them.[21] Finally, in 1989 the AFL-CIO established an Organizing Institute to recruit, train, and place skilled organizers and to provide technical assistance in the design and conduct of organizing drives. This was an institutional reform that involved the federation even more deeply in the labor-organizing function.[22]

These various efforts of the AFL-CIO in the 1980s to revitalize the labor movement through expanded organizing, institutional reforms, and political change clearly helped to bridge the deep divide of the previous decade between the dominant and dissident wings of the labor leadership. As the federation implemented the reforms proposed by the Political Works Committee and the Committee on the Evolution of Work, dissident union leaders increasingly acknowledged the change both in the direction of the AFL-CIO under Kirkland and, as a result, in their relations with the federation and its leadership.[23] No dissident made the point more clearly than IAM President William Winpisinger. The most unabashed critic of the AFL-CIO leadership in the late 1970s, Winpisinger described himself a decade later as a "team player" in the AFL-CIO, explaining that "the fact is, things did change. Kirkland undertook initiatives."[24]

But any reconciliation between the Meany and Reuther wings of labor in the 1980s was limited and conditional. It was so, first of all, because a fault line continued to run through the labor movement over the foreign policies of the United States government and the international operations of the AFL-CIO. Indeed, this was the central political and institutional conflict in the AFL-CIO during the 1980s, and although it was most intense in regard to Central America, it extended to détente with the Soviet Union, the nuclear freeze proposal, the level of defense spending, and the Cold War basis of U.S. and AFL-CIO foreign policy.[25]

So deep-rooted was the split over foreign policy in the labor movement that not even the end of the Cold War healed it. In the first major foreign-policy issue of the post-Cold War era, the 1991 Persian Gulf war, labor leaders divided yet again, and in the now familiar pattern. In a signed letter to the *Washington Post,* nine union presidents in the Reuther wing expressed grave reservations about the prospect of war in the Persian Gulf just days before U.S. troops were deployed there, while AFL-CIO President Lane Kirkland declared the full support of the AFL-CIO for the Gulf War as soon as the deployment occurred.[26]

Rapprochement between the two wings of the labor leadership was also limited and conditional because the dissident unions remained skeptical of their factional rivals and continued to act independently of the AFL-CIO. It was largely the dissident unions, not those in the dominant wing, that participated in the federation's new organizing campaigns and political programs in the 1980s, as AFL-CIO President Kirkland and Secretary-Treasurer Donohue could not elicit broad or deep support among affiliates in the dominant wing for the changes the federation had adopted.[27] Dissident labor leaders, though pleased with the growth of their influence and the new initiatives of the AFL-CIO, consequently retained a good deal of skepticism about the will and ability of the federation's leadership and dominant unions to revive organized labor. This is indicated by the fact that in 1986—a time well into the efforts of the AFL-CIO to accommodate the dissident unions—dissident labor leaders established two new organizations, the Economic Policy Institute (EPI) and Jobs with Justice (JWJ), to strengthen the political and organizing capacities of unions and to revive the labor-liberal coalition. In both cases, dissident union leaders acted independently of the AFL-CIO leadership and in ways the latter did not approve or support.

Together with the foreign-policy conflicts, the formation of EPI and JWJ shows the continuing division of the dissident labor leadership from the AFL-CIO and its dominant unions. These new organizations were successors to the Progressive Alliance, Citizen Labor Energy Coalition, and National Labor Committee, and they carried forward in time, while extending and revising, the political and organizing strategies of the dissident unions. They are therefore instructive about the further evolution of these unions during the 1980s and 1990s.

New Political Organizations of the Dissident Unions

Technically a tax-exempt, nonprofit educational foundation, in more common parlance the Economic Policy Institute is a think tank, a combined research institute and advocacy organization. Though it was founded by a group of economists including Lester Thurow, Ray Marshall, Robert Reich, Barry Bluestone, Robert Kuttner, and Jeff Faux, a number of dissident unions played a crucial role in the formation and leadership of EPI.[28] The State, County and Municipal Employees (AFSCME), Auto Workers (UAW), Steel Workers (USWA), Mine Workers (UMW), Machinists (IAM), Communications Workers (CWA), Service Employees (SEIU), and Food and Commercial Workers (UFCW) unions collectively contributed nearly half a million dollars to EPI—over half of its budget—during its first year, and more importantly made a five-year commitment to fund the institute.[29] This union money helped EPI secure its second key source of funds, grants from progressive foundations.[30] AFSCME President Gerald McEntee played the lead role in arranging union funding for EPI, and he and four other union presidents—Morton Bahr of CWA, Owen Bieber of UAW, Richard Trumka of UMW, and Lynn Williams of USWA—assumed one-third of the seats on EPI's board of directors.[31]

EPI was established to "widen the debate about policies for the new economic era America has entered."[32] As its president, Jeff Faux, explained, the institute was organized to compete with the conservative think tanks, like the Heritage Foundation and American Enterprise Institute (AEI), that had "dominated the debate and skewed it to the right."[33] In opposition to the laissez-faire and pro-business orientation of Heritage, AEI, and other think tanks on the right, the economic research and policy analysis of EPI would promote an active role for government in the national and international economies. The early research and policy agenda of EPI suggested an intent to address mainstream concerns about growth, productivity, and competitiveness, but in ways that would incorporate and validate public investment, high-wage employment, income redistribution, managed trade, collective bargaining, and other liberal commitments. In order to influence both elite policy makers and broader public debates, EPI published high-quality research by competent scholars, disseminated it through the print and electronic media, held periodic seminars and conferences on current issues and policies, and issued a regular series of briefing papers to national policy makers, citizen groups, and the media.[34]

EPI carried forward much of the political strategy of the earlier organizations of the dissident unions, though in new and different ways. In the first place, it renewed the kind of collaboration between unions and intellectuals that the Progressive Alliance had initiated, provoking speculation that it might revive "the kind of alliance between unions and academe that helped shape economic policy in the 1940s and 1950s."[35] Next, EPI operated to strengthen the labor-liberal wing of the Democratic Party in intra- as well as interparty battles. It was formed to counteract the growing support for market-based growth strategies, conservative fiscal policies, and anti-union competitiveness schemes among Democratic politicians, exemplified by the 1985 organization of the Democratic Leadership Council (DLC), which received substantial corporate financial backing. EPI founder Robert Kuttner, President Jeff Faux, and institute staff and affiliated economists regularly engaged in polemical and scientific debates with neoliberal ideas and

DLC proposals, consistently defending active government, collective bargaining, and redistributive policies as compatible with growth, productivity, and competitiveness.[36]

Further, EPI influentials like Kuttner and Faux were among the leading exponents of a left-populist strategy for Democratic liberals, and the institute proposed a variety of institutional and policy reforms that could be described as anticorporate or populist, including a single-payer system of universal health insurance, legal changes to facilitate unionization of employees, increases in the minimum wage and other measures to reduce income inequality, reregulation of the financial system, and reorganization of the Federal Reserve System.[37] EPI research and policy proposals also sought to integrate managed trade policy with strategies to promote economic development in poor countries. Like the National Labor Committee in its later stages, EPI argued for a regulated, rather than laissez-faire, world economy, one that would protect labor rights and social standards in the developed countries yet also ensure more equitable treatment of developing nations.[38]

Finally, union funding of EPI represented an investment in the modernization of labor's political techniques. Through EPI, labor finally achieved a place in the world of think tanks, which had become an important force in American politics.[39] Much more effectively than the Progressive Alliance, which was strongly attracted to the think-tank model, EPI represented the adaptation of the dissident unions to a political order that placed considerable weight on the deployment of expert research and advocacy in public and policy debates.

In sum, the Economic Policy Institute embodied a political strategy quite similar to that developed earlier by the Progressive Alliance, Citizen Labor Energy Coalition, and National Labor Committee. At the same time, EPI was a distinctive type of political organization for the dissident unions. It was a genuine think tank and had a singular focus on economic policy, as dissident labor leaders and liberal economists recognized that changed conditions required a new and active defense of liberal economic policies. Further, EPI was always more autonomous of its labor sponsors than were the earlier organizations. The fact that union leaders financed EPI and sat on its board of directors indicated the intellectual and political affinity between them and EPI's professional economists, not the "ownership" and control of the latter by the former.

The Economic Policy Institute has never had the resources that Heritage, AEI, and some other conservative think tanks possess, and it is difficult to evaluate the impact it has had on public policy. But over the years EPI produced a substantial body of high-quality research—conducted not only by the institute's staff but also by respected academic economists attracted to EPI's political mission or research agenda—and achieved a relatively high level of visibility and credibility in the national media, among liberal Democrats in Congress, and in public debates. The institute maintained its support among labor leaders and remains today an organization based on an alliance of unions and intellectuals. The share of its funding contributed by labor unions has declined from EPI's early years, as progressive foundations have supplied more of its finances, but both the number of unions that support EPI and the union share of seats on the institute's board of directors increased from 1986 to 2001.[40] Researchers have also circulated between the staffs of EPI and the AFL-CIO in recent years. To the benefit of organized labor and many other liberals, EPI secured a place for itself in intra-Democratic and national economic and social-policy debates.

Jobs with Justice was founded by Morton Bahr, president of the Communications Workers of America (CWA), at the urging of the union's organizing director, Larry Cohen.[41] Its purpose was to mobilize union and community support on worker-rights issues. Bahr initially established JWJ as a national committee of ten unions, but by 1991 it had grown to include twenty-five unions—the most active of which were CWA, AFSCME, IAM, SEIU, NEA, UNITE, UAW, UE, UFCW, UMW, USWA, Hotel Employees and Restaurant Employees (HERE), and American Postal Workers Union (APWU)—and a number of civil-rights, women's, senior-citizen, student, and other organizations.[42] Jobs with Justice thus became, like the Progressive Alliance and Citizen Labor Energy Coalition before it, a national coalition of dissident unions with other liberal groups, and one that was financed by its labor members.[43]

But Jobs with Justice was more than a national committee; it was also organized as a national network of local union-community alliances in support of worker rights. By the early twenty-first century, this network included union-community coalitions in over forty cities in twenty-nine states, apparently including some sunbelt states, an accomplishment that eluded PA, CLEC, and NLC.[44] Although close to the organizational model of the Citizen Labor Energy Coalition, JWJ developed an even more decentralized structure. Since it placed a premium on grass-roots activism, the role of the national JWJ committee was to provide financial and technical assistance to the local alliances of unions and community groups (of women, minorities, consumers, seniors, and others) and to coordinate their activity when regional or national campaigns on labor rights or other issues were undertaken.[45]

Unlike earlier organizations of the dissident unions, JWJ focused primarily on issues of direct concern to workers and unions, especially their rights to organize and to negotiate collective agreements. As CWA's Larry Cohen pointed out, JWJ was formed in response to "the difficult organizing climate of the late 1980s" and was intended to develop methods of "organizing the unorganized" and of "revitalizing unions."[46] The network of local alliances operated chiefly to mobilize the support of many unions and community groups in an area for a group of workers or a union engaged in a difficult organizing campaign or contract fight. This cultivation of cross-union solidarity and community outreach sought to expand the scope of conflict and alter the balance of power in such disputes, so that a particular union or group of workers could overcome the disadvantages that labor law and its administration impose on them. The national JWJ coalition also coordinated the local alliances in campaigns to revise federal labor law and to pressure regional National Labor Relations Board (NLRB) offices to administer existing labor laws more expeditiously and fairly.[47] Jobs with Justice operated on the assumptions that labor should provide opportunities for its community and political allies to assist it in organizing and contract campaigns, and that many community and liberal groups would in fact assist labor in these campaigns because they realize that strong unions can in turn provide crucial organizational and financial support for their causes.[48]

But Jobs with Justice also engaged broader economic and social issues in national politics. In the early 1990s, JWJ was deeply engaged in the battle for health-care reform as an advocate for universal health insurance. In the same period, it also supported the efforts of the National Education Association—through an organization called the Campaign for New Priorities—to shift federal spending priorities from military to domestic needs.[49] More recently, JWJ has devoted considerable attention and effort to "living wage" campaigns in a number of cities and states, battles over welfare reform, reforms of corporate governance, and the issues of global economic justice—trade, development, labor rights, international finance—that the National Labor Committee had earlier taken up.[50]

Given the limited attention that scholars have paid to JWJ, it is difficult to evaluate its effectiveness and influence. Its participation in high-profile industrial disputes, such as those involving Eastern Airlines in the late 1980s, and in national policy campaigns, like those for labor law and health-care reform in the early 1990s, did not achieve victories. On the other hand, at the local level JWJ coalitions mounted successful campaigns in aid of many different types of workers involved in labor-management conflicts, including municipal transport workers, janitors, cafeteria workers, newspaper employees, construction workers, office and technical employees in the publishing industry, telecommunications workers, and others.[51]

JWJ also made interesting innovations in the political alliances and organizing strategies of unions.[52] It joined with the U.S. Students Association to form the Student–Labor Action Project (SLAP), one of the most serious attempts by the modern labor movement to ally with college students and campus activism. Even more important, it pioneered the development of Worker Rights Boards in some twenty cities to facilitate organizing or contract campaigns. These boards include religious, academic, governmental, and other community leaders; though they lack legal authority, they investigate labor-management disputes, issue findings, and both cooperate with and pressure employers to resolve disputes with workers.[53] The contribution of Jobs with Justice to labor rights was recognized by the Institute for Policy Studies, which awarded JWJ its Letelier-Moffitt Human Rights

Award for 2002.[54] A decade earlier, the National Labor Committee had received the same award.

Like EPI, Jobs with Justice continued the political strategy developed by the Progressive Alliance, Citizen Labor Energy Coalition, and National Labor Committee. It built coalitions between unions and other liberal groups, pressured Democratic politicians to favor progressive policies, advocated populist or anti-corporate reforms (on issues like health insurance and executive compensation), promoted a foreign policy focused less on military might and more on the global market, and updated the political tactics of unions to include grass-roots activism and other innovations. But, again like EPI, JWJ also differed from the earlier organizations of the dissident unions, especially in its focus on the bedrock union issues of organizing and collective bargaining. The earlier organizations were premised on the assumption that coalition building with nonlabor groups and movements required an emphasis on broad social issues, but JWJ sought to build a broad alliance primarily around issues crucial to the growth and strength of organized labor. JWJ's direct engagement with labor's organizing and bargaining problems indicates that the dissident unions had become increasingly anxious about, and active on, the critical issues of union decline and revival.

With few exceptions, the unions that created the Economic Policy Institute and Jobs with Justice in 1986 were the same ones that had founded and led the Progressive Alliance, Citizen Labor Energy Coalition, and National Labor Committee. The formation of EPI and JWJ strongly suggests that in the latter half of the 1980s dissident labor leaders remained dissatisfied with the efforts of the AFL-CIO and its dominant faction to revive unionism and the labor-liberal alliance, even though they recognized and appreciated the progress that the federation had made during the decade. These new organizations clearly show that the dissident unions remained committed to independent action, to the political strategy forged by PA, CLEC, and NLC, and to the pursuit of union revival.

The Sweeney Rebellion and Regime

Although the factional split in the labor leadership and the political organizations of the dissident unions are central to a full understanding of the 1995 leadership contest at the AFL-CIO and the new regime that emerged from it, they were neither immediate nor sufficient causes of the upheaval at the federation. After all, before 1995 the dissidents took no concrete steps to frontally challenge the incumbent leadership for control of the nation's labor federation. Specific events of the early to mid-1990s triggered the insurgency.

The immediate cause of the 1995 upheaval at the AFL-CIO was a series of political defeats the labor movement suffered in the early 1990s. The elections of 1992 restored unified Democratic control of the national government for the first time since 1980 and revived hope in the labor movement of policy gains and improved organizing prospects. But within the first two years of the Clinton administration, organized labor suffered bitter defeats on the budget, health care, trade, and labor-law reform, and in 1994 the Republican Party won majority control of both houses of Congress for the first time in forty years.[55] This string of defeats, and above all the loss of what had long been labor's last line of political defense, Democratic control of the House of Representatives, precipitated the insurgent "New Voice" campaign against the federation's "old guard." As John Sweeney later said of the Republican capture of Congress in 1994: "We waited for the top leader of the AFL-CIO to raise his voice or sound his trumpet—but the silence was deafening."[56] Only then did the insurgents move in earnest to dislodge the federation leadership, and their election was clearly aided by the ascent of Republicans to power in Congress, which strengthened the case for a new political strategy for labor.

Another, related spur to the insurgency was the ongoing decline of union density, which fell from 23.2 percent of the nonagricultural work force in 1980 to 16.1 percent in 1990 and 15.5 percent in 1994.[57] In his post facto explanation of the rising dissatisfaction that led to the insurgency, Sweeney noted that "in the 1980s and 1990s . . . labor's share of the workforce dramatically declined, and with it our bargaining power, political clout, and media visibility."[58] In the 1980s, dissident labor leaders had been willing to cooperate with the established leadership of the AFL-CIO in an effort to improve the labor movement's ability to organize new members. But when the political defeats of the early to mid-1990s made clear to the dissidents that union decline had not only continued but reached a critical point, they decided that a new and more vigorous leadership of the labor movement was needed.

Although these were the proximate causes of the upheaval at the AFL-CIO, the history of factional division in labor, and the many political organizations of the dissident unions, clearly served as important historical sources of and political influences on the "Sweeney Rebellion" and the new AFL-CIO leadership. Their role and influence can be seen in four areas: the composition of the unions and labor leaders that initiated the insurgency; the support coalitions that emerged around the competing candidates in the 1995 election; the makeup of the leading personnel in the Sweeney administration; and the goals and strategies of the Sweeney regime.

First, the unions and leaders that initiated the insurgent campaign were drawn entirely from the bloc of dissident unions that had formed and led PA, CLEC, NLC, EPI, and JWJ. The co-instigators of the insurgency were Gerald McEntee, president of the American Federation of State, County and Municipal Employees (AFSCME), and John Sweeney, president of the Service Employees International Union (SEIU). AFSCME and SEIU were both core unions of PA, CLEC, NLC, EPI, and JWJ, and Sweeney and especially McEntee were personally active in those organizations. In early 1995, McEntee and Sweeney formed a "Committee for Change," composed of the presidents of eleven AFL-CIO unions, that publicly advocated a changing of the guard at the federation and eventually selected Sweeney as its nominee. The eleven unions on the committee represented only about one-seventh of all AFL-CIO unions, but they held a much larger percentage—close to a majority—of the votes to be cast for the presidency of the federation, because such votes are weighted by union size and the committee included many of the largest unions in the AFL-CIO.[59] All of the eleven unions represented on this committee had belonged to one or (usually) more of PA, CLEC, NLC, EPI, and JWJ.

Second, the support coalitions assembled by John Sweeney and Thomas Donohue during the campaign and election broadly reflected the long-standing division between the dissident and dominant wings of organized labor. By way of qualification, it should immediately be noted that the breakdown of the vote in the 1995 AFL-CIO presidential election did not in all cases follow the preexisting division between dominant and dissident unions. Several dissident unions, including such core unions of PA, CLEC, NLC, EPI, and JWJ as the Communications Workers, Food and Commercial Workers, and UNITE, voted for Donohue rather than Sweeney. On the other hand, several building trades and transportation unions, mainstays of the dominant wing of the federation for nearly half a century, voted for Sweeney over Donohue.[60] These unions voted contrary to their long-standing factional alignments for a variety of reasons, including the personal loyalties (which do not always coincide with political loyalties) of union presidents; the commitment of labor leaders to institutional protocol; internal union divisions over the candidates; concerns about the survival or unity of the labor movement; and possibly strategic voting (i.e., voting for the expected winner).[61]

Despite these important exceptions, the old division between the Meany and Reuther wings of labor shaped the alignments in the 1995 election. Taylor Dark's analysis of the vote shows that Sweeney's base of support lay crucially among large ex-CIO industrial unions, public employee unions, and the biggest unions in the private service sector, whereas Donohue's key bases of support were craft unions in the building, maritime, and food trades and in the communications and entertainment sectors.[62] This pattern closely corresponds to the analysis presented in Chapter 8 of the bases of the dominant and dissident wings of the labor leadership, and Dark himself concluded that Donohue depended disproportionately on "unions that had previously backed Kirkland and Meany," while Sweeney relied on "a coalition of 'outsiders' who had long been relegated to the margins of the federation power structure."[63] Moreover, the unions that joined and led PA, CLEC, NLC, EPI, and JWJ were critical to Sweeney's victory. Close to half of the unions that supported Sweeney had belonged to one or more of those organizations, and Sweeney won by holding a large majority (about two-thirds) of the core unions of those organizations while also securing the support of some traditionally more conservative unions.

Third, many of the leading personnel in the new administration of the AFL-CIO were recruited from the unions that had organized PA, CLEC, NLC, EPI, and JWJ. The victory of the insurgent slate meant that all of the top three executive offices of the federation were filled from these unions. Elected with Sweeney were Linda Chavez-Thompson from AFSCME, who became executive vice president of the AFL-CIO, and Richard Trumka from the Mine Workers union (UMW), who became secretary-treasurer of the federation. The Sweeney team also reorganized existing and created new departments at the AFL-CIO, and it usually placed people from PA, CLEC, NLC, EPI, and JWJ unions in top departmental positions. The director of the Political Department was drawn from the Communications Workers union (CWA), by way of Secretary Robert Reich's Department of Labor; the head of the reorganized Department of International Affairs was recruited from the Machinists union (IAM); the head of the new Corporate Affairs Department came from the Clothing and Textile Workers union (ACTWU); and the director of the new Working Women's Department was chosen from Sweeney's own union (SEIU).[64]

Further, Gerald McEntee, whom Sweeney acknowledged as the "political strategist" of the new regime, was placed at the head of the federation's Committee on Political Education (COPE).[65] Lastly, by expanding the AFL-CIO Executive Council by eighteen seats, the Sweeney leadership not only added more women and people of color to the council but also granted additional seats on it to several core unions of the dissident political organizations, including SEIU, AFSCME, UAW, and USWA. These appointments and other actions indicated that the new AFL-CIO would be strongly shaped by the dissident unions that had coalesced in PA, CLEC, NLC, EPI, and JWJ.[66]

Finally, and most important, the goals of the insurgents and the strategies of the new AFL-CIO leadership reveal the substantial influence of the Progressive Alliance, Citizen Labor Energy Coalition, National Labor Committee, Economic Policy Institute, and Jobs with Justice. A major goal of the insurgents was to develop and project a much stronger public voice for organized labor.[67] As Sweeney stated after his victory, the insurgents "yearned for a strong voice and a visible presence in the debates of the 1990s."[68] The new AFL-CIO leadership moved on three fronts—communications, policy research, and grass-roots mobilization—to accomplish this goal. It attempted to improve the public image and strengthen the public voice of the labor movement through media outreach, use of new communications technologies, expanded contact with intellectuals, and establishment of a new Department of Public Affairs at the AFL-CIO.[69] The AFL-CIO's new Department of Public Policy expanded and reoriented policy research in order to define labor's issue agenda, develop and promote progressive policies, and respond to conservative think tanks.[70] And the new director of the AFL-CIO's Political Department made grass-roots lobbying and electoral campaigns the basis of the federation's political strategy and strength.[71] Under Sweeney, the

AFL-CIO also placed more emphasis on the state federations of labor and local central labor councils as instruments of grass-roots political mobilization.[72]

Another fundamental commitment of the insurgents was to restore a broad social mission to the labor movement. As Sweeney put it: "When we participate in politics, we shouldn't act as one more special interest group. We need to act as a social movement that represents working people throughout the society—union members and nonmembers alike."[73] Among other things, according to Sweeney, this meant that unions had to meet the needs of different workers, reach beyond the workplace into the community, and bridge divisions of color and culture.[74] Once again, the new federation leadership moved on three fronts—a class or populist agenda, coalition building, and a new foreign policy—to realize this lofty aspiration. In pursuit of a legislative program that would mobilize unionists and at the same time win support from the broader working population, the new AFL-CIO promoted what its political director called a "working class economic agenda," focused on such issues as the minimum wage, trade, part-time or contingent work, and income inequality.[75] Emblematic of what one union official called the "new populist tone of the AFL-CIO" was the "Executive Pay Watch" page that the federation added to its Web site.[76]

Further, following his election Sweeney declared that labor would reach out to "our allies: civil-rights groups, women's groups, churches and synagogues, community activists, environmentalists," and he later added the "gay and lesbian and student and intellectual communities" to his list of labor's "natural allies."[77] Labor activists and journalists have since documented the AFL-CIO's efforts to align unions with Latino and Asian immigrant workers, social-welfare advocates, working women, and liberal intellectuals.[78] Finally, the new leadership of the AFL-CIO reoriented labor's foreign policy in the aftermath of the Cold War, something the federation's old guard had been unable to do.[79] The Sweeney team reorganized the federation's Department of International Affairs, put it under new leadership, and consolidated the old regional foreign-policy institutes into a new Solidarity Center. The international activism of the AFL-CIO was refocused on promotion of labor and human-rights standards in trade and investment agreements, ending abuses of labor rights in developing countries, and coordinating organizing and bargaining efforts with a wide range of unions overseas in order to deal more effectively with transnational corporations.[80]

These, then, were the elements of AFL-CIO politics after 1995: strengthening labor's public voice, developing its research and policy capacities, mobilizing grass-roots influence, promoting a working-class agenda and populist issues, allying with other liberal groups, and reorienting labor's foreign policy. They not only represent the same broad impulse to revive social activism and liberal politics in the labor movement that was evident in PA, CLEC, NLC, EPI, and JWJ, they also largely reproduce the specific political strategy developed by those earlier political organizations.

The dissident unions and their political organizations influenced the labor organizing as well as political commitments and strategies of the New Voice campaign and the Sweeney-led AFL-CIO. The New Voice campaign promised to aggressively expand union organizing, and after its election the Sweeney team attempted in a variety of ways to fulfill that pledge.[81] The post-1995 AFL-CIO expanded its Organizing Institute and created a new Organizing Department in order to train more union organizers and provide more strategic and technical assistance to union organizing drives, established "Street Heat" and "Union Cities" programs in order to mobilize rank-and-file unionists and municipal labor councils and their affiliates in support of organizing campaigns, and otherwise shifted federation resources toward labor organizing. It also strongly encouraged its affiliated unions to commit at least 30 percent of their budgets to organizing new members, to cooperate in multi-union organizing campaigns, and to develop and diffuse a "culture of organizing" throughout their organizations.[82]

Both the emphasis on organizing new members and many of the organizing strategies of the new AFL-CIO reveal the influence of earlier dissident labor leaders and their organizations. Beginning in the late 1960s, Walter Reuther and Jerry Wurf tried to prod the labor movement to expand organizing efforts, and they especially promoted multi-union organizing campaigns and a more central, directive role for the AFL-CIO in labor organizing. The initiatives of the Sweeney team described here faithfully adhered to this tradition of thought. Although Jobs with Justice developed a much more decentralized approach to labor organizing (though it, too, favored multi-union organizing campaigns), its promotion of cross-union solidarity and rank-and-file mobilization in support of organizing drives was also replicated by the AFL-CIO under Sweeney.

In sum, the dissident unions and labor leaders that had united in the Progressive Alliance, Citizen Labor Energy Coalition, National Labor Committee, Economic Policy Institute, and Jobs with Justice initiated the insurgent New Voice campaign, contributed strongly to the election of the Sweeney ticket, provided most of the leadership of the post-1995 AFL-CIO, and deeply shaped the political and organizing commitments and strategies of the Sweeney-led AFL-CIO. The PA, CLEC, NLC, EPI, and JWJ provided dissidents in the labor leadership with a history, extending over a decade and a half, of organization and collective action that built up the trust, cooperation, and cohesion that enabled them to mount and sustain an effective challenge to the long-entrenched leadership of the AFL-CIO. They also crystallized the commitments and pioneered the strategies that the dissidents proclaimed in the 1995 election campaign and then adopted as official policy when they assumed control of the AFL-CIO. The program and strategies of the New Voice campaign and Sweeney regime did not emerge out of thin air in 1995; they were developed over many years by the dissident unions in PA, CLEC, NLC, EPI, and JWJ, and by their predecessors dating back to 1968. The New Voice campaign and Sweeney regime carried forward and institutionalized the fundamental projects of the dissident wing of labor for a quarter-century: to revive unionism and rebuild the labor-liberal coalition.

The Record of the "New AFL-CIO"

In the years after 1995, the Sweeney regime kept faith with these projects of the dissident unions from which it sprang. The "new AFL-CIO," as Sweeney supporters called it, made substantial efforts to revive unionism and strengthen the labor-liberal alliance. But intentions and efforts are one thing, results another. So how did the new AFL-CIO fare? Did it revive unionism and strengthen the labor-liberal coalition, or at least make progress toward these goals? Here we consider the Sweeney regime's record on union revival; the next chapter examines its contribution to strengthening the labor-liberal coalition.

For the dissident labor leaders who gained control of the AFL-CIO in 1995, as for their predecessors, reviving unionism meant two things above all else: (a) strengthening labor's political influence by changing and improving its political strategy and operations, and (b) increasing union membership and density by expanding and improving labor organizing. On both the political and organizing fronts, the Sweeney regime significantly increased the level of activity and resources, made strategic shifts and innovations, and achieved some notable victories.[83] It thereby made important progress toward reviving unionism. But the political and organizing successes of the Sweeney regime were limited and largely confined to the late 1990s. In the early years of the new millennium, the old pattern of political setbacks and membership decline resumed. As a result, just a decade after the "Sweeney Rebellion," the American labor movement was beset by even more serious internal divisions.

As many journalists and scholars have concluded, organized labor's political influence increased after 1995, in large part because of the efforts of the new leadership at the AFL-CIO.[84] The Sweeney regime expanded and improved both labor's electoral activity and its lobbying and opinion-shaping campaigns, resulting in some important policy victories in the second half of the 1990s.

Post-1995 advances in voter mobilization and campaigning improved labor's electoral performance. The new AFL-CIO put more activists and resources into registering, educating, and mobilizing union members and others in union households to vote. Labor registered half a million new voters for the 1998 elections and 2.3 million new voters for the 2000 elections.[85] Although it was widely reported in the media, and by the AFL-CIO, that labor sharply increased the union household share of the electorate—the percentage of all voters who were members of union households—in the late 1990s, Richard Freeman has cast strong doubt on this claim.[86] However, the more reliable data that he presents permit a more modest claim: expanded voter mobilization by unions held the union household share of the electorate steady in the second half of the 1990s despite declining union density. According to Freeman's calculations, the union household share of the electorate in 2000 remained at about 25 percent, much higher than the 13.5 percent rate of unionization in that year.[87]

Moreover, the new AFL-CIO and its affiliates devoted much more money and effort to educating union and other voters on issues and candidates.[88] This strategy usually had the desired effect of increasing the rate of Democratic voting among union members and other voters in union households. Polls conducted for the AFL-CIO showed increased rates of Democratic voting by union members in presidential elections, from 55 percent in 1992 to about 64 percent in 1996 and 63 percent in 2000, and in congressional elections from 60 percent in 1994 to 62 percent in 1996 and to 70 percent in 1998 and 2000.[89] According to National Election Studies (NES) data, the percentage of members of union households that voted Democratic in presidential elections increased from 68 percent in 1992 to 75 percent in 1996, though it fell into the low 60s in 2000 and to 60 percent in 2004 (according to 2004 exit poll data; NES data for 2004 were not yet available). NES data on congressional elections show that the percentage of members of union households that voted Democratic increased from 59 percent in 1996 to 67 percent in 2000 and from 57 percent in the midterm elections of 1998 to 63 percent in those of 2002.[90]

Organized labor also increased the scale and improved the effectiveness of its campaign activity after 1995. The AFL-CIO and many unions spent more on media advertising on candidates and issues in both presidential and congressional campaigns, although such spending was scaled back somewhat after the $35 million campaign of 1996 in order to avoid backlash effects.[91] They also increased their financial contributions to Democratic candidates and party committees. According to the Center for Responsive Politics, labor political action committee (PAC) contributions to federal candidates increased from under $34 million in 1992 to $46.3 million in 1996, $52.5 million in 2000, and $53.7 million in 2004.[92] Partly for this reason, the Democratic Party and its candidates became more dependent on unions for money than they had been previously; for instance, Democrats in the House of Representatives received 45 percent of their total political action committee (PAC) contributions from unions in 1996, up from 32 percent in 1992.[93] In addition, the post-1995 federation and its affiliates deployed thousands of organizers and activists, both paid and volunteer, in successive election campaigns. Studies of union campaign activity have concluded that after 1995, labor's media ads, financial contributions, and campaign activists were more effectively targeted so as to maximize the number of Democrats elected to Congress.[94]

Labor's expanded and improved electoral activity after 1995 had a favorable impact on election outcomes. Its main accomplishment was to progressively reduce the size of Republican majorities in Congress in the elections of 1996, 1998, and 2000.[95] This *was* an accomplishment, given the advantages of incumbent candidates in congressional elections and the historical tendency for the party of the president to lose seats in midterm elections.[96] Organized labor also made important contributions to President Clinton's reelection in 1996 and to Vice President Gore's popular vote victory in 2000.[97]

Labor also conducted more effective lobbying and opinion-shaping campaigns in the years after John Sweeney's victory. Pointing out that "[t]he current national leaders understand the changed political and media environment better than previous leaders," Herbert Asher and his colleagues have shown that after 1995, organized labor "modernized its lobbying and communication efforts" by shifting from an "insider" to an "outsider" strategy that relied on mobilization of union members, grass-roots lobbying, issue advocacy, and coalition building.[98] They believe that this outsider strategy revived labor influence on public opinion, the policy agenda, and legislation, and point to labor victories on a variety of issues, including the minimum wage, portable health benefits, Medicare and Medicaid spending, workplace safety regulations, and fast-track trade authority, in support of their view.[99] In a detailed analysis of trade policy that confirms this view, James Shoch attributed labor's dramatic defeats of fast-track trade authority for the president in 1997 and again in 1998 to its new and effective combination of "Washington lobbying, coalition building, issue advertising, and grassroots mobilization," a product of the "revitalization of the AFL-CIO's political operations under its new president, John Sweeney."[100]

As just suggested, the new AFL-CIO's expanded and improved electoral and lobbying campaigns combined to increase support for labor among Democratic officeholders and to win victories for unions in national policy making. COPE scores, compiled by the federation's Committee on Political Education to measure the percentage of labor-backed bills that members of Congress vote for, provide evidence of growing Democratic support for the labor movement. From the 103rd Congress (1993–95) through the 105th (1997–99), average COPE scores for Democrats in the House of Representatives rose from just over 80 to just over 90 percent; after dipping into the upper 80 percent range in the 106th Congress (1999–2001), they again rose above 90 percent in the 107th Congress (2001–3).[101]

More impressive were the policy victories that labor won in the second half of the 1990s despite Republican control of Congress. The most striking of these were the 1997 and 1998 defeats of legislation that would have renewed fast-track trade authority for presidents, under which the Congress must vote on trade agreements negotiated by the president without having the opportunity to amend them first. These were impressive victories not only because unions and other opponents prevailed over the business community and major wings of both political parties, but because they constituted "the first time that a trade liberalization proposal had been rejected in the entire post-World War II era."[102] But as noted earlier in this discussion, organized labor also prevailed on other issues of economic and social policy, including minimum-wage, health-care, regulatory, and labor legislation.[103]

Especially noteworthy is labor's success at fending off Republican-sponsored anti-union legislation at both national and state levels. Although in 1996 Congress passed the Team Act, which in labor's view weakened the prohibition against company unions in the National Labor Relations Act, unions successfully prevailed on President Clinton to veto it despite strong corporate pressure on him to sign the law.[104] Labor's lobbying influence in the House of Representatives—with moderate Republicans as well as Democrats—also defeated the so-called Paycheck Protection Act, which would have obstructed labor political action by requiring unions to receive prior written permission from members before spending dues money on political activities.[105] Intensive mobilization of union and other voters subsequently defeated "paycheck protection" ballot propositions in California, Oregon, and other states.[106] Analysts attribute these policy victories largely to labor's more aggressive and effective electoral, lobbying, and educational campaigns in the years after 1995.

There is, then, good reason to credit the Sweeney regime for reviving labor's political influence. But it is also clear that this revival was limited and that some of its accomplishments were short-lived. The labor movement's primary electoral goal after 1995 was to shift majority control of Congress to the Democratic Party while keeping the White House in Democratic hands, and failure to achieve it (though through no fault of its own in the case of the 2000 electoral college vote and its aftermath) marked the limit of labor's revived electoral influence. Further, most of the policy victories that labor achieved in the second half of the 1990s were defensive rather than offensive (they protected past gains rather than won new ones), and of course labor also lost important policy battles in those years, including the bitter 2000 trade-policy fight over "permanent normal trade relations" with China.[107] Policy defeats became commonplace for labor during the first administration of George W. Bush, ranging from tax and regulatory legislation through trade and labor policies. Even labor's most stunning victory of the late 1990s, its defeat of fast-track trade legislation, was reversed in 2002, when the Republican Congress granted fast-track trade authority to President Bush.[108] Finally, labor's limited electoral gains through 2000 largely evaporated in 2002 and 2004, as President Bush won reelection and Republicans increased the size of their congressional majorities.[109]

This pattern of initial advances followed by reversals also characterized the new AFL-CIO's efforts to boost union membership through expanded and improved organizing. The Sweeney regime made several organizational and policy changes at the AFL-CIO that were intended to enhance the organizing capacities of the labor movement. Chief among these were expansion of the Organizing Institute, formation of an Organizing Department, creation of the "Street Heat" and "Union Cities" programs, shift of federation resources toward labor organizing, and promotion of multi-union organizing campaigns. In addition, the Sweeney regime persuaded unions to raise the share of their budgets devoted to organizing from 3 to 10 percent, on average, in just four years (i.e., by 1999).[110]

These efforts probably contributed to the growth of union membership from 16.3 million in 1996 to 16.5 million in 1999 and to the stabilization of union density at 13.9 percent from 1998 to 1999.[111] These late-1990s improvements in membership and density trends were the first such gains for the labor movement in two decades. They provided grounds for optimism about the prospects of the new AFL-CIO to revive unionism. With the turn of the new century, however, neither the advances nor the optimism were sustained. From 1999 to 2003, union membership declined from 16.5 million to 15.8 million, and union density fell from 13.9 percent to 12.9 percent.[112] This resumption of union decline might have been a cyclical phenomenon in part, shaped by the recession of 2001, the subsequent "jobless recovery," and a Republican National Labor Relations Board. But deeper forces were at work, as well. Quite apart from the business cycle and election outcomes, labor organizing remained extremely difficult in the United States, for the same reasons as before 1995, namely, employer opposition to unions and unfavorable labor laws (including their interpretation and administration).[113]

The new AFL-CIO and its affiliated unions responded to the resumption of union decline in the new millennium in two ways. First, they experimented with new approaches to labor organizing, or more accurately, made new or increased use of organizing approaches that had long been known. Two organizing approaches in particular commanded union attention. One continued to rely on representation (or certification) elections conducted by the National Labor Relations Board (NLRB) to organize new members but pressured employers to remain neutral during the organizing drives and campaigns that precede these elections. Another approach bypassed NLRB certification elections, seeking instead to organize new members by pressuring or inducing employers to grant voluntary recognition to unions upon showing that a majority of employees signed union authorization cards.[114] The key to both approaches is union pressure on or incentives for employers, either to remain neutral during an organizing campaign prior to a certification election or to voluntarily recognize a union as bargaining agent once a majority of employees has signed union authorization cards.

Unions have explored two ways—one political, the other contractual—of generating the requisite pressure on or incentives for employers. In the first method, unions persuade elected government officials to publicly intervene in organizing drives to pressure employers to remain neutral or to grant voluntary recognition. Such intervention has ranged from elected officials publicly exhorting employers to respect the legal right of their workers to unionize, or criticizing employers that violated that right, to the use or threat of officials' legislative, budgetary, or regulatory powers to compel employer neutrality or recognition.[115] At least one study has indicated that unions have a significantly higher win rate in certification elections in which elected officials intervened than in those in which they did not.[116] The more that government officials rely on union votes, money, and other resources for their election, the greater is the pressure on them to comply with union requests for assistance in organizing campaigns. Increased union political influence can pay dividends in organizing new members.[117]

The second or contractual method seeks to elicit employer neutrality or recognition through the process of collective bargaining. Unions that represent employees at certain of a firm's facilities increasingly use the negotiation of labor contracts as a means of organizing employees at the firm's nonunion facilities. They do this by winning neutrality or recognition provisions in the contract, either through the threat of economic pressure (e.g., a strike) on the employer or, more likely, through granting concessions to employers on other contract issues.[118] Unfortunately, as yet there seems to be little if any reliable evidence on the effectiveness of this method of organizing.[119]

Although the labor movement's first response to the resumption of union decline takes the prevailing legal framework of labor organizing as a given, the second seeks to alter it. The AFL-CIO and its member unions renewed the quest for reform of the nation's labor laws. Although by the late 1970s, dissident labor leaders had concluded that labor-law reform was necessary to any substantial revival of unionism, those who launched the "Sweeney Rebellion" tended to deemphasize it. Both in their 1995 campaign and in their early years at the helm of the AFL-CIO, the Sweeney team focused on what the labor movement itself could do to organize new members even in an unfavorable legal environment. That approach was dictated by three considerations: (a) previous attempts at labor-law reform had failed, including President Clinton's Commission on the Future of Worker-Management Relations in 1993–94; (b) Republican control of Congress after 1994 eliminated any immediate prospects for labor-law reform of the sort unions favored; and (c) labor in fact needed to expand and improve its own organizing efforts and strategies.

But even before union decline resumed in 2000, the Sweeney regime resurrected the goal of labor-law reform. Although post-1995 improvements in labor's organizing capacities, efforts, and strategies had led to the first union membership gains in quite some time, those gains had only stabilized union density. Union revival required a significant increase in the rate of unionization, and for that unions needed labor-law reform, though in the prevailing political circumstances it could be conceived only as a long-term goal or demand.

Thus, in 1999 the AFL-CIO launched a new "Voice@Work" campaign to establish the right of workers to form unions as "a basic human and civil right" and to build "broad public and political support for organizing."[120] The campaign included efforts to expose the unfair and illegal tactics used by employers to interfere with the right of workers to freely choose whether to join a union; to educate government officeholders and candidates about employer resistance to unionization and to persuade them, as a condition of union endorsement and support, to sign a "Statement of Principles" supporting the right of workers to unionize; and to enlist the support of religious, political, environmental, civic, and other groups and leaders for restoring an effective right to form unions.[121]

In the near-term, Voice@Work was to assist organizing campaigns that encountered stiff employer resistance, and in this respect it mirrored the approach of Jobs with Justice, expanding the scope of conflict—to include the public, politicians, and group allies—in organizing drives in order to shift the balance of power toward workers. The ultimate goal of the campaign, though, was labor-law reform. As the AFL-CIO explained, "In the future, we will ask them [elected officials] to change our nation's labor laws so that workers can join a union as freely as they choose a house of worship or a neighborhood in which to live."[122] By late 2003, Voice@Work began to mobilize support for a bill, introduced into Congress by Senator Edward Kennedy (D-MA) and Representative George Miller (D-CA) and titled the Employee Free Choice Act, that requires recognition of unions as bargaining agents when a majority of employees has signed union authorization cards.[123]

Both of organized labor's responses to the ongoing decline of union membership and density—experimentation with new methods of organizing workers and a long-term campaign for labor-law reform—are necessary and promising. They have not yet yielded gains in the number or percentage of organized workers, however; nor could they have, for by their very nature they are responses that require considerable time to work. But more time is just what some unions were not willing to grant the Sweeney regime. As was perhaps inevitable for a leadership team that came to power pledged to revive union membership and influence, when, after 2000, those goals seemed to be receding rather than approaching, it came under criticism, and stresses and strains emerged not just within the AFL-CIO but within the bloc of dissident unions that had put John Sweeney in power.

The recrudescence of internal divisions in the labor movement began in 2001, when the Carpenters union (CJA) disaffiliated from the AFL-CIO, its new president complaining that the federation "was frittering away his members' money on projects other than helping unions organize."[124] The Carpenters were not alone in thinking that the AFL-CIO could and should have done more to boost organizing and union membership. In the summer of 2003, four unions that remained affiliated to the federation, the Service Employees (SEIU); Needletrades, Industrial, and Textile Employees (UNITE); Hotel and Restaurant Employees (HERE); and Laborers Union (LIU), joined with the Carpenters in the New Unity Partnership (NUP) to cooperate on organizing. NUP criticized the record of the Sweeney regime on union revival and argued that the federation needed to be reorganized so that the union movement could be strategically and financially refocused on labor organizing and membership growth.[125] NUP's criticisms and reform proposals ignited an intense and healthy debate in the AFL-CIO over strategies of union revival or, as some argued, survival.

Although NUP disbanded, by 2005 it was reconstituted, with the addition of two large unions, the Teamsters (IBT) and Food and Commercial Workers (UFCW), as the Change to Win Coalition. In May, the coalition issued a proposal, *Restoring the American Dream: Building a 21st Century Labor Movement That Can Win,* for a "revitalized and restructured labor federation" that would make organizing for membership growth its top priority.[126] The proposal explicitly called for reform of the AFL-CIO and either could have been submitted for approval at the federation's July 2005 convention or could have served as a campaign platform in a contest for the AFL-CIO presidency, which was up for election at the convention. Indeed, during the year preceding the convention, there was much speculation that the coalition would mount a challenge to John Sweeney, though there were also fears that at least the Service Employees (SEIU)—Sweeney's old union, whose current president, Andrew Stern, had emerged as Sweeney's most vocal critic—would leave the federation, as Stern had threatened.[127]

In response to the debate over the future of the labor movement, the Sweeney regime had already issued its own reform proposal, *Winning for Working Families,* in April of 2005.[128] Although it patiently rehearsed the many changes and accomplishments of the Sweeney regime over the prior decade, it acknowledged the need for, and recommended, further reforms of the organization and governance of the labor movement and of its organizing and political programs. A serious effort at further change to promote union revival, the proposal was also clearly an attempt to placate critics and head off divisive convention debates, a challenge for the AFL-CIO presidency, and defection of affiliates from the federation. Then, the appearance of the Change to Win Coalition's reform proposal in May spurred the Sweeney regime to order staff reductions, departmental consolidation, and program elimination at the AFL-CIO, in order to streamline the federation and free resources for organizing, and to revise its own reform proposals in *Winning for Working Families.*[129]

These moves were intended to accommodate critics and preserve labor unity, but to leaders of the Change to Win Coalition they were "too little too late," a desperate attempt by an exhausted leadership to maintain power.[130] As the July convention neared, however, it was still unclear what exactly the new dissidents, as the media referred to them, would do. In the event, the Change to Win Coalition neither contested the AFL-CIO presidential election, as the dissidents of 1995 had done, nor attempted to win convention approval of the reforms it had proposed in *Restoring the American Dream.* No doubt it rejected these options because it represented a small minority of the federation's affiliated unions (though it contained a large minority of the federation's combined individual membership). Instead, on the eve of the convention, four of the seven Change to Win Coalition unions declared that they would boycott it. Two of the boycotting unions, the Service Employees (SEIU) and Teamsters (IBT), went further and announced their disaffiliation from the federation.[131] Within a few days, the Food and Commercial Workers union (UFCW) also disaffiliated, and the merged UNITE-HERE and other Coalition unions subsequently followed suit.

The boycott and disaffiliations elicited bitter denunciations from the Sweeney leadership, as well as expressions of concern from Democratic politicians and strategists. Unlike four of the members of the Change to Win Coalition, the rest of the unions that had supported John Sweeney ten years earlier remained loyal, and the convention returned him and his fellow executive officers to a third term and also adopted many of the reforms the AFL-CIO proposed in *Winning for Working Families*. Still, a decade after the Sweeney Rebellion, and on the fiftieth anniversary of the 1955 merger of the AFL and CIO, the federation fractured and the Change to Win Coalition moved to establish itself as a separate labor federation. Whether it will succeed and endure as an independent federation is an open question, but for now the American labor movement is divided into rival federations for the first time since 1954.

The causes and consequences of this division of the labor movement will be long and hotly debated. Different strategies of union revival, rooted in sectoral differences, were a key source of the schism. The most important strategic difference between the Sweeney regime and the Change to Win Coalition seems to be the relative priority that each attaches to politics and organizing as means to revive unionism.[132] During its first decade, the Sweeney regime emphasized political action to achieve a labor-friendly government that would in the short run improve union-organizing success and in the long run reform labor law. The Change to Win Coalition concluded that this approach had failed and argued that political change could not occur until union membership and density were considerably expanded by a more intensive focus on organizing.[133] The AFL-CIO leadership responded that politics and organizing were too interdependent for one to be accorded higher priority than the other, but relative to its new rival, it still placed greater emphasis on political action as imperative for union revival.[134]

Sectoral differences underlie this strategic split. The Change to Win Coalition is largely an alliance between large service-sector unions (or general unions with major service-sector contingents) like the Service Employees, Hotel and Restaurant Employees, and Food and Commercial Workers, and building trades unions like the Carpenters and Laborers. Service- and building-trades unions operate in economic sectors that have recently experienced consumer-driven employment growth and are unhampered by international trade competition. As a result, they may now be less dependent on government than other unions and more inclined toward a strategy that emphasizes organizing the growing workforce over mobilizing political influence. But unions cannot dispense with politics altogether, and the Change to Win Coalition seems to suggest that large service-sector unions have shifted toward the political model long associated with building-trades unions, for it insists that the labor movement must focus its program on "workplace-centered and worker oriented" issues and adopt a more bipartisan approach to politics.[135]

If service-sector unions have moved into alignment with building-trades unions (and the Teamsters), manufacturing and public-employee unions appear to remain at the core of the Sweeney regime. It is striking that no major manufacturing or public-employee union, such as the Auto Workers, Steel Workers, Machinists, State, County and Municipal Employees, or Teachers, joined Change to Win. These unions operate in economic sectors with stagnant or declining employment levels that are either profoundly affected by trade policy or directly dependent on government spending; they are thus the unions most dependent on political action and inclined toward the strategic approach of the Sweeney regime. For this reason, the Sweeney regime also continues to attach more importance to a broad labor political program that can attract liberal allies, despite preconvention concessions to Change to Win's call for a more focused workplace/worker program.[136]

Only time and debate will tell if this analysis of the division in the labor movement has merit. Even more uncertain than the sources of the current schism in organized labor are its likely consequences. Supporters of the Change to Win unions see not dangers but opportunities for growth in the split, and this possibility cannot be ruled out. But it does not seem likely. What remains most unconvincing in the Change to Win strategy is its claim that unions possess sufficient resources to make major organizing gains *absent labor-law reform* but lack sufficient resources to make the political changes necessary for labor-law reform.[137]

Labor-law reform is necessary for substantial union revival, because current labor law neither protects the right of employees to freely form or join a union nor accounts for economic changes, such as the growth of a "contingent" workforce, that have implications for labor organizing.[138] There is no way to achieve labor-law reform other than through politics, and the political resources of organized labor are at least as great as its economic or organizing resources. The electoral setbacks of 2000–2004 did not prove that AFL-CIO political strategy had failed, as Change to Win claimed.[139] They were in good measure products of the antiquated and undemocratic electoral college, an extraordinary intervention of the Supreme Court into the electoral process, the pervasive gerrymandering of congressional districts, and the terrorist attacks of September 11, 2001.

The battle for labor-law reform is a long-term one, and unions must do what they can to organize and grow in the meantime. The Change to Win Coalition has potentially useful ideas about how to do that. But the Sweeney regime does not slight the need for labor-law reform, political action, and a broad liberal program, and it now seems to hold these in better balance with the need to further expand and improve organizing efforts. Supporters of both sides can now only hope that they seek peace rather than wage war.

CHAPTER 10

The Labor-Liberal Coalition: Retrospect and Prospect

Introduction

Much of the political history of the United States since the late 1960s is encapsulated in the phrase "the decline of the labor-liberal coalition." But as long and deep as the decline of that coalition proved to be, it never reached the point of complete collapse, and from its onset, unions and liberals made repeated efforts to revive and strengthen their alliance. Those efforts, too, are part of the political history of this country during the past thirty to forty years, though they have not received the attention they deserve. In important ways, the Progressive Alliance, Citizen Labor Energy Coalition, and National Labor Committee, together with their predecessors and successors, did revive and strengthen the labor-liberal coalition. So, too, did the leadership change at the AFL-CIO in 1995. Convergent changes in the social composition of unionism and liberalism facilitated this revitalization of their political alliance.

Yet this revival of the labor-liberal coalition was limited, and in certain key respects the coalition's decline continued apace. It remains today in a weak and defensive position in American politics. Now and for the future, the two most serious problems afflicting the labor-liberal coalition and inhibiting its revival are the ongoing decline of union density and the continuing fragmentation of liberalism. A third problem, only recently emerged and of uncertain severity, is the division of the labor movement into rival federations. Until these problems are solved or alleviated, the business-conservative alliance will continue to rule the roost of American politics. They can be alleviated, if not completely solved, though it will be a long and difficult task. Over the past generation, unions bore much of the burden of rebuilding the labor-liberal coalition; in the future, liberals need to assume more of that responsibility.

The Limited Revival of the
Labor-Liberal Coalition

The Progressive Alliance, Citizen Labor Energy Coalition, and National Labor Committee, together with Democratic Agenda, Economic Policy Institute, and Jobs with Justice, collectively rebuilt and strengthened the labor-liberal coalition, but not to the point of substantially altering the balance of political power between it and the rival business-conservative alliance. These organizations were neither inconsequential nor earth-shaking; they made modest but important contributions to the revival of the labor-liberal alliance and its influence in the Democratic Party and national politics, but they did not overcome key limits on its power or reverse the deepest sources of its decline. Their experience suggests that a major revival of a powerful labor-liberal coalition—if such a thing is indeed possible—will be a long and gradual process, one that these organizations initiated but could not complete.

More important than this general conclusion, however, is to specify both the ways in which these organizations renewed and strengthened the labor-liberal coalition and the reasons why they did not effect a major change in the balance of political power in the United States. To begin, it will be useful to recall the distinction between the internal strength (or unity) and the external power of the labor-liberal coalition. The former refers to the strength of the bonds of mutual support between unions and liberals; the latter to the power of their alliance in national politics, which is always relative to the influence of the rival business-conservative alliance. Together with their predecessors and successors, PA, CLEC, and NLC enhanced both the internal unity and the external power of the labor-liberal alliance, but they increased the former more than the latter.

Given the conflicts that disrupted the labor-liberal coalition in and after the late 1960s, its revival required the rebuilding of trust and cooperation between unions and liberals. The organizations discussed in this book accomplished that task, and thus strengthened the bonds of mutual support between unions and liberals, to a considerable degree. Several aspects of these organizations and their histories suggest this conclusion. For one thing, these organizations represented six separate cases, all initiated within roughly a decade, in which unions and liberals directly allied or (in one case) cooperated extensively. Further, they united dissident unions with a variety of liberal groups and movements across a wide range of issues and policies, from party reform through energy, foreign, and economic policy to labor law.

Moreover, none of the organizations discussed in this book experienced serious conflicts of interest or principle between their union and liberal partners. Although some of them, like the Progressive Alliance, were short-lived, this was not because of internal conflicts. The tensions and disputes that did arise in these organizations tended to divide some unions from others and some liberals from others (as in the decision whether to back President Carter or Senator Kennedy for the Democratic presidential nomination in 1980), and they were managed. Finally, these organizations provided forums in which labor and liberal leaders and activists regularly met, discussed issues and strategy, and sought agreement. Their collective record suggests a rising level of mutual support and collaboration, and a widening scope of issue agreement, between unions and liberals after the mid-1970s, especially in contrast to the dominant trend of the previous decade.

Although all of the organizations discussed in this book helped to strengthen the bonds of mutual support between unions and liberals, it seems likely that the National Labor Committee made a particularly important contribution to this outcome, given the crucial role that Cold War foreign policy had played in fragmenting the labor-liberal coalition. Though I am unaware of relevant empirical evidence on this point, it might well be that the quick and forceful opposition by the dissident unions in NLC to Reagan administration policy in Central America went a long way toward repairing the damage that had been done to the progressive reputation of the labor movement by the AFL-CIO's vocal support for the war in Vietnam, as well as toward encouraging liberals to again view unions as worthy and reliable allies.

It is true, of course, that growing Republican control of the national government after the late 1970s, and growing centrist influence in the Democratic Party after the mid-1980s, strongly encouraged labor and liberals to reunite and collaborate. But after the trials and tribulations of the previous decade, unions and liberals still had to make deliberate efforts to support and cooperate with each other. In large part, they did this through the organizations discussed in this book. The result was an internally strengthened labor-liberal coalition.

These organizations also enhanced the external power of that coalition, though to a more limited degree. Along with strengthening its internal unity, which is an element of external power, they increased the political influence of the labor-liberal coalition in four other ways: (a) by providing more and better coordination between unions and liberals; (b) by building up the institutional infrastructure of the labor-liberal coalition; (c) by developing and testing effective political strategies for the coalition; and (d) by expanding the types of power resources that the coalition mobilized.

Once their coalition had fragmented, unions and liberals needed to develop new means and opportunities to coordinate their political activity if they were going to recoup their influence in the Democratic Party and national politics. They needed ways to hammer out common positions, plan unified campaigns, pool scarce resources, and cooperate in the various realms of political action (electoral, legislative, public debates, etc.). The organizations discussed in this book provided the principal means and opportunities for this kind of coordination between unions and liberals from the mid-1970s on. Of special importance were the efforts of these organizations to better coordinate dissident unions and liberal interest groups with liberal Democratic officeholders. Such coordination was one of the reasons that these organizations could exert some influence on issues like plant closures, energy costs, and Central America, and could contest and limit growing centrist influence in the Democratic Party.

These organizations also bolstered the political influence of the labor-liberal coalition by building up its institutional infrastructure, the ongoing network of organizations and capabilities through which the coalition competes in political and policy-making arenas. Of the six organizations discussed in this book, some were short-lived but others proved quite durable, and even those that disbanded tended to leave institutional legacies. The Citizen Labor Energy Coalition lasted five or six years as an independent organization, but it largely created the association of statewide citizen groups known as Citizen Action, which survived the passing of CLEC by some fifteen years and even continues, reorganized and renamed (US Action), to this day. The National Labor Committee ceased being a coalition of labor unions contesting Cold War foreign policy in Central America after a little over a decade, but it remains up to the present as a lively staff organization that has raised public awareness about the off-shoring of U.S. manufacturing jobs and the exploitation of female labor in the global apparel industry. Jobs with Justice has endured for nearly two decades not only as a national organization but also as a nationwide network of local union-community alliances. The Economic Policy Institute has grown since 1986 and secured a prominent position in the hotly competitive world of think tanks. Citizen Action/US Action, the National Labor Committee, national and local JWJ alliances, and EPI represent sustained institutional accretions to the labor-liberal coalition that expanded and improved its capacities for electoral mobilization, grass-roots lobbying, and the shaping of mass opinion and elite policy debates.

Yet another way that PA, CLEC, NLC, and the other organizations strengthened the labor-liberal coalition was by developing and testing such effective political strategies as coalition building, grass-roots activism, populism, and policy research and advocacy. All six of the organizations discussed in this book adopted at least three of these strategies, while practicing and experimenting with different versions of them. None of these four strategies was really new. All of them had been effectively used by ascendant corporate and conservative forces and had become requirements of national political influence. By adopting and refining these strategies, the organizations examined in this book helped the labor-liberal coalition to adapt to a new political order and to compete against the business-conservative alliance. As suggested in the case studies, the organizations deployed these strategies with some success.

Finally, the organizations discussed in this book augmented the political influence of the labor-liberal coalition by expanding the types of power resources that it mobilized. In particular, they enabled the labor-liberal coalition to mobilize grass-roots activists and issue or policy research—two increasingly important political resources—to a greater degree and more effectively than before. These power resources in turn improved the effectiveness of the coalition's electoral, lobbying, and opinion-shaping activities.

In these four ways, the Progressive Alliance, Citizen Labor Energy Coalition, National Labor Committee, and the organizations that preceded and succeeded them enhanced the external power of the labor-liberal coalition. That they did so is evident in the modest successes that these organizations achieved on the issues they engaged, from placing the social costs of plant closures on the legislative agenda to protecting low-income citizens against the full costs of energy deregulation, limiting U.S. assistance to authoritarian regimes and proxy armies in Central America, and providing an updated and intellectually credible defense of active government. As modest as these successes were, it is entirely possible that even they would not have been achieved absent the political coordination, institutional development, strategic experimentation, and resource mobilization that these organizations provided. In an era of labor and liberal decline, these organizations maximized the influence that unions and liberals could exert, however limited and defensive that influence remained.

Beyond that, they laid the groundwork for a more powerful labor-liberal coalition in the future. These organizations acknowledged the decline of the labor-liberal coalition and took the first steps to arrest and reverse it. Later organizations (like the Economic Policy Institute and Jobs with Justice) built on the foundations of earlier ones (like the Progressive Alliance and Citizen Labor Energy Coalition) but learned from their mistakes; experimented with new or different partners, issues, and methods; and discovered how to build more durable institutions. Collectively and over time, they developed some successful or at least promising coordination methods, institutional capacities, political strategies, and power resources. Conceivably, this kind of process could continue over a protracted period and lead to a substantially stronger labor-liberal coalition. If it does, much of the credit will be owed to the labor leaders who formed and led these organizations. As the liberal activist Heather Booth has said, "Bill Winpisinger, Doug Fraser, Jerry Wurf and others were remarkable. The roles they played took courage and a deep commitment to a progressive vision as well as to their unions and the labor movement. Their creating alliances between unions and the broader progressive community helped to herald in a new era of progressive politics and we still are building on their legacy today."[1]

If the organizations examined in this book succeeded at increasing the internal strength and the external power of the labor-liberal coalition, they did so only to a limited extent. They made modest or incremental gains in both areas, not the kind of major advances required to alter sharply the balance of power in American politics. What did these organizations not accomplish that was necessary for a more substantial revival of the labor-liberal coalition? They left four problems, or areas of continuing weakness, in the labor-liberal coalition: (a) residual liberal fragmentation; (b) relatively low coalition density; (c) insufficient power resources; and (d) lack of a permanent and comprehensive factional organization.

First, although PA, CLEC, NLC, and the other organizations strengthened the bonds of mutual support between unions and liberals, they did not fully unify or integrate the many species of liberal groups and movements, including organized labor. They did not, and probably could not, overcome the underlying fragmentation of liberalism that has characterized American politics since the 1960s. Through the late twentieth and into the present century, liberal groups and movements—labor, civil rights, feminism, environmentalism, community organizing, and others—remained socially and politically distinctive and organizationally autonomous, separate groups and movements with particular goals and priorities as well as shared and overlapping interests. If these groups and movements are now more likely to see their various goals and priorities as compatible and worthy of support, in large part because of the efforts of the organizations examined in this book, they still do not clearly treat the causes of other groups and movements as their own, and there is no overarching set of political principles or demands that serves to strongly unite them. In short, the internal strength of the labor-liberal coalition is still lacking, if improved, and to some extent the coalition remains as much or more an instrumental as an organic alliance, one that pursues the separate goals of the partners as much or more as their common or shared interests.

A second problem that the organizations examined in this book did not fully remedy was the relatively low density of the labor-liberal coalition, that is, the relatively low share of all unions or liberals that actively participated in and supported the coalition. This problem was most acute on the labor side of the alliance. The persistence of the split between the Meany and Reuther wings of organized labor, right up to the 1995 battle for control of the nation's labor federation, meant that a major segment of the labor movement did not participate in the organizations that sought to revive the labor-liberal coalition and, more generally, that many unions and the AFL-CIO leadership incompletely supported that coalition. However much the organizations discussed in this book strengthened the labor-liberal alliance, the persistence of labor disunity continued to weaken it by limiting union participation, support, and resources. For a time at least, the 1995 leadership change at the AFL-CIO went a long way toward solving this problem, as the Sweeney regime committed the federation to strong support for the labor-liberal coalition. It remains unclear what exactly the current division of the labor movement into rival federations will mean for the density of the coalition, but in general it does not improve its prospects.

The problem of the relatively low density of the labor-liberal coalition also existed, if less acutely, on the liberal side. Liberal interest groups like Common Cause, Public Citizen, and Natural Resources Defense Council, among others, did not join the organizations that sought to rebuild the labor-liberal coalition and generally showed little interest in the concerns of unions. Jobs with Justice was the first of these organizations to enlist liberal support for the specific institutional interests of unions, and this was an important step in rebuilding the labor-liberal coalition. But liberal interest groups of many kinds could still do much more to support an embattled labor movement.

Third, although the organizations that rebuilt the labor-liberal coalition mobilized new types of power resources, they did not significantly expand the amounts of crucial resources—votes, money, activists, offices—at its disposal, especially compared to the levels of those resources mobilized by the business-conservative alliance. They did not and could not do so due to the ongoing decline of both union density and Democratic electoral success. The unionized share of the labor force continued to decline over the history of these organizations, from about 25 percent in 1978 to just under 15 percent in 1995 and just under 13 percent in 2003.[2] To a point, unions can compensate for membership decline and increase their political resources and influence despite it, for instance by increasing dues and voter turnout among remaining members.[3] But the decline of membership and density limited the political resources that unions could *potentially* mobilize, and that was and is critical given the magnitude of the discrepancy in political resources between the labor-liberal and business-conservative alliances. Unions and liberals needed to mobilize much greater resources in order to compete more effectively for national power, but union decline reduced the number and percentage of voters that unions could mobilize and influence, the amounts of money that unions could raise from member dues and from voluntary contributions by union households to union political action committees, and the number of staff and rank-and-file activists that unions could deploy in electoral and legislative campaigns.

Democratic electoral success also continued to decline over the history of the organizations that rebuilt the labor-liberal coalition. After dominating presidential elections between 1932 and 1964, Democrats lost the elections of 1968 and 1972. Then, of the eight presidential elections held between 1976 and 2004 (inclusive), the Republican Party won five and the Democratic Party only three, despite the popular-vote plurality that Vice President Albert Gore received in 2000. Moreover, using a measure of presidential ideology very similar to that used by Americans for Democratic Action to rate members of Congress, Andrew Taylor found that the only two presidents the Democratic Party elected after 1968, Jimmy Carter and Bill Clinton, were "the Democrats' two least liberal post-war presidents."[4] Finally, although the number of Democrats elected to the House of Representatives and Senate fluctuated between the 95th (1977–79) and

108th (2003–5) Congresses, the trend was one of decline, from 292 to 206 in the House and from 62 to 48 in the Senate. This meant that the Democratic Party lost majority control of the Senate between 1980 and 1986 and of both houses of Congress in 1994, and it remained the minority party in the legislative branch of the national government for the next twelve years.

In sum, the power resources, from votes and dollars to activists and officeholders, that the labor-liberal organizations could mobilize remained limited because those organizations did not reverse the decline of union density or of Democratic electoral success. By way of qualification, it should be noted that liberal influence did increase in segments of the Democratic Party across the three decades from the 1970s through the 1990s. The percentages of Democratic voters and activists—the latter mainly convention delegates and party leaders—who identified themselves as liberal and/or held liberal views on policy issues increased over those decades.[5] Further, Democratic members of Congress, in both the House and Senate, became considerably more liberal in their voting records, as judged by the ratings of the liberal organization Americans for Democratic Action, from at least the late 1970s through the mid-1990s.[6] It is possible, but by no means certain, that the organizations discussed in this book played a role in this revival of liberal influence, although the rising liberalism of congressional Democrats was primarily due to the electoral effects of the Voting Rights Act of 1965.[7] But this growth of liberal influence in the Democratic Party was stymied by Republican presidents, moderate Democratic presidents, and the declining number of congressional Democrats—that is, by Democratic electoral decline and the growth of centrist influence in the presidential wing of the party.

Fourth and finally, the organizations discussed in this book did not institutionalize a factional organization in the Democratic Party by means of which the labor-liberal coalition could continuously and comprehensively compete with centrist Democrats for control of the party's machinery, candidates, program, and electoral strategy. Unions and liberals needed such an organization. Virtually from the moment that George McGovern lost the 1972 presidential election, moderates in the party organized to gain control of it. Their initial organization, the Coalition for a Democratic Majority (CDM), was not notably successful, but their second effort, the Democratic Leadership Council (DLC) and affiliated Progressive Policy Institute (PPI), organized in the wake of the party's next severe electoral defeat in 1984, proved more durable and influential.[8] Even before the DLC was established, but especially afterward, it was evident to labor leaders and liberal activists and politicians that they needed to organize within their own party to prevent it from tacking to the right. That was one of the reasons that the organizations discussed in this book were formed and was why liberal Democratic politicians formed the Coalition for Democratic Values (CDV) in 1990.[9]

But none of these groups proved to be the full-fledged and durable factional organization that the Democratic Party's labor-liberal wing needed. Some were ill suited to the task because of narrow issue agendas or memberships, others were well suited on those grounds but for different reasons were short-lived. Neither singly nor in combination did they establish a comprehensive and lasting institutional framework for factional politics by the labor-liberal coalition. This was probably most consequential in presidential politics, where Democratic centrists and neoliberals had their greatest influence, but it affected other segments of the party and other political arenas, as well. For the labor-liberal coalition, power within the Democratic Party does not guarantee influence in national politics and policy making, but its absence guarantees marginalization in the larger political system.

Democratic Agenda, Progressive Alliance, Citizen Labor Energy Coalition, National Labor Committee, Economic Policy Institute, and Jobs with Justice enhanced both the internal strength and external power of the labor-liberal coalition. They bolstered its political influence at the times they existed and contributed to a long-term rebuilding of the coalition and its power. But these organizations did not, and quite likely could not, solve all the problems and remedy all the weaknesses of the labor-liberal coalition, and as a result they did not affect a substantial redistribution of national political power. If a major revival of the labor-liberal coalition occurs at all, probably as a result of a long and uneven process, these organizations will have a strong claim to have initiated that process and taken the critical first steps.

1995 and the Labor-Liberal Coalition

The fortunes of the labor-liberal coalition are shaped by the internal politics of both unionism and Democratic liberalism. The 1995 leadership change at the AFL-CIO was a major development in the internal politics of the labor movement. What were its consequences for the labor-liberal alliance? The AFL-CIO leadership change further strengthened both the internal unity and the external power of the labor-liberal coalition but, once again, only to a limited degree.

The leadership change at the AFL-CIO was a product of factional conflict in organized labor, including the political organizations of the dissident unions. For the Sweeney regime, the political legacy of those organizations was a strengthened but still relatively weak and defensive labor-liberal coalition. Its own impact on that coalition is best examined by focusing on the four problems that the earlier organizations had not solved and that continued to limit labor-liberal unity and power, namely, the persistence of liberal fragmentation, the low density of the labor-liberal coalition, the comparatively meager power resources it mobilized, and the lack of a full-scale and durable labor-liberal factional organization in the Democratic Party.

The Sweeney victory in the 1995 AFL-CIO presidential election further strengthened the internal unity of the labor-liberal coalition. The earlier organizations of the dissident unions had already done this, but it made a difference when the dissidents gained control of the nation's labor federation, the principal voice of the labor movement in public affairs. The post-1995 AFL-CIO largely made good on John Sweeney's pledge to ally more strongly with a variety of liberal groups and movements, and this helped dissipate lingering liberal hostility or skepticism toward the AFL-CIO. Considering how disruptive of the labor-liberal coalition foreign policy had been over the past quarter-century, it was particularly important that after 1995, the official foreign-policy positions of organized labor conformed much more closely to those of liberals. The Sweeney regime, moreover, was much more openly and actively supportive of two liberal causes, immigrant and gay and lesbian rights, than the earlier political organizations of the dissident unions had been. But although the leadership change at the federation further strengthened the bonds of mutual support between labor and liberals in these ways, it did not resolve the underlying fragmentation of liberal groups and movements any more than the earlier organizations of the dissident unions.

The leadership change at the AFL-CIO probably had its greatest impact on the labor-liberal coalition by increasing its density. From the late 1960s on, the opposition of George Meany and Lane Kirkland to liberal foreign policies and party strategies meant that the AFL-CIO did not fully support the labor-liberal alliance. The Sweeney regime placed the nation's labor federation much more solidly and completely behind the labor-liberal coalition. In addition, after the leadership change, factional conflict initially subsided. Thus, after 1995 a relatively united labor movement strongly supported the alliance with liberals, for the first time in at least a quarter-century. The greater density of the labor-liberal coalition meant that it had greater resources at its disposal, although they continued to lag well behind those of the rival alliance. Of course, after 1995, many individual unions still did little to support or participate in the labor-liberal alliance. More recently, and ominously, the redivision of the labor movement into separate federations raises the question of whether part of it might opt out of, or reduce its commitment to, that alliance, decreasing its density yet again.

The consequences of the power shift at the AFL-CIO for the problem of the labor-liberal coalition's comparatively meager power resources were mixed. On the one hand, by aligning the labor federation much more closely with liberal politics, and by mobilizing labor's political resources more effectively, the Sweeney regime increased the power resources at the disposal of the labor-liberal coalition. The Sweeney leadership increased labor's campaign contributions and media spending, its rates of voter turnout and Democratic voting, and the numbers of activists it deployed in electoral and legislative campaigns, and these increased resources supported a broad range of liberal candidates and policies. On the other hand, the inability of the Sweeney regime to increase union membership and density—or even to halt their decline—meant that the post-1995 labor movement did not succeed, any more than the earlier organizations of the dissident unions, at substantially increasing the power resources mobilized by the labor-liberal coalition, especially in comparison with the resource-rich business-conservative alliance.

Finally, the leadership change at the AFL-CIO helped to remedy the problem of the lack of a labor-liberal factional organization in the Democratic Party. In 1996 a new labor-liberal factional organization, called the Campaign for America's Future (CAF), was organized. The AFL-CIO did not take the initiative in launching CAF, but those who did were encouraged to do so by the changing of the guard at the Federation, and John Sweeney and many other union leaders took seats on CAF's advisory board and provided some of the organization's finances. In existence nearly a decade now, CAF remains a vigorous labor-liberal caucus in the Democratic Party. How effective it has been as a factional organization, and how it has dealt with the problem of liberal fragmentation, are issues in need of research and analysis. But the Campaign for America's Future is the closest thing to a full-scale and durable factional organization in the Democratic Party that the labor-liberal coalition has yet produced, and the Sweeney leadership at the AFL-CIO was one of the reasons why. The Campaign for America's Future will be discussed more fully at the end of this chapter.

All told, when the Reuther wing of American unionism gained control of the AFL-CIO, it further strengthened the labor-liberal coalition, chiefly by aligning the nation's labor federation more solidly with liberal politics, increasing the power resources that the labor movement put at the coalition's disposal, and helping to form a labor-liberal factional organization in the Democratic Party. But the post-1995 AFL-CIO was not able, any more than the earlier organizations of the dissident labor leadership, to solve the deepest problems of the labor-liberal coalition, especially the fragmentation of liberalism and the decline of unionism, which continue to limit, respectively, the internal unity and the external influence of the coalition. The shift of power in the U.S. labor movement incrementally strengthened the labor-liberal coalition, but in the only way that counts—compared to the rival business-conservative alliance—that coalition remains weak and defensive.

The Changing Social Foundations of Labor-Liberal Politics

After the late 1970s, both the internal unity and, to a lesser degree, the external power of the labor-liberal coalition were revived and strengthened, but only within the limits of ongoing union decline, liberal fragmentation, and Democratic electoral defeat. The trend of labor-liberal politics over the past quarter-century was one of incremental advances amidst continuing weakness.

Did this trend have a social basis or a sociological explanation? I have argued that the decline of the labor-liberal coalition, especially in its first phase between 1968 and 1972, was rooted in the diverging social bases of unionism and liberalism in that era, as youth, blacks, women, and educated middle-class professionals recomposed the liberal wing of the Democratic Party. By the same logic, the limited revival and incremental strengthening of the labor-liberal coalition over the last quarter-century reflected a *partial reconvergence* of the social bases of the labor movement and Democratic liberalism in this period, as organized labor incorporated more of the social groups that earlier constituted New Politics liberalism. Empirical evidence for these claims is provided in Tables 1–4.

Tables 1 and 2 summarize information contained in Tables 3 and 4, which are in the appendix. Tables 3 and 4 use data from the American National Election Studies (ANES), 1948–2002 Cumulative Data File, to compare the social characteristics of union members with those of Democratic voters and self-identified liberals in 1952, 1972, and 1992. Table 3 provides the percentages of union members and of Democratic voters who were 17–24 years old, black, female, suburbanites, professionals, in the 34th–67th (or middle) percentile of family income, and college educated in each of those three years. Table 4 contains the percentages of union members and of self-identified liberals that possessed those characteristics in 1972 and 1992 (ANES did not collect data on self-identified liberals in 1952). Data on both Democratic voters and self-identified liberals are included because they are not identical groups and because both the labor-liberal coalition and the labor-Democratic Party alliance are important.

Tables 1 and 2 summarize this data in a way that more readily allows us to compare the social characteristics of union members and of Democratic voters across the years 1952, 1972, and 1992, and those of union members and of self-identified liberals across the years 1972 and 1992. They show the differences, given in percentage points, in the percentages of union members and Democratic voters, or of union members and self-identified liberals, that possessed the vari-

Table 1. Differences (in Percentage Points) in the
Percentages of Union Members and Democrats with
Selected Social and Demographic Characteristics

	1952	1972	1992
Age (17–24)	1.9	4.8	3.6
Black	2.3	9.4	6.7
Female	33.9	34.1	25.6
Suburban	1.5	4.6	8.1
Professional	4.3	12.6	2.9
Income (34th–67th Percentile)	4.4	11.2	8.4
College Degree	3.7	12.8	6.6

Table 2. Differences (in Percentage Points) in the
Percentages of Union Members and Liberals with Selected
Social and Demographic Characteristics

	1972	1992
Age (17–24)	14.4	6.6
Black	4.2	0.7
Female	27.5	20.5
Suburban	0.6	8.8
Professional	20.0	10.6
Income (34th–67th Percentile)	13.6	8.0
College Degree	20.7	17.7

Source: American National Election Studies, 1948–2002
Cumulative Data File

ous social and demographic characteristics in the relevant years. For example, Table 1 indicates that in 1952 there was a difference of 1.9 percentage points in the percentages of union members and of Democratic voters who were seventeen to twenty-four years of age. (The 1.9 percentage point difference is arrived at by subtracting the 4.6 percent of Democratic voters from the 6.5 percent of union members who were seventeen to twenty-four years of age in 1952, according to the data in Table 3.)

Tables 1 and 2 are meant to show whether, over time, the social composition of unions and of Democrats or liberals diverged or converged. If the percentage-point difference between union members and Democratic voters, or between union members and self-identified liberals, increases from one year to the next on a given social or demographic characteristic, then unions and Democrats or liberals diverged on that characteristic; if the percentage-point difference decreases, then they converged. To judge whether the social composition of union members and of Democrats or liberals diverged or converged in general or overall, we must of course look at all of the selected characteristics.

The tables clearly indicate that the social composition of union members and Democratic voters diverged between 1952 and 1972 and that the social composition of union members and of both Democratic voters and self-identified liberals converged between 1972 and 1992. Comparing 1952 and 1972, we see that the percentage-point differences between union members and Democratic voters increased on every one of the selected social or demographic characteristics, although the increase on gender was small. By contrast, comparing 1972 with 1992 shows that the percentage-point differences between union members and Democratic voters decreased on every characteristic except suburban residence. Likewise, between 1972 and 1992, the percentage-point differences between union members and self-identified liberals decreased on every characteristic except suburban residence. So, as has often been claimed in this book and elsewhere, unionists and Democrats became socially less similar between 1952 and 1972, whereas unionists, Democrats, and liberals became socially more similar between 1972 and 1992. The divergent social bases of unionism and Democratic liberalism strained their alliance in the earlier period, but their reconvergent social bases strengthened it in the later period.

The underlying data in Tables 3 and 4 also indicate that the divergence in the social bases of unionism and Democratic liberalism in the 1952–72 period was due to the greater increase of youth, blacks, and college-educated professionals among Democratic voters than among union members and that the reconvergence of their social bases in the 1972–92 period was due to the greater increase of blacks, females, and college-educated professionals among union members than among either Democratic voters or self-identified liberals. (For example, seventeen-to-twenty-four-year-olds increased by 13.6 percentage points as a share of Democratic voters, but only by 6.9 percentage points as a share of union members, between 1952 and 1972; on the other hand, those with college degrees increased by 13.3 percentage points as a share of union members, but only by 7.1 percentage points as a share of Democratic voters, between 1972 and 1992.) In other words, in the 1972–92 period, the labor movement finally incorporated on a substantial scale many of the social groups that had recomposed Democratic liberalism in the previous twenty-year period, so that it more closely resembled the social composition of the liberal wing of the Democratic Party in 1992 than it had in 1972.

Prospects of the Labor-Liberal Coalition

The data presented above show that differences remain in the social composition of organized labor and Democratic liberalism, despite the trend of reconvergence. These differences might limit the internal unity, and thereby the political power, of the labor-liberal coalition. But the most serious social discontinuities between unions and liberal Democrats have by now been reduced if not overcome, and their respective social bases will never be perfectly congruent. The future prospects of the labor-liberal coalition rest more crucially on two other problems: union decline and liberal fragmentation. The problem of union decline was considered in the previous chapter, which concluded that reform of the nation's labor laws is necessary for a substantial revival of union membership and density. Few things would increase the political power of the labor-liberal coalition more than a sharp upturn in union density. But the future of that coalition also depends on whether the fragmentation of liberalism, a fundamental fact of American politics since the 1960s, can be further alleviated.

Since at least the late 1970s, liberal thinkers and activists have worried about the fragmentation of liberalism, assuming that it weakens liberals in ideological and political competition, and searched for ways to overcome it. It has become common among scholars and activists to analyze the fragmentation of liberalism by means of various binary distinctions: New Deal versus New Politics liberalism, materialist versus postmaterialist left, class versus identity politics, and others. Whatever the differences among these formulations, their shared assumption of two different and rival strands of liberalism understates the extent of liberal fragmentation. There are at least three distinct varieties of liberalism today: New Deal (or labor) liberalism, civil-rights liberalism (which might also be called multicultural liberalism or identity politics), and public-interest liberalism. I leave aside a fourth variant, neoliberalism, which is a centrist current among Democratic Party elites that lacks strong claim to the mantle of modern reform liberalism.

New Deal liberalism is commonly and rightly understood as the commitment to active government—active use of the fiscal and regulatory authority of the state—to manage the economy and provide social welfare. Developed during the economic crisis of the 1930s, but with sources in earlier Populist and Progressive movements, it sought to promote relief and recovery from the Great Depression and to effect economic, social, and political reforms. New Deal liberalism established, or at least initiated the development of, a national regulatory-welfare state to achieve stable economic growth and a greater degree of economic security and equality among citizens. In the process, it altered power relations and redressed class inequalities in both the private economy and the public sphere, most notably by facilitating the unionization of industrial workers and recognizing social rights to employment, insurance, and other elements of a decent standard of living. In the 1930s and 1940s, New Deal liberalism was at once deeply time-bound and surprisingly anticipatory. Its social policies reflected the racial and gender exclusions of the era, but it also contained many elements of social and cultural modernism and prefigured the later development of both civil-rights and public-interest (environmental and consumer) liberalism. From the mid-1930s on, decisive social and institutional support for New Deal liberalism was provided by wage earners and organized labor, especially its industrial unionist wing.[10]

However much it was transformed or moderated, New Deal liberalism remained the dominant public philosophy for a generation after the 1930s and continues today as a weakened and embattled yet still influential approach to government. Now seven decades past its formative period, it might well be referred to as *labor liberalism* for two reasons. It relies even more heavily than in the past on the institutional support and advocacy of organized labor and of intellectuals and political activists allied to it. And unions took up much of the task of modifying and updating New Deal liberalism as time passed. The Reuther wing of the labor movement in particular sought to unite and adapt the New Deal tradition to new social movements and New Politics liberals in the 1960s and 1970s and to the end of the Cold War and the globalization of the economy in the 1980s and 1990s. For example, it supported the extension of active government to affirmative-action programs for minorities and women and to managed trade and international-labor standards in world markets. Labor liberalism today generally advocates active government, cultural pluralism, and regulation of the global economy. Its bedrock remains the use of the state to regulate the private economy and to promote economic security and social equality. Because unions defend active government as necessary to ensure the economic well-being of "working people" or "working families," labor liberalism represents a form of class politics.[11]

Civil-rights liberalism emerged with the black civil-rights movement of the 1950s and 1960s, which sought the destruction of the Jim Crow system in the South, the prohibition of racially discriminatory behavior (in education, housing, and employment) throughout the nation, and the integration of minorities into the institutions and opportunities of American society. The core demand of this movement was for equal civil rights for African Americans, a demand that was understood to promote equality, liberty, inclusion, and recognition. The initial judicial and legislative accomplishments of the civil-rights movement, *Brown v. Board of Education* in 1954, the Civil Rights Act of 1964, and the Voting Rights Act of 1965, were victories for equal civil rights and legal equality. But the failure of these policies to achieve economic and social (as distinct from legal) equality led to an evolution from a nondiscrimination model to an affirmative action model of civil-rights policy, which established preferences (in education and employment) for minorities and other protected groups that had suffered discrimination in the past or "adverse impacts" in the present. As affirmative-action programs elicited a white/conservative backlash, and even criticism from some liberals, they were retrenched, but they remain, together with the classic nondiscrimination laws and rulings, the cornerstone of civil-rights policy.[12]

Civil-rights liberalism quickly expanded well beyond its original African-American social base and political organizations. The success of the black civil-rights movement in obtaining desegregation rulings, antidiscrimination legislation, antipoverty and affirmative-action programs, and cultural recognition led other groups that had suffered discrimination or disadvantage—women, Hispanic and Asian Americans, gays and lesbians, the disabled—to model their demands, strategies, and organizations on those of black Americans. Broadly speaking, then, civil-rights liberalism consists of demands for equal civil rights, affirmative-action programs, and cultural recognition by minorities or subaltern groups, and has been and is the primary political orientation of African, Hispanic, and Asian Americans; women; gays and lesbians; and others. Indeed, the development of civil-rights liberalism included an even broader "rights revolution" that not only extended existing rights to excluded groups but created—through judicial as well as legislative action—new rights, including those to privacy and to safe consumer products and workplaces.[13]

Throughout its different phases and expansion, the fundamental commitment of civil-rights liberalism was to extend the legal and regulatory authority of the national government over both public and private institutions and behavior in order to ensure equality, liberty, inclusion, and recognition for a wider range of social groups. Because these groups organize politically and assert demands based on their particular social identities (of race, ethnicity, gender, sexual orientation), civil-rights liberalism is often referred to as *identity politics*. And, because this variant of contemporary liberalism values the diversity of cultures or ways of life among these and other groups, or even denies the reality or value of a common nationhood in the United States, it is also sometimes referred to as *multicultural liberalism*.

Public-interest liberalism maintains that government should be responsive to the public interest as it emerges from a democratic process of deliberation and debate, not promote special interests or passively accept market outcomes. It regards both corporate business and bureaucratic government as threats to the public interest and aims to reform and hold accountable both sets of institutions. Strongly reminiscent of, and to some extent modeled on, the Progressive movement of the first two decades of the twentieth century, public-interest liberalism arose between the mid-1960s and mid-1970s with the formation of three inter-related sets of interest groups: environmental, consumer, and government or political-reform groups like Common Cause and Public Citizen. These groups have always drawn their membership and support principally from the white, well-educated, professional middle and upper-middle classes. They claim to represent not the private or special interests of particular occupations or identities, but public interests—in a healthy natural environment, safe consumer products, and an accountable and responsive government—that were traditionally unorganized and unrepresented. The mission of these public-interest groups has been to achieve "civic balance" by organizing and representing these public interests as an effective counterweight to the private or special interests that had long dominated policy making and administration.[14]

In the 1960s and 1970s, public-interest groups and their allies in Congress enacted environmental, consumer, and government (including campaign finance) reform legislation that significantly expanded the regulatory authority of the national government over the economic activity of private business and the political activity of special interests. Public-interest liberalism added a new layer of regulatory agencies (Environmental Protection Agency, Occupational Safety and Health Administration, Consumer Product Safety Commission, Federal Election Commission) to national government yet harbored a deep distrust of bureaucratic government as susceptible to "capture" by the very firms and interests it is supposed to regulate. It sought to ensure the responsiveness of regulatory agencies to the public interest by organizing public-interest groups as a counterweight to special-interest influence, securing the right of private citizens to sue regulatory agencies, placing public-interest representatives within these agencies, and winning protections for agency whistle-blowers. A potent force between 1965 and 1975, public-interest liberalism has been under attack since the late 1970s; it retains significant, if diminished, organizational strength and political influence.[15]

These three variants of contemporary liberalism have much in common, but also many differences. Commonalities exist in both their policy demands and their political strategies. Their most important common policy preference was and remains expansion of the regulatory authority of the national government over both the market and private business and state and local governments. They have all demanded that the national government regulate market transactions and limit corporate discretion, whether in order to promote economic stability and industrial democracy, prohibit discriminatory behavior in employment and housing, or ensure a healthy environment and safe consumer products. They all usually favored extension of national regulatory authority over state and local governments, as well, in order to prohibit discriminatory or unjust laws, ensure uniform rights or standards, solve problems of national scope, or prevent the mobility of private capital from undermining public regulation and social standards through interlocal and interstate competition for business investment. All three variants of liberalism have supported expansion of national regulatory authority in part in order to promote greater economic, social, or political equality. In short, a shared commitment to national regulatory authority and egalitarian norms binds the three varieties of liberalism together and, indeed, defines them all as liberal.

Commonalities also exist in the broad political strategies of the New Deal/labor, civil-rights, and public-interest strands of liberalism. Sustained by social movements and the interest groups they generated, all three versions of liberalism operated in and through the Democratic Party to shape government and public policy. To a considerable extent, they confronted and contested the same political opponents: the business-conservative alliance organized as the Republican Party in interparty competition, and southern conservatives and more recently southern and suburban centrists in intraparty competition. The shared experience, since the late 1970s, of being embattled in both inter- and intraparty politics and in ideological competition made all three variants of contemporary liberalism more conscious of their need for mutual support and coordination, as the organizations studied in this book suggest.

These commonalities among the three versions of contemporary liberalism are general or abstract in character, however, and admit of important differences on specifics. Thus the three strands of liberalism are distinctive and, in some respects, in tension. Three dimensions of difference should be emphasized. The first is that the New Deal/labor, civil-rights, and public-interest versions of liberalism have distinct if overlapping social and institutional bases. New Deal/labor liberalism remains rooted in the working or wage-earning classes and the labor unions that represent them. Civil-rights liberalism draws its main support from racial minorities and women and their respective social movements and interest groups. Public-interest liberalism rests on environmental, consumer, and government reform groups and the broader professional middle and upper-middle classes from which they draw their principal support.

Second, the three strands of liberalism have distinct if overlapping agendas and priorities. New Deal/labor liberalism focuses on management of the economy, provision of social welfare, and protection of worker rights to achieve economic security and equality and industrial democracy. Civil-rights liberalism emphasizes the extension of rights, opportunities, and recognition to minorities and other excluded groups in pursuit of a more equal, inclusive, and tolerant society. Public-interest liberalism centers on ensuring the health and safety of the natural environment and consumer products as critical components of an improved and sustainable quality of life.

Although all three traditions of contemporary liberalism support the regulatory state, their priorities for government regulation vary. New Deal/labor liberalism stresses the regulation of corporate power and behavior in product, capital, and especially labor markets, where government authority regulates wages, hours, working conditions, and other aspects of employment both directly and indirectly (through legal support for collective bargaining). Civil-rights liberalism advocates national regulation of state and local governments, employers, and public accommodations to guarantee nondiscrimination and affirmative action toward targeted groups. Public-interest liberalism promotes government regulation of business in product and capital markets and of political organizations in campaign finance and lobbying "markets."

Third and finally, the three strands of contemporary liberalism differ in their political strategies. They entail different organizing principles and axes of political conflict: for New Deal/labor liberalism, class; for civil-rights liberalism, race and gender (and other nonclass social identities); for public-interest liberalism, a set of civic principles (environmentalism, consumerism, good government) to which persons of any social background or identity can subscribe (though in practice mainly middle- and upper-middle-class professionals do so). As a result, they also have distinct strategic orientations: that of New Deal/labor liberalism is populist and majoritarian, seeking and legitimating power by appeal to and mobilization of the nonrich, wage-earning majority; that of civil-rights liberalism emphasizes protection of minority rights and political appeals and mobilization based on discrete social identities; and that of public-interest liberalism privileges public over private interests and pursues them through staff-dominated organizations that appeal to and mobilize educated opinion by means of policy expertise.

This combination of commonalities and differences means that there is much that binds New Deal/labor, civil-rights, and public-interest liberalisms together and just as much that pulls them apart. As the case studies in this book suggest, at the level of their organizations, leaders, and activists, the three liberal traditions are quite capable of mutual support and coordination, but they are far from unified around an overarching set of commitments or a single strategy. Although it may well be possible to further develop their mutual support and collaboration, it seems unlikely that any deep integration of their demands or strategies is possible. For although what they share is significant, at bottom the New Deal/ labor, civil-rights, and public-interest traditions of liberalism are socially diverse, organizationally autonomous, and politically distinctive. It is very difficult to imagine how or under what conditions this fragmentation of liberalism could be overcome.

But it also bears emphasis that the fragmentation of liberalism is not as damaging today as it was two or three decades ago, because the common experience of political decline taught different types of liberals the necessity of mutual support and coordination, and because the organizations examined in this book united them and built trust and cooperation among them. Further gains along this line, which require patient and undramatic efforts, are more likely than either a genuine integration of the three types of liberalism or the willing subordination of any of them to the others.

In this light, it is worth considering briefly the labor-liberal factional organization Campaign for America's Future (CAF), established in July of 1996. Founded by Roger Hickey and Robert Borosage, who remain its codirectors, CAF was a response to three developments. One was the growing dominance of the business-conservative alliance in national politics, which CAF was formed to contest. A second was the 1995 leadership change at the AFL-CIO, which CAF's founders viewed as an opportunity to organize a more active and influential labor-liberal alliance. The third development was the centrism of the Clinton administration, which required the liberal wing of the Democratic Party to organize itself for intraparty influence. Though more than a factional organization, CAF was clearly intended to challenge the influence of centrist Democrats and their factional organization, the Democratic Leadership Council (DLC), and to promote liberal or progressive policies, strategies, and candidates within the Democratic Party. It formed an allied think tank, the Institute for America's Future (IAF), as a counterpoint to the DLC-linked Progressive Policy Institute.[16]

From the start, Campaign for America's Future was based on a strategy for uniting the disparate groups and movements of the liberal wing of the Democratic Party. The strategy was described by a knowledgeable journalist as "an attempt to unite the Left, which has increasingly become fragmented by identity and single-issue politics, around two propositions: that economic inequality and insecurity are the overriding problems this country confronts and that an activist government can and must provide the means to overcome them."[17] CAF cofounders Hickey and Borosage themselves explained to the New York Times that an agenda focused on the economic conditions of working people, especially the erosion of their living standards over the previous two decades, could unite liberals across racial, ethnic, class, and other divisions.[18] By the mid-1990s, this strategy of surmounting liberal fragmentation by focusing on the growing economic insecurity and inequality that afflicted white male workers, women, minorities, and families with children alike, was advocated by a number of prominent liberal thinkers and activists.[19] Noting the range of liberal activists in attendance at CAF's founding conference, encompassing the labor, civil-rights, women's, environmental, consumer, and other movements, journalistic observers were inclined to see in CAF evidence of emerging liberal consensus on this strategy.[20]

Were they right? Did CAF's strategy effectively unite all three strands of liberalism in the Democratic Party? The question arises, of course, because CAF's strategy represents the New Deal tradition much more clearly and emphatically than it does the other variants of liberalism.[21] As that strategy dictates, CAF's agenda and program are focused on economic and social-welfare issues of New Deal provenance, and it asks all liberals to unite around them. CAF affirms the New Deal version of liberalism as the one that is or should be capable of integrating or unifying the others.

There are at least a few reasons to think the strategy has succeeded. First, CAF is now a decade old; its survival and continuing vigor suggest that its strategy is at least viable. Second, CAF in fact appears to enjoy support from all three strands of contemporary liberalism. Its 130–member board of advisors includes leaders of labor unions, civil-rights organizations, environmental and consumer organizations, and community-organizing groups, along with a large number of other political activists and intellectuals.[22] This suggests that leaders and activists from all three liberal traditions are concerned about the growth of economic inequality and insecurity in recent decades and support the economic and social-welfare policies that CAF promotes to reduce them. Third, CAF has made a particular effort to integrate environmental and consumer concerns into its predominantly economic/social-welfare agenda and recently devised an energy policy that has strong support from both environmental groups like the Sierra Club and numerous industrial unions.[23] So perhaps the New Deal tradition does have adaptive and integrative capacities.

Still, there are grounds for skepticism about CAF's success at unifying the various strands of liberalism. Civil-rights and public-interest liberals have distinctive priorities that are not at the center of CAF's agenda and program and cannot be fully assimilated into the economic and social-welfare policies that are. It is therefore hard to see how they could be entirely satisfied with CAF as a liberal factional organization. Granted that they support it, the question is how actively and strongly they do so, since they must pursue their primary concerns and highest priorities outside it. And this in turn raises questions about CAF's ability to fully mobilize labor-liberal influence in the Democratic Party.

In truth, relatively little is known about CAF, because little if any scholarly research and analysis have been done on it. I express these doubts not to criticize CAF but to raise questions that should be examined and debated. In fact, I think there are good moral and political grounds for the strategy CAF adopted. It just seems unlikely that such a strategy will truly integrate or unify the three strands of contemporary liberalism, not because CAF is inadequate to the task but because the task itself probably cannot be accomplished. CAF could nevertheless be a very useful organization. If the New Deal, civil-rights, and public-interest traditions of liberalism cannot be fully unified, it remains vitally important that they communicate, recognize common interests, and cooperate as much as possible. If CAF serves that more limited purpose, it will still make an important contribution.

Apart from its strategy, the paucity of research on CAF makes it difficult to evaluate its effectiveness as a factional organization. It is worthy of note that CAF did not enlist elected liberal Democratic officeholders to serve as advisors, evidently preferring to serve as an external pressure on them. Although this decision protects CAF from becoming a mere instrument of incumbent liberal Democratic officeholders, it also limits CAF's ability to coordinate the party's labor-liberal activists and interest groups with its liberal officeholders. A full-blown party factional organization would include the party's ideologically compatible officeholders, as the Democratic Leadership Council does for party centrists, since maximum factional influence requires policy and strategic coordination of activists and groups with them.

If CAF remains or becomes an effective factional organization, it will certainly help the labor-liberal coalition. But that coalition faces daunting problems and challenges. The only solutions to the problems of union decline and liberal fragmentation are long-term and difficult. As if this were not trouble enough, the recent redivision of the labor movement renders the coalition's prospects even more uncertain. Although the labor-liberal coalition is down, it is not out, and there is no reason to think that it was a creature of the twentieth century that has no place or role in the twenty-first. But neither are there grounds for thinking that a major revival of that coalition and its influence are imminent. Its revival will be long and hard if it does occur. And much of the burden of that revival now rests on the shoulders of liberals. Over the past quarter-century, it was organized labor, its Reuther wing in particular, that assumed much of the responsibility for rebuilding and strengthening that coalition. But labor's focus might now shift inward to its own divisions. It is time for liberals, including those in civil-rights and public-interest organizations and those elected to office under the banner of the Democratic Party, to do more to support the labor movement and labor-law reform. It is in their self-interest to do so, for the future of the labor-liberal Democratic alliance depends on it.

APPENDIX

Table 3. Percentages of Union Members and Democrats with Selected Social and Demographic Characteristics

	1952		1972		1992	
	Union N = 294	Democrat N = 518	Union N = 380	Democrat N = 566	Union N = 260	Democrat N = 793
Age (17–24)	6.5	4.6	13.4	18.2	3.5	7.1
Black	10.2	7.9	11.8	21.2	15.0	21.7
Female	13.6	47.5	25.8	59.9	32.7	58.3
Suburban	29.3	27.8	33.9	29.3	48.5	40.4
Professional	8.2	12.5	10.0	22.6	26.9	29.8
Income (34th–67th Percentile)	28.9	24.5	47.9	36.7	38.0	29.6
College Degree	1.7	5.4	6.3	19.1	19.6	26.2

Table 4. Percentages of Union Members and Liberals with Selected Social and Demographic Characteristics

	1972		1992	
	Union N = 380	Liberal N = 400	Union N = 260	Liberal N = 504
Age (17–24)	13.4	27.8	3.5	10.1
Black	11.8	16.0	15.0	14.3
Female	25.8	53.3	32.7	53.2
Suburban	33.9	33.3	48.5	39.7
Professional	10.0	30.0	26.9	37.5
Income (34th–67th Percentile)	47.9	34.3	38.0	30.0
College Degree	6.3	27.0	19.6	37.3

Source: American National Election Studies, 1948–2002 Cumulative Data File

NOTES

Introduction

1. Among the many works that argue that the labor-liberal coalition declined after the late 1960s are David Brody, *Workers in Industrial America: Essays on the Twentieth Century Struggle* (New York: Oxford University Press, 1980), ch. 6; Thomas Byrne Edsall, *The New Politics of Inequality* (New York: Norton, 1984); Kevin Boyle, *The UAW and the Heyday of American Liberalism, 1945–1968* (Ithaca, N.Y.: Cornell University Press, 1995); David Plotke, *Building a Democratic Political Order: Reshaping American Liberalism in the 1930s and 1940s* (Cambridge, U.K.: Cambridge University Press, 1996); and Judith Stein, *Running Steel, Running America: Race, Economic Policy, and the Decline of Liberalism* (Chapel Hill: University of North Carolina Press, 1998).

2. Works that date the decline of the labor-liberal coalition from the late 1940s include Nelson Lichtenstein, "From Corporatism to Collective Bargaining: The Eclipse of Social Democracy in the Postwar Era," in Steve Fraser and Gary Gerstle, eds., *The Rise and Fall of the New Deal Order, 1930–1980* (Princeton, N.J.: Princeton University Press, 1989), 122–52; Ira Katznelson, "Was the Great Society a Lost Opportunity?" in Fraser and Gerstle, eds., *The Rise and Fall of the New Deal Order*, 185–211; Frances Fox Piven, "Structural Constraints and Political Development: The Case of the American Democratic Party," in Piven, ed., *Labor Parties in Postindustrial Societies* (New York: Oxford University Press, 1992); and Alan Brinkley, *The End of Reform: New Deal Liberalism in Recession and War* (New York: Vintage Books, 1996). The view that the labor-liberal coalition did not substantially decline after the late 1960s and remained a vital influence in American politics is developed in J. David Greenstone, "Introduction to the Phoenix Edition," in Greenstone, *Labor in American Politics* (Chicago: University of Chicago Press, 1977); and Taylor E. Dark, *The Unions and the Democrats: An Enduring Alliance* (Ithaca, N.Y.: Cornell University Press, 1999).

3. Kevin Boyle's important work exemplifies the tendency to overstate the decline of the labor-liberal coalition, frequently invoking its "collapse" and "death throes." See Boyle, *The UAW and the Heyday of American Liberalism*, esp. the introduction; and Kevin Boyle, introduction, in Boyle, ed., *Organized Labor and American Politics, 1894–1994: The Labor-Liberal Alliance* (Albany: State University of New York Press, 1998), 1–11.

Chapter 1: Understanding the Labor-Liberal Coalition

1. This point is conceded even by the most forceful advocates of the view that labor has been allied with the Democratic Party. See J. David Greenstone, *Labor in American Politics* (New York: Vintage Books, 1969), 57, 322–43; Taylor E. Dark, *The Unions and the*

Democrats: An Enduring Alliance (Ithaca, N.Y.: Cornell University Press, 1999), 53–63, 107–14.

2. Reuther quoted in David Brody, *Workers in Industrial America: Essays on the Twentieth Century Struggle* (New York: Oxford University Press, 1980), 229.

3. Greenstone, *Labor in American Politics*, 325–30.

4. Ibid., 323, 352; Graham K. Wilson, *Unions in American National Politics* (London: MacMillan, 1979), 61–62; Thomas Byrne Edsall, *The New Politics of Inequality* (New York: Norton, 1984), 46, 144; Karen Orren, "Union Politics and Postwar Liberalism in the United States, 1946–1979," in Orren and Stephen Skowronek, eds., *Studies in American Political Development: An Annual,* Volume 1 (New Haven, Conn.: Yale University Press, 1986), 215–52.

5. Nicol C. Rae, *Southern Democrats* (New York: Oxford University Press, 1994); James C. Glaser, *Race, Campaign Politics, and the Realignment in the South* (New Haven, Conn.: Yale University Press, 1997).

6. Greenstone, *Labor in American Politics*, 360–71; Ruth Horowitz, *Political Ideologies of Organized Labor: The New Deal Era* (New Brunswick, N.J.: Transaction Books, 1978), 207–38; Marick F. Masters and John T. Delaney, "The Causes of Union Political Involvement: A Longitudinal Analysis," *Journal of Labor Research* 6 (Fall 1985): 341–62; Gary Marks, "Variations in Union Political Activity in the United States, Britain, and Germany from the Nineteenth Century," *Comparative Politics* (October 1989): 83–104; Daniel B. Cornfield, "Union Decline and the Political Demands of Organized Labor," *Work and Occupations* 3 (August 1989): 292–322; William Form, *Segmented Labor, Fractured Politics: Labor Politics in American Life* (New York: Plenum Press, 1995), 18–22.

7. Form, *Segmented Labor, Fractured Politics*, 18–22; Greenstone, *Labor in American Politics*, 360–71; and Cornfield, "Union Decline."

8. Form, *Segmented Labor, Fractured Politics*, 22.

9. Form, *Segmented Labor, Fractured Politics*, 18–22; Greenstone, *Labor in American Politics*, 360–71; Horowitz, *Political Ideologies of Organized Labor*, 207–38; Cornfield, "Union Decline"; Irving Bernstein, *The Lean Years: A History of the American Worker, 1920–1933* (Baltimore: Penguin Books, 1966), ch. 2; Richard B. Freeman, "Unionism Comes to the Public Sector," *Journal of Economic Literature* (March 1986): 41–86; Edwin F. Beal, Edward D. Wickersham, and Philip K. Kienast, *The Practice of Collective Bargaining* (Homewood, Ill.: Richard D. Irwin), chs. 1–3.

10. Andrew Battista, "Political Divisions in Organized Labor, 1968–1988," *Polity* 2 (Winter 1991): 173–97.

11. Taylor E. Dark, "Debating Decline: The 1995 Race for the AFL-CIO Presidency," *Labor History* 3 (August 1999): 323–43.

12. See the sources cited in note 9.

13. Everett Carl Ladd Jr., with Charles D. Hadley, *Transformations of the American Party System*, 2nd ed. (New York: Norton, 1978), 211–27, 284–91, 333–42, 383–86; Alonzo L. Hamby, *Liberalism and Its Challengers: From FDR to Bush*, 2nd ed. (New York: Oxford University Press, 1992), viii–x, chs. 5, 6; Jeff Manza and Clem Brooks, *Social Cleavages and Political Change: Voter Alignments and U.S. Party Coalitions* (Oxford, U.K.: Oxford University Press, 1999), 24–26, 67–69, 232–33; Jeffrey M. Berry, *The New Liberalism: The Rising Power of Citizen Groups* (Washington, D.C.: Brookings Institution Press, 1999), ch. 3.

14. See Ladd with Hadley, *Transformations of the American Party System*, 211–27, 284–91, 333–42, 383–86; Benjamin Ginsberg and Martin Shefter, "A Critical Realignment? The

New Politics, the Reconstituted Right, and the 1984 Elections," in Michael Nelson, ed., *The Elections of 1984* (Washington, D.C.: Congressional Quarterly Press, 1985), 1–25; Byron E. Shafer, "Partisan Elites, 1946–1996," in Shafer, ed., *Partisan Approaches to Postwar American Politics* (New York: Chatham House, 1998), 75–141.

15. See William E. Leuchtenburg, *Franklin D. Roosevelt and the New Deal, 1932–1940* (New York: Harper and Row, 1963); James L. Sundquist, *Dynamics of the Party System: Alignment and Realignment of Political Parties in the United States,* rev. ed. (Washington, D.C.: Brookings Institution, 1983), ch. 10; David Plotke, *Building a Democratic Political Order: Reshaping American Liberalism in the 1930s and 1940s* (Cambridge, U.K.: Cambridge University Press, 1996); John Gerring, *Party Ideologies in America, 1828–1996* (Cambridge, U.K.: Cambridge University Press, 1998), ch. 6; Gary Gerstle, *American Crucible: Race and Nation in the Twentieth Century* (Princeton, N.J.: Princeton University Press, 2001), ch. 4.

16. See Ladd with Hadley, *Transformations of the American Party System,* 221–31, 333–42, 383–86; Richard L. Rubin, *Party Dynamics: The Democratic Coalition and the Politics of Change* (New York: Oxford University Press, 1976), 98–106; Ginsberg and Shefter, "A Critical Realignment?"; Benjamin Ginsberg and Martin Shefter, *Politics by Other Means* (New York: Basic Books, 1990), ch. 2; Shafer, "Partisan Elites," 101–14.

17. See Jeffrey C. Isaac, *The Poverty of Progressivism: The Future of American Democracy in a Time of Liberal Decline* (Lanham, Md.: Rowman and Littlefield, 2003), ch. 3; Todd Gitlin, "Beyond Identity Politics: A Modest Precedent," in Steven Fraser and Joshua B. Freeman, eds., *Audacious Democracy: Labor, Intellectuals, and the Social Reconstruction of America* (Boston: Houghton Mifflin, 1997), 152–63.

18. See Greenstone, *Labor in American Politics,* introduction, ch. 2; Alan Draper, *A Rope of Sand: The AFL-CIO Committee on Political Education, 1958–1967* (New York: Praeger, 1989), introduction; Form, *Segmented Labor, Fractured Politics,* ch. 12; Dark, *The Unions and the Democrats,* introduction, ch. 2.

19. See Dark, *The Unions and the Democrats,* 4–6.

20. See Greenstone, *Labor in American Politics,* 57, 322–43; Dark, *The Unions and the Democrats,* 53–63, 107–14; Peter Bruce, "Political Parties and Labor Legislation in Canada and the U.S.," *Industrial Relations* 2 (Spring 1989): 124–27; James MacGregor Burns, *The Deadlock of Democracy: Four-Party Politics in America* (Englewood Cliffs, N.J.: Prentice Hall, 1967), 199–200; James L. Sundquist, *Politics and Policy: The Eisenhower, Kennedy, and Johnson Years* (Washington, D.C.: Brookings Institution, 1968), 395–96, 403–15.

21. Rubin, *Party Dynamics,* ch. 5; Nicol C. Rae, "Party Factionalism, 1946–1996," in Shafer, ed., *Partisan Approaches to Postwar American Politics,* 41–74.

22. Ibid., esp. 56–70, including Table 2.6, p. 65.

23. In this book I analyze the rise and decline of the labor-liberal coalition in national politics. An anonymous reviewer for University of Illinois Press pointed out that analysis of the labor-liberal coalition in local, state, and regional politics would be illuminating and might alter our understanding of when and how that coalition arose and declined. This is a good point. However, the focus of this book on national politics is entirely legitimate, and serious analysis of the labor-liberal coalition at local, state, or regional levels would have added considerably to its length. It would be very useful to have detailed studies of the rise and decline of the labor-liberal coalition in various localities and states.

24. Julie Greene, "Negotiating the State: The Transformation of Labor's Political Culture in Progressive America," in Kevin Boyle, ed., *Organized Labor and American Politics,*

1894–1994: The Labor-Liberal Alliance (Albany: State University of New York Press, 1998), 71–102.

25. See Form, *Segmented Labor, Fractured Politics,* ch. 12; Dark, *The Unions and the Democrats,* ch. 2. See also Draper, *A Rope of Sand,* ch. 1, conclusion.

26. See Dark, *The Unions and the Democrats,* ch. 2; and Form, *Segmented Labor, Fractured Politics,* 260–65.

27. See Andrew Martin, *The Politics of Economic Policy in the United States: A Tentative View from a Comparative Perspective,* Sage Professional Papers in Comparative Politics, Series No. 01-040, Vol. 4 (Beverly Hills, Calif.: Sage, 1973), 35–40; John D. Stephens, *The Transition from Capitalism to Socialism* (Urbana: University of Illinois Press, 1979), 89–98; David R. Cameron, "Social Democracy, Corporatism, Labour Quiescence and the Representation of Economic Interest in Advanced Capitalist Society," in John H. Goldthorpe, ed., *Order and Conflict in Contemporary Capitalism: Studies in the Political Economy of Western European Nations* (Oxford, U.K.: Clarendon Press, 1984), 143–78.

28. Dark, *The Unions and the Democrats,* 29–31, ch. 2, esp. Table 2.1 on p. 38.

29. Ibid., 21–31, 195–201.

Chapter 2: *The Rise of the Labor-Liberal Coalition*

1. J. David Greenstone, *Labor in American Politics* (New York: Vintage Books, 1969), 29–38; Melvyn Dubofsky, *The State and Labor in Modern America* (Chapel Hill: University of North Carolina Press, 1994), 51–83; Julie Greene, "Negotiating the State: The Transformation of Labor's Political Culture in Progressive America," in Kevin Boyle, ed., *Organized Labor and American Politics, 1894–1994: The Labor-Liberal Alliance* (Albany: State University of New York Press, 1998), 71–102.

2. Dubofsky, *The State and Labor,* 83.

3. James L. Sundquist, *Dynamics of the Party System: Alignment and Realignment of Political Parties in the United States,* rev. ed. (Washington, D.C.: Brookings Institution, 1983), 182; Greenstone, *Labor in American Politics,* 34–35.

4. Greene, "Negotiating the State."

5. Dubofsky, *The State and Labor,* chs. 2, 3.

6. Greenstone, *Labor in American Politics,* 36–48; Ruth Horowitz, *Political Ideologies of Organized Labor: The New Deal Era* (New Brunswick, N.J.: Transaction Books, 1978), 10, 19, 172–77, ch. 8. I borrow the idea and terminology of a "CIO reformation" from Horowitz.

7. Everett Carl Ladd Jr., with Charles D. Hadley, *Transformations of the American Party System,* 2nd ed. (New York: Norton, 1978), ch. 1; Sundquist, *Dynamics of the Party System,* ch. 10.

8. Greenstone, *Labor in American Politics,* 40–44.

9. Irving Bernstein, *The Lean Years: A History of the American Worker, 1920–1933* (Baltimore: Penguin Books, 1966), 84–88.

10. Ibid., 91–93, 222–26, 345–55; Horowitz, *Political Ideologies of Organized Labor,* 27–46; Alan Draper, *A Rope of Sand: The AFL-CIO Committee on Political Education, 1958–1967* (New York: Praeger, 1989), 12–15.

11. Michael Rogin, "Voluntarism: The Political Functions of an Anti-Political Doctrine," in David Brody, ed., *The American Labor Movement* (New York: Harper and Row, 1971), 100–118, esp. 111–15.

12. John H. M. Laslett, "Socialism and the American Labor Movement," in Brody, ed., *The American Labor Movement,* 67–82; John H. M. Laslett, "Samuel Gompers and the Rise of American Business Unionism," in Melvyn Dubofsky and Warren Van Tine, eds., *Labor Leaders in America* (Urbana: University of Illinois Press, 1987), 62–88.

13. Robert H. Zieger, *American Workers, American Unions,* 2nd ed. (Baltimore: Johns Hopkins University Press, 1994), ch. 1.

14. Robert H. Zieger, *The CIO, 1935–1955* (Chapel Hill: University of North Carolina Press, 1995), chs. 1, 4.

15. Horowitz, *Political Ideologies of Organized Labor,* 232.

16. John Barnard, *Walter Reuther and the Rise of the Auto Workers* (Boston: Little, Brown, 1983), 213.

17. Murray quoted in Kim Moody, *An Injury to All: The Decline of American Unionism* (London: Verso, 1988), 58.

18. Greenstone, *Labor in American Politics,* 41, 67, 366–71; Horowitz, *Political Ideologies of Organized Labor,* 220–30.

19. Zieger, *American Workers, American Unions,* 23, 60.

20. Ibid., 100–101.

21. Irving Bernstein, *Turbulent Years: A History of the American Worker, 1933–1941* (Boston: Houghton Mifflin, 1971), 771–74.

22. Horowitz, *Political Ideologies of Organized Labor,* 243–46.

23. Ibid., ch. 8, 243–46.

24. Greenstone, *Labor in American Politics,* 40 (emphasis in the original).

25. Melvin Dubofsky and Warren Van Tine, "John L. Lewis and the Triumph of Mass-Production Unionism," in Dubofsky and Van Tine, eds., *Labor Leaders,* 195; Melvin Dubofsky and Warren Van Tine, *John L. Lewis: A Biography* (Urbana: University of Illinois Press, 1986), abridged ed., ch. 12; Zieger, *The CIO,* 20.

26. Steven Fraser, "Sidney Hillman: Labor's Machiavelli," in Dubofsky and Van Tine, eds., *Labor Leaders,* 216–22; Steven Fraser, *Labor Will Rule: Sidney Hillman and the Rise of American Labor* (New York: The Free Press, 1991), ch. 12.

27. Horowitz, *Political Ideologies of Organized Labor,* chs. 4–8.

28. Greenstone, *Labor in American Politics,* 49–52.

29. Zieger, *The CIO,* 20–21, ch. 2; Dubofsky and Van Tine, "John L. Lewis and the Triumph of Mass-Production Unionism," 197–98; David Brody, *Labor in Crisis: The Steel Strike of 1919* (Urbana: University of Illinois Press, 1987; originally published 1965), ch. 6.

30. Greenstone, *Labor in American Politics,* ch. 2; Horowitz, *Political Ideologies of Organized Labor;* David Plotke, *Building a Democratic Political Order: Reshaping American Liberalism in the 1930s and 1940s* (Cambridge, U.K.: Cambridge University Press, 1996); Dubofsky, *The State and Labor,* chs. 5–7; Zieger, *The CIO.*

31. There are intimations of this in Greenstone, *Labor in American Politics;* and in Plotke, *Building a Democratic Political Order.*

32. Dubofsky, *The State and Labor,* 201–8; Plotke, *Building a Democratic Political Order,* ch. 8.

33. Barbara S. Griffith, *The Crisis of American Labor: Operation Dixie and the Defeat of the CIO* (Philadelphia: Temple University Press, 1988); Zieger, *The CIO,* 227–41.

34. Michael Goldfield, *The Decline of Organized Labor in the United States* (Chicago: University of Chicago Press, 1987), 10, Table 1.

35. Sundquist, *Dynamics of the Party System,* ch. 15; Ladd with Hadley, *Transformations of the American Party System,* chs. 3–5; David G. Lawrence, *The Collapse of the Democratic Presidential Majority* (Boulder, Colo.: Westview Press, 1997), chs. 3, 4.

36. Plotke, *Building a Democratic Political Order,* 341–44.

37. James Gilbert, *Another Chance: Postwar America, 1945–1985,* 2nd ed. (Chicago: Dorsey Press, 1986), 88–89; Plotke, *Building a Democratic Political Order,* ch. 11.

38. Nelson Lichtenstein, "From Corporatism to Collective Bargaining: Organized Labor and the Eclipse of Social Democracy in the Postwar Era," in Steve Fraser and Gary Gerstle, eds., *The Rise and Fall of the New Deal Order, 1930–1980* (Princeton, N.J.: Princeton University Press, 1989), 122–52; Ira Katznelson, "Was the Great Society a Lost Opportunity?" in Fraser and Gerstle, eds., *The Rise and Fall of the New Deal Order,* 185–211; and Frances Fox Piven, "Structural Constraints and Political Development: The Case of the American Democratic Party," in Piven, ed., *Labor Parties in Postindustrial Societies* (New York: Oxford University Press, 1992), 235–64. All emphasize the political defeats and strategic failures of the labor-liberal coalition in the late 1940s. The most systematic and persuasive response to this perspective is Plotke's *Building a Democratic Political Order,* esp. chs. 7–9.

39. Dubofsky, *The State and Labor,* 197.

40. Ibid., 199–208; Plotke, *Building a Democratic Political Order,* ch. 8.

41. Goldfield, *The Decline of Organized Labor,* 10, Table 1.

42. Ladd with Hadley, *Transformations of the American Party System,* ch. 2; Sundquist, *Dynamics of the Party System,* ch. 15. A somewhat more complicated picture is drawn by Lawrence, *The Collapse of the Democratic Presidential Majority,* ch. 3.

43. Plotke, *Building a Democratic Political Order,* 221–22, Tables 7.1 and 7.2.

44. Lichtenstein, "From Corporatism to Collective Bargaining," 128–33; Katznelson, "Was the Great Society a Lost Opportunity?" 189–95; Alan Brinkley, *The End of Reform: New Deal Liberalism in Recession and War* (New York: Vintage Books, 1995), epilogue.

45. Plotke, *Building a Democratic Political Order,* 346; Zieger, *The CIO,* 321–22; Nelson Lichtenstein, "Walter Reuther and the Rise of Labor-Liberalism," in Dubofsky and Van Tine, eds., *Labor Leaders in America,* 292–95.

46. Zieger, *The CIO,* 312–22; Plotke, *Building a Democratic Political Order,* 262–67.

47. Zieger, *The CIO,* 322.

48. James L. Sundquist, *Politics and Policy: The Eisenhower, Kennedy, and Johnson Years* (Washington, D.C.: Brookings Institution, 1968), 60–73, 296–302.

49. Adolph Sturmthal, *Left of Center: European Labor Since World War II* (Urbana: University of Illinois Press, 1983), ch. 1; Denis MacShane, *International Labour and the Origins of the Cold War* (Oxford, U.K.: Clarendon Press/Oxford University Press, 1992), chs. 7, 8; Zieger, *The CIO,* ch. 9.

50. David Brody, *Workers in Industrial America: Essays on the Twentieth Century Struggle* (New York: Oxford University Press, 1980), 222–29; Lichtenstein, "From Corporatism to Collective Bargaining," 137–39; Zieger, *The CIO,* 261–77.

51. Zieger, *The CIO,* 277–93; Sturmthal, *Left of Center,* ch. 4.

52. Works that are highly critical of labor-liberal anticommunism and enlistment in the Cold War include Ronald Radosh, *American Labor and United States Foreign Policy: The Cold War in the Unions from Gompers to Lovestone* (New York: Vintage Books, 1969); Henry Berger, "Organized Labor and American Foreign Policy," in Irving Louis Horowitz, John C. Leggett, and Martin Oppenheimer, eds., *The American Working Class: Prospects for the 1980s* (Brunswick, N.J.: Transaction Books, 1979), 193–213; Mike Davis, *Prisoners of the American Dream* (London: Verso, 1986), chs. 2, 5; Daniel Cantor and Juliet Schor,

Tunnel Vision: Labor, the World Economy, and Central America (Boston: South End Press, 1987). Works that are more sympathetic without being uncritical include Barnard, *Walter Reuther and the Rise of the Auto Workers,* ch. 7; MacShane, *International Labour and the Origins of the Cold War,* chs. 6–8, 15; Zieger, *The CIO,* chs. 9, 11, and conclusion; and Plotke, *Building a Democratic Political Order,* ch. 10.

53. Sturmthal, *Left of Center,* chs. 1, 4; MacShane, *International Labour and the Origins of the Cold War,* chs. 1, 6–8, 15.

54. Recognition of these consequences is evident in scholars such as Zieger, *The CIO,* chs. 9, 11, conclusion; and Plotke, *Building a Democratic Political Order,* ch. 10, who grant legitimacy to anticommunism and the Cold War from liberal or social-democratic perspectives. An important statement of the impact of the Cold War on U.S. economic and trade policy is Robert Kuttner, *The End of Laissez-Faire: National Purpose and the Global Economy after the Cold War* (New York: Knopf, 1991).

55. Ibid., 376.

56. Greenstone, *Labor in American Politics,* 50–55; Graham K. Wilson, *Unions in American National Politics* (London: MacMillan, 1979), 7–8, 37–38; Zieger, *American Workers, American Unions,* 114–19; Byron E. Shafer, "Partisan Elites, 1946–1996," in Shafer, ed., *Partisan Approaches to Postwar American Politics* (New York: Chatham House, 1998), 87.

57. Ibid., 49–58; Wilson, *Unions in American National Politics,* 17, 37; Zieger, *American Workers, American Unions,* 114–19.

58. Ibid., 336–43, 355–59; Wilson, *Unions in American National Politics,* ch. 4.

59. Sundquist, *Politics and Policy,* 389–410.

60. Ibid., 296–302; Greenstone, *Labor in American Politics,* 49–52, 322–25, 355–59; Taylor E. Dark, *The Unions and the Democrats: An Enduring Alliance* (Ithaca, N.Y.: Cornell University Press, 1999), 93.

61. Bernstein, *Turbulent Years,* ch. 14; Davis, *Prisoners of the American Dream,* ch. 2; Zieger, *American Workers, American Unions,* 69.

62. Ibid., 699–703.

63. Arthur J. Goldberg, *AFL-CIO: Labor United* (New York: McGraw-Hill, 1956), 42–47, 197–208, 214–16; Joel Seidman, "Efforts toward Merger: 1935–1955," *Industrial and Labor Relations Review* 3 (April 1956): 353–70; Greenstone, *Labor in American Politics,* 52–59; Horowitz, *Political Ideologies of Organized Labor,* 234–37, 244–46.

64. Seidman, "Efforts toward Merger," 363, 369–70; Victor G. Reuther, *The Brothers Reuther and the Story of the UAW* (Boston: Houghton Mifflin, 1976), ch. 25, esp. 362–63; Zieger, *The CIO,* chs. 12, 13.

65. Goldberg, *AFL-CIO,* 62–71, 102; Seidman, "Efforts toward Merger," 361–62, 369–70; Draper, *A Rope of Sand,* 28–39.

66. Draper, *A Rope of Sand,* 38.

67. Ibid., 30.

68. Goldberg, *AFL-CIO; Industrial and Labor Relations Review* 3 (April 1956).

69. Draper, *A Rope of Sand,* 76–93, 106–19; Greenstone, *Labor in American Politics,* ch. 10.

70. Wilson, *Unions in American National Politics,* 38; Brody, *Workers in Industrial America,* 231; Nicol C. Rae, *Southern Democrats* (New York: Oxford University Press, 1994), 67.

71. Sundquist, *Politics and Policy,* 471–78.

72. Ibid., chs. 1–8; Allen J. Matusow, *The Unraveling of America: A History of Liberalism in the 1960s* (New York: Harper and Row, 1984), chs. 7–9.

73. Davis, *Prisoners of the American Dream*, 100; Lichtenstein, "From Corporatism to Collective Bargaining," 145; Katznelson, "Was the Great Society a Lost Opportunity?" 194–95; Thomas Ferguson and Joel Rogers, *Right Turn: The Decline of the Democrats and the Future of American Politics* (New York: Hill and Wang, 1986), 51–57.

74. Sundquist, *Politics and Policy*, chs. 1–8; Greenstone, *Labor in American Politics*, ch. 10; Kevin Boyle, *The UAW and the Heyday of American Liberalism, 1945–1968* (Ithaca, N.Y.: Cornell University Press, 1995), chs. 7, 8; Dark, *The Unions and the Democrats*, ch. 3.

75. Greenstone, *Labor in American Politics*, 69–70, 315, 336.

76. Ladd with Hadley, *Transformations of the American Party System*, 121–24; Lawrence, *The Collapse of the Democratic Presidential Majority*, 36–37.

77. Lichtenstein, "From Corporatism to Collective Bargaining"; Katznelson, "Was the Great Society a Lost Opportunity?"; Piven, "Structural Constraints and Political Development"; Brinkley, *The End of Reform*, epilogue.

78. Plotke, *Building a Democratic Political Order*, esp. ch. 11; Judith Stein, *Running Steel, Running America: Race, Economic Policy, and the Decline of Liberalism* (Chapel Hill: University of North Carolina Press, 1998), esp. the conclusion.

79. David Vogel, *Fluctuating Fortunes: The Political Power of Business in America* (New York: Basic Books, 1989), 21–22, 26; Andrew Martin, "The Politics of Economic Policy in the United States," *Sage Professional Papers in Comparative Politics*, Series No. 01-040 (Beverly Hills, Calif.: Sage, 1973), 48–52.

80. Martin, "The Politics of Economic Policy," 53.

81. Stein, *Running Steel, Running America*, 26–36, ch. 3.

82. Dark, *The Unions and the Democrats*, 59–63; Gordon L. Clark, *Unions and Communities under Siege: American Communities and the Crisis of Organized Labor* (Cambridge, U.K.: Cambridge University Press, 1989), ch. 10; Peter Bruce, "Political Parties and Labor Legislation in Canada and the U.S.," *Industrial Relations* 2 (Spring 1989): 122–27.

83. Robert Axelrod, "Where the Votes Come From: An Analysis of Electoral Coalitions, 1952–1968 (and 1972 Addendum)," in Charles M. Rehmus, Doris B. McLaughlin, and Frederick H. Nesbitt, eds., *Labor and American Politics: A Book of Readings*, rev. ed. (Ann Arbor: University of Michigan Press, 1983), Table 1, 388, 389–90.

84. Katznelson, "Was the Great Society a Lost Opportunity?" 199–205; Stein, *Running Steel, Running America*, ch. 3.

85. Axelrod, "Where the Votes Come From," Table 1, 388. Of course, the categories of union members and black citizens overlap.

86. Zieger, *American Workers, American Unions*, 174.

87. Martin, "The Politics of Economic Policy"; Ira Katznelson, "Considerations on Social Democracy in the United States," *Comparative Politics* 11 (October 1978): 77–99; John D. Stephens, *The Transition from Capitalism to Socialism* (Urbana: University of Illinois Press, 1979), 149–56; Bruce, "Political Parties and Labor Legislation," 115–41. In short, the labor-liberal coalition in the United States was unable to develop the "full employment welfare state" as far as European social democracy did.

Chapter 3: The Decline of the Labor-Liberal Coalition

1. Alan Draper, *A Rope of Sand: The AFL-CIO Committee on Political Education, 1958–1967* (New York: Praeger, 1989), 117–28; Alan J. Matusow, *The Unraveling of America: A History of Liberalism in the 1960s* (New York: Harper and Row, 1984), 214.

2. See Everett Carl Ladd Jr., with Charles D. Hadley, *Transformations of the American Party System*, 2nd ed. (New York: Norton, 1978), 211–31, 333–42, 383–86; Graham K. Wilson, *Unions in American National Politics* (London: MacMillan, 1979), chs. 3, 4; Thomas Byrne Edsall, *The New Politics of Inequality* (New York: Norton, 1984), 48–63, 157–62; Benjamin Ginsberg and Martin Shefter, "A Critical Realignment? The New Politics, the Reconstituted Right, and the 1984 Election," in Michael Nelson, ed., *The Elections of 1984* (Washington, D.C.: Congressional Quarterly Press, 1985), 1–25; Byron E. Shafer, "Partisan Elites, 1946–1996," in Byron E. Shafer, ed., *Partisan Approaches to Postwar American Politics* (New York: Chatham House, 1998), 101–14; Nicol C. Rae, "Party Factionalism, 1946–1996," in Shafer, ed., *Partisan Approaches*, 56–59.

3. Matusow, *The Unraveling of America*, chs. 11, 12; Maurice Isserman and Michael Kazin, "The Failure and Success of the New Radicalism," in Steve Fraser and Gary Gerstle, eds., *The Rise and Fall of the New Deal Order, 1930–1980* (Princeton, N.J.: Princeton University Press, 1989), 212–42; Peter Levy, *The New Left and Labor in the 1960s* (Urbana: University of Illinois Press, 1994).

4. Kay Lehman Schlozman and John T. Tierney, *Organized Interests and American Democracy* (New York: Harper and Row, 1986), ch. 4; Jeffrey M. Berry, *The Interest Group Society*, 3rd ed. (New York: Longman, 1997), ch. 2; David Vogel, *Fluctuating Fortunes: The Political Power of Business in America* (New York: Basic Books, 1989), chs. 3, 4.

5. Ladd with Hadley, *Transformations of the American Party System*, ch. 4; Shafer, "Partisan Elites," 103–9; Vogel, *Fluctuating Fortunes*, 95–100.

6. Taylor E. Dark, *The Unions and the Democrats: An Enduring Alliance* (Ithaca, N.Y.: Cornell University Press, 1999), ch. 4.

7. Ladd with Hadley, *Transformations of the American Party System*, 383–86; Shafer, "Partisan Elites," 101–14.

8. Ginsberg and Shefter, "A Critical Realignment?"; Shafer, "Partisan Elites," 111–13; Dark, *The Unions and the Democrats*, ch. 4.

9. See the sources cited in note 2.

10. Levy, *The New Left and Labor*, esp. 4–6, 187–88.

11. J. David Greenstone, *Labor in American Politics* (New York: Vintage Books, 1969), 342–43; Wilson, *Unions in American National Politics*, 70–72.

12. Archie Robinson, *George Meany and His Times* (New York: Simon and Schuster, 1981), 20; James R. Green, *The World of the Worker: Labor in Twentieth-Century America* (New York: Hill and Wang), 241; Stanley Aronowitz, *From the Ashes of the Old: American Labor and America's Future* (New York: Basic Books, 1998), 75–76.

13. Vogel, *Fluctuating Fortunes*, 39, 160–63.

14. Ibid., 232.

15. Ibid., 51–53 and 83–87.

16. Dona Cooper Hamilton and Charles V. Hamilton, "The Dual Agenda of African American Organizations since the New Deal: Social Welfare Policies and Civil Rights," *Political Science Quarterly* 3 (1992): 435–52; Anne N. Costain, "Women Lobby Congress," in Anne N. Costain and Andrew S. McFarland, *Social Movements and American Political Institutions* (Lanham, Md.: Rowman and Littlefield, 1998), ch. 10.

17. Vogel, *Fluctuating Fortunes*, chs. 7, 8.

18. William B. Gould, *Black Workers in White Unions: Job Discrimination in the United States* (Ithaca, N.Y.: Cornell University Press, 1977); Herbert Hill, "The AFL-CIO and the Black Worker: Twenty-Five Years after the Merger," *The Journal of Intergroup Relations* 10

(Spring 1982): 5–78; Alice H. Cook, "Women and Minorities," in George Strauss, Daniel G. Gallagher, and Jack Fiorito, eds., *The State of the Unions* (Madison, Wis.: Industrial Relations Research Association, 1991), ch. 7.

19. Gould, *Black Workers,* esp. the introduction; Hill, "The AFL-CIO and the Black Worker."

20. Kim Moody, *An Injury to All: The Decline of American Unionism* (London: Verso, 1988), 255–57, 272–81; Ruth Milkman, "Women Workers, Feminism, and the Labor Movement since the 1960s," in Milkman, ed., *Women, Work, and Protest* (Boston: Routledge and Kegan Paul, 1985), 311–14.

21. Patricia Cayo Sexton and Brendan Sexton, *Blue Collars and Hard Hats: The Working Class and the Future of American Politics* (New York: Vintage Books, 1971), 266–71; Andrew Levison, *The Working-Class Majority* (New York: Coward, McCann, and Geoghagen, 1974), 185–89, 222–23.

22. Kevin Boyle, *The UAW and the Heyday of American Liberalism, 1945–1968* (Ithaca, N.Y.: Cornell University Press, 1995), ch. 7; Judith Stein, *Running Steel, Running America: Race, Economic Policy, and the Decline of Liberalism* (Chapel Hill: University of North Carolina Press, 1998), chs. 2–4.

23. Milkman, "Women Workers, Feminism, and the Labor Movement," 304; Robert Zieger, *American Workers, American Unions,* 2nd ed. (Baltimore: Johns Hopkins University Press, 1994), 164; Stanley Aronowitz, *Working Class Hero: A New Strategy for Labor* (New York: Pilgrim Press, 1983), 135–43; Leon Fink and Brian Greenberg, *Upheaval in the Quiet Zone: A History of Hospital Workers' Union, Local 1199* (Urbana: University of Illinois Press, 1989).

24. Dark, *The Unions and the Democrats,* 80–83.

25. William Crotty, *Party Reform* (New York: Longman, 1983); Dark, *The Unions and the Democrats,* 76–87.

26. Boyle, *The UAW and the Heyday of American Liberalism,* 236.

27. Ladd with Hadley, *Transformations of the American Party System,* 211–31, 333–42, 383–86; Ginsberg and Shefter, "A Critical Realignment?"; and Shafer, "Partisan Elites," 101–14.

28. Philip S. Foner, *American Labor and the Indochina War: The Growth of Union Opposition* (New York: International, 1971), 20, 88, passim; Zieger, *American Workers, American Unions,* 171–72.

29. Foner, *American Labor,* 89; Henry Berger, "Organized Labor and American Foreign Policy," in Irving Louis Horowitz, John C. Leggett, and Martin Oppenheimer, eds., *The American Working Class: Prospects for the 1980s* (New Brunswick, N.J.: Transaction Books, 1979), 199.

30. Levy, *The New Left and Labor,* 46–54.

31. John P. Windmuller, "The Foreign Policy Conflict in American Labor," *Political Science Quarterly* 82 (June 1967): 218–20; Dark, *The Unions and the Democrats,* 73; Boyle, *The UAW and the Heyday of American Liberalism,* chs. 9, 10.

32. Ibid., 226, note 50; Levy, *The New Left and Labor,* 55–56; Foner, *American Labor,* 48–63.

33. Foner, *American Labor,* 64–115; *Business Week,* July 1, 1972, 15.

34. Foner, *American Labor,* 48–97.

35. Ibid., 64–97.

36. Levy, *The New Left and Labor,* 55–63.

37. Crotty, *Party Reform.*

38. Ibid., 131.

39. Dark, *The Unions and the Democrats,* 77–87.

40. Wilson, *Unions in American National Politics,* 43, 48–49; Crotty, *Party Reform,* 132; Dark, *The Unions and the Democrats,* 85.

41. Ibid., 43; Joseph Goulden, *Jerry Wurf: Labor's Last Angry Man* (New York: Atheneum, 1982), 216.

42. Ibid., 43–44; Dark, *The Unions and the Democrats,* 87–90; Levison, *The Working-Class Majority,* 240–47.

43. A. H. Raskin, "Labor: A Movement in Search of a Mission," in Seymour Martin Lipset, ed., *Unions in Transition: Entering the Second Century* (San Francisco: Institute for Contemporary Studies, 1986), 34.

44. Wilson, *Unions in American National Politics,* 33–34.

45. Goulden, *Jerry Wurf,* 217–18; Levison, *The Working-Class Majority,* 245.

46. Alan Ehrenhalt, "The Labor Coalition and the Democrats: A Tenuous Romance," in Charles M. Rehmus and Doris B. McLaughlin, eds., *Labor and American Politics* (Ann Arbor: University of Michigan Press, 1983), 216; Levison, *The Working-Class Majority,* 245–46.

47. Ladd with Hadley, *Transformations of the American Party System,* 344–45; Kenneth S. Baer, *Reinventing Democrats: The Politics of Liberalism from Reagan to Clinton* (Lawrence: University Press of Kansas, 2000), 30–32.

48. Ehrenhalt, "The Labor Coalition and the Democrats," 217; Dark, *The Unions and the Democrats,* 102–3.

49. Ehrenhalt, "The Labor Coalition and the Democrats," 215–19; Wilson, *Unions in American National Politics,* 32–35, 48–49.

50. Ehrenhalt, "The Labor Coalition and the Democrats," 218–19; Wilson, *Unions in American National Politics,* 33–34, 48.

51. Ehrenhalt, "The Labor Coalition and the Democrats," 100–103.

52. William Berman, *America's Right Turn: From Nixon to Bush* (Baltimore: Johns Hopkins University Press, 1994), 37–52.

53. Edsall, *The New Politics of Inequality,* 13–15, 45, 208–15; Ray Marshall, *Unheard Voices: Labor and Economic Policy in a Competitive World* (New York: Basic Books, 1987), 39–46, ch. 3; Bennett Harrison and Barry Bluestone, *The Great U-Turn: Corporate Restructuring and the Polarizing of America* (New York: Basic Books, 1988), chs. 1, 5; Vogel, *Fluctuating Fortunes,* 9, 136; Sheldon Danziger and Peter Gottschalk, *America Unequal* (New York and Cambridge, Mass.: Russell Sage Foundation and Harvard University Press, 1995), ch. 1.

54. Vogel, *Fluctuating Fortunes,* 136–44; Margaret Weir, *Politics and Jobs: The Boundaries of Employment Policy in the United States* (Princeton, N.J.: Princeton University Press, 1992), 130–36.

55. Weir, *Politics and Jobs,* 100–103, 157–62; Vogel, *Fluctuating Fortunes,* ch. 7; Edsall, *The New Politics of Inequality,* 13–15, 207–30; Harrison and Bluestone, *The Great U-Turn,* ch. 4; Marshall, *Unheard Voices,* ch.2.

56. Harrison and Bluestone, *The Great U-Turn,* chs. 2, 4; Richard B. Freeman and James L. Medoff, *What Do Unions Do?* (New York: Basic Books, 1984), 52–60, 239; Weir, *Politics and Jobs,* 154–59.

57. Vogel, *Fluctuating Fortunes,* 231.

58. Ibid., 169–86, 232–33.

59. Ibid., 8–10, 228–33, 272–76, 290–91.

60. Alan Crawford, *Thunder on the Right: The "New Right" and the Politics of Resentment* (New York: Pantheon Books, 1980); Mike Davis, *Prisoners of the American Dream* (London: Verso, 1986), ch. 4; Thomas Byrne Edsall with Mary D. Edsall, *Chain Reaction: The Impact of Race, Rights, and Taxes on American Politics* (New York: Norton, 1991); Gillian Peele, *Revival and Reaction: The Right in Contemporary America* (Oxford, U.K.: Clarendon Press, 1984); Kevin P. Phillips, *Post-Conservative America: People, Politics, and Ideology in a Time of Crisis* (New York: Vintage Books, 1982).

61. In addition to the sources cited in the previous note, see also Ladd with Hadley, *Transformations of the American Party System*, 333–61.

62. Richard N. Block, John Beck, and Daniel H. Krueger, *Labor Law, Industrial Relations and Employee Choice* (Kalamazoo, Mich.: W. E. Upjohn Institute, 1996); Gordon L. Clark, *Unions and Communities under Siege: American Communities and the Crisis of Organized Labor* (Cambridge, U.K.: Cambridge University Press, 1989); Davis, *Prisoners of the American Dream*, ch. 3; Edsall, *The New Politics of Inequality*, ch. 4; Freeman and Medoff, *What Do Unions Do?* ch. 15; Sheldon Friedman, Richard W. Hurd, Rudolph A. Oswald, and Ronald L. Seeber, eds., *Restoring the Promise of American Labor Law* (Ithaca, N.Y.: ILR Press, 1994); Michael Goldfield, *The Decline of Organized Labor in the United States* (Chicago: University of Chicago Press, 1987); Harrison and Bluestone, *The Great U-Turn*; Marshall, *Unheard Voices*, ch. 5; Paul Weiler, *Governing the Workplace: The Future of Labor and Employment Law* (Cambridge, Mass.: Harvard University Press, 1990).

63. Edsall, *The New Politics of Inequality*, ch. 3; Harrison and Bluestone, *The Great U-Turn*; Vogel, *Fluctuating Fortunes*, chs. 7, 8.

64. See the sources in the previous note.

65. Edsall, *The New Politics of Inequality*, 72–73.

66. Ibid., ch. 2; Peele, *Revival and Reaction*, ch. 4.

67. Ibid.; Benjamin Ginsberg, "Money and Power: The New Political Economy of American Elections," in Thomas Ferguson and Joel Rogers, eds., *The Political Economy: Readings in the Politics and Economics of American Public Policy* (Armonk, N.Y.: M. E. Sharpe, 1984), 163–79.

68. Goldfield, *The Decline of Organized Labor*, 11, Table 2.

69. Ibid., chs. 1 and 9; Davis, *Prisoners of the American Dream*, 120–27, 131–32; Edsall, *The New Politics of Inequality*, 151–55; Freeman and Medoff, *What Do Unions Do*, ch. 15, esp. 232, 240.

70. See the sources cited in the previous note.

71. Edsall, *The New Politics of Inequality*, 165–70, 259, note 39.

72. Marcus D. Pohlman and George S. Crisci, "Support for Organized Labor in the House of Representatives: The 89th and 95th Congresses," *Political Science Quarterly* 4 (Winter 1982–83): 639–52; quote at 647.

73. Edsall, *The New Politics of Inequality*, 156; Vogel, *Fluctuating Fortunes*, 153–57; Dark, *The Unions and the Democrats*, 107–14.

74. Vogel, *Fluctuating Fortunes*, 141–44, 157–58; Weir, *Politics and Jobs*, ch. 5.

75. Ibid., 211.

76. Edsall, *The New Politics of Inequality*, 37–49.

77. Ibid., 74–75; Berman, *America's Right Turn*, 50–52.

78. Baer, *Reinventing Democrats*, 32.

79. Ibid., 32–33; Rae, "Party Factionalism," 57.

80. Robert Kuttner, *The Life of the Party: Democratic Prospects in 1988 and Beyond* (New York: Viking, 1987), 60.

81. Leo Troy, "The Rise and Fall of American Trade Unions: The Labor Movement from FDR to RR," in Lipset, ed., *Unions in Transition,* 75–112; Ladd with Hadley, *Transformations of the American Party System.*

82. Moody, *An Injury to All;* Alonzo L. Hamby, *Liberalism and Its Challengers, from F.D.R. to Bush,* 2nd ed. (New York: Oxford University Press, 1992), esp. the preface.

83. Freeman and Medoff, *What Do Unions Do?* ch. 15; Goldfield, *The Decline of Organized Labor.*

84. The sources cited in note 82 exemplify these difficulties.

Chapter 4: Labor Redivided

1. Arthur J. Goldberg, *AFL-CIO: Labor United* (New York: McGraw-Hill, 1956), 42–71; J. David Greenstone, *Labor in American Politics* (New York: Vintage Books, 1969), 39–58; Ruth Horowitz, *Political Ideologies of Organized Labor: The New Deal Era* (New Brunswick, N.J.: Transaction Books, 1978), 234–46.

2. Goldberg, *AFL-CIO,* 119–20; Victor Reuther, *The Brothers Reuther and the Story of the UAW: A Memoir* (Boston: Houghton Mifflin, 1976), ch. 25; Robert H. Zieger, *American Workers, American Unions,* 2nd ed. (Baltimore: Johns Hopkins University Press, 1994), 158–63; Robert H. Zieger, *The CIO, 1935–1955* (Chapel Hill: University of North Carolina Press, 1995), ch. 13.

3. Goldberg, *AFL-CIO,* 62–71, 102; Alan Draper, *A Rope of Sand: The AFL-CIO Committee on Political Education, 1855–67* (New York: Praeger, 1989), 28–39.

4. James R. Green, *The World of the Worker: Labor in Twentieth Century America* (New York: Hill and Wang, 1980), 222–24; Kim Moody, *An Injury to All: The Decline of American Unionism* (New York: Verso, 1988), ch. 3.

5. Graham K. Wilson, *Unions in American National Politics* (London: MacMillan, 1979), 7–9; Kevin Boyle, *The UAW and the Heyday of American Liberalism, 1945–1968* (Ithaca, N.Y.: Cornell University Press, 1995), 156–57; Walter Galenson, *The American Labor Movement, 1955–1995* (Westport, Conn.: Greenwood Press, 1996), 30.

6. John Barnard, *Walter Reuther and the Rise of the Auto Workers* (Boston: Little, Brown, 1983), 177–98; Boyle, *The UAW and the Heyday of American Liberalism,* 156–58, 219–28; Taylor E. Dark, *The Unions and the Democrats: An Enduring Alliance* (Ithaca, N.Y.: Cornell University Press, 1999), 69–75; Reuther, *The Brothers Reuther,* 365–81.

7. Ibid., 195.

8. Boyle, *The UAW and the Heyday of American Liberalism,* 246–48.

9. Nelson Lichtenstein, "Walter Reuther and the Rise of Labor-Liberalism," in Melvyn Dubofsky and Warren Van Tine, eds., *Labor Leaders in America* (Urbana: University of Illinois Press, 1987), 298–99.

10. Joseph Goulden, *Jerry Wurf: Labor's Last Angry Man* (New York: Atheneum, 1982), ch. 7; Reuther, *The Brothers Reuther,* 379; Sumner Rosen, "The United States: A Time for Reassessment," in Solomon Barkin, ed., *Worker Militancy and Its Consequences, 1965–1975: New Directions in Western Industrial Relations* (New York: Praeger, 1975), 335.

11. Andrew Battista, "Political Divisions in Organized Labor, 1968–1988," *Polity* 2 (Winter 1991): 173–97, esp. 186–91.

12. Robert Zieger, "George Meany: Labor's Organization Man," in Dubofsky and Van

Tine, eds., *Labor Leaders in America;* Mike Davis, *Prisoners of the American Dream* (London: Verso, 1986), 263–64; Dark, *The Unions and the Democrats,* 69–75.

13. John P. Windmuller, "The Foreign Policy Conflict in American Labor," *Political Science Quarterly* 82 (June 1967): 222–26.

14. Ibid., 229–31; Wilson, *Unions in American National Politics,* ch. 7; Zieger, *American Workers, American Unions,* 170–74.

15. John Herling, "Change and Conflict in the AFL-CIO," *Dissent* (Fall 1974): 479–85; David Brody, *Workers in Industrial America: Essays on the Twentieth Century Struggle* (New York: Oxford University Press, 1980), 227–28; Zieger, *American Workers, American Unions,* 170–74; Davis, *Prisoners of the American Dream,* 263.

16. Dark, *The Unions and the Democrats,* 77–87.

17. William Crotty, *Party Reform* (New York: Longman, 1983), 118–37.

18. Dark, *The Unions and the Democrats,* 69–75.

19. Ibid., 80–81.

20. Battista, "Political Divisions in Organized Labor," 186–91.

21. Windmuller, "The Foreign Policy Conflict in Organized Labor," 218–20, 222–26.

22. Wilson, *Unions in American National Politics,* 41–43; Dark, *The Unions and the Democrats,* 77–87.

23. Dark, *The Unions and the Democrats,* 69–75, 85–89.

24. Reuther, *The Brothers Reuther,* 367–71.

25. These proposals are summarized in Galenson, *The American Labor Movement,* 33.

26. Maurice F. Neufeld, "Structure and Government of the AFL-CIO," *Industrial and Labor Relations Review* 3 (April 1956): 371–90, esp. 381–82.

27. Galenson, *The American Labor Movement,* 23, 32–33; Lichtenstein, "Walter Reuther and the Rise of Labor-Liberalism," 298.

28. Ibid., 32.

29. Barnard, *Walter Reuther,* 196–97.

30. Galenson, *The American Labor Movement,* 32–35; Barnard, *Walter Reuther,* 195–99.

31. AFL-CIO, *Proceedings of the Tenth Constitutional Convention of the AFL-CIO, 1973,* 319.

32. Ibid.

33. Ibid., 320.

34. Ibid., 319–20, 325.

35. Ibid., quotes at 320 and 325.

36. Ibid., 320.

37. Herling, "Change and Conflict in the AFL-CIO," 482.

38. AFL-CIO, *Proceedings of the Tenth Constitutional Convention of the AFL-CIO, 1973,* 324.

39. Ibid., 324–25.

40. Ibid., 325.

41. Ibid., 326–27.

42. Ibid., 322–24, 327.

43. Ibid., 322.

44. Nick Kotz, "Can Labor's Tired Leaders Deal with a Troubled Movement?" *New York Times Magazine,* September 4, 1977, 10ff; "Labor Tries to Revitalize Itself," *Business Week,* September 12, 1977, 38–39; Brendan Sexton, "Progressive Stirrings in the American Unions," *Dissent* (Fall 1977): 347–50.

45. In addition to the sources cited in the previous note, see "Uphill All the Way: Interview: William W. Winpisinger," *Challenge* (March–April 1978): 44–53; William W. Winpisinger, *Reclaiming Our Future: An Agenda for American Labor*, edited by John Logue (Boulder, Colo.: Westview Press, 1989), including the introduction by Logue; and "Interview: The UAW's Doug Fraser Looks Ahead," *The Nation*, September 3, 1977, 171–76.

46. A. H. Raskin, "Big Labor Strives to Break Out of Its Rut," *Fortune*, August 27, 1979, 37; Lowell Turner and Richard W. Hurd, "Building Social Movement Unionism," in Lowell Turner, Harry C. Katz, and Richard W. Hurd, *Rekindling the Movement: Labor's Quest for Relevance in the 21st Century* (Ithaca, N.Y.: Cornell University Press, 2001), 18–19.

47. "Labor Tries to Revitalize Itself," 39.

48. Kotz, "Can Labor's Tired Leaders Deal with a Troubled Movement?" 30.

49. Ibid., 31 (quote); "Labor Tries to Revitalize Itself," 38–39; Sexton, "Progressive Stirrings in the American Unions," 348.

50. See the sources cited in the previous note.

51. "Labor Tries to Revitalize Itself," 39.

52. Ibid., 38–39; Herling, "Change and Conflict in the AFL-CIO," 483–84.

53. Quoted in Kotz, "Can Labor's Tired Leaders Deal with a Troubled Movement?" 10.

54. Sexton, "Progressive Stirrings in the American Unions," 348.

55. Gary M. Fink, "Labor Law Revision and the End of the Postwar Labor Accord," in Kevin Boyle, ed., *Organized Labor and American Politics, 1894–1994: The Labor-Liberal Alliance* (Albany: State University of New York Press, 1998), 244; Sexton, "Progressive Stirrings in the American Unions," 349.

56. "Labor Tries to Revitalize Itself," 39; Sexton, "Progressive Stirrings in the American Unions," 349.

57. See Kotz, "Can Labor's Tired Leaders Deal with a Troubled Movement?" 31; John Logue, "Introduction: William Winpisinger and the American Labor Movement," in Winpisinger, *Reclaiming Our Future*, 11.

58. Ibid.

59. Michael Harrington, *Taking Sides: The Education of a Militant Mind* (New York: Holt, Rinehart, and Winston, 1985), 153; Michael Harrington, *The Long-Distance Runner: An Autobiography* (Holt, 1988), 14–15; Michael Massing, "From Bolshevism to Reaganism: Trotsky's Orphans," *New Republic* (June 1987), 18–22.

60. Massing, "From Bolshevism to Reaganism," 19.

61. Gillian Peele, *Revival and Reaction: The Right in Contemporary America* (Oxford, U.K.: Oxford University Press, 1984), introduction and ch. 1; Robert Kuttner, *The Life of the Party: Democratic Prospects in 1988 and Beyond* (New York: Viking, 1987), 155–67.

62. Harrington, *The Long-Distance Runner*, 14; Kuttner, *The Life of the Party*, ch. 5; Peele, *Revival and Reaction*, introduction.

63. Ibid.; Massing, "From Bolshevism to Reaganism"; Moody, *An Injury to All*, 292–93.

64. Massing, "From Bolshevism to Reaganism," 20; Moody, *An Injury to All*, 293.

65. Harrington, *The Long-Distance Runner*, 13–14; Harrington, *Taking Sides*, 154–55.

66. Ibid., 15–25, quote at 25.

67. Ibid., 47; Stanley Aronowitz, "The Labor Movement and the Left in the United States," *Socialist Review*, 44 (1979): 9–59.

68. Ibid., 100–102; *Business Week*, September 24, 1979, 130–31; Aronowitz, "The Labor Movement and the Left in the United States"; idem., "Remaking the American Left, Part

One: Currents in American Radicalism," *Socialist Review* 67 (1983): 10–50; *Democratic Left,* Sept.–Oct. 1989, 18ff.

69. Ibid., 100–102.

70. Ibid., 103–4.

71. Ibid., 103–11.

72. Ibid., 114.

73. See Kenneth S. Baer, *Reinventing Democrats: The Politics of Liberalism from Reagan to Clinton* (Lawrence: University Press of Kansas, 2000), 80.

74. See Nicol C. Rae, "Party Factionalism, 1946–1996," in Byron E. Shafer, ed., *Partisan Approaches to Postwar American Politics* (New York: Chatham House, 1998), 66.

75. Reuther, *The Brothers Reuther;* Boyle, *The UAW and the Heyday of American Liberalism.*

76. Harrington, *The Long-Distance Runner,* 187–90.

77. Massing, "From Bolshevism to Reaganism"; Harrington, *The Long-Distance Runner,* 144, 160–73.

78. See "Socialism Is No Longer a Dirty Word to Labor," *Business Week,* September 24, 1979.

79. Kotz, "Can Labor's Tired Leaders Deal with a Troubled Movement?" 8ff; "Labor Tries to Revitalize Itself," 38–39.

Chapter 5: *The Progressive Alliance*

1. David Vogel, *Fluctuating Fortunes: The Political Power of Business in America* (New York: Basic Books, 1989), ch. 7.

2. *The Economist,* February 17, 1979, 44; *Solidarity,* October 15–30, 1978, 3–7; *Newsweek,* October 30, 1978, 31; *In These Times,* March 14–20, 1979, 2.

3. Progressive Alliance, "Statement of Principles," January 15, 1979.

4. *Newsweek,* October 30, 1978, 31.

5. Ira Katznelson, "A Radical Departure: Social Welfare and the Election," in Thomas Ferguson and Joel Rogers, eds., *The Hidden Election* (New York: Pantheon, 1981), 337–38; Jack W. Germond and Jules Witcover, "Liberal Alliance Falls Apart at Strange Time," *The Washington Star,* March 23, 1981.

6. See the series by Philip Shabecoff in the *New York Times,* April 29, May 15, May 25, June 18, 1978; *Congressional Quarterly Almanac 34,* 1978, 284–87; Thomas Ferguson and Joel Rogers, "Labor Law Reform and Its Enemies," *The Nation,* January 6–13, 1979, 1, 17–20.

7. The first quoted phrase is from Ferguson and Rogers, "Labor Law Reform," 1; the second is from Thomas B. Edsall, *The New Politics of Inequality* (New York: Norton, 1984), 128.

8. Ibid.

9. William T. Moye, "Presidential Labor-Management Committees: Productive Failures," *Industrial and Labor Relations Review* 1 (October 1980): 51–66.

10. Douglas Fraser, letter of resignation from the Labor-Management Group, July 17, 1978.

11. Ibid.

12. David Brody, *Workers in Industrial America: Essays on the Twentieth Century Struggle* (New York: Oxford University Press, 1980), 245–51.

13. Ibid., ch. 5; Thomas A. Kochan, Harry C. Katz, and Robert B. McKersie, *The Transformation of American Industrial Relations* (New York: Basic Books, 1986), ch. 2; Richard Edwards and Michael Podgursky, "The Unravelling Accord: American Unions in Crisis," in Richard Edwards, Paolo Garonna, and Franz Todtling, eds., *Unions in Crisis and Beyond: Perspectives from Six Countries* (Dover, Mass.: Auburn House, 1986), 14–60.

14. Fraser, letter of resignation.

15. Douglas Fraser, telephone interview, April 8, 1987.

16. *UAW Washington Report,* October, 1978, 3; *U.S. News and World Report,* October 9, 1978, 80; Marcus D. Pohlman and George S. Crisci, "Support for Organized Labor in the House of Representatives: The 89th and 95th Congresses," *Political Science Quarterly* 4 (Winter 1982–83): 639–52.

17. Douglas Fraser, letter of invitation to the initial planning meeting of the Progressive Alliance, September 19, 1978; Douglas Fraser, telephone interview, April 8, 1987.

18. Fraser, letter of invitation; Douglas Fraser, "Revitalized Left Needed for Principled Politics against Corporate Power," *In These Times,* June 6–12, 1979, 18.

19. Fraser, letter of resignation; Fraser, letter of invitation; Fraser, "Revitalized Left Needed."

20. Fraser, telephone interview, April 8, 1987; Douglas Fraser, "Functions of the Progressive Alliance," memo of May 3, 1979; Michael Harrington, telephone interview, April 13, 1987.

21. This list includes only the most important unions in the Alliance, as judged by levels of participation, leadership and staff positions, and financial support. Among the many liberal organizations that joined the Progressive Alliance were American Civil Liberties Union, Association of Community Organizations for Reform Now, Campaign for Economic Democracy, Children's Defense Fund, Consumer Federation of America, Environmental Action Federation, Federation of Southern Cooperatives, Friends of the Earth, Leadership Conference on Civil Rights, Martin Luther King Center, Massachusetts Fair Share, National Association for the Advancement of Colored People, National Council of La Raza, National Council of Negro Women, National Council of Senior Citizens, National Lawyers Guild, National Organization of Women, National Urban League, National Women's Political Caucus, Ohio Public Interest Campaign, Sierra Club, United States Student Association, and Women's Action Alliance. Progressive Alliance, "Membership Organizations," n.d.

22. Fraser, letter of invitation.

23. Fraser, telephone interview, April 8, 1987.

24. *Solidarity,* October 15–30, 1978, 5.

25. Political Process Commission, "Mandate for the Subcommission on Political Parties," January 16, 1980; Christopher Arterton, telephone interview, April 3, 1987.

26. *Solidarity,* October 15–30, 1978, 5.

27. Fraser, letter of invitation, 3, and the "Tentative Agenda" appended to this letter.

28. Fraser, telephone interview, April 8, 1987; Fraser, "Functions of the Progressive Alliance"; Michael Harrington, telephone interview, April 13, 1987.

29. Douglas Fraser, "Functions of the Progressive Alliance"; "Notes of 4/23/79 Meeting"; memo from Edgar James to Stephen Schlossberg and Don Stillman, April 9, 1979.

30. Progressive Alliance, "Democratic Credo: Economic Bill of Rights," n.d.

31. Progressive Alliance, "Instructions for the Commissions," January 14, 1979.

32. Memo from Marcus Raskin and Jacob Clayman to Issues Commission, May 19,

1980; Marcus Raskin, "Issues Commission Report" to the Progressive Alliance Executive Board, October 29, 1980.

33. Marcus Raskin, memo of April 9, 1980.

34. Fraser, "Functions of the Progressive Alliance."

35. Fraser, letter of invitation; Fraser, "Revitalized Left Needed"; and Progressive Alliance, "Statement of Principles."

36. Progressive Alliance, "Resolution for a Commission on Party Accountability."

37. See Crotty, *Party Reform,* 37, 42–43, 107–9.

38. Ibid., 107–9.

39. For an account of the final report of the Platform Accountability Commission, see the *National Journal,* May 26, 1984, 1026.

40. Douglas Fraser, "Functions of the Progressive Alliance"; Fraser, telephone interview, April 8, 1987; Terry Herndon, telephone interview, April 15, 1987; *Newsweek,* October 30, 1978, 31.

41. Douglas Fraser, "Progressive Alliance Organizing Projects," memo of May 7, 1979.

42. Political Process Commission, "Mandate for the Subcommission on Political Parties."

43. Edgar James, interview, Washington, D.C., July 16, 1986; Bill Dodds, memo of April 1, 1980.

44. Fraser, "Progressive Alliance Organizing Projects"; Fraser, "Revitalized Left Needed"; David M. Gordon, "Toward a Progressive Strategy on Economic Issues for the 1980s," January 1980 (paper prepared for the Progressive Alliance).

45. Memo from Marcus Raskin and Jacob Clayman to Issues Commission, May 19, 1980; David Gordon, telephone interview, April 17, 1987.

46. David Gordon, telephone interview, April 17, 1987.

47. Samuel Bowles, David M. Gordon, and Thomas E. Weisskopf, *Beyond the Waste Land: A Democratic Alternative to Economic Decline* (Garden City, N.Y.: Anchor Books, 1984); David Gordon, telephone interview, April 17, 1987.

48. "The Progressive Alliance," undated brochure; Progressive Alliance, "Regulatory Controversy: The Case of Health and Safety," March 7 and 8, 1980.

49. Fraser, "Progressive Alliance Organizing Projects." Stillman had previously published an important paper on the issue: Don Stillman, "The Devastating Impact of Plant Relocations," *Working Papers* 4 (July–August 1978), reprinted in Mark Green et al., eds., *The Big Business Reader,* rev. ed. (New York: Pilgrim Press, 1983), 137–48.

50. Barry Bluestone and Bennet Harrison, *Capital and Communities: The Causes and Consequences of Private Disinvestment* (Washington, D.C.: The Progressive Alliance, 1980). Bluestone and Harrison's report for the alliance was later published commercially in revised and expanded form; see Barry Bluestone and Bennett Harrison, *The Deindustrialization of America: Plant Closings, Community Abandonment, and the Dismantling of Basic Industry* (New York: Basic Books, 1982).

51. Raskin, "Issues Commission Report."

52. "The Progressive Alliance" (brochure); "Plant Closings Strategy Packet," edited by William Schweke and published jointly by the Progressive Alliance and the Conference on Alternative State and Local Policies, January 1980, 6.

53. Raskin, "Issues Commission Report"; "Notes of 4/23/79 Meeting"; "The Progressive Alliance" (brochure); and "Plant Closings Strategy Packet."

54. Ibid.

55. Statement of Barry Bluestone and Bennett Harrison before the House Committee on Small Business, Subcommittee on Antitrust, February 12, 1980.

56. Bluestone and Harrison, *Capital and Communities,* ch. 8.

57. *Congressional Quarterly Weekly Report,* July 9, 1988, 1919; and August 6, 1988, 2216.

58. John T. Addison and Barry T. Hirsch, "The Economic Effects of Employment Regulation: What Are the Limits?" in Bruce E. Kaufman, ed., *Government Regulation of the Employment Relationship* (Madison, Wis.: Industrial Relations Research Association, 1997), 125–78, esp. 153–56.

59. See Robert B. Reich and John D. Donahue, *New Deals: The Chrysler Revival and the American System* (New York: Penguin Books, 1986).

60. Bill Dodds, interview, July 14, 1986, Washington, D.C. For a different view, see "UAW Seat on Chrysler Board: What It Means for Workers," *Solidarity,* November 19, 1979.

61. Reich and Donahue, *New Deals,* 244–45.

62. On LICIT, see Kevin P. Phillips, *Staying on Top: Winning the Trade War* (New York: Vintage Books, 1986), 30–33, 70–71, 149.

63. Ibid., 101.

64. "Interview: Douglas Fraser," *Challenge* 1 (March-April 1979): 33–39; "Interview: William Winpisinger," *Challenge* 1 (March–April 1978): 44–53.

65. Edsall, *The New Politics of Inequality,* 237–38.

66. Bill Dodds, interview, July 14, 1986, Washington, D.C.; Kim Moody, *An Injury to All: The Decline of American Unionism* (London: Verso, 1988), 148–52.

67. Douglas Fraser, letter of April 27, 1981.

68. Germond and Witcover, "Liberal Alliance Falls Apart at Strange Time."

69. Christopher Arterton, telephone interview, April 3, 1987.

70. See *New York Times,* May 1, 1981, B16, and July 2, 1981, A14.

71. Edsall, *The New Politics of Inequality,* 143, 171; and Vogel, *Fluctuating Fortunes,* 257–60.

72. Edsall, *The New Politics of Inequality,* 171; I. M. Destler, *American Trade Politics* (Washington, D.C., and New York: Institute for International Economics and the Twentieth Century Fund, 1986), 72–73.

73. Moody, *An Injury to All,* 148–56; Andrew Battista, "Labor and Coalition Politics: The Progressive Alliance," *Labor History* 3 (Summer 1991): 401–21.

74. Reich and Donahue, *New Deals,* 99.

75. Leo Troy and Neil Sheflin, *Union Sourcebook* (West Orange, N.J.: IRDIS, 1985), 3–16, Table 3.71.

76. Germond and Witcover, "Liberal Alliance Falls Apart at Strange Time."

77. Terry Herndon, telephone interview, April 15, 1987; Bill Dodds, telephone interview, June 18, 1987.

78. Douglas Fraser, telephone interview, April 8, 1987.

79. Ibid.

80. Ibid.

81. Rademase Cabrera, interview, July 16, 1986, Washington, D.C.; Joann Howse, interview, July 15, 1986, Washington, D.C.; see also Germond and Witcover, "Liberal Alliance Falls Apart at Strange Time."

82. Terry Herndon, telephone interview, April 15, 1987; Heather Booth, telephone interview, March 20, 1987; Michael Harrington, telephone interview, April 13, 1987.

83. Douglas Fraser, telephone interview, April 8, 1987.

84. Michael Harrington, telephone interview, April 13, 1987.

85. William Serrin, "Working for the Union: An Interview with Douglas A. Fraser," *American Heritage* 2 (February–March 1985): 57–64; John Barnard, *Walter Reuther and the Rise of the Auto Workers* (Boston: Little, Brown, 1983); Kevin Boyle, *The UAW and the Heyday of American Liberalism, 1945–1968* (Ithaca, N.Y.: Cornell University Press, 1995); and Nelson Lichtenstein, *The Most Dangerous Man in Detroit: Walter Reuther and the Fate of American Labor* (New York: Basic Books, 1995).

Chapter 6: The Citizen Labor Energy Coalition

1. Peter B. Levy, *The New Left and Labor in the 1960s* (Urbana: University of Illinois Press, 1994), 154–55, 162.

2. The statewide citizen groups involved with Booth in the formation of CLEC were Massachusetts Fair Share, Connecticut Citizen Action Group, Ohio Public Interest Campaign, Illinois Public Action Council, and Oregon Fair Share. Heather Booth, interview, Washington, D.C., June 18, 1993; Harry Boyte, Heather Booth, and Steve Max, *Citizen Action and the New American Populism* (Philadelphia: Temple University Press, 1986), ch. 3.

3. Heather Booth, interview, Washington, D.C., June 18, 1993; John Logue, "William Winpisinger and the American Labor Movement," introduction to William W. Winpisinger, *Reclaiming Our Future: An Agenda for American Labor* (Boulder, Colo.: Westview Press, 1989), 1–19.

4. Memo from Jerry Thompson to Heather Booth and Bob Lawson, March 2, 1978; memo from Bob Lawson to William Winpisinger and CLEC staff, September 19, 1978; Heather Booth, interview, Washington, D.C., June 18, 1993; Robert Creamer, interview, Chicago, Ill., June 22, 1992; Robert Brandon, interview, Washington, D.C., June 17, 1993.

5. In addition to the Machinists union (IAM), the unions that joined CLEC included the United Auto Workers (UAW), American Federation of State, County and Municipal Employees (AFSCME), Oil, Chemical and Atomic Workers (OCAW), United Food and Commercial Workers (UFCW), National Education Association (NEA), Amalgamated Clothing and Textile Workers (ACTWU), United Steelworkers of America (USWA), Sheet Metal Workers (SMWIA), Service Employees International Union (SEIU), Communication Workers of America (CWA), Allied Industrial Workers (AIW), United Electrical Workers (UE), National Football League Players Association (NFLPA), Bakery Workers (BCTW), Electrical Workers (IUE), Ladies Garment Workers (ILGWU), American Federation of Government Employees (AFGE), and the Bricklayers Union (BAC). Memo from Jerry P. Thompson to Heather Booth and Bob Lawson, February 28, 1978; memo from Jerry Thompson to Heather Booth and Bob Lawson, March 2, 1978; Notes by William Winpisinger, Energy Coalition Luncheon, March 16, 1978; letter from William Winpisinger to union presidents, March 24, 1978; CLEC, "Unions on the Current Board (Executive Committee)," n.d.; memo from Bob Brandon to George Poulin, June 24, 1982; memo from Robert Brandon to William Winpisinger, July 28, 1982; William Winpisinger, telephone interview, March 23, 1995; Heather Booth, interview, Washington, D.C., June 18, 1993; Ken Rolling, interview, Chicago, Ill., June 25, 1992.

6. CLEC, "Citizen Labor Energy Coalition," April 28, 1978; letter from Robert M. Brandon to Mr. Ken Young, May 20, 1981; CLEC, "A History of the Citizen Labor Energy

Coalition," August 1983; CLEC, "Discussion Paper: Future Options and Strategies for CLEC," n.d.; Heather Booth, interview, Washington, D.C., June 18, 1993; Robert Creamer, interview, Chicago, Ill., June 22, 1992; Ken Rolling, interview, Chicago, Ill., June 25, 1992; Robert Brandon, interview, Washington, D.C., June 17, 1993; Bob Hudek, interview, Chicago, Ill., June 25, 1992.

7. CLEC, "Discussion Paper: Future Options and Strategies," n.d.; memo from Bob Lawson to CLEC Staff, February 8, 1979; Betsy Reid, "Status Report on the Development of a Statewide, Multi-issue Organization in Maryland," March 1981; Dan Kaemerer, "Status Report on the Development of a Statewide, Multi-issue Organization in Wisconsin," March 1981; CLEC, "A History of the Citizen Labor Energy Coalition," August 1983; Robert Brandon, interview, Washington, D.C., June 17, 1993; Robert Creamer, interview, Chicago, Ill., June 22, 1992; Don Wiener, interview, Chicago, Ill., June 24, 1992; Bob Hudek, interview, Chicago, Ill., June 25, 1992; Ken Rolling, interview, Chicago, Ill., June 25, 1992; David Moberg, "Activists Regroup for Reagan Years," *In These Times,* December 10–16, 1980.

8. William Winpisinger, telephone interview, March 23, 1995; Notes by William Winpisinger, Energy Coalition Luncheon, March 16, 1978; Outline of Remarks by William Winpisinger, Energy Coalition Planning Committee Meeting, April 19, 1978; letter from William Winpisinger to IAM Executive Council and Grand Lodge Representatives, May 31, 1978; memo from Bob Lawson to William Winpisinger and CLEC Staff, September 19, 1978; letter from Robert M. Brandon to Mr. Ken Young, May 20, 1981.

9. William Winpisinger, telephone interview, March 23, 1995.

10. Memo from Jerry Thompson to Heather Booth and Bob Lawson, March 2, 1978; memo from Bob Lawson, Heather Booth, and Barbara Shailor to CLEC Members, April 26, 1978; CLEC, "Citizen Labor Energy Coalition," April 28, 1978; memo from William Winpisinger to Executive Committee Members of Citizen Labor Energy Coalition, May 1, 1978; memo from Barbara Shailor to William Winpisinger, June 13, 1978; minutes of CLEC Executive Committee Meeting, November 14, 1978; memo from Ken Rolling to Heather Booth, May 24, 1979; minutes of May 22–23 CLEC Staff Meeting, May 24, 1979; memo from Heather Booth to William Winpisinger, William Hutton, Tim Sampson, Bob Creamer, Mike Ansara, and CLEC Staff, June 26, 1980; letter from Robert M. Brandon to Mr. Ken Young, May 20, 1981; Heather Booth, interview, Washington, D.C., June 18, 1993; Robert Brandon, interview, Washington, D.C., June 17, 1993; Ken Rolling, interview, Chicago, Ill., June 25, 1992; John Herbers, "Grass-Roots Groups Go National," *New York Times Magazine,* September 4, 1983, 22ff; Moberg, "Activists Regroup for Reagan Years."

11. CLEC, "Citizen Labor Energy Coalition National Staff," n.d.; Don Wiener, interview, Chicago, Ill., June 24, 1992; Heather Booth, interview, Washington, D.C., June 18, 1993; Ken Rolling, interview, Chicago, Ill., June 25, 1992.

12. CLEC, "Financial Report," November 14, 1978; letter from Bob Lawson to David Hunter, Stern Fund, October 10, 1978; minutes of CLEC Executive Committee Meeting, November 14, 1978; memo from Heather Booth to William Winpisinger, February 1, 1979; CLEC, "Citizen Labor Energy Coalition Consolidated Income Statement and Proposed Budget," April 1, 1979; memo from CLEC Staff to Executive Board, April 29, 1979; CLEC, "Labor Unions: Contributions/Memberships," December 27, 1979; memo from Ken Rolling to CLEC Staff, July 7, 1980; memo from Bob Hudek to CLEC Regional Organizers, August 14, 1980; letter from Robert M. Brandon to Mr. Ken Young, May 20, 1981; memo from Bob Brandon to George Poulan, June 24, 1982; memo from Robert Brandon to William Winpisinger, July 28, 1982; memo from Ken Rolling to CLEC Staff, January 17, 1983;

letter from Robert Brandon to Lou Brogna, September 20, 1983; Ken Rolling, interview, Chicago, Ill., June 25, 1992; Betsy Reid, interview, Washington, D.C., June 16, 1993; Bob Hudek, interview, Chicago, Ill., June 25, 1992; William Winpisinger, telephone interview, March 23, 1995.

13. Memo from Bob Lawson to CLEC Executive Committee, September 15, 1978; minutes of CLEC Executive Committee Meeting, November 14, 1978; letter from William Winpisinger to IAM Executive Council, Grand Lodge Representatives, et al., May 31, 1978; CLEC, "Regional Conferences," n.d.; Bob Lawson, "Citizen Labor Energy Coalition Progress Report," February 20, 1979; CLEC, "Citizen Labor Energy Coalition Consolidated Income Statement and Proposed Budget," April 1, 1979; memo from Bob Lawson to CLEC Staff, February 8, 1979; CLEC, "State Progress Reports," June 1980; CLEC, "A History of the Citizen Labor Energy Coalition," August 1983, 1, 4; Bob Hudek, interview, Chicago, Ill., June 25, 1992; Ken Rolling, interview, Chicago, Ill., June 25, 1992; Betsy Reid, interview, Washington, D.C., June 16, 1993.

14. Memo from Bob Lawson to CLEC Staff, February 8, 1979; Bob Lawson, "Citizen Labor Energy Coalition Progress Report," February 20, 1979; CLEC, "State Progress Reports," June 1980; CLEC, "A History of the Citizen Labor Energy Coalition," August 1983; Ken Rolling, interview, Chicago, Ill., June 25, 1992; Bob Hudek, interview, Chicago, Ill., June 25, 1992.

15. CLEC, "Citizen Labor Energy Coalition," April 28, 1978; CLEC, "Funding Proposal," n.d.; CLEC, "Building a Solid Foundation for National Energy Policy," reprinted from a 1978 issue of *The Machinist*; CLEC, "Energy Crisis Fact Sheet," n.d.; Statement of Robert M. Brandon to the Democratic Party Platform Advisory Committee on Energy, October 23, 1979.

16. Ibid.

17. CLEC, "Policy Statement for Energy Coalition," April 20, 1978; CLEC, "Citizen Labor Energy Coalition," April 28, 1978; CLEC, "Proposed Statement of Purpose and Structure," April 19, 1978; CLEC, "Proposed Campaign against Energy Profiteering," February 17, 1979; CLEC, "Natural Gas Decontrol Fact Sheet," n.d.; CLEC, "Draft Study to Determine the Jobs Impact of Energy Conservation and Solar Energy," n.d.; CLEC, "A History of the Citizen Labor Energy Coalition," August 1983.

18. CLEC, "Citizens' Energy Program," n.d. (1979); CLEC, "A Call for a Day of National Protest," n.d. (1979); CLEC, "A History of the Citizen Labor Energy Coalition," August 1983.

19. CLEC, "Citizen Labor Energy Coalition," April 28, 1978; CLEC, "Funding Proposal," n.d.; Bob Lawson, "Citizen Labor Energy Coalition Progress Report," February 20, 1979; letter from Robert M. Brandon to Mr. Ken Young, May 20, 1981; CLEC, "A History of the Citizen Labor Energy Coalition," August 1983.

20. CLEC, "Campaign on Utility Rate Reform: Working Draft," August 17, 1978; CLEC Utility Rate Reform Task Force, "Campaign," October 12, 1978; CLEC, "Campaign on Utility Rate Reform," October 12, 1978; CLEC, Press Release on Utility Shut-offs, Nov. 14, 1978; CLEC Press Release on Winter Shut-off Campaign, November 21, 1978; Bob Lawson, "Speech of January 8, 1979"; Bob Lawson, "Citizen Labor Coalition Progress Report," February 20, 1979; CLEC Utility Rate Reform Task Force, "Victories," April 30, 1979; CLEC Utility Rate Reform Task Force, "Report: Overview," July 30, 1980; CLEC Utility Rate Reform Task Force, "CLEC Victories," April 1, 1980; memo from Bob Hudek to Utility Rate Reform Task Force, March 31, 1980; CLEC, "A History of the Citizen Labor

Energy Coalition," August 1983; *Citizen Power* 3, August 1981; *Citizen Power* 5, Spring 1982; *Citizen Power* 9, June 1983. *Citizen Power* was the newspaper that CLEC published.

21. Memo from CLEC Commission on Pricing, Profits, and Industry Structure to CLEC National Board, August 1, 1980; CLEC, "Summary of Minutes: CLEC Board of Directors Meeting of November 20, 1980"; CLEC, "State Oil Tax Campaigns," July 31, 1980; CLEC, "State Taxation of Windfall Profits," March 25, 1980; memo from Bob Hudek to CLEC Staff, October 6, 1980; CLEC, "Campaigns to Enact State Profit Taxes on Major Oil Companies," December 7, 1981; memo from Bob Hudek to Oil Tax Campaign Participants, February 13, 1981; CLEC, "State Oil Profits Tax Campaigns: Update," June 24, 1981; memo from Scott Hempling to Affiliates and Friends of CLEC, May 4, 1982.

22. CLEC, "State Oil Tax Campaigns," July 31, 1980; memo from Bob Hudek to Oil Tax Campaign Participants, February 13, 1981; CLEC, "State Oil Profits Tax Campaigns: Update," June 24, 1981; CLEC, "Campaigns to Enact State Profit Taxes on Major Oil Companies," December 7, 1981; memo from Scott Hempling to Affiliates and Friends of CLEC, May 4, 1982; CLEC, *Citizen Power* 3, August 1981; CLEC, *Citizen Power* 5, Spring 1982.

23. CLEC, "Citizen Labor Energy Coalition," April 28, 1978; CLEC, "Draft Study to Determine Jobs Impact of Energy Conservation and Solar Energy," n.d.; CLEC, "Job Campaign Through Energy Conservation and Solar Energy," September 30, 1978; memo from CLEC Staff to CLEC Executive Committee, November 3, 1978; "Speech by Bob Lawson of January 8, 1979"; Bob Lawson, "Citizen Labor Energy Coalition Progress Report," February 20, 1979; CLEC National Office, "Jobs and Energy: Targeted Cities Weatherization Campaign," July 1980; CLEC, "Summary of Minutes: CLEC Board of Directors Meeting," November 20, 1980.

24. CLEC, "Summary of Minutes: CLEC Board of Directors Meeting," November 20, 1980; CLEC, "A History of the Citizen Labor Energy Coalition," August 1983, 3.

25. CLEC Press Release, "Coalition Launches Campaign against Major Oil Companies," May 1, 1979; Statement of Robert M. Brandon, Washington Director, Citizen Labor Energy Coalition, Before House Energy and Power Subcommittee, May 17, 1979; CLEC, "Crude Oil Decontrol," May 9, 1979; memo from Ken Rolling to Members of CLEC, May 10, 1979; CLEC Press Release, "Grassroots Activities Set to Fight against Oil Companies," September, 4, 1979; CLEC, "A Call for a Day of National Protest," n.d.; CLEC, "Organizing Plans for Big Oil Protest Day," n.d.; memo from Robert Brandon to CLEC Organizers, July 17, 1980; CLEC, "A History of the Citizen Labor Energy Coalition," August 1983; *Kansas City Star,* May 3, 1979; *Wall Street Journal,* May 2, 1979; Walter Rosenbaum, *Energy, Politics, and Public Policy* (Washington, D.C.: Congressional Quarterly Press, 1981), 145–51; Congressional Quarterly, eds., *Energy and Environment: The Unfinished Business* (Washington, D.C.: Congressional Quarterly Press, 1985), 20–23; David Vogel, *Fluctuating Fortunes: The Political Power of Business in America* (New York: Basic Books, 1989), 178–81.

26. Helen Dewar, "Citizen Groups Say Oil Profits Are Understated," *Washington Post,* November 15, 1979; Vogel, *Fluctuating Fortunes,* 180–81; Rosenbaum, *Energy, Politics, and Public Policy,* 149–51; Congressional Quarterly, eds., *Energy and Environment,* 22–23.

27. Vogel, *Fluctuating Fortunes,* 177–78; Rosenbaum, *Energy, Politics, and Public Policy,* 152–59; Congressional Quarterly, eds., *Energy and Environment,* 28–29.

28. CLEC, "Policy on Natural Gas Pricing," April 20, 1978; CLEC, "Proposed Action Agenda on Natural Gas," April 19, 1978; CLEC, "Natural Gas Update," November 11, 1978; "Bob Lawson Speech," January 8, 1979.

29. CLEC, "Natural Gas Decontrol Means Higher Gas Bills, Inflation," August 18, 1981;

CLEC, "Natural Gas Decontrol Will Add to Jobless Totals," August 18, 1981; CLEC, "Decontrol Won't Aid Gas Production, Conservation," August 18, 1981; memo from CLEC to Newspaper Editors and Energy Reporters, March 17, 1981; CLEC Press Release, "Gas Decontrol to Cost 3.4 Million Jobs, Study Says," June 24, 1981; CLEC Press Release, "Coalition Kicks Off National Lobbying Effort to Stop Natural Gas Decontrol," February 19, 1981; memo from AFL-CIO and CLEC to District Coordinators, n.d.; CLEC, "Natural Gas Campaign Summary," March 9, 1981; memo from Don Wiener and Bob Brandon to CLEC Affiliates and Allies, February 1981; CLEC, "Labor, Citizen Groups Mount Campaign to Stop Gas Decontrol," August 18, 1981; CLEC, *Citizen Power*, August 1981, 4; CLEC, "Preventing Backdoor Decontrol: The FERC Strategy," June 24, 1981; memo from Scott Hempling to Staff and Friends in the Natural Gas Campaign, November 25, 1981; memo from CLEC to Labor Unions and National Organizations, February 11, 1982; memo from CLEC Staff to Board of Directors and Friends, October 11, 1982; CLEC, "Background on the Natural Gas Decontrol Debate," n.d.; CLEC Campaign to Stop Gas Decontrol, "List of State Coordinators," n.d.; CLEC, *Citizen Power*, Spring 1982, 1; CLEC, "Natural Gas Decontrol Fact Sheet," n.d.; memo from Robert A. Brandon to CLEC Board of Directors, March 22, 1982; CLEC Press Release, "Coalition Hails Grass Roots Efforts That Win Congressional Majority," April 7, 1982; memo from CLEC to National Organizations, April 20, 1982; Robert D. Hershey, "Reagan Ends Push on Gas Decontrol," *New York Times*, March 2, 1982; Congressional Quarterly, eds., *Energy and Environment*, 30–31; Ed Rothschild, interview, Washington, D.C., June 17, 1993; Don Wiener, interview, Chicago, Ill., June 24, 1992; Robert Creamer, interview, Chicago, Ill., June 22, 1992.

30. In the House of Representatives the NGCRA was HR2154, and its primary sponsors were Representatives Gephardt (D-MO) and Glickman (D-KA); in the Senate it was S996, sponsored by Senators Eagleton (D-MO) and Kassebaum (R-KA). *Congressional Quarterly Weekly Report*, March 5, 1983, 446, noted that CLEC had "become an important voice in the natural gas debate" and "played the lead role in crafting the principal alternative to the administration plan."

31. Memo from Natural Gas Campaign Staff to Affiliates and Allies, July 8, 1983; CLEC, "Gas Protest Day Sweeps the Country," n.d.; memo from CLEC Staff to Staff Directors, January 16, 1984; memo from Campaign to Stop Natural Gas Decontrol to Allies, April 13, 1984; memo from CLEC Staff to Allies, July 28, 1984; *Congressional Quarterly Weekly Report*, March 5, 1983, 443–47; CLEC, *Citizen Power*, June 1983, 1–2; Congressional Quarterly, eds., *Energy and Environment*, 31.

32. Rosenbaum, *Energy, Politics, and Public Policy*, 143.

33. Examples of the energy industry's vigilance and resistance include the following: the American Petroleum Institute alerted its members to CLEC's campaign to impose state taxes on oil firms; oil and natural-gas companies expended considerable resources and effort to block CLEC's Natural Gas Consumer Relief Act; Mobil took out full-page ads in major newspapers to rebut CLEC's analysis of oil company profits; and the Natural Gas Supply Association created a front organization that imitated CLEC's door-to-door canvass and commissioned a report that red-baited CLEC. CLEC, "Building a Solid Foundation for National Energy Policy"; William Winpisinger, "An Open Statement to the Delegates at the 1978 Midterm Democratic Conference," December 9, 1978; CLEC, "Policy Statement for Energy Coalition," April 20, 1978; CLEC Press Release, "Coalition Launches Campaign against Major Oil Companies," May 1, 1979; IAM, "A National Citizen Action/Labor Co-

alition on Energy Policy," n.d.; CLEC Energy Industry Task Force, "Proposal to CLEC Board," December 12, 1979; memo from Committee on Pricing, Profits, and Industry Structure to CLEC National Board, August 1, 1980; memo from Scott Hempling to Affiliates and Friends of CLEC, May 4, 1982; letter from Robert Brandon to Mr. Robert W. Stewart, June 13, 1983; letter from Ken Rolling to Mr. Richard W. Zemin, May 29, 1983; memo from Natural Gas Campaign Staff to Affiliates and Allies of CLEC, July 8, 1983; CLEC, "A History of the Citizen Labor Energy Coalition," August 1983; Ed Rothschild, interview, Washington, D.C., June 17, 1993; Betsy Reid, interview, Washington, D.C., June 16, 1993.

34. Bob Lawson, "Citizen Labor Energy Coalition Progress Report," February 20, 1979; CLEC, "State Progress Reports," June 1980; CLEC, *Citizen Power,* August 1981, 3; memo from CLEC Campaign Staff to CLEC Affiliates and Allies, December 28, 1982; memo from CLEC Staff to CLEC Board of Directors and Friends, October 11, 1982; CLEC, "A History of the Citizen Labor Energy Coalition," August 1983; Bob Hudek, interview, Chicago, Ill., June 25, 1992; Ken Rolling, interview, Chicago, Ill., June 25, 1992; Rosenbaum, *Energy, Politics, and Public Policy,* 141–42, 204–7.

35. Memo from Bob Lawson to William Winpisinger and CLEC Staff, September 19, 1978; Bob Lawson, speech of January 8, 1979; Robert Creamer, interview, Chicago, Ill., June 22, 1992; Robert Brandon, interview, Washington, D.C., June 17, 1993.

36. David Moberg, "How Far Will Populists Go?" *In These Times,* August 6–19, 1986; Herbers, "Grass-roots Groups Go National"; Jack Germond and Jules Witcover, "Closing In on Mainstream," syndicated column of August 5, 1987; Salim Muwakkil, "Opening New Doors for the Left," *In These Times,* May 18–24, 1988; Robert Creamer, interview, Chicago, Ill., June 22, 1992; Robert Brandon, interview, Washington, D.C., June 17, 1993; Heather Booth, interview, Washington, D.C., June 18, 1993; William Winpisinger, telephone interview, March 23, 1995; Robert Kuttner, *The Life of the Party: Democratic Prospects in 1988 and Beyond* (New York: Viking, 1987), 144–50.

37. Robert Creamer, interview, Chicago, Ill., June 22, 1992; Ken Rolling, interview, Chicago, Ill., June 25, 1992; Bob Hudek, interview, Chicago, Ill., June 25, 1992; Don Wiener, interview, Chicago, Ill., June 24, 1992; Robert Brandon, interview, Washington, D.C., June 17, 1993; William Winpisinger, telephone interview, March 23, 1995.

38. CLEC, "Citizen Labor Energy Coalition," April 28, 1978; CLEC Press Release, "Grassroots Activities Set to Fight against Oil Companies," September 4, 1979; *Wall Street Journal,* May 2, 1979; CLEC, "A Call for A Day of National Protest," n.d.; CLEC, "Background on the Natural Gas Decontrol Debate," n.d.; letter from Robert M. Brandon to Mr. Ken Young, May 20, 1981; memo from Natural Gas Campaign Staff to Canvass Directors and Supervisors, September 23, 1983; memo from Natural Gas Campaign Staff to Affiliates and Allies, July 8, 1983; CLEC, "A History of the Citizen Labor Energy Coalition," August 1983; Don Wiener, interview, Chicago, Ill., June 24, 1992; Ken Rolling, interview, Chicago, Ill., June 25, 1992; Bob Hudek, interview, Chicago, Ill., June 25, 1992; Ed Rothschild, interview, Washington, D.C., June 17, 1993; Robert Brandon, interview, Washington, D.C., June 17, 1993.

39. Memo from Bob Lawson to CLEC Staff, February 8, 1979; CLEC, "Proposed Campaign against Energy Profiteering," February 17, 1979; memo from Heather Booth to CLEC Board Members, March 5, 1980; CLEC, "Labor, Citizen Groups Mount Campaign to Stop Decontrol," August 18, 1981; memo from Robert A. Brandon to CLEC Board of Directors, March 22, 1982; CLEC Press Release, "Coalition Hails Grass Roots Efforts that Win Con-

gressional Majority," April 7, 1982; *Citizen Power* 9, June 1983, 1–2; Bob Hudek, interview, Chicago, Ill., June 25, 1992; Ed Rothschild, interview, Washington, D.C., June 17, 1993.

40. CLEC, "Proposed Statement of Purpose and Structure," April 19, 1978; memo to CLEC Executive Committee from CLEC Staff, n.d.; CLEC, "Preliminary Outline: Natural Gas Strategy," April 6, 1982; CLEC, "A History of the Citizen Labor Energy Coalition," August 1983; Ken Rolling, interview, Chicago, Ill., June 25, 1992; Heather Booth, interview, Washington, D.C., June 18, 1993; William Winpisinger, telephone interview, March 23, 1995; Moberg, "Activists Regroup for Reagan Years"; Moberg, "Citizen Groups Seek Effective National Politics"; Herbers, "Grass-roots Groups Go National"; Vogel, *Fluctuating Fortunes,* ch. 5.

41. CLEC, "Preliminary Outline: Natural Gas Strategy," April 6, 1982; memo from CLEC Central Staff to CLEC Staff and Allies, April 30, 1982; memo from CLEC Washington Office to Staff and Affiliates of CLEC, July 13, 1982; memo from CLEC Campaign Staff to CLEC Affiliates and Allies, November 10, 1982; memo from Robert Brandon to William Winpisinger, July 28, 1982; CLEC, "A History of the Citizen Labor Energy Coalition," August 1983; Don Wiener, interview, Chicago, Ill., June 24, 1992; Ken Rolling, interview, Chicago, Ill., June 25, 1992; William Winpisinger, telephone interview, March 23, 1995.

42. William Winpisinger, "An Open Statement to the Delegates at the 1978 Mid-term Democratic Conference," December 9, 1978; Statement of Robert M. Brandon, Washington Director of the Citizen Labor Energy Coalition, to the Democratic Party Platform Advisory Committee on Energy, October 23, 1979; CLEC, "Draft: Heating Oil Price Controls/Oil Industry Accountability Campaign," November 13, 1979; memo from CLEC Washington Office to CLEC Organizers, March 28, 1980; letter from Michael Podhorzer to Gene Gessow, Democratic National Committee, April 15, 1982; letter from Michael Podhorzer to the Energy and Environment Task Force, Democratic National Committee, April 16, 1982; memo from CLEC Central Staff to CLEC Staff and Allies, April 30, 1982; William Winpisinger, telephone interview, March 23, 1995.

43. Memo from CLEC Washington Office to Staff and Affiliates of CLEC, July 13, 1982; CLEC, "A History of the Citizen Labor Energy Coalition," August 1983; John Judis, "Playing for Keeps," *In These Times,* June 16, 1982.

44. CLEC, "Citizen Labor Energy Coalition," April 28, 1978; William W. Winpisinger, "Outline of Remarks by William W. Winpisinger, Energy Coalition Planning Committee Meeting," April 19, 1978; CLEC, "A National Citizen Action-Labor Coalition on Energy Policy," n.d.; CLEC, "Citizens' Energy Program," n.d. Important statements of the left-populist strategy include: Boyte, Booth, and Max, *Citizen Action;* Robert Kuttner, *The Life of the Party;* Harold Meyerson, "Why the Democrats Keep Losing: The Abandonment of Economic Populism," *Dissent,* Summer 1989, 305–10; and Jeff Faux, "A New Conversation: How to Rebuild the Democratic Party," *American Prospect,* Spring 1995, 35–43.

45. James L. Sundquist, *Dynamics of the Party System: Alignment and Realignment of Political Parties in the United States,* rev. ed. (Washington, D.C.: Brookings Institution, 1983), 352–411; Benjamin Ginsberg and Martin Shefter, "A Critical Realignment? The New Politics, the Reconstituted Right, and the 1984 Elections," in Michael Nelson, ed., *The Elections of 1984* (Washington, D.C.: Congressional Quarterly Press, 1985), 1–25; Thomas Byrne Edsall with Mary D. Edsall, *Chain Reaction* (New York: Norton, 1992).

46. On the vulnerability of populist coalitions to racial politics, see Robert Huckfeldt and Carol W. Kohfeld, *Race and the Decline of Class in American Politics* (Urbana and Chicago: University of Illinois Press, 1989), esp. ch. 5; and Edsall, *Chain Reaction.*

47. Heather Booth, telephone conversation of May 14, 1996.
48. William Winpisinger, telephone interview, March 23, 1995.
49. Heather Booth, interview, Washington, D.C., June 18, 1993.

Chapter 7: The National Labor Committee

1. Morris J. Blachman, William M. LeoGrande, and Kenneth Sharpe, eds., *Confronting Revolution: Security through Diplomacy in Central America* (New York: Pantheon Books, 1986); Nora Hamilton, Jeffrey A. Frieden, Linda Fuller, and Manuel Pastor Jr., eds., *Crisis in Central America: Regional Dynamics and U.S. Policy in the 1980s* (Boulder, Colo.: Westview Press, 1988).

2. In addition to the sources cited in the previous note, see Christian Smith, *Resisting Reagan: The U.S. Central America Peace Movement* (Chicago: University of Chicago Press, 1996), chs. 2, 3. Smith discusses Reagan administration plans for direct U.S. military intervention in Central America at pp. 24–34; see also on this topic Blachman et al., *Confronting Revolution,* 309–16.

3. The views and policies of the AFL-CIO on Central America during the 1980s will be documented in detail later.

4. David Dyson, interview, New York City, May 10, 1993.

5. Jack Sheinkman, interview, New York City, May 11, 1993; David Dyson and Daniel Cantor, "Anaheim and After: A Proposal for General Support Funding of the National Labor Committee," September 1986; NLC, "Background on the National Labor Committee," n.d.; National Labor Committee in Support of Democracy and Human Rights in El Salvador, *The Search for Peace in Central America,* May 1985.

As of 1985, the membership of the National Labor Committee was as follows, with all members being presidents of their respective unions unless otherwise noted: Jack Sheinkman, secretary-treasurer, ACTWU; Douglas Fraser, president emeritus, UAW; William Winpisinger, IAM; Morton Bahr, Communications Workers of America (CWA); Owen Bieber, UAW; Kenneth Blaylock, American Federation of Government Employees (AFGE); Kenneth Brown, Graphic Communications International Union (GCIU); Bernard Butsavage, International Molders and Allied Workers Union (IMAW); William Bywater, International Union of Electrical Workers (IUE); Cesar Chavez, United Farm Workers of America (UFW); John DeConcini, Bakery, Confectionary and Tobacco Workers Union (BCTW); Murray Finley, ACTWU; Mary Hatwood Futrell, National Education Association (NEA); James Herman, International Longshoremen's and Warehousemen's Union (ILWU); Keith Johnson, International Woodworkers of America (IWA); James Kane, United Electrical Workers (UE); Frank Martino, International Chemical Workers Union (ICW); Gerald McEntee, American Federation of State, County and Municipal Employees (AFSCME); Joseph Misbrener, Oil, Chemical and Atomic Workers (OCAW); Henry Nicholas, National Union of Hospital and Health Care Employees (NUHHCE); Charles Perlik, The Newspaper Guild (TNG); Carl Scarbrough, United Furniture Workers of America (UFWA); Vincent Sombrotto, National Association of Letter Carriers (NALC); John Sweeney, Service Employees International Union (SEIU); and J.C. Turner, International Union of Operating Engineers (IUOE). National Labor Committee in Support of Democracy and Human Rights in El Salvador, *The Search for Peace in Central America,* May 1985, 3–4; National Labor Committee in Support of Democracy and Human Rights in El Salvador, *El Salvador: Critical Choices,* June 1989, inside front cover; and National

Labor Committee Education Fund in Support of Worker and Human Rights in Central America, *Haiti After the Coup: Still in the Hands of Thugs,* April 1993, 4–5.

6. Jack Sheinkman, interview, New York City, May 11, 1993; David Dyson, interview, New York City, May 10, 1993; Daniel Cantor, interview, May 11, 1993.

7. Dave Slaney, "Solidarity and Self-Interest," *NACLA: Report on the Americas,* May–June 1988, 30; Sean Sweeney, *Labour Imperialism or Democratic Internationalism? U.S. Trade Unions and the Conflict in El Salvador and Nicaragua, 1981–1989,* Ph.D. diss., University of Bath, 1990, 291–92. The industrial sectors of NLC unions were determined based on data on union membership by industry group in Bureau of Labor Statistics, *Directory of National Unions and Employee Associations, 1979,* Appendix A.

8. The membership figure was calculated from data in Courtney D. Gifford, *Directory of U.S. Labor Organizations, 1988–89 Edition* (Washington, D.C.: Bureau of National Affairs, 1988), 42, 47, and Appendix A. David Dyson, interview, New York City, May 10, 1993; Dave Dyson and Bill Patterson, memo to Don Stillman, November 16, 1983; Jack Sheinkman, letter to Henry Nicholas, June 3, 1986; David Dyson, memo to El Salvador Contacts, June 29, 1989; Kitty Krupat, "From War Zone to Free Trade Zone: A History of the National Labor Committee," in Andrew Ross, ed., *No Sweat: Fashion, Free Trade, and the Rights of Garment Workers* (New York: Verso, 1997), 73; Daniel Cantor, interview, New York City, May 11, 1993; Charles Kernaghan, interview, New York City, May 12, 1993.

9. Daniel Cantor, interview, New York City, May 11, 1993; Jack Sheinkman, interview, New York City, May 11, 1993.

10. National Labor Committee in Support of Democracy and Human Rights in El Salvador and New York City Labor Committee in Support of Democracy and Human Rights in El Salvador, "And Now We Too Must Speak Out," *New York Times,* March 26, 1982; National Labor Committee, "Background on the National Labor Committee," n.d., 3.

11. Jack Sheinkman, interview, New York City, May 11, 1993.

12. National Labor Committee and New York City Labor Committee, "And Now We Too Must Speak Out"; David Dyson and Daniel Cantor, "Anaheim and After: A Proposal for General Support Funding of the National Labor Committee," September 1986, 6, 9.

13. National Labor Committee and New York City Labor Committee, "And Now We Too Must Speak Out"; Jack Sheinkman, interview, New York City, May 11, 1993; David Dyson, interview, New York City, May 10, 1993; National Labor Committee, "Background on the National Labor Committee," n.d.

14. Jack Sheinkman, interview, New York City, May 11, 1993; David Dyson, interview, New York City, May 10, 1993; Daniel Cantor, interview, New York City, May 11, 1993; David Dyson and Daniel Cantor, "Anaheim and After: A Proposal for General Support Funding of the National Labor Committee," September 1986, 4–5; Slaney, "Solidarity and Self-Interest," 28–36.

15. The four reports published by the National Labor Committee in Support of Democracy and Human Rights in El Salvador were *El Salvador: Labor, Terror, and Peace* (July 1983); *The Search for Peace in Central America* (May 1985); *El Salvador: Critical Choices* (June 1989); and *El Salvador 1990: Arena Repression Unites the Salvadoran Labor Movement* (September 1990).

16. National Labor Committee and New York City Labor Committee, "And Now We Too Must Speak Out"; NLC, *El Salvador: Labor, Terror, and Peace,* 3–7, 11–15; NLC, *The Search for Peace in Central America,* 7–10, 14–15, 24; NLC, *El Salvador: Critical Choices,*

4–8, 13–15; NLC, *El Salvador 1990: ARENA Repression Unites the Salvadoran Labor Movement,* 3–5; David Dyson, "Testimony of April 27, 1988," 1–6.

17. National Labor Committee and New York City Labor Committee, "And Now We Too Must Speak Out"; NLC, *El Salvador: Labor, Terror, and Peace,* 18–19; NLC, *The Search for Peace in Central America,* 13–16, 24, 27; NLC, *El Salvador: Critical Choices,* 12–15; NLC, *El Salvador 1990: ARENA Repression Unites the Salvadoran Labor Movement,* 1–2, 13–14; David Dyson, "Testimony of April 27, 1988," 4–6, 17. The Contadora process was initiated in 1983 by Panama, Mexico, Columbia, and Venezuela to promote a regional political settlement of the conflicts in Central America, and the Arias Plan, proposed later in the decade by the Costa Rican president Oscar Arias, was likewise a framework for a region-wide negotiated settlement of Central American conflicts. Because the Contadora process and Arias Plan favored regional settlement of Central American conflicts by means of political negotiations, in which the United States would have no direct role or influence, the Reagan administration was hostile toward both. The Arias Plan, for which President Arias received a Nobel Prize in 1987, led to the Esquipulas Accord of that year, which provided a framework under which the governments and oppositions of Nicaragua, El Salvador, and other Central American nations negotiated treaties that concluded their military conflicts.

18. NLC, *The Search for Peace in Central America,* 17–25.

19. NLC, *El Salvador: Labor, Terror, and Peace,* 1–2; NLC, *The Search for Peace in Central America,* 3–5; NLC, *El Salvador: Critical Choices,* 2–3; NLC, *El Salvador 1990,* "Preface"; NLC, *Labor Rights Denied, El Salvador: An On-Site Investigation by a Delegation of Labor-Legislative-Religious Leaders,* December 1988, 3–4; Jack Sheinkman, interview, New York City, May 11, 1993; David Dyson, interview, New York City, May 10, 1993; Daniel Cantor, interview, New York City, May 11, 1993.

20. National Union of Salvadoran Workers (UNTS), "Proposal for Tour of the United States by a Delegation from the National Union of Salvadoran Workers (UNTS)," n.d.; NLC, "Freed Salvadoran Labor Leader Meets N.Y. Union Leaders," press release, June 20, 1989; David Dyson, memo to (ACTWU) General Office Staff, June 21, 1989; NLC, *El Salvador 1990,* "Preface."

21. David Dyson, "Testimony before House Appropriations Subcommittee on Foreign Operations," May 17, 1985; David Dyson, "Testimony of April 27, 1988"; Jack Sheinkman, letter to Henry Nicholas, June 3, 1986; Jack Sheinkman, letter to William Winpisinger, 1 October 1987; NLC, "Funding El Salvador: Debate in the U.S. Congress," March–April 1989; NLC, "Funding El Salvador: Legislative Overview," April 26, 1989; Jack Sheinkman, letter to the Honorable Dante Fascell, May 22, 1989; David Dyson and Charles Kernaghan, memo to Labor Contacts, November 1989; David Dyson and Charles Kernaghan, memo to Labor Contacts, April 25, 1990; Charles Kernaghan, memo to National Labor Committee Contacts, October 21, 1991.

22. NLC, "An Appeal to the People of the U.S.," photocopy, n.d.; Jack Sheinkman, interview, New York City, May 11, 1993; David Dyson, interview, New York City, May 10, 1993; Daniel Cantor, interview, New York City, May 11, 1993; Sweeney, *Labour Imperialism or Democratic Internationalism?* 548–52, 570–73.

23. NLC, "Cities Committees," n.d.; Ben Davis, letter to David Dyson, July 25, 1988; Denys Everingham and Bruce Bodner, letter to Labor Committee Supporters, n.d.; Tess Ewing, letter to Brothers and Sisters, June 1, 1988; Tess Ewing, letter to Dave Dyson, May 26, 1989; Scott Harding, letter to Dave Dyson, June 24, 1988; "Interview with David

Dyson," *Labor Report on Central America,* 1988 (prepublication transcription); Slaney, "Solidarity and Self-Interest," 28–36; Labor Coalition on Central America, *Labor Action,* February 1990; Labor Coalition on Central America, *Labor Action,* April/May 1990; Jack Sheinkman, interview, New York City, May 11, 1993; David Dyson, interview, New York City, May 10, 1993; Daniel Cantor, interview, New York City, May 11, 1993.

24. Jack Sheinkman, interview, New York City, May 11, 1993.

25. National Labor Committee and New York City Labor Committee, "And Now We Too Must Speak Out"; Jack Sheinkman, letter to Supporters, October 17, 1984; David Dyson, letter to Ken Blaylock, December 23, 1986; David Dyson, letter to John DeMars, November 17, 1987; NLC, *Labor Rights Denied: El Salvador,* 3; NLC, "Funding El Salvador: Legislative Overview," April 26, 1989; David Dyson, memo to General Office Staff, June 21, 1989; David Dyson, memo to El Salvador Contacts, June 29, 1989; David Dyson and Charles Kernaghan, memo to Labor Contacts, November 1989; NLC, "An Appeal to President Bush and Congress: Statement Agreed to at Labor-Religious Dialogue for Peace in El Salvador," December 20, 1989; Jack Sheinkman, memo to Members of the National Labor Committee, January 18, 1990; Sweeney, *Labour Imperialism or Democratic Internationalism?* 578–80.

26. Jack Sheinkman, letter to William Winpisinger, October 1, 1987; Union of Salvadoran Workers (UNTS), "Proposal for Tour of the United States by a Delegation from the Union of Salvadoran Workers (UNTS), n.d.; David Dyson, letter to John DeMars, November 17, 1987; "Interview with David Dyson," *Labor Report on Central America,* 1988; David Dyson, memo to General Office Staff, June 21, 1989; David Dyson, memo to El Salvador Contacts, June 29, 1989; NLC, *El Salvador: Critical Choices,* June 1989, 3; David Dyson and Charles Kernaghan, memo to Labor Contacts, April 25, 1990; Smith, *Resisting Reagan,* 97–99; NLC, "Funding El Salvador: Legislative Overview," April 26, 1989.

27. Smith, *Resisting Reagan,* 365–72; William M. LeoGrande, Douglas C. Bennett, Morris J. Blachman, and Kenneth E. Sharpe, "Grappling with Central America: From Carter to Reagan," in Blachman, LeoGrande, and Sharpe, eds., *Confronting Revolution,* ch. 12; Cynthia Arnson, "The Reagan Administration, Congress, and Central America: The Search for Consensus," in Hamilton, Frieden, Fuller, and Pastor Jr., eds., *Crisis in Central America,* ch. 2; Philip Brenner and William M. LeoGrande, "Congress and Nicaragua: The Limits of Alternative Policy Making," in James A. Thurber, ed., *Divided Democracy: Cooperation and Conflict between the President and Congress* (Washington, D.C.: CQ Press, 1991), ch. 11; Cynthia J. Arnson and Philip Brenner, "The Limits of Lobbying: Interest Groups, Congress, and Aid to the Contras," in Richard Sobel, ed., *Public Opinion in U.S. Foreign Policy: The Controversy over Contra Aid* (Lanham, Md.: Rowman and Littlefield, 1993), 191–219.

28. Brenner and Leogrande, "Congress and Nicaragua," 243–44; Arnson, "The Reagan Administration, Congress, and Central America," 51; Arnson and Brenner, "The Limits of Lobbying."

29. Buhl quoted in Smith, *Resisting Reagan,* 246.

30. See the sources listed in note 28.

31. Jack Sheinkman, interview, New York City, May 11, 1993; Dan Cantor, memo to Local Committees, November 25, 1985; NLC, "Funding El Salvador: Legislative Overview," April 26, 1989; "Interview with David Dyson," *Labor Report on Central America,* 1988.

32. "The Kissinger Commission Report," *Free Trade Union News,* February 1984, 1–2; Lane Kirkland, "The Challenge in Latin America," *Free Trade Union News,* July–August

1984, 1, 2, 8; AFL-CIO, "Resolution No. 34 (As Amended), AFL-CIO Convention, October 1985"; AFL-CIO, *Trade Union Rights, Peace and Democracy in Central America: Report of a Delegation of AFL-CIO Presidents to Nicaragua and El Salvador,* September 1987, 1–12; AFL-CIO/American Institute for Free Labor Development, "A Critique of the Americas Watch Report on Labor Rights in El Salvador," June 10, 1988; American Institute for Free Labor Development, *Source Book: El Salvador,* November 1988, section titled "El Salvador: Key Issues"; American Institute for Free Labor Development, *Source Book: Nicaragua,* November 1988, section titled "Nicaragua: Key Issues"; Aaron Bernstein, "Is Big Labor Playing Global Vigilante?" *Business Week,* November 4, 1985, 92–93; David Moberg, "Teaching the AFL-CIO Some New Tricks," *In These Times,* November 13–19, 1985, 5–6; Henry Bernstein, "U.S. Unionists Split on Strategy for Central American Aid," *Los Angeles Times,* May 14, 1986.

33. Lane Kirkland, letter to Principal Officers of State and Local Central Bodies, March 24, 1983; ACTWU, "Resolution on El Salvador, Submitted to the 1983 Convention of the AFL-CIO"; Lane Kirkland, letter to Mr. Frank Hammer, September 13, 1984; Lane Kirkland, "The Challenge in Latin America"; ACTWU, "Resolution on El Salvador, Submitted to the 1985 Convention of the AFL-CIO"; AFL-CIO, "Resolution No. 34 (As Amended), AFL-CIO Convention, October 1985"; AFL-CIO, "Our Values: An Introduction," n.d.; AFL-CIO Executive Council, "Resolution on Central America and the Caribbean," February 1988; AFL-CIO Executive Council, "Statement on Central America," February 23, 1989; Jack Sheinkman, letter to Tom Donahue, May 10, 1990; Labor Coalition on Central America, *Labor Action,* July/August 1990, 10; James Ridgeway, "Lane Kirkland Snubs the Lech Walesa of El Salvador," *Village Voice,* May 29, 1984; Henry Weinstein, "AFL-CIO Supports Arias Peace Proposal," *Los Angeles Times,* October 28, 1987; Slaney, "Solidarity and Self-Interest," 30; William M. LeoGrande, "Through the Looking Glass: The Kissinger Report on Central America," *World Policy Journal,* Winter 1984, 251–84.

34. ACTWU, "Resolution on El Salvador, Submitted to the 1983 Convention of the AFL-CIO"; ACTWU, "Resolution on El Salvador, Submitted to the 1985 Convention of the AFL-CIO"; AFL-CIO, "Resolution No. 34 (As Amended), AFL-CIO Convention, October 1985"; Weinstein, "AFL-CIO Supports Arias Peace Proposal"; Slaney, "Solidarity and Self-Interest," 30.

35. Faye Hansen, "The AFL-CIO and the Endowment for Democracy," *Economic Notes,* May–June 1985, 12–15; "The Kissinger Commission Report," *Free Trade Union News,* February 1984, 1–2; Jack Germond and Jules Witcover, "'Contra' Debate Shows New Foreign Policy Stance by Labor," *Baltimore Sun,* March 23, 1986; Bureau of National Affairs, *Daily Labor Report,* January 9, 1988.

36. AFL-CIO, "Floor Debate on Resolution No. 34," AFL-CIO Convention, October 1985 (transcription); AFL-CIO, "Resolution No. 34 (As Amended), AFL-CIO Convention, October 1985"; David Moberg, "Teaching the AFL-CIO Some New Tricks," 5–6; Washington Area Labor Committee, *The Labor Link,* Spring 1986, 1; Harry Bernstein, "U.S. Unionists Split on Strategy for Central American Aid," *Los Angeles Times,* May 14, 1986; William Serrin, "Reagan Bid Stirring Longstanding Labor Debate," *New York Times,* March 4, 1986; Weinstein, "AFL-CIO Supports Arias Peace Proposal"; David Dyson and Daniel Cantor, memo to City Committees, Local Unions, Friends, and Supporters, November 6, 1987; Kenneth Crowe, "AFL-CIO Opposes Aid to Contras," *Newsday,* October 28, 1987.

37. Brenner and LeoGrande, "Congress and Nicaragua," 232; AFL-CIO Executive Council, "Resolution on Central America and the Caribbean," February 1988; David Dyson,

letter to John DeMars, November 17, 1987; "Interview with David Dyson," *Labor Report,* 1988.

38. Jack Sheinkman, interview, New York City, May 11, 1993.

39. Jack Sheinkman, letter to Tom Donahue, May 10, 1990; Daniel Cantor and Juliet Schor, *Tunnel Vision: Labor, The World Economy, and Central America* (Boston: South End Press, 1987), 77–78; Paul Garver, "Beyond the Cold War: New Directions for Labor Internationalism," *Labor Research Review* (Spring 1989): 61–71; AFL-CIO, *Trade Union Rights, Peace and Democracy in Central America,* 2, 7–12; American Institute for Free Labor Development, *Source Book: Nicaragua,* section entitled "Nicaragua: Key Issues"; NLC, *The Search for Peace in Central America,* 17–19; Lane Kirkland, letter to Principal Officers of State and Local Central Bodies, March 24, 1983; Bernstein, "Is Big Labor Playing Global Vigilante?"; Bernstein, "U.S. Unionists Split on Strategy for Central American Aid"; Al Weinrub and William Bollinger, *The AFL-CIO in Central America* (Oakland, Calif.: Labor Network on Central America), 1987, 21–26; Tom Barry and Deb Preusch, *AIFLD in Central America* (Albuquerque, N.M.: Inter-Hemispheric Education Resource Center), 1986), 31–40; AFL-CIO/American Institute for Free Labor Development, "A Critique of the Americas Watch Report," 3–15.

40. David Dyson, interview, New York City, May 10, 1993; Jean Weisman, "U.S. Labor Leaders Help Win Release of Ten Salvadoran Trade Unionists" (photocopy; source unknown); Lane Kirkland, letter to Principal Officers of State and Local Central Bodies, March 24, 1983; Tom Kahn, memo to State Federations and Central Bodies, August 22, 1986; Slaney, "Solidarity and Self-Interest," 30–31.

41. The favored red-baiting techniques were on display in Tom Kahn, memo to State Federations and Central Bodies, August 22, 1986; John T. Joyce, letter of April 1, 1987; Albert Shanker, "Where We Stand," *New York Times,* April 19, 1987.

42. Lane Kirkland, letter to Principal Officers of State and Local Central Bodies, March 24, 1983; Fred Solowey, interview, Washington, D.C., June 16, 1993; Slaney, "Solidarity and Self-Interest," 30–32.

43. Lane Kirkland, letter to Principal Officers of State and Local Central Bodies, March 24, 1983; Charlie Dee, letter to Mr. Lane Kirkland, April 20, 1983; Charlie Dee, letter to Mr. Irving Brown, May 19, 1983; Tom Kahn, memo to State Federations and Central Bodies, August 22, 1986; Eric Thiel, memo to Tom Kahn, Director of International Affairs, AFL-CIO, August 27, 1986; Bernstein, "Is Big Labor Playing Global Vigilante?"; Slaney, "Solidarity and Self-Interest," 30–32; Cantor and Schor, *Tunnel Vision.*

44. NLC, press release, October 16, 1984; Jose Arnulfo Grande et al., letter to National Labor Committee, November 30, 1984; Weisman, "U.S. Labor Leaders Help Win Release of Ten Salvadoran Trade Unionists"; Jack Sheinkman, interview, New York City, May 11, 1993; David Dyson, interview, New York City, May 10, 1993; Ridgeway, "Lane Kirkland Snubs the Lech Walesa of El Salvador."

45. David Dyson, interview, New York City, May 10, 1993; Labor Coalition on Central America, *Labor Action,* July/August 1990, 2, 10, 15; Sweeney, *Labour Imperialism or Democratic Internationalism?* 310–19.

46. Krupat, "From War Zone to Free Trade Zone," 69; Jack Sheinkman, interview, New York City, May 11, 1993; David Dyson, interview, New York City, May 10, 1993; Isabelle Letelier, letter to Jack Sheinkman, June 26, 1989.

47. Robert H. Zieger, *The CIO, 1935–1955* (Chapel Hill: University of North Carolina Press, 1995), ch. 9, 328–32, 374–76; Denis MacShane, *International Labour and the Origins*

of the Cold War (Oxford, U.K.: Clarendon Press, 1992), chs. 6–8; John Barnard, *Walter Reuther and the Rise of the Auto Workers* (Boston: Little, Brown, 1983), ch. 7; David Plotke, *Building a Democratic Political Order: Reshaping American Liberalism in the 1930s and 1940s* (Cambridge, U.K.: Cambridge University Press, 1996), ch. 10; John P. Windmuller, "The Foreign Policy Conflict in American Labor," *Political Science Quarterly* 82 (June 1967): 205–34; Adolph Sturmthal, *Left of Center: European Labor since World War II* (Urbana: University of Illinois Press, 1983), chs. 1–4, 16. More critical analyses of American labor's Cold War commitments include Ronald Radosh, *American Labor and United States Foreign Policy* (New York: Vintage Books, 1969); Henry Berger, "Organized Labor and American Foreign Policy," in I. L. Horowitz, J. C. Leggett, and M. Oppenheimer, eds., *The American Working Class: Prospects for the 1980s* (New Brunswick, N.J.: Transaction Books, 1979), ch. 7; and Cantor and Schor, *Tunnel Vision.*

48. Allen J. Matusow, *The Unraveling of America: A History of Liberalism in the 1960s* (New York: Harper and Row, 1984), ch. 13; Jerel A. Rosati, *The Politics of United States Foreign Policy* (Fort Worth, Tex.: Harcourt Brace, 1999), 2nd ed., 398–405, 460–66; Sturmthal, *Left of Center,* ch. 16; Windmuller, "The Foreign Policy Conflict in American Labor."

49. Windmuller, "The Foreign Policy Conflict in American Labor"; Cantor and Schor, *Tunnel Vision,* 34–48; Kim Moody, *An Injury to All: The Decline of American Unionism* (London: Verso, 1988), 288–96; Sturmthal, *Left of Center,* ch. 16.

50. Robert H. Zieger, "George Meany: Labor's Organization Man," in Melvyn Dubofsky and Warren Van Tine, eds., *Labor Leaders in America* (Urbana: University of Illinois Press, 1987), ch. 14; Walter Galenson, *The American Labor Movement, 1955–1995* (Westport, Conn.: Greenwood Press, 1996), ch. 14; Radosh, *American Labor and United States Foreign Policy,* ch. 14; Taylor Dark, *The Unions and the Democrats: An Enduring Alliance* (Ithaca, N.Y.: Cornell University Press, 1999), 66, 102; Michael Massing, "From Bolshevism to Reaganism: Trotsky's Orphans," *New Republic,* June 1987, 18–22; Jack Clark, "The 'Ex' Syndrome," *NACLA: Report on the Americas,* May/June 1988, 26; Bernstein, "Is Big Labor Playing Global Vigilante?"

51. David Dyson, interview, New York City, May 10, 1993; Fred Solowey, interview, Washington, D.C., June 16, 1993; National Labor Committee and New York City Labor Committee, "And Now We Too Must Speak Out"; Cantor and Schor, *Tunnel Vision,* 3–5, 12–18; Slaney, "Solidarity and Self-Interest," 29; Hobart Spalding, "The Two Latin American Foreign Policies of the U.S. Labor Movement," *Science and Society* (Winter 1992–93): 421–39.

52. Andrew Battista, "Political Divisions in Organized Labor, 1968–1988," *Polity* (Winter 1991): 173–97; Steve Early and Suzanne Gordon, "The Union Label: Today's Hardhats Are Peaceniks," *Boston Globe,* April 19, 1987; Sean Sweeney, interview, New York City, May 12, 1993; Andrew Battista, "The Economic and Social Bases of Liberal Unionism," prepared for the 1990 Annual Meeting of the Midwest Political Science Association, Chicago, Ill.

53. David Dyson, interview, New York City, May 10, 1993.

54. National Labor Committee and New York City Labor Committee, "And Now We Too Must Speak Out"; Jack Sheinkman, interview, New York City, May 11, 1993; Fred Solowey, interview, Washington, D.C., June 16, 1993; Slaney, "Solidarity and Self-Interest," 29; Cantor and Schor, *Tunnel Vision,* 12–13; David Dyson, interview, New York City, May 10, 1993; Daniel Cantor, interview, New York City, May 11, 1993; Graham K. Wilson, *Unions in American National Politics* (London: MacMillan, 1979), ch. 3; AFL-CIO, "Floor Debate on Resolution No. 34, AFL-CIO Convention, October 1985" (transcript); Sweeney, *Labour Imperialism or Democratic Internationalism?* 35–38, 636–45.

55. Jack Sheinkman, interview, New York City, May 11, 1993.

56. Jack Sheinkman, "Preface" to NLC, *Worker Rights and the New World Order: El Salvador, Honduras, Guatemala,* June 1991, 1.

57. David Dyson, interview, New York City, May 10, 1993; Charles Kernaghan, interview, New York City, May 12, 1993; Ron Blackwell, interview, New York City, May 14, 1993; Krupat, "From War Zone to Free Trade Zone," 71; Smith, *Resisting Reagan,* 348–54; NLC, *Paying to Lose Our Jobs,* September 1992, 1–2.

58. NLC, *Paying to Lose Our Jobs,* September 1992; NLC, "Partial News Coverage as of December 11, 1992"; NLC, "Summary of 1994 Accomplishments," n.d.; Charles Kernaghan, interview, New York City, May 12, 1993; Barbara Briggs, "Aiding and Abetting Corporate Flight: U.S. AID in the Caribbean Basin," *Multinational Monitor,* January/February 1993, 37–41; Krupat, "From War Zone to Free Trade Zone," 71–73; Bureau of National Affairs, *Daily Labor Report,* October 1, 1992; Erin Day, "Foreign Aid's Role in Private Sector Promotion in Developing Countries: The Controversy over the U.S. Agency for International Development," Congressional Research Service, CRS Report 92–931 F, December 11, 1992.

59. NLC, "Summary of 1995 Accomplishments," n.d.; NLC, "The 'Authentic Gap': How Would You Like Your Daughter to Work for the Gap?", November/December 1995; Charles Kernaghan, memo to NLC Contacts, December 16, 1995; NLC, "Disney Alert," July 25, 1996; NLC, "An Open Letter to Walt Disney Co.," May 29, 1996; NLC, *The U.S. in Haiti: How to Get Rich on Eleven Cents an Hour,* January/February 1996; Barry Bearak, "Kathie Lee and the Sweatshop Crusade," *Los Angeles Times,* June 14, 1996; Krupat, "From War Zone to Free Trade Zone," 51–63; Don Stillman, "Charles Kernaghan: The Labor Activist Who Made Kathie Lee Cry," *WorkingUSA,* July/August 1998, 30–41, 75–79.

60. For varied assessments of NLC's approach to the problem of sweatshops, see the contributions by Ross, Cavanagh, Krupat, Piore, and Howard in Ross, ed., *No Sweat;* Stillman, "Charles Kernaghan"; and David Moberg, "Lessons from the Victory at Phillips Van Heusen," *WorkingUSA,* May–June 1998, 39–49.

61. The major study of the U.S. Central America peace movement is Smith, *Resisting Reagan;* see also Arnson and Brenner, "The Limits of Lobbying."

Chapter 8: *The Political Strategy and Social Bases of the Dissident Unions*

1. Douglas Fraser, "Revitalized Left Needed for Principled Politics against Corporate Power," *In These Times,* June 6–12, 1979; William W. Winpisinger, *Reclaiming Our Future: An Agenda for American Labor* (Boulder, Colo.: Westview Press, 1989), ch. 7.

2. Douglas Fraser, letter of resignation from the Labor Management Group, July 17, 1978.

3. Seymour Melman, *The Permanent War Economy,* rev. ed. (New York: Simon and Schuster, 1985), 245–47; Andrew Battista, "The Economic and Social Bases of Liberal Unionism," paper presented to the 1990 Annual Meeting of the Midwest Political Science Association, Chicago, 7–10.

4. Taylor E. Dark, *The Unions and the Democrats: An Enduring Alliance* (Ithaca, N.Y.: Cornell University Press, 1999), ch. 4.

5. Kay Lehman Schlozman and John T. Tierney, *Organized Interests and American Democracy* (New York: Harper and Row, 1986), chs. 7, 8; Jeffrey M. Berry, *The Interest*

Group Society, 3rd ed. (New York: Longman, 1997), ch. 6; Darrell M. West and Burdett A. Loomis, *The Sound of Money: How Political Interests Get What They Want* (New York: Norton, 1998), chs. 1, 2.

6. Andrew Battista, "Political Divisions in Organized Labor, 1968–1988," *Polity* 2 (Winter 1991): 187–89.

7. J. David Greenstone, *Labor in American Politics* (New York: Vintage Books, 1969), 369–71; Ruth Horowitz, *Political Ideologies of Organized Labor: The New Deal Era* (New Brunswick, N.J.: Transaction Books, 1978), 201–38; Graham K. Wilson, *Unions in American National Politics* (London: MacMillan, 1979), 57–86.

8. The figures in this paragraph were calculated from data contained in Bureau of Labor Statistics, *Directory of National Unions and Employee Associations, 1979* (Washington, D.C.: GPO, 1980), 21–49; and in Gary Fink, ed., *Labor Unions* (Westport, Conn.: Greenwood Press, 1977), Appendix 1 and Appendix 3.

9. Horowitz, *Political Ideologies of Organized Labor,* 234–35; Kim Moody, *An Injury to All: The Decline of American Unionism* (London: Verso, 1988), 194, 213.

10. The figures in this paragraph were calculated from data contained in Bureau of Labor Statistics, *Directory of National Unions,* Appendix I.

11. Ruth Milkman, "Women Workers, Feminism, and the Labor Movement Since the 1960s," in Milkman, ed., *Women, Work, and Protest* (Boston and London: Routledge and Kegan Paul, 1985), 306 (Table 2).

12. William B. Gould, *Black Workers in White Unions: Job Discrimination in the United States* (Ithaca, N.Y.: Cornell University Press, 1977), 365, 387, 398; Hector Figueroa, "The Growing Force of Latino Labor," *NACLA: Report on the Americas* 30 (November/December 1996): 19–24.

13. Bureau of Labor Statistics, *Earnings and Other Characteristics of Organized Workers, May 1980* (Washington, D.C.: GPO, 1981), 18–19.

14. Greenstone, *Labor in American Politics,* 361–71; Horowitz, *Political Ideologies of Organized Labor,* 220–33.

15. Steven Fraser, *Labor Will Rule: Sidney Hillman and the Rise of American Labor* (New York: The Free Press, 1991); Kevin Boyle, *The UAW and the Heyday of American Liberalism, 1945–1968* (Ithaca, N.Y.: Cornell University Press, 1995).

16. Moody, *An Injury to All,* 272–81; Daniel B. Cornfield, "Union Decline and the Political Demands of Organized Labor," *Work and Occupations* 16 (August 1989): 292–322; William Form, *Segmented Labor, Fractured Politics: Labor Politics in American Life* (New York: Plenum Press, 1995), 22, 330.

17. Stanley Aronowitz, *Working Class Hero: A New Strategy for Labor* (New York: Pilgrim Press, 1983), 135–43; Leon Fink and Brian Greenberg, *Upheaval in the Quiet Zone: A History of Hospital Workers' Union, Local 1199* (Urbana: University of Illinois Press, 1989).

18. Peter B. Levy, *The New Left and Labor in the 1960s* (Urbana: University of Illinois Press, 1994); Dark, *The Unions and the Democrats;* Taylor E. Dark, "Debating Decline: The 1995 Race for the AFL-CIO Presidency," *Labor History* 3 (August 1999): 323–44.

19. Leo Troy, "The Rise and Fall of American Trade Unions: The Labor Movement from FDR to RR," in Seymour Martin Lipset, ed., *Unions in Transition: Entering the Second Century* (San Francisco: Institute for Contemporary Studies, 1986), 75–109; Leo Troy, "Public Sector Unionism: The Rising Power Center of Organized Labor," *Government Union Review* 3 (Summer 1988): 1–35. See also Kenneth R. Weinstein and August Stofferahn, *From Meany to Sweeney: Labor's Leftward Tilt,* The Heritage Foundation, Backgrounder No. 1094, October 4, 1996, available at www.heritage.org/library/categories/govern/bgl094.

20. Troy, "Public Sector Unionism," 7–9; Troy, "The Rise and Fall of American Trade Unions," 104–7.

21. Ibid.; Weinstein and Stofferahn, *From Meany to Sweeney*, 1–3, 8.

22. Harold Meyerson, "Solidarity Sometimes," *American Prospect*, September 24–October 8, 2001, 6–7; William Form, *Segmented Labor, Fractured Politics*, 18–22.

23. Thomas Edsall, *The New Politics of Inequality* (New York: Norton, 1984), 143–44, 170–72.

24. David Vogel, *Fluctuating Fortunes: The Political Power of Business in America* (New York: Basic Books, 1989), 181–86, 255–60; Walter Galenson, *The American Labor Movement, 1955–1995* (Westport, CT: Greenwood Press, 1996), 134–49.

25. Christopher L. Erickson, "Collective Bargaining in the Aerospace Industry in the 1980s"; Jeffrey Keefe and Karen Boroff, "Telecommunications Labor-Management Relations after Divestiture"; and Richard P. Chaykowski, Terry Thomason, and Harris L. Zwerling, "Labor Relations in American Textiles," chs. 3, 8, and 9, respectively, of Paula B. Voos, ed., *Contemporary Collective Bargaining in the Private Sector* (Madison, Wis.: Industrial Relations Research Association, 1994).

26. Edsall, *The New Politics of Inequality*, 171.

27. Thomas A. Kochan, Harry C. Katz, and Robert B. McKersie, *The Transformation of American Industrial Relation* (New York: Basic Books, 1986), chs. 5, 6.

28. International Association of Machinists, *Let's Rebuild America* (Washington, D.C.: IAM, 1983); Industrial Union Department (AFL-CIO), *Crossroads for America: Choosing a Better Future for American Industry and the American People* (Washington, D.C.: IUD, 1986); Ray Marshall, *Unheard Voices: Labor and Economic Policy in a Competitive World* (New York: Basic Books, 1987), ch. 9; Robert Kuttner, *The End of Laissez-Faire: National Purpose and the Global Economy after the Cold War* (New York: Knopf, 1991), ch. 4; Jeff Faux, *The Party's Not Over: A New Vision for the Democrats* (New York: Basic Books, 1996), ch. 6.

29. Moody, *An Injury to All*, xx and chs. 1, 3, 7.

30. Ibid. See also Kim Moody, "Building a Labor Movement for the 1990s: Cooperation and Concessions or Confrontation and Coalition," in Jeremy Brecher and Tim Costello, eds., *Building Bridges: The Emerging Grassroots Coalition of Labor and Community* (New York: Monthly Review Press, 1990), 216–28; Eric Mann, "Labor-Community Coalitions as a Tactic for Labor Insurgency," in Brecher and Costello, *Building Bridges*, 113–32.

31. Mike Davis, *Prisoners of the American Dream* (London: Verso, 1986), chs. 2, 7; Michael Goldfield, *The Decline of Organized Labor in the United States* (Chicago: University of Chicago Press, 1987), ch. 11.

32. See David Brody, *Workers in Industrial America: Essays on the Twentieth Century Struggle* (New York: Oxford University Press, 1980), ch. 5; Greenstone, *Labor in American Politics*, ch. 2; and Form, *Segmented Labor, Fractured Politics*, ch. 12.

33. For such arguments and evidence, see Greenstone, *Labor in American Politics*, ch. 10; Richard B. Freeman and James L. Medoff, *What Do Unions Do?* (New York: Basic Books, 1984), ch. 14; and Dark, *The Unions and the Democrats*, esp. chs. 7, 8, and conclusion.

34. Moody, *An Injury to All*, 148–52; Davis, *Prisoners of the American Dream*, 179–80, 266–67.

35. Stan Weir, "Doug Fraser's Middle Class Coalition," *Radical America*, January–February 1979, 19–29; Moody, *An Injury to All*, chs. 7, 8, 14; Moody, "Building a Labor Movement for the 1990s"; Jeremy Brecher and Tim Costello, "Concluding Essay: Labor-Community

Coalitions and the Restructuring of Power," in Brecher and Costello, eds., *Building Bridges,* 325–45.

36. Steven J. Rosenstone, Roy L. Behr, and Edward H. Lazarus, *Third Parties in America,* 2nd ed. (Princeton, N.J.: Princeton University Press, 1996); Paul S. Herrnson and John C. Green, eds., *Multi-Party Politics in America* (Lanham, Md.: Rowman and Littlefield, 1997); Douglas J. Amy, *Real Choices, New Voices* (New York: Columbia University Press, 1993).

37. Freeman and Medoff, *What Do Unions Do?* 217–20; Kochan, Katz, and McKersie, *The Transformation of American Industrial Relations,* 134–37; R. Bean, *Comparative Industrial Relations: An Introduction to Cross-National Perspectives* (New York: St. Martin's Press, 1985), ch. 6.

38. Andrew Martin, *The Politics of Economic Policy in the United States: A Tentative View from a Comparative Perspective,* Sage Professional Papers in Comparative Politics, Series No. 01-040, Vol. 4 (Beverly Hills: Sage, 1973); John D. Stephens, *The Transition from Capitalism to Socialism* (Urbana: University of Illinois Press, 1979), 87, ch. 4; David R. Cameron, "Social Democracy, Corporatism, Labor Quiescence and the Representation of Economic Interest in Advanced Capitalist Society," in John H. Goldthorpe, ed., *Order and Conflict in Contemporary Capitalism* (Oxford, U.K.: Oxford University Press, 1984), 143–78.

39. Thomas Ferguson and Joel Rogers, "The State of the Unions," *The Nation,* April 28, 1979, 462–65.

40. Aronowitz, *Working Class Hero,* 193–98.

41. Stanley Aronowitz, *The Death and Rebirth of American Radicalism* (New York: Routledge, 1996), 51.

42. See Form, *Segmented Labor, Fractured Politics,* 335; Dark, *The Unions and the Democrats,* 139.

Chapter 9: *Toward, and Beyond, 1995*

1. Harold Meyerson, "A Second Chance: The New AFL-CIO and the Prospective Revival of the American Labor Movement," in Jo-Ann Mort, ed., *Not Your Father's Union Movement: Inside the AFL-CIO* (London and New York: Verso, 1998), 133–44; Taylor E. Dark, "Debating Decline," *Labor History* 3 (August 1999): 323–43.

2. Observers as different as Mike Davis and Taylor Dark claimed that the split between the Meany and Reuther wings was repaired by the early 1980s. Mike Davis, *Prisoners of the American Dream* (London: Verso, 1986), 261–67; Taylor E. Dark, *The Unions and the Democrats: An Enduring Alliance* (Ithaca, N.Y.: Cornell University Press, 1999), 141, 145.

3. As has been argued in Dark, "Debating Decline."

4. John Logue, "Introduction: William Winpisinger and the American Labor Movement," in William W. Winpisinger, *Reclaiming Our Future: An Agenda for American Labor* (Boulder, Colo.: Westview Press, 1989), 11; Andrew Battista, "Political Divisions in Organized Labor, 1968–1988," *Polity* 2 (Winter 1991): 194–95.

5. Thomas Byrne Edsall, *The New Politics of Inequality* (New York: Norton, 1984), 167.

6. Ibid., 168; Amy Foerster, "Confronting the Dilemmas of Organizing: Obstacles and Innovations at the AFL-CIO Organizing Institute," in Lowell Turner, Harry C. Katz, and Richard W. Hurd, eds., *Rekindling the Movement: Labor's Quest for Relevance in the 21st Century* (Ithaca, N.Y.: Cornell University Press, 2001), 158–60.

7. Ibid.; Foerster, "Confronting the Dilemmas of Organizing," 158 (quote).

8. Dark, *The Unions and the Democrats,* 127.

9. Bill Keller, "Once a Washington Power, Labor Now Plays Catch-Up in Lobbying and Politics," *Congressional Quarterly Weekly Report,* September 4, 1982, 3; William Form, *Segmented Labor, Fractured Politics: Labor Politics in American Life* (New York: Plenum Press, 1995), 302–4, 315–16; Dark, *The Unions and the Democrats,* 148.

10. Edsall, *The New Politics of Inequality,* 164–69; Dark, *The Unions and the Democrats,* 126–33.

11. Ibid., 168–69; Dark, *The Unions and the Democrats,* 128.

12. Dark, *The Unions and the Democrats,* 130–31; Lane Kirkland, "It Has All Been Said Before . . .," in Seymour Martin Lipset, ed., *Unions in Transition: Entering the Second Century* (San Francisco: Institute for Contemporary Studies, 1986), 402–3.

13. Compare Edsall, *The New Politics of Inequality,* 169–176, with Dark, *The Unions and the Democrats,* 135–40.

14. *The Changing Situation of Workers and Their Unions,* a Report by the AFL-CIO Committee on the Evolution of Work (Washington, D.C.: AFL-CIO, February 1985).

15. Ibid., quote at 7; Kirkland, "It Has All Been Said Before . . .," 393–404; Walter Galenson, *The American Labor Movement, 1955–1995* (Westport, Conn.: Greenwood Press, 1996), 59–63.

16. Ibid., 8–16.

17. Ibid., 17–34.

18. Kirkland, "It Has All Been Said Before . . .," 402; Galenson, *The American Labor Movement,* 58.

19. Ibid., 401–2.

20. Ibid., 402.

21. Ibid., 403.

22. Foerster, "Confronting the Dilemmas of Organizing," 158–60; Galenson, *The American Labor Movement,* 70.

23. Joseph Clark, "Labor Remains in Politics," *Dissent* (Spring 1985): 154–59; William Serrin, "Labor's Changing Outlook: Can Unions Achieve a Comeback?" *New York Times,* February 22, 1986, A8.

24. Logue, "Introduction: William Winpisinger," 11.

25. See Winpisinger, *Reclaiming Our Future,* chs. 3, 4; Logue, "Introduction: William Winpisinger."

26. Al Weinrub, "Labor Challenges Persian Gulf War," *Labor Action,* March 1991, 13.

27. Michael A. Pollock, "Pink Collar Workers: The Next Rank and File?" *Business Week,* February 24, 1986, 116; Turner, Katz, and Hurd, eds., *Rekindling the Movement,* chs. 1, 7, 8.

28. "The Economic Policy Institute," brochure, n.d.

29. Paul Taylor, "Analyzing Alternatives in Labor's Think Tank," *Washington Post,* February 19, 1987, A25.

30. Ibid.

31. Timothy B. Clark, "Waging a New Debate," *National Journal,* January 3, 1987, 46; "The Economic Policy Institute."

32. "The Economic Policy Institute."

33. Quoted in Clark, "Waging a New Debate."

34. "The Economic Policy Institute"; Clark, "Waging a New Debate"; Taylor, "Analyzing Alternatives."

35. Taylor, "Analyzing Alternatives"; Clark, "Waging a New Debate."

36. Robert Kuttner, *The Life of the Party: Democratic Prospects in 1988 and Beyond* (New York: Viking, 1987); Jeff Faux, *The Party's Not Over: A New Vision for the Democrats* (New York: Basic Books, 1996). Important examples of the many impressive economic and policy studies issued by EPI over the years include Lawrence Mishel and Paula B. Voos, eds., *Unions and Economic Competitiveness* (Armonk, N.Y.: M.E. Sharpe, 1992); Todd Schafer and Jeff Faux, eds., *Reclaiming Prosperity: A Blueprint for Progressive Economic Reform* (Armonk, N.Y.: M.E. Sharpe, 1996); Robert A. Blecker, ed., *U.S. Trade Policy and Global Growth: New Directions in the International Economy* (Armonk, N.Y.: M.E. Sharpe, 1996).

37. Schafer and Faux, eds., *Reclaiming Prosperity.*

38. See Schafer and Faux, eds., *Reclaiming Prosperity,* Section IV; and Blecker, ed., *U.S. Trade Policy.*

39. Edsall, *The New Politics of Inequality,* 117–20; Andrew Rich and R. Kent Weaver, "Advocates and Analysts: Think Tanks and the Politicization of Expertise," in Allan J. Cigler and Burdett A. Loomis, eds., *Interest Group Politics,* 5th ed. (Washington, D.C.: Congressional Quarterly Press, 1998), 235–54.

40. Information in this paragraph was obtained from EPI's Web site, www.epinet.org, in September of 2002.

41. Andrew Banks, "Jobs with Justice: Florida's Fight against Worker's Abuse," in Jeremy Brecher and Tim Costello, eds., *Building Bridges: The Emerging Grassroots Coalition of Labor and Community* (New York: Monthly Review Press, 1990), 28.

42. David Moberg, "Jobs with Justice Helps Unions Broaden Support," *In These Times,* October 9–15, 1991, 7 (quote); Steve Early and Larry Cohen, "Jobs with Justice: Building a Broad-Based Movement for Workers' Rights," *Social Policy* (Winter 1994): 7–18.

43. Early and Cohen, "Jobs with Justice," 14.

44. The current number of local alliances is given at the JWJ Web site, www.jwj.org.

45. See Banks, "Jobs with Justice"; Moberg, "Jobs with Justice"; Early and Cohen, "Jobs with Justice."

46. Early and Cohen, "Jobs with Justice," 14.

47. Ibid., 15–16.

48. Ibid., 17.

49. Moberg, "Jobs with Justice."

50. There is considerable information about the agenda of JWJ at its Web site, www.jwj.org.

51. Banks, "Jobs with Justice"; Moberg, "Jobs with Justice"; Early and Cohen, "Jobs with Justice."

52. In addition to the sources cited in the previous note, see also Steve Early, "Membership-Based Organizing," in Gregory Mantsios, ed., *A New Labor Movement for The New Century* (New York: Monthly Review Press, 1998), 82–103, esp. 99–101.

53. Information on the Student–Labor Action Project and on the Worker Rights Boards is available at the JWJ Web site, www.jwj.org.

54. See the JWJ Web site, www.jwj.org.

55. Galenson, *The American Labor Movement,* ch. 9; Dark, *The Unions and the Democrats,* ch. 9.

56. John J. Sweeney, *America Needs a Raise: Fighting for Economic Security and Social Justice* (Boston: Houghton Mifflin, 1996), 90.

57. Dark, *The Unions and the Democrats,* 15, Table 1.1.

58. Sweeney, *America Needs a Raise,* 88.

59. Sweeney, *America Needs a Raise,* 91–92; Dark, *The Unions and the Democrats,* 178–84; Dark, "Debating Decline"; Harold Meyerson, "Bomb Throwers of Bal Harbor," *LA Weekly,* March 10–16, 1995; Meyerson, "A Second Chance," 4–15.

60. Dark, "Debating Decline," 336–37, Table 1.

61. Ibid., 331, 338; Meyerson, "A Second Chance," 11.

62. Ibid., 335–41, esp. 335 and 340.

63. Ibid., 335.

64. *AFL-CIO News,* November 6, 1995, and February 5, 1996.

65. Sweeney, *America Needs a Raise,* 108.

66. *AFL-CIO News,* February 5, 1996.

67. Dark, *The Unions and the Democrats,* 178–80; Meyerson, "Bomb Throwers of Bal Harbor."

68. Sweeney, *America Needs a Raise,* 90.

69. Jo-Ann Mort, "Finding a Voice: The AFL-CIO Communicates," in Mort, ed., *Not Your Father's Union Movement,* 43–54.

70. Marc Baldwin, "Public Policy and the Two-Thirds Majority," in Mort, ed., *Not Your Father's Union Movement,* 133–44.

71. Steve Rosenthal, "Building to Win, Building to Last: The AFL-CIO Political Program," in Mort, ed., *Not Your Father's Union Movement,* 99–112.

72. Dark, "Debating Decline," 334, 341; Rosenthal, "Building to Win, Building to Last," 106, 109.

73. Sweeney, *America Needs a Raise,* 106.

74. Ibid., 123–24.

75. Rosenthal, "Building to Win, Building to Last," 102; Baldwin, "Public Policy and the Two-Thirds Majority."

76. Mort, "Finding a Voice," 49.

77. Sweeney, *America Needs a Raise,* 133; John J. Sweeney, "America Needs a Raise," in Steven Fraser and Joshua B. Freeman, eds., *Audacious Democracy: Labor, Intellectuals, and the Social Reconstruction of America* (Boston: Houghton Mifflin, 1997), 18.

78. Meyerson, "A Second Chance: The New AFL-CIO," 20–23; Harold Meyerson, "Rolling the Union On: John Sweeney's Movement Four Years Later," *Dissent* (Winter 2000): 51–52; Baldwin, "Public Policy and the Two-Thirds Majority," 141–42; Karen Nussbaum, "Women in Labor: Always the Bridesmaid?" in Mort, ed., *Not Your Father's Union Movement,* 66–67; Steven Fraser and Joshua B. Freeman, introduction, in Fraser and Freeman, eds., *Audacious Democracy,* 1–12.

79. Meyerson, "Bomb Throwers of Bal Harbor," 29–30; Meyerson, "A Second Chance: The New AFL-CIO," 8.

80. Meyerson, "A Second Chance: The New AFL-CIO," 17, 25–26; Barbara Shailor, "A New Internationalism: Advancing Workers' Rights in the Global Economy," in Mort, ed., *Not Your Father's Union Movement,* 145–56.

81. Sweeney, *America Needs a Raise,* 84–87, 123–33; Meyerson, "A Second Chance," 2, 16–17.

82. Ibid., 125–26; Meyerson, "A Second Chance," 16–18; Richard Bensinger, "When We Try More, We Win More: Organizing the New Workforce," in Mort, ed., *Not Your Father's Union Movement,* 27–41; Jill Kriesky, "Structural Change in the AFL-CIO: A Regional Study of Union Cities' Impact," in Turner, Katz, and Hurd, eds., *Rekindling the Movement,* 129–54; Amy Foerster, "Confronting the Dilemmas of Organizing," 155–81.

83. Dark, *The Unions and the Democrats,* ch. 8; Mort, ed., *Not Your Father's Union Movement;* Turner, Katz, and Hurd, eds., *Rekindling the Movement;* Asher et al., *American Labor Unions in the Electoral Arena* (Lanham, Md.: Rowman and Littlefield, 2001), chs. 5, 8; David Moberg, "Empowering Workers," available at www.ourfuture.org/readarticle.

84. Turner, Katz, and Hurd, eds., *Rekindling the Movement,* 1, 275; David Moberg, "It's Payback Time," *The Nation,* July 1, 2002, 19; Harold Meyerson, "Organize or Die," *The American Prospect,* September 2003, 40–41; Herbert B. Asher et al., *American Labor Unions,* 104–5, ch. 8; James Shoch, "Organized Labor versus Globalization: NAFTA, Fast Track, and PNTR with China," in Turner, Katz, and Hurd, *Rekindling the Movement,* 276, 293–97; Taylor E. Dark, "Organized Labor in the 1998 Elections," available at www .taylordark.com/1998update.html, 2, 6–9.

85. Dark, "Organized Labor in the 1998 Elections," 4; Peter L. Francia, "Protecting America's Workers in Hostile Territory: Unions and the Republican Congress," in Paul S. Herrnson, Ronald G. Shaiko, and Clyde Wilcox, eds., *The Interest Group Connection: Electioneering, Lobbying, and Policymaking in Washington* (Washington, D.C.: Congressional Quarterly Press, 2005), 219.

86. Richard B. Freeman, "What Do Unions Do . . . to Voting?" National Bureau of Economic Research, Working Paper 9992, September 2003, available at www.nber.org/ papers/w9992. I originally repeated the erroneous claim in this book, and I am indebted to an anonymous reader for University of Illinois Press for bringing the error to my attention and for providing the reference to Freeman's important paper.

87. Ibid., 40, Table 1, and 15–16.

88. Asher et al., *American Labor Unions,* 96–105; Dark, "Organized Labor in the 1998 Elections"; Robert Biersack and Marianne H. Viray, "Interest Groups and Federal Campaign Finance: The Beginning of a New Era," in Herrnson, Shaiko, and Wilcox, eds., *The Interest Group Connection,* 49–74, esp. 59–63; Francia, "Protecting America's Workers."

89. These figures were culled from various sources, including Dark, *The Unions and the Democrats;* Dark, "Organized Labor in the 1998 Elections"; and Biersack and Viray, "Interest Groups and Federal Campaign Finance."

90. National Election Studies, Center for Political Studies, University of Michigan, *The NES Guide to Public Opinion and Electoral Behavior,* Table 9A.1 and Table 9B.1, available at www.umich.edu/nes/nesguide.htm.

91. Dark, "Organized Labor in the 1998 Elections"; Biersack and Viray, "Interest Groups and Federal Campaign Finance"; Francia, "Protecting America's Workers."

92. These figures are from www.opensecrets.org/pacs/sector.htm.

93. Asher et al., *American Labor Unions,* 98.

94. See the sources cited in note 91.

95. Asher et al., *American Labor Unions,* 102–5, 166–68.

96. Ibid., 102; Dark, "Organized Labor in the 1998 Elections," 6–7.

97. Ibid., 102–3, 166–67.

98. Ibid., 21–22, 96–97, 104–5, 168.

99. Ibid., 163–66.

100. Shoch, "Organized Labor versus Globalization," 275–77.

101. See Francia, "Protecting America's Workers," 220–21, esp. Figure 11–2.

102. Shoch, "Organized Labor versus Globalization," 275.

103. Asher et al., *American Labor Unions,* 163–66; Francia, "Protecting America's Workers," 220–23.

104. Dark, *The Unions and the Democrats*, 174–75.

105. Dark, "Organized Labor in the 1988 Elections," 2.

106. Ibid., 2–3, 7; Asher et al., *American Labor Unions*, 77–78.

107. Shoch, "Organized Labor versus Globalization."

108. Francia, "Protecting America's Workers," 223–25.

109. Larry J. Sabato, ed., *Divided States of America: The Slash and Burn Politics of the 2004 Presidential Election* (New York: Pearson Longman, 2006), esp. chs. 4, 12.

110. Asher et al., *American Labor Unions*, 96.

111. Ibid., 26; Lowell Turner and Richard W. Hurd, "Building Social Movement Unionism: The Transformation of the American Labor Movement," in Turner, Katz, and Hurd, *Rekindling the Movement*, 24.

112. These Census Bureau figures on union membership and density are available at www.census.gov/prod/2004pubs/04statab/labor.pdf.

113. Richard B. Freeman and James L. Medoff, *What Do Unions Do?* (New York: Basic Books, 1984), ch. 15; Thomas A. Kochan, Harry C. Katz, and Robert B. McKersie, *The Transformation of American Industrial Relations* (New York: Basic Books, 1986), chs. 2, 3; Ray Marshall, *Unheard Voices: Labor and Economic Policy in a Competitive World* (New York: Basic Books, 1987), ch. 5; Michael Goldfield, *The Decline of Organized Labor in the United States* (Chicago: University of Chicago Press, 1987); Gordon L. Clark, *Unions and Communities under Siege: American Communities and the Crisis of Organized Labor* (Cambridge, U.K.: Cambridge University Press, 1989), Parts I, III, and V; Paul C. Weiler, *Governing the Workplace: The Future of Labor and Employment Law* (Cambridge, Mass.: Harvard University Press, 1990), ch. 3; Sheldon Friedman, Richard W. Hurd, Rudolph A. Oswald, and Ronald L. Seeber, eds., *Restoring the Promise of American Labor Law* (Ithaca, N.Y.: ILR Press, 1994); Bruce Western, *Between Class and Market: Postwar Unionization in the Capitalist Democracies* (Princeton, N.J.: Princeton University Press, 1997).

114. Under court decisions issued after passage of the 1947 Taft-Hartley Act, employers can voluntarily grant recognition to unions if a majority of their employees sign union authorization cards. Unions so recognized have the same legal rights as those certified by the NLRB following a representation election. Card check recognition avoids lengthy election campaigns with their plentiful opportunities for employers to interfere with employees' free choice of whether or not to unionize. The difficulty, of course, lies in securing the employer's voluntary recognition of the union once a majority of employees has signed cards authorizing a union as their bargaining agent. See William B. Gould IV, *A Primer on American Labor Law*, 3rd ed. (Cambridge, Mass.: MIT Press, 1993), 82–88; Richard N. Block, John Beck, and Daniel H. Kruger, *Labor Law, Industrial Relations and Employee Choice* (Kalamazoo, Mich.: W. E. Upjohn Institute for Employment Research), 13–14.

115. David Moberg, "It's Payback Time: Labor-Backed Politicians Are Being Asked to Return the Favor in Union Fights," *The Nation*, July 1, 2002, 19.

116. The study was conducted by Kate Bronfenbrenner of Cornell University and is cited in Moberg, "It's Payback Time."

117. Ibid.; Moberg, "Empowering Workers"; Dark, "Organized Labor in the 1998 Elections," 8.

118. Moberg, "Empowering Workers," 8; David Moberg, "Labor Fights for Rights," *The Nation*, September 15, 2003, 24; Bill Fletcher Jr. and Richard W. Hurd, "Overcoming Obstacles to Transformation: Challenges on the Way to a New Unionism," in Turner,

Katz, and Hurd, eds., *Rekindling the Movement,* 200–202; Hoyt N. Wheeler, *The Future of the American Labor Movement* (Cambridge, U.K.: Cambridge University Press, 2002), 75.

119. Fletcher and Hurd, "Overcoming Obstacles to Transformation," 201, assert that this method has not worked well but do not fully explain the basis of this judgment.

120. AFL-CIO, "National Organizing Summit," August 6, 2001, available at www.aflcio .org/aboutaflcio/ecouncil/ec08062002.cfm.

121. The quote is from AFL-CIO, "Remarks by AFL-CIO President John Sweeney, Organizing Press Conference," February 26, 2003, available at www.aflcio.org/mediacenter/ prsptm/sp02262003.cfm; see also AFL-CIO, "Voice@Work—The Freedom to Choose a Union Involving Public Officials," July 31, 2001, available at www.aflcio.org/aboutaflcio/ ecouncil/ec07312001.cfm; and Moberg, "Labor Fights for Rights."

122. AFL-CIO, "Voice@Work—The Freedom to Choose a Union Involving Public Officials."

123. American Rights at Work, "In the News," available at www.americanrightsatwork .org/news.

124. Meyerson, "Organize or Die," 39.

125. David Moberg, "Organize, Strategize, Revitalize," *In These Times,* January 16, 2004, available at www.inthesetimes.com/site/main/print/681/; Christopher Hayes, "The Fight for Our Future," *In These Times,* February 14, 2005, 15–20.

126. *Restoring the American Dream: Building a 21st Century Labor Movement That Can Win,* 2, available at www.unitetowin.org.

127. David Moberg, "Which Comes First: Growth or Clout?" *In These Times,* April 18, 2005, 14–15; Harold Meyerson, "Labor's Civil War," *The American Prospect,* June 2005, 45–50.

128. *Winning for Working Families: Recommendations from the Officers of the AFL-CIO for Uniting and Strengthening the Union Movement,* April 2005 (revised June 7), available at www.aflcio.org/aboutus/ourfuture/upload/executive_officers.pdf.

129. Meyerson, "Labor's Civil War."

130. Ibid.

131. Steven Greenhouse, "Four Major Unions Plan to Boycott AFL-CIO Event," *New York Times,* July 25, 2005, A1; Ron Fournier, "Organized Labor Continues to Splinter," Associated Press article, *Johnson City Press,* July 26, 2005, 1A.

132. Compare the Change to Win Coalition's *Restoring the American Dream* with the Sweeney regime's *Winning for Working Families.* See also Steven Greenhouse, "Labor Chief and Critics Quarrel Anew," *New York Times,* March 2, 2005; Moberg, "Which Comes First: Growth or Clout?"

133. Ibid., 1.

134. *Winning for Working Families,* 5, 10–12.

135. See *Restoring the American Dream,* 4.

136. *Winning for Working Families,* 11; *Restoring the American Dream,* 4.

137. *Restoring the American Dream,* 1.

138. Moberg, "Empowering Workers"; Paul Osterman, Thomas A. Kochan, Richard M. Locke, and Michael J. Piore, *Working in America: A Blueprint for the New Labor Market* (Cambridge, Mass.: MIT Press, 2002).

139. *Restoring the American Dream,* 1, 4.

Chapter 10: The Labor-Liberal Coalition

1. Heather Booth, letter to author, May 17, 2006.

2. Taylor E. Dark, *The Unions and the Democrats: An Enduring Alliance* (Ithaca, N.Y.: Cornell University Press, 1999), 15, Table 1.1; Census Bureau, www.census.gov/prod/2004pubs/2004statab/labor.pdf.

3. Ibid., ch. 1.

4. Andrew J. Taylor, "The Ideological Development of the Parties in Washington, 1947–1994," *Polity* 2 (Winter 1996): 273–92, quote at 290.

5. National Election Studies, Center for Political Studies, University of Michigan, *The NES Guide to Public Opinion and Electoral Behavior,* Tables 3.1.1 and 3.1.3, "Liberal-Conservative Self-Identification 1972–2002," at www.umich.edu/nes/nesguide/nesguide.htm; Jeffrey M. Stonecash, *Class and Party in American Politics* (Boulder, Colo.: Westview Press, 2000), 79, Table 4.11; Samuel J. Eldersveld and Hanes Walton Jr., *Political Parties in American Society,* 2nd ed., (Boston: Bedford/St. Martin's, 2000), 162–66.

6. Taylor, "The Ideological Development of the Parties"; Tim Groseclose, Steven D. Levitt, and James M. Snyder Jr., "Comparing Interest Group Scores across Time and Chambers: Adjusted ADA Scores for the U.S. Congress," *American Political Science Review* 1 (March 1999): 33–51.

7. Nicol C. Rae, *Southern Democrats* (New York: Oxford University Press, 1994), ch. 4.

8. Jon F. Hale, "The Making of the New Democrats," *Political Science Quarterly* 2 (1995): 207–32; Rae, *Southern Democrats,* ch. 5; Kenneth S. Baer, *Reinventing Democrats: The Politics of Liberalism from Reagan to Clinton* (Lawrence: University Press of Kansas, 2000).

9. See Baer, *Reinventing Democrats,* 184.

10. William E. Leuchtenburg, *Franklin D. Roosevelt and the New Deal, 1932–1940* (New York: Harper and Row, 1963); David Plotke, *Building a Democratic Political Order: Reshaping American Liberalism in the 1930s and 1940s* (Cambridge, U.K.: Cambridge University Press, 1996).

11. See the AFL-CIO Web site, www.aflcio.org; John J. Sweeney, *America Needs a Raise: Fighting for Economic Security and Social Justice* (Boston: Houghton Mifflin, 1996); Jo-Ann Mort, ed., *Not Your Father's Union Movement: Inside the AFL-CIO* (London: Verso, 1998).

12. David B. Robertson and Dennis R. Judd, *The Development of American Public Policy: The Structure of Policy Restraint* (Glenview, Ill: Scott, Foresman, 1989), ch. 6; Eric Foner, *The Story of American Freedom* (New York: Norton, 1998), ch. 12; John Gerring, *Party Ideologies in America, 1828–1996* (Cambridge, U.K.: Cambridge University Press, 1998), ch. 7; Hugh Davis Graham, "Since 1964: The Paradox of American Civil Rights Regulation," in Morton Keller and R. Shep Melnick, *Taking Stock: American Government in the Twentieth Century* (Cambridge, U.K.: Cambridge University Press and Woodrow Wilson Center Press, 1999), 187–218; Otis L. Graham Jr., "Liberalism after the Sixties: A Reconnaissance," in William H. Chafe, ed., *The Achievement of American Liberalism: The New Deal and Its Legacies* (New York: Columbia University Press, 2003), 293–325.

13. John D. Skrentny, *The Minority Rights Revolution* (Cambridge, Mass.: Harvard University Press, 2004).

14. David Vogel, *Fluctuating Fortunes: The Political Power of Business in America* (New York: Basic Books, 1989), ch. 5; David Vogel, *Kindred Strangers: The Uneasy Relationship*

between Politics and Business in America (Princeton, N.J.: Princeton University Press, 1996), ch. 5; Andrew S. McFarland, *Common Cause: Lobbying in the Public Interest* (Chatham, N.J.: Chatham House, 1984), introduction and chs. 2, 9; Peter Levine, *The New Progressive Era: Toward a Fair and Deliberative Democracy* (Lanham, Md.: Rowman and Littlefield, 2000), 54–60.

15. Jeffrey M. Berry, *The New Liberalism: The Rising Power of Citizen Groups* (Washington, D.C.: Brookings Institution Press, 1999).

16. Bob Herbert, "In America: Can We Talk?" *New York Times,* July 8, 1996, A13; Julie Kosterlitz, "Reconciliation on the Left," *National Journal,* August 3, 1996, 1668; "Home Economics," *The Nation,* August 12, 1996, 5; Jules Witcover, "Rallying the Left," *Baltimore Sun,* June 9, 2003. These and other sources on CAF can be accessed through links on its Web site, www.ourfuture.org.

17. Kosterlitz, "Reconciliation on the Left."

18. Herbert, "In America."

19. Harold Meyerson, "A Second Chance: The New AFL-CIO and the Prospective Revival of American Labor," in Mort, ed., *Not Your Father's Union Movement,* 1–26; Jeff Faux, *The Party's Not Over: A New Vision for the Democrats* (New York: Basic Books, 1996); Michael Tomasky, *Left for Dead: The Life, Death, and Possible Resurrection of Progressive Politics in America* (New York: The Free Press, 1996); Todd Gitlin, "Beyond Identity Politics: A Modest Precedent," in Steven Fraser and Joshua B. Freeman, eds., *Audacious Democracy: Labor, Intellectuals, and the Social Reconstruction of America* (Boston: Houghton Mifflin, 1997), 152–63; Theda Skocpol and Stanley Greenberg, "A Politics for Our Time," in Greenberg and Skocpol, eds., *The New Majority: Towards a Popular Progressive Politics* (New Haven, Conn.: Yale University Press, 1997), 1–20.

20. See Kosterlitz, "Reconciliation on the Left," and *The Nation* (editorial), "Home Economics."

21. Theda Skocpol and Stanley Greenberg rightly link CAF with the post-1995 AFL-CIO and the Economic Policy Institute as the key advocates of "economic or labor-oriented populism" in the Democratic Party. Skocpol and Greenberg, "A Politics for Our Times," 12–15.

22. The names and affiliations of CAF's "advisors" are provided on the organization's Web site, www.ourfuture.org/aboutus/founders.cfm.

23. Steven Greenhouse, "Unions Back Research Plan for Energy," *New York Times,* June 6, 2003; see also CAF's Web site and its manifesto "Take Back America."

INDEX

Abel, I. W., 49

Alliance for Labor Action, 49, 63

Amalgamated Clothing and Textile Workers Union: as dissident union, 49, 65, 71, 76, 152, 154; and merger with International Ladies Garment Workers Union, 143; and National Labor Committee, 79, 125–26, 143; and Sweeney regime, 178

Amalgamated Clothing Workers Union, 31, 49

Amalgamated Meat Cutters, 49, 65

American Enterprise Institute, 99, 150, 171, 172

American Federation of Labor: alliance with Democratic Party in Progressive era, 27–28; business unionism of, 29; and Cold War, 35–36, 139; craft unions of 11, 13; industrial unions of, 19, 30; Labor League for Political Education, 37; 1955 merger with CIO, 3, 37–39; schism with CIO, 3, 13, 29–30, 31–32, 33, 37–38; voluntarism of, 28–29

American Federation of Labor–Congress of Industrial Organizations (AFL-CIO): American Institute for Free Labor Development, 124, 128, 134, 136; A. Philip Randolph Institute, 75; Building and Construction Trades Department, 72, 73; and Central America, 79, 122, 123–24, 133–39; and Citizen Labor Energy Coalition, 104, 107, 112, 116; and Cold War, 123–24, 139–42, 149; Committee on Political Education, 37, 43, 51, 52, 64, 178, 183; Committee on the Evolution of Work, 168–69; Corporate Affairs Department, 178; and Democratic Party, 50–52, 168; Department of International Affairs, 64, 75, 78, 123–24, 134, 137–38, 140, 178, 179; Department of Organization and Field Services, 75; Department of Public Affairs, 178; Department of Public Policy, 168; and election of 1972, 51; and election of 1976, 51–52; Executive Council, 49, 51, 52, 64, 68, 71–72, 73, 103, 150, 178; Free Trade Union Institute, 75, 135; Industrial Union Department, 62, 68, 71; and international labor solidarity, 124, 136–39; Labor Institute of Public Affairs, 168; and labor law reform, 72–73, 186–87; and labor-liberal coalition, 18–19, 24, 37–39, 44–48, 122, 196, 199–201; Legislative Action Committees, 168; and National Labor Committee, 125, 133–36; and New Left, 104, 158; and New Politics liberals, 45–48, 50–52, 59, 64–65; 1955 merger, 3, 37–39, 48, 61–62; 1995 presidential election in, 5, 6, 13, 19–20, 143, 165–67, 175–81; Organizing Department, 180, 184; Organizing Institute, 169, 180, 184; Political Department, 178; political divisions in, 3, 13–15, 61–67, 74–80, 165–90; political strategy of, 64–65, 149–50, 178–90, 181–87; Political Works Committee, 168; and public employee unions, 12; and Reagan administration, 123–24, 134, 166; and service sector unions, 12; and Social Democrats USA, 74–79; Solidarity Center, 179; Sweeney regime in, 165–66, 178–90, 199–201; and 2005 schism, 187–90; and union decline, 3–4, 67–73; and union revival, 167–70, 180–87; and Vietnam war, 48–50, 145, 149; Voice@ Work campaign, 186–87; Working Women's Department, 178

American Federation of State, County and Municipal Employees: and Citizen Labor Energy Coalition, 105, 107, 119; as dissident union, 4, 49, 50, 51, 52, 63, 65, 69–70, 71, 76, 152; and Economic Policy Institute, 170–71; and Jobs with Justice, 173; and National Labor Committee, 126; and Progressive Alliance, 86; support for comparable worth, 45–46; and Sweeney regime, 176–78

American Federation of Teachers, 68, 75

American Newspaper Guild, 49, 65

American Postal Workers Union, 173

Americans for Democratic Action, 10, 198

Americas Watch, 130, 132

Amnesty International, 130

antiwar movement, 49, 50, 74

ANDREW BATTISTA is an associate professor of political science at East Tennessee State University.

The University of Illinois Press
is a founding member of the
Association of American University Presses.

Composed in 10.5/13 Adobe Minion Pro
at the University of Illinois Press
Manufactured by Thomson-Shore, Inc.

University of Illinois Press
1325 South Oak Street
Champaign, IL 61820-6903
www.press.uillinois.edu